THE COLOUR OF DEMOCRACY
RACISM IN CANADIAN SOCIETY

Frances Henry • Carol Tator • Winston Mattis • Tim Rees

HARCOURT
BRACE
CANADA

Harcourt Brace & Company, Canada

Toronto   Montreal   Fort Worth   New York   Orlando
Philadelphia   San Diego   London   Sydney   Tokyo

Canadian Cataloguing in Publication Data

Main entry under title:

The Colour of democracy : racism in Canadian society

Includes bibliographical references and index.
ISBN 0-7747-3255-5

1. Racism–Canada   2. Canada–Race relations.
3. Canada–Social conditions. I. Henry, Frances,
1931–

FC104.C76 1995   305.8'00971   C94-930705-X
F1035.A1C7 1995

Publisher: Heather McWhinney
Editor and Marketing Manager: Daniel J. Brooks
Projects Co-ordinator: Megan Mueller
Director of Publishing Services: Jean Davies
Editorial Manager: Marcel Chiera
Supervising Editor: Semareh Al-Hillal
Production Editor: Kathleen M. Vanderlinden
Production Manager: Sue-Ann Becker
Production Supervisor: Carol Tong
Copy Editor: John Eerkes
Cover Design: Brett Miller
Interior Design: The Brookview Group
Typesetting and Assembly: Debbie Fleming
Printing and Binding: Hignell Printing Limited

Cover Art: William Ronald, *Pierre Elliott Trudeau*, 1982–83. Oil on canvas, 304.8 x 182.8 cm. Image provided by the Art Gallery of Ontario. Reproduced with the permission of the artist.

∞ This book was printed in Canada on acid-free paper.

1 2 3 4 5   99 98 97 96 95

This book is dedicated to the memory of Dr. Wilson Head,
whose life was committed to the pursuit of a
more just and equitable society
and to the elimination of racism in Canada.
His vision and tireless efforts have inspired and guided all of us
engaged in anti-racism.

About the Authors

▼▼▼▼▼▼▼▼▼▼▼▼▼▼▼▼▼▼▼▼▼▼▼▼▼▼▼▼▼▼

Frances Henry, a professor of social anthropology and scholar in the field of race and ethnic relations, is one of the first researchers in Canada to carry out studies on the dynamics of racism. One of her earliest studies on racist attitudes found that 51 percent of Canadians had somewhat or very racist beliefs (Henry, 1978). Her ground-breaking field study of racial discrimination in employment provided dramatic evidence of the extensive barriers that affect Black jobseekers (Henry and Ginzberg, 1984). As a professor at York University, she has taught courses on racism for more than two decades and published widely on the subject.

Carol Tator worked on the frontlines of the anti-racism movement in one of the first voluntary race relations organizations in Canada. She has participated in many coalitions formed by people of colour and other equality seekers and has been involved in many organizations working to dismantle racist structures and systems. Ms. Tator has contributed to a number of government inquiries and task forces on racism and has worked in the areas of anti-racist policy development, program implementation and evaluation, strategic planning, training, and research.

Winston Mattis has experience in community development, employment equity, organizational change, and public administration. He has a particular understanding of racism as it affects the Black community in Canada and has worked on the frontlines of both the voluntary and the private sector. His particular interest is in policing, justice, and the law.

Tim Rees has worked in the race-relations field in a variety of capacities in the public, private, and voluntary sectors for the past two decades. As a policy and program manager with the Ontario government, he assisted in the development of Ontario's first policies on multiculturalism and race relations. He currently works with the Municipality of Metropolitan Toronto as a senior policy consultant on anti-racism. Mr. Rees is also the editor of the first and only anti-racism journal in Canada, *Currents: Readings in Race Relations*, published by the Urban Alliance on Race Relations.

As private consultants, all four authors have worked extensively with public-sector institutions to address racism in the institutions' policies, programs, and practices. Their work with large and complex organizations has focussed on assisting these agencies to analyze barriers to access, participation, and equity in the major arenas of Canadian society. They have provided consultation to municipal, provincial, and federal government agencies, boards of education, colleges and universities, human service delivery organizations, media corporations, and law enforcement and justice agencies. As anti-racism consultants, they have conducted numerous research studies and surveys, directed community consultations, reviewed organizational systems, and provided training to the staff and management of major mainstream organizations.

Preface

▼ ▼ ▼ ▼ ▼ ▼ ▼ ▼ ▼ ▼

This book's approach to the subject of racism in Canada attempts to link theory to practice, thought to experience, the personal to the political, the community to the state, and advocacy to social change. Its authors reflect both academic and practical perspectives.

The text provides a multidimensional analysis of racism by discussing, first, how dominant or majority group values, norms, and conflicting ideologies affect the development and maintenance of inequitable social, economic, and cultural systems and structures in Canada. Second, racism is analyzed by looking at how it is manifested in government, education, media, human services, employment, justice, and law enforcement. Third, the concept of democratic racism is applied to explain why racism continues to flourish in the policies and practices of media and cultural organizations, schools and universities, social and health care agencies, police forces, and justice agencies.

Fourth, the text examines the ways in which Canadian society has responded to racism. It documents the struggle for racial justice and equity and the obstacles that prevent them from becoming a reality.

Finally, a word about the authors' purpose in writing this book. The objective of writing a book on racism in Canada was to link the growing theoretical knowledge of the academic community with the first-hand experience of those involved in the struggle against racism. The challenge of writing this text was to make it accessible to students of various disciplines who wish to deepen their understanding of racism as both ideology and practice. It was also written to enhance the knowledge and skills of those who work in fields related to the practice of anti-racism. The authors hope that *The Colour of Democracy: Racism in Canadian Society* will challenge racist beliefs and ideologies, behaviours, and practices and lead to the development, implementation, and institutionalization of new strategies, models, and mechanisms for the development of a more just and equitable society.

ACKNOWLEDGEMENTS

The book documents the nature and dynamics of racism as it affects the everyday life of people of colour in Canada and as it is manifested in Canadian culture and institutions. Across Canada, there are individuals who have been steadfast in their efforts to challenge racial prejudice and discrimination in all of its insidious forms. They come from various walks of life and include community activists, writers and artists, educators, bureaucrats, advocates and consultants, academics and practitioners. They are people of colour, Aboriginal people, and "mainstream" Canadians. They are Muslims, Jews, Christians, Hindus, and members of other faiths.

We are deeply indebted to the contribution of our many friends and colleagues who share our vision of making Canada a more just and equitable society for *all* Canadians. We owe our sincere thanks to all those who shared suggestions for the development of this book.

The authors would also like to thank Jeffrey Reitz at the University of Toronto and Allan Dutton of the Canadian Anti-Racism Education and Research Society. Their helpful comments and suggestions assisted in the fine-tuning of this book.

A NOTE FROM THE PUBLISHER

Thank you for selecting *The Colour of Democracy: Racism in Canadian Society*, by Frances Henry, Carol Tator, Winston Mattis, and Tim Rees. The authors and publisher have devoted considerable time to the careful development of this book. We appreciate your recognition of this effort and accomplishment.

We want to hear what you think about *The Colour of Democracy*. Please take a few minutes to fill out the stamped reader reply card at the back of the book. Your comments and suggestions will be valuable to us as we prepare new editions and other books.

Brief Contents

▼▼▼▼▼▼▼▼▼▼▼▼▼▼▼▼▼▼▼▼▼▼

Contents

▼ ▼ ▼ ▼ ▼ ▼ ▼ ▼

CHAPTER 5
RACISM AND THE JUSTICE SYSTEM 133

CHAPTER 6
RACISM AND HUMAN-SERVICE DELIVERY 153

PART THREE
Racism in Educational and Cultural Institutions

Introduction

▽ ▽ ▽ ▽ ▽ ▽ ▽ ▽ ▽ ▽ ▽ ▽ ▽ ▽

"I am not a racist."

"She/he is not a racist."

"This is not a racist institution."

"Canada is not a racist society."

In spite of the historical and contemporary evidence of racism as a pervasive and intractable reality in Canada, the above statements have become mantras, which, when repeated, cast an illusory spell that has allowed Canadians to ignore the harsh reality of a society divided by colour and ethnicity. Canada suffers from historical amnesia. Its citizens and institutions function in a state of collective denial. Canadians have obliterated from their collective memory the racist laws, policies, and practices that have shaped their major social, cultural, political, and economic institutions for 300 years.

Racist beliefs and practices, although widespread and persistent, are frequently invisible to everyone but those who suffer from them. White Canadians tend to dismiss evidence of their racial prejudice and their differential treatment of minorities. Victims' testimonies are unheard and their experiences unacknowledged. Public sector agencies conduct extensive consultations and then fail to translate their knowledge into substantive initiatives. Government bodies establish task forces and commissions of inquiry on racism to demonstrate their grave concern, their findings and recommendations are ignored. Academics produce empirical studies documenting the ways in which **people of colour** are denied power, equity, and rights, and the studies are then buried. Politicians and the power elite rationalize the racial barriers that prevent people of colour from fully participating in education, employment, media, justice, human services, and the arts.

In recent years, racism has received increased attention. Racial unrest in Vancouver, Toronto, Montreal, and Halifax, and the demands of racial-minority communities for greater participation in Canadian society, have become difficult to ignore. As a result, various levels of government and public sector organizations such as boards of education, police forces, and human services and cultural organizations have developed policies and programs and modified some of their traditional practices to respond to demands for equity. Money has been allocated, racial-minority communities have been consulted, and people of colour have been hired and appointed to serve in previously all-White organizations and institutions.

However, fundamental racial inequality continues to affect the lives of people of colour in Canada. Racial prejudice and discrimination are a ubiquitous reality in the workplace and the classroom. The racist assumptions and practices of the print and electronic media marginalize racial minorities by portraying them as invisible and by depicting them as outsiders. Arts and cultural organizations ignore and exclude the creative images, words, and voices of people of colour. Patterns of policing and the attitudes and behaviour of police officers are marked by overt prejudice and the differential treatment of people of colour, particularly Blacks. The justice system fails to give fair and equal treatment to racial minorities. Racial barriers impair the delivery of services by social and health-care agencies.

In each of these sectors, resistance to equity policies and programs and the backlash against anti-racism initiatives exists among individuals, organizations, and systems. Widespread opposition to any change in the status quo dramatically reduces the effectiveness of any efforts to promote equity.

At the federal level of government, there is no policy to deal with racism. Some argue that multiculturalism, as a public policy enshrined in legislation, provides a framework for legitimizing cultural and racial diversity and for ensuring the rights of all Canadians. Yet, despite the Multiculturalism Act's affirmation of the pluralistic nature of Canadian society, Canadians appear deeply ambivalent about the public recognition of other cultures, the freedom of non-White racial and non-European cultural groups to maintain their unique identities, and the right of minorities to function in a society free of racism.

Canada's racist heritage has bequeathed to both earlier and present generations of Canadians a powerful set of perceptions and behavioural patterns regarding people of colour. A deeply entrenched system of White dominance perpetuates inequity and oppression against the socially and economically disadvantaged.

However, racism as a commanding force in this country is constantly challenged and denied by applying the arguments of democratic liberalism. In a society that espouses equality, fairness, tolerance, social harmony, and respect for individual rights, the existence of racial prejudice, discrimination, and disadvantage is difficult to acknowledge and therefore remedy. Canadians have a deep attachment to the assumptions that in a democratic society individuals are rewarded solely on the basis of their individual merit and that no one group is singled out for discrimination. Consistent with these liberal, democratic values is the assumption that physical differences such as skin colour are irrelevant in determining one's status. Therefore, those who experience racial bias or differential treatment are considered somehow responsible for their state, resulting in a "blame it on the victim" syndrome.

This conflict between democratic liberalism and the collective racism of the dominant culture creates a dissonance in Canadian society. There is a constant and fundamental moral tension between the everyday experiences of people of colour and the perceptions of those who have the power to re-define that reality—politicians, bureaucrats, educators, judges, journalists, and the corporate elite. While lip service is paid to the need to ensure equality in a pluralistic society, most Canadian individuals, organizations, and institutions are far more committed to maintaining or increasing their own power.

The multiplicity of ways in which these values conflict is the subject of this book. It examines this phenomenon and analyzes the impact of "demo-cratic racism" on Canadian society and its institutions.

TERMINOLOGY

One of the first challenges that confronts anyone analyzing racism is identi-fying an appropriate terminology. One must search for words that them-selves are not viewed as racist and, at the same time, clearly and accurately communicate what racism means. As the phenomenon of racism continues to show diverse manifestations, so too does the language modify.

Although colour remains the nucleus of the race classification system, paradoxically, it bears little relation to the actual skin tones of human beings. No White person is truly white, nor is any Black individual completely devoid of colour. Whites do not consider themselves part of the colour spec-trum but rather identify their group as constituting the universal norm. However, the gradations of colour from white to black associated with various racial groups have economic, social, and cultural consequences. The ideology that defines Whites as superior renders people of different colours inferior.

As we demonstrate in every chapter of this book, skin colour has an important relationship to one's status and position in Canadian society. Therefore, references to colour in this text are used in their political sense and the terms "Black" and "White" are capitalized to reflect this context. The reader will note that references citing British literature or experiences use the term Black inclusively, to refer to people of colour. However, in all other discussions, Black refers specifically to people of African descent.

The terms "mainstream," "Anglo," and "the **dominant group**" are used interchangeably throughout this book to refer to the group in Canadian society that maintains the power to define itself and its culture as the norm.

Although the phrases "racial minorities" and "people of colour" appear frequently in this book, they are used cautiously. Referring to groups of people who represent four fifths of the world's population as minorities, is, at the very least, inaccurate. Furthermore, huge distinctions exist among racial minorities or people of colour. There are, for example, in each of the groups examined in this book, significant differences that relate to class and gender. The experiences of recent affluent immigrants from Hong Kong, who come to Canada with significant resources and business skills, bear little similarity to those of the unskilled worker who is a third-generation Canadian or the Chinese refugee fleeing from political persecution.

In using the phrases "racial minorities" and "people of colour," we are referring to groups of people who because of their physical characteristics are subjected to differential and unequal treatment in Canada. Their minority status is the result of a lack of access to power, privilege, and prestige in relation to the White majority group. Although there are significant differences among "racial minorities" or "people of colour," members of these diverse communities share a history of exposure to racial bias and discriminatory barriers based on the colour of their skin. So, for the purposes of this book, they are grouped together.

Finally, what do we mean by "race" and "racism"? Our theoretical perspective is that race is a socially constructed phenomenon (see chapters 1 and 2 for more detailed definitions) based on the erroneous assumption that physical differences such as skin colour, hair colour and texture, and facial features are related to intellectual, moral, or cultural superiority. The concept of race has no basis in biological reality and, as such, has no meaning independent of its social definitions. But, as a social construction, race significantly affects the lives of people of colour.

Racism (more correctly, "social racism") refers to the assumptions, attitudes, beliefs, and behaviours of individuals as well as to the institutional policies, processes, and practices that flow from those understandings. It is reflected in the collective belief systems of the dominant culture, and it is woven into the laws, language, rules, and norms of Canadian society

Another term frequently used in this book, "racialization," often appears in studies on racism produced in the United Kingdom, particularly those that use a political economy perspective. It is less familiar to North American readers. It has been defined as:

> processes by which meanings are attributed to particular objects, features and processes, in such a way that the latter are given special significance and carry or are embodied with a set of additional meanings. (Miles, 1989:70)

Skin colour as a feature of race therefore carries with it more than the signification of "colour"; it also includes a set of meanings attached to the cultural traits of those who are a certain colour. The assertion that "Blacks are prone to commit crimes" therefore signifies that members of a racial group, identified by their skin colour, have a propensity for certain behaviour. Ideological racialization refers to the ways in which discourse concerning a set of principles becomes imbued with racial dimensions.

In Canada the debate about immigration has become racialized because substantial numbers of immigrants are now people of colour. Restricting immigration therefore becomes a means of excluding these groups. The racialization of crime results in the stigmatization of certain groups. For example, racialization in the media results in news stories and editorials in which Blacks figure prominently in crimes that are also committed by members of other groups.

PERSPECTIVE

Before embarking on an analysis of racism in Canadian society, some of the text's limitations should be noted. The authors have tried to provide a national perspective on racism in Canada and, wherever possible, to draw on the experiences and expertise of theoreticians and practitioners across the country. However, for the past two decades, Ontario has been one of the primary scenes of the anti-racism struggle in Canada. It has the greatest number of people of colour in its population, and its minority communities, especially in Toronto, have perhaps been more politicized and more insistent on ensuring that racism become part of the public agenda.

The authors' work as educators, consultants, and practitioners has provided them with direct knowledge of the organizational and institutional processes occurring in each of the arenas described in Part Two. Although they document the events, issues, and activities in other Canadian jurisdictions as well as in the United States and the United Kingdom, they believe that the text's focus on Ontario will be of interest and educational value to readers everywhere.

Important gaps exist in this text with respect to Aboriginal peoples. The evidence of racism in Canada is most graphically manifested in the 400-year relationship between a White racist society and oppressed Aboriginal indigenous peoples. However, although this book makes numerous references to the impact of racism on indigenous peoples, its focus is on people of colour or racial minorities who live in Canada as the result of relatively recent immigration. An attempt has been made to identify and analyze some of those dimensions of racism that are common to both groups, particularly in the chapter on the justice system, but the relationship of Aboriginal peoples to the state is significantly different from its relationship to racial minorities. The position of Aboriginal peoples is governed by treaties and legislation. Their role and status is determined by formal mechanisms, and the solutions to their systemic racial oppression lie in a unique set of strategies (e.g., self-government) that are unavailable to other people of colour. The authors believe that their contribution to anti-racism is most effectively realized by concentrating on areas in which they are confident of their expertise. The huge and well-documented field of studies of racism against Aboriginal peoples is better left to specialists in this field.

Throughout this text, there are frequent references to the British experience with racism and anti-racism. Although important differences exist between Canada and the United Kingdom, many similarities exist with respect to the patterns of bias and discrimination against people of colour. Moreover, an extensive body of literature documents racism in British society, its effects on the victims, and various strategies for dismantling racist ideologies, structures, and practices (Rex, 1988; Benyon and Solomos, 1987; Hall, 1991; Gilroy, 1987). The British evidence, therefore, is both timely and relevant to the discussion of racism and anti-racism in Canadian society.

The United Kingdom is, in many ways, a model for Canadian society. It has had a similar pattern of immigration from the Commonwealth of

Nations. Immigrants of colour from the Caribbean and Asia began arriving in large numbers in Britian more than twenty years before they did so in Canada. Thinking that they would be well received as members of the Commonwealth, immigrants of colour in Britain were shocked at the racism they faced in employment, housing, social services, policing, and the justice system (Gilroy, in CCCS, 1982; Hall, 1978).

FRAMEWORK

Part One establishes a framework for understanding the nature of democratic racism. Chapter 1 introduces the reader to the concept of democratic racism by examining a central ideological struggle in Canadian society: the conflict between the image of a country with a strong and cherished tradition of democratic liberalism and the reality of persistent and pervasive inequality based on colour. While individuals, organizations, institutions, and the state vigorously deny the presence of racism, it flourishes in this liberal democratic country, deeply affecting the daily lives of people of colour. This chapter looks at how democratic racism functions in terms of individual and collective belief systems and behaviour. It challenges the many myths that prevent Canadians from confronting and responding to racism.

Chapter 2 provides a brief overview of theories of racism developed in the United States, the United Kingdom, and Canada. It also provides definitions of terms used in the study of racism. It then turns to the problems of assessing and measuring racism.

Chapter 3 reviews some of the evidence of racism in Canada by looking at the experiences of specific groups in the history of this country. It also draws on the findings of task forces, government inquiries, research, and polls and surveys conducted over the past two decades. One of the main thrusts of this chapter, however, is to demonstrate the extent of individual and everyday racism in Canada. The documented experiences of people of colour provide commanding evidence of racism in Canada. Hate-group activity and the proliferation of White-supremacist groups further demonstrate individual prejudice and discrimination in Canadian society. The final section of this chapter draws on the evidence of employment and housing discrimination to demonstrate how deeply embedded racism is in the fabric of Canadian society.

Part Two examines a number of key institutions in Canadian society—particularly service providers in the public and voluntary sectors—within which racism continues to be a significant source of tension, conflict, and oppression. The chapters in this part—on policing, the justice system, and the human services—demonstrate how the policies, programs, procedures, and delivery systems of the major institutions in Canada discriminate against people of colour. The analysis of these key institutions illuminates the nature of racism in Canada as it is articulated in both overt and covert organizational behaviour.

Chapter 4 analyzes racism in Canadian law-enforcement agencies. It explores the culture of policing, the racialization of crime, and the overpolicing and underpolicing of minority communities. The chapter then critically examines the responses of police forces across Canada in areas such as training, policy development, employment equity, community relations, and the use of force.

Chapter 5 examines the justice system from the perspective of the differential treatment of racial minorities in the granting of bail, sentencing, and minority representation in the system. Case studies highlight the attitudes of justice system officials.

Chapter 6 examines the models and delivery of human services. It shows how racism is reflected in the professional values, assumptions, and practices of social workers and other human services practitioners. It emphasizes the role, position, and status of "minority" workers as an example of how mainstream organizations operate in a racist manner.

In continuing to examine the institutional arenas in Canadian social structure, Part Three analyzes racism in education, the media, and culture and the arts. These areas develop, protect, and support a society's values, beliefs, and systems. The chapters in this part focus on the ways in which the ideology of racism is supported and sustained in these institutional defenders of Canada's collective belief system. They also show how the myths and assumptions of democratic racism are employed to avoid the necessity of acknowledging that the ideology of racism is central to the definition of Canada.

Chapter 7 looks at one of the most powerful socializing agents in society, the educational system, and at the ways in which racism pervades the teaching process and the learning environment and forms an intrinsic part of the organizational structure of schools and classrooms. It explores the ways in which Eurocentric and assimilationist values and ideologies influence curriculum and teaching practices. Examples are presented of the ways in which racial bias and differential treatment affect the educational opportunities of students of colour, particularly Black children.

Chapter 8 continues the examination of educational institutions by focussing on universities. It challenges the widespread notion that universities are free of racism by discussing the lack of minority representation in hiring, promotion, and tenure decisions; the prevalance of Eurocentric curriculum; and racial tensions and harassment among students and between students and faculty.

Chapter 9 analyzes cultural racism by looking at the Eurocentric values and assumptions of arts and cultural organizations in Canada. The power of White culture to define the standards of excellence and professionalism in the arts and to determine what images and voices are outside the boundaries of mainstream culture is an important dimension of cultural racism. This chapter analyzes the appropriation of minority cultural experiences and symbols by people outside those cultures as another manifestation of racism. It examines the barriers to participation in the arts in the context of the underrepresentation of racial minority artists and writers in art galleries, museums, publishing houses, art councils, unions, and associations. The chapter's two case studies illustrate the cycle of racism and the response of the **dominant group** to those who challenge racist actions.

Chapter 10 focusses on the mass media and explores how the print and electronic media use their enormous influence to marginalize racial minorities in Canada. It shows how the media, contrary to public myth, are linked to political, social, and corporate elites and legitimate White power structures. It also provides an analysis and examples of influential power-brokers shaping the agendas, information, and images circulated by media organizations in the public domain.

Part Four provides an analysis of the impact of democratic racism on the state and society by focussing on the ways in which organizations in every sector of Canadian society have maintained, reinforced and reproduced racist ideologies and practices. By examining the change process used by many of these agencies, it is possible to identify some powerful and widespread forms of resistance to change in organizations that declare their commitment to anti-racism.

Chapter 11 poses the question, What role does the state play in perpetuating and reproducing racism? This chapter looks at the laws, policies, and processes of various levels of government that affect the lives of people of colour in Canadian society. The Canadian Charter of Rights and Freedoms, provincial human rights codes and commissions, and municipal race-relations advisory committees are briefly examined. The analysis of state responses includes a critique of the limitations of policies such as the Multiculturalism Act and employment equity legislation.

Chapter 12 analyzes the weaknesses of the approaches and strategies identified in the preceding chapters to deal with racism in Canadian society and institutions. In exploring resistance to change, it shows again how democratic racism works: individuals and organizations continue to assert their commitment to fairness and equality for all, while at the same time opposing measures that would ensure racial equity.

Chapter 13 concludes the book by discussing how democratic racism has often led to the failure of new policies, programs, and practices to alleviate the oppression of people of colour in the social, cultural, economic, and political arenas. Analyzing the weaknesses of many of the current approaches also allows for some reflection on strategies for change. Three central measures are examined as possible future directions: community empowerment; mechanisms for monitoring and evaluating new policies, programs, and practices and a process for responding to institutional resistance; and the development of organizational and administrative measures and accountability systems based on a recognition of the pervasiveness of racism in the central institutions of Canadian society.

Readers may notice an occasional dearth of research documentation on Canada, especially in the chapters on justice, policing, and cultural organizations. One of the main reasons for this omission is that there is relatively little published research on racism in Canadian institutions. The authors therefore cite many American and British sources and rely extensively on their personal experiences.

REFERENCES

Benyon J., and J. Solomos, (eds.). (1987). *The Roots of Urban Unrest*. Oxford: Pergamon Press.

Gilroy, P. (1982). In Centre for Contemporary Cultural Studies, *The Empire Strikes Back*. London: Hutchinson.

_____. (1987). *There Ain't No Black in the Union Jack: The Cultural Politics of Race and Nation*. London: Hutchinson.

Hall, S. (1991). "Old and New Identities: Old and New Ethnicities." In A. King (ed.), *Culture, Globalization, and the World System*. Binghampton: N.Y., Department of Art History, State University of New York.

_____, et al. (1978). *Policing the Crisis*. London: Macmillan.

Henry, F. (1978). *Dynamics of Racism in Toronto*. North York: York University.

_____, and E. Ginzberg. (1984). *Who Gets the Work? A Test of Racial Discrimination in Employment*. Toronto: Urban Alliance on Race Relations.

Miles, R. (1989). *Racism*. London: Routledge.

Rex, J. (1988). *The Ghetto and the Underclass*. Aldershot, U.K. and Brookfield, Vt.: Avebury.

PART
ONE

▼▼▼▼▼▼▼▼▼▼▼▼▼▼▼▼▼▼▼▼▼▼▼▼▼▼▼▼▼▼▼▼▼▼▼▼▼▼▼

Perspectives
on Racism

▼▼▼▼▼▼▼▼▼▼▼▼▼▼▼▼▼▼▼▼▼▼▼▼▼

*This part introduces the concept of democratic racism and
provides a general perspective on racism. A discussion of the theoretical
explanations of racism, as documented by social science literature,
is presented in Chapter 2. Chapter 3 reviews the evidence of racism
in Canadian society, drawing on historical examples
as well as current studies, polls, and surveys.*

▼▼▼

Chapter 1

▼▼▼▼▼▼▼▼▼▼▼▼

The Ideology of Racism

We are at one of those critical junctures where two ideals are in conflict. There's the principle of the legal equality of all. There's the fact that there are serious inequalities in our society, many of which can only be remedied by treating people unequally. Which puts liberals like myself at war with ourselves. (Richard Gwyn, *The Toronto Star*, July 18, 1993)

This chapter examines the **ideology** of **racism** in Canada today. It begins with a brief examination of the function of ideology as the basis of social behaviour and then explores the nature of **racist** ideology. This ideology provides the foundation for understanding the racist **attitudes** and behaviours of individuals, the maintenance of racist policies and practices in Canadian **institutions**, and the promulgation of racist doctrines and laws by the state. The chapter analyzes the role and functions of racist ideology and introduces the concept of **democratic racism**. The last section of this chapter examines the powerful myths that help perpetuate and reinforce both individual and collective belief systems.

Democratic racism is an ideology that permits and sustains people's ability to maintain two apparently conflicting sets of values. One set consists of a commitment to a liberal, democratic society motivated by the egalitarian values of fairness, justice, and equality. Conflicting with these values are attitudes and behaviours that include negative feelings about people of colour and that result in differential treatment of them or **discrimination** against them. Democratic racism, in its simplest form, is an ideology that reduces the conflict between maintaining a commitment to both egalitarian and non-egalitarian values.

INTRODUCTION

WHAT IS IDEOLOGY?

Ideology is a set of beliefs, perceptions, assumptions, and values that provide members of a group with an understanding and an explanation of their world. At another level, ideology provides a framework for "organizing, maintaining and transforming relations of power and dominance in society" (Fleras and Elliot, 1992:54).

Ideology influences the ways in which people interpret social, cultural, political, and economic systems and structures, and it is linked to their perceived needs, hopes, and fears. Ideological formations are not static but organic and constantly evolving, often as a result of contradictory experiences (Hall, 1983).

People are often unaware of their ideologies:

> It is indeed a peculiarity of ideology that it imposes (without appearing to do so) obviousness as obviousness which we cannot fail to recognize and before which we have the inevitable and natural reaction of crying out (aloud or in the still small voice of conscience): "That's obvious! That's right! That's true!" (Althusser, 1971:127)

Within these everyday ideological constructs, ideas about **race**, gender, and class are produced, preserved, and promoted. These ideas form the basis for social behaviour. Therefore, understanding ideology is crucial to an understanding of the marginalization, **exclusion**, and domination of people of colour in Canadian society.

THE DEFINITION AND FUNCTION OF RACIST IDEOLOGY

Racist ideology provides the conceptual framework for the political, social, and cultural structures of inequality and systems of dominance based on race, as well as the processes of exclusion and marginalization of people of colour that characterize Canadian society.

The cognitive dimensions of racism are located in collective patterns of thought, knowledge, and beliefs as well as individual attitudes, perceptions, and behaviours. "Racism as ideology includes the whole range of concepts, ideas, images and institutions that provide the framework of interpretation and meaning for racial thought in society" (Essed, 1990:44). Racist ideology therefore organizes, preserves, and perpetuates the power structures in a society. It creates and preserves a system of dominance based on race and is communicated and reproduced through agencies of socialization and cultural transmission, such as the mass media, schools and universities, religious doctrines, symbols and images, art, music and literature. It is reflected and regenerated in the very language we read, write, and speak.

THE ELUSIVE NATURE OF RACISM

One of the most complex aspects of racism is its elusive and changing nature. The most commonly accepted concept of racism in Canada is one that refers to the individual expression of overt feelings or actions. Racism is generally understood to refer to physical assaults that have been perpetrated by bigoted individuals, racial slurs and **harassment** in schools or in the

Figure 1.1
IDEOLOGY AND ITS EFFECTS

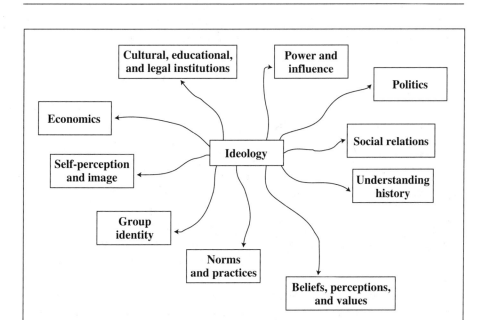

workplace, defacing property with racial graffiti, and similar overt acts. There seems to be an extremely limited understanding of racism in public discourse. Racism manifests itself not only within individuals, but also in groups, organizations, institutions, at the state level, and is embedded in the value system of society. In each arena, racism assumes a different form. This will be discussed in more detail in Chapter 2. It has: "a geographic, social and historical specificity.... In any country, at any point of time, the realization of racist practice will be of a specific nature" (Brandt, 1986:67–68).

Racism is not a natural element in society, just waiting for a series of events to trigger its manifestations:

> It has no natural and universal law of development. It does not always assume the same shape. There have been many significantly different *racisms*—each historically specific and articulated in a different way.... Racism is always historically specific in this way, whatever common features it may appear to share with other similar social phenomena.... It always assumes specific forms which arise out of the *present*—not the past—conditions and organization of society. (Hall, 1978:26)

Thus the ways in which racism manifests itself at any particular time are fluid, dynamic, and ever-changing. They are affected by the social contexts in which racism develops.

In a similar vein, the study of racism provides "a picture...of historically variant racism both continuously and discontinuously transformed from one period to another. Subject, objects and modes alter. Developments and changes in racist discourse are demonstrated to be functions of dominant interests, aims, and purposes" (Goldberg, l990:xiii).

Another important dimension of racism is its ability to be so subtly expressed or indirectly implied that its targets are not even aware of it. Conversely, racism is sometimes visible only to its victims. It remains indiscernible to others, who therefore deny its existence.

The subtle and ever-changing nature of racism helps to explain both its persistence over time and the difficulties of defining and measuring it. However, although many are confused by the term, racism rests on this mystification of social relations—the necessary illusions that secure the order of public authority (Gilroy, 1987).

Racist ideology forms part of "common sense." Racist thinking, according to this view, is natural and forms part of the ways in which ordinary people view the world—they do not need to have specialized knowledge about **minority groups** to be racist. "Common sense" racism is not based on theory, nor does it have a unified body of knowledge to support it; it contains a "storehouse of knowledge" that guides the thinking of "the practical struggle of everyday life of the popular masses" (Lawrence, 1982:49)

The construction of and belief in a racist ideology helps people to understand the increasingly complex societies in which they live. Thus, recently unemployed people can easily blame the new immigrants who have taken their jobs away. People who are fearful in their homes and on the streets can now blame all those Black people who commit crimes. Teachers whose Black students are underachieving can believe that it has nothing to do with their racial attitudes or classroom practices. The corporate manager is able to justify a refusal to hire those who are racially "different" on the basis of not wanting to disrupt the harmony of the workforce.

Racist assumptions and beliefs provide a ready explanation for the stress experienced by people who live in a country undergoing rapid social and cultural change:

> Racism is not a set of a false pleas which swim around in the head. They're not a set of mistaken perceptions. They have their basis in real material conditions of existence. They arise because of concrete problems of different classes and groups in society. Racism represents the attempt ideologically to construct those conditions, contradictions, and problems in such a way that they can be dealt with and deflected in the same moment. (Hall, 1978:35)

Ideology may go far beyond beliefs and attitudes; it carries with it a predisposition to behave in negative, derogative, or discriminatory ways toward members of the targeted group. An ideology of racism therefore carries more power than a set of mere attitudes (Hall et al., 1978).

THE CONCEPT OF DEMOCRATIC RACISM

The primary characteristic of democratic racism—the most appropriate model for understanding how and why racism continues in Canada—is the justification of the inherent conflict between the egalitarian values of justice and fairness and the racist ideologies reflected in the collective mass-belief system as well as the racist attitudes, perceptions, and assumptions of individuals.

Racist beliefs and practices continue to pervade Canadian society. Attitude surveys have found that many Canadians hold racist views. In the first such survey carried out in Canada, 16 percent of Canadian adults were found to be confirmed bigots, while a further 35 percent held somewhat intolerant views. Another 30 percent leaned toward tolerance, and the remaining 20 percent were extremely tolerant (Henry, 1978). Later surveys and polls support these findings (see Chapter 3). Most Canadians therefore hold some degree of racist attitudes. But, living in a society that believes in democracy, most Canadians also recognize that these attitudes are socially unacceptable. In order to maintain their racist beliefs while championing democratic values, Canadians have developed the ideology of democratic racism—a set of justificatory arguments and mechanisms that permit these contradictory ideologies to coexist.

Democratic racism therefore, results from the retention of racist beliefs and behaviours in a "democratic" society. The obfuscation and justificatory arguments of democratic racism are deployed to demonstrate continuing faith in the principles of an egalitarian society while at the same time under-mining and sabotaging those ideals.

Before discussing this ideology as it pertains to Canada, it is useful to analyze it in the context of the United Kingdom and the United States. In the former, the concept of "new racism" has been elaborated, while in the latter "aversive racism" has appeared in the literature. These aspects of racism, identified by critical English theorists, are also relevant to Canada and are included in democratic racism.

NEW RACISM IN THE UNITED KINGDOM

Distancing themselves from the crude ideas of biological inferiority and superiority, the new racists have defined a national British **culture** that is homogeneously White. It is concerned with:

> mechanisms of inclusion and exclusion. It specifies who may legitimate-ly belong to the national community and simultaneously advances reasons for the segregation or banishment of those whose "origin"... assigns them elsewhere. [West Indians, and Asians, for different reasons] are judged to be imcompatible with authentic forms of Englishness.... Alien cultures come to embody a threat which, in turn, invites the con-clusion that national decline and weakness have been precipitated by the arrival of Blacks. (Gilroy, 1987: 45–46)

Scholars in the United Kingdom have analyzed the trend toward the increasing racialization of state policies "in all areas of social life" (CCCS, 1982:19). For at least the past two decades, observers have noted the lack of sympathy and support for racial-equality initiatives on the part of the central government (Ball and Solomos, 1990). The policy interventions of the central government have tended to affirm a deep-seated commitment to the rights of the White majority rather than minority communities. Herman Ouseley notes that the failure "to implement radical race equality policies...was the result of inadequate attempts by national and local politicians" (Ball and Solomos, 1990). Such state policies reinforce the racist thinking of much of the population.

Lawrence (1982) has identified a number of racial ideologies characteristic of the Conservative-run state in Great Britain. At their heart is a definition of "British" that clearly excludes people of colour from former (and present) Commonwealth countries. This definition affirms the "naturalness" of British values, British culture, and especially British family life. Within the politics of nationalism, sovereignty, and cultural **identity**, it defines the nation as a unified *cultural* community (Gilroy, 1987). Thus, White anti-racists are regarded as having been influenced by "alien" ideas.

Although new racism no longer espouses doctrines of racial superiority (there are exceptions, particularly in academia and the extreme right), it nevertheless denigrates people of colour. The myths that fuel new racism often derive from a negative evaluation of other cultures rather than a focus on race. This ideology, for example, expresses itself in a negative evaluation of Black culture, particularly the "deviant" Black family and the "aberrant" behaviour of Black youth. Thus, although police officials do not consider themselves racist, they believe that Blacks are culturally disposed to criminal behaviour. Further, the media, while not admitting racism, publishes report after report in which derogatory cultural characteristics are highlighted.

New racism cites pathological cultural patterns as major reasons for criminal behaviour, poverty, poor achievement in school, and an assortment of other social problems. Blacks show their inferiority by a propensity for loud music and raucous conversation. New racists therefore cloak their negative attitudes toward other groups by claiming that while they do not believe in racial superiority, not all cultures are equally valid. The cultural behaviour of the "others," such as Blacks, demonstrates that they are not the same as Whites and cannot be part of the national culture.

When race is identified with identity and culture, careful language enables people to "speak about race without mentioning the word" (Gilroy, 1987:53). The crude and overtly racist labels of the far right are avoided, but the new racism can be articulated by the choice of carefully coded language:

> "'They,' despite the good qualities of some of 'them,' are held to be different from 'us' and would, on the whole, be better off back in 'their' countries." (Billig et al., 1988:107)

Another form of discourse in which overt racism is avoided occurs in the "two-handedness of the 'on the one hand, on the other hand' formulation. Having stated an opposition to racism or to **prejudice**, the way is then opened for an expression of racist or prejudiced views"(Billig et al., 1988:109). These formulations appear in an ideology in which traditional racism is eschewed but a newer, masked, and more subtle form is allowed expression. Modern racism is expressed in a rhetorical context, demonstrated in comments such as "I'm not a racist, but…" which are followed by an overtly racist statement.

AVERSIVE RACISM IN THE UNITED STATES

In the United States, a new form of democratic racism has been explored by social psychologists, who analyze the individual's attitudes. Gaertner and Dovidio (1986) present the results of studies of racism among the "well intentioned":

> Our work has focused on those White Americans, who, in terms of racism and public policy, seem "well intentioned." That is, they genuinely profess egalitarianism, as well as the desire to ameliorate the consequences of racism and poverty. However, we believe that the racial attitudes of many of these well-intentioned people may be characterized by a special type of ambivalence: aversiveness. (Gaertner and Dovidio, 1981:208)

Their analysis builds on what was earlier identified as "aversive racism" (Kovel, 1970). In this pioneering work, Kovel distinguished "dominative" racists—strong hard-core bigots who are prepared to act on their attitudes—from "aversive" racists. The latter also believe in White supremacy, but do nothing about it. Aversive racists are prejudiced but do not act in discriminatory ways. Some avoid contact with Blacks and other minorities, but when contact is unavoidable, they are polite.

Other aversive racists, however, "are impelled by a strong social conscience, consider themselves liberals and, despite their sense of aversion (which may not be admitted inwardly) do their best within the given structure of society to ameliorate the conditions of the Negro" (Kovel, 1970:55). They believe in fairness and equality for all and pride themselves on their strong social conscience. They may not be aware of their aversion to Blacks (or other minorities) and appear to have a positive racial attitude. Gaertner and Dovidio note that this attitude is superficial, ambiguous, and complex. Their studies have identified a number of characteristics of aversive racists, including the following:

- Aversive racists consider themselves prejudice-free, but attempt to avoid contact with the minority group to which they are averse.
- Aversive racists think of themselves as politically liberal and non-discriminatory. In a situation in which clearly prescribed norms call for tolerant behaviour, they will behave appropriately. However, in

situations in which there are no clear prescriptive norms, they may indulge in discriminatory behaviour because it would not be obvious.

- Aversive racists' positive actions toward minority groups relate less to a genuine effort to help minorities or to implement egalitarian values but to reaffirm their own lack of prejudice. This attitude may result in tokenism—aversive racists affirm that they are prejudice-free by making trivial gestures that preclude the necessity for extensive, costly action. (Gaertner, 1976:208)

Aversive racism therefore "represents a particular type of ambivalence in which the conflict is between feelings and beliefs associated with a sincerely egalitarian value system and unacknowledged negative feelings and beliefs about Blacks" (Gaertner and Dovidio, 1986:62). Moreover, this type of racism does not necessarily include feelings of hate or hostility, nor will it usually express itself in hostile or discriminatory behaviour. Aversive racism involves "discomfort, uneasiness, disgust, and sometimes fear, which tend to motivate avoidance rather than intentionally destructive behaviours" (Gaertner and Dovidio, 1986:63).

Aversive racism stems from socialization and is reinforced by social and cultural factors. In the United States, for example, the denigration of Black culture, Black **stereotypes**, and the constant association with poverty, crime, and delinquency reinforces negative racial attitudes. Moreover, the differential distribution of social, economic, and political power between Blacks and Whites further reinforces these attitudes.

SYMBOLIC RACISM

Closely aligned to the aversive form, symbolic racism is an attitude in which "abstract moral assertions are made about Blacks' behaviour as a group, concerning what Blacks deserve, how they ought to act, whether or not they are treated equitably, and so on" (Sears and McConahay, 1973:138). Symbolic racism manifests itself in acts that are rationalized on a nonracial basis but that actually maintain the racial status quo by continuing discrimination against Blacks" (Sears and McConohay, 1973:24). In the United States, these acts include voting for White rather than Black candidates, opposing affirmative-action programs, and opposing desegregation in housing and education. In Canada, opposing **affirmative action** and **employment equity** is an act of symbolic racism.

Other aspects of symbolic racism have relevance for Canada. For example, unlike the older "redneck" bigotry, which denied equal rights and opportunities for people of colour, symbolic racism allows a person to uphold these values but still believe that Blacks are too pushy because they are making too many demands for equality too quickly. Moreover, Whites who hold these views may not feel personally threatened by Black claims to equality but feel that their values are endangered: Black assertiveness may be regarded as a threat to the very fabric of society. Another important component of symbolic racism is that, as its name implies, it operates through symbols rather than overt discrimination. Thus, there is opposition to welfare, Black politicians, and fair housing laws because they symbolize the unreasonable demands being made by Blacks. In sum, then, symbolic racism

> is the expression in terms of abstract ideological symbols and symbolic behaviours of the feeling that Blacks are violating cherished values and making illegitimate demands for changes in the racial status quo. (McConahay and Hough, 1976:38)

DEMOCRATIC RACISM

Although democratic racism pertains largely to ideology and stresses the role of value differences as these are reflected in systems and institutions, individuals are largely responsible for the development of policies and the implementation of procedures that regulate systems and institutions. Thus democratic racism is related to new racism, aversive racism, and symbolic racism. It differs from them by positing a value conflict.

Democratic racism is an ideology in which two conflicting sets of values are made congruent to each other. Commitments to democratic principles such as justice, equality, and fairness conflict but coexist with attitudes and behaviours that include negative feelings about minority groups and differential treatment of and discrimination against them.

One of the consequences of the conflict is a lack of support for policies and practices that might ameliorate the low status of people of colour. These policies and practices tend to require changes in the existing social, economic, and political order, usually by state intervention. The intervention, however, is perceived to be in in conflict with and a threat to liberal democracy. Thus democratic racism holds that the spread of racism should only be dealt with—if at all—by leaving basic economic structures and societal relations essentially unchanged (Gilroy, 1987). Efforts to combat racism that require intervention to change the social, economic, and political order will lack political support. More importantly, they will lack legitimacy, according to the egalitarian principles of liberal democracy.

THE MYTHS OF DEMOCRATIC RACISM

How is democratic racism manifested in the daily lives, opinions, and feelings of people? What are the values, assumptions, and arguments of democratic racism? As Wellman (1977) has noted, the maintenance of a wide array of myths and misconceptions about racism has permitted a pattern of denial that has led to a wholly inadequate response to racism.

Following are some assumptions and beliefs commonly articulated in Canada that reflect democratic racism.

Racism Cannot Exist Within a Democratic Society.

This is the classic statement of denial in the face of overwhelming evidence to the contrary. The assumption here is that because Canada is a society that upholds the ideals of democracy, it could not possibly be racist. When racism is shown to exist, it tends to be identified as either a psychological problem or the result of "undemocratic" traditions that are disappearing from the Canadian scene.

Canada's constitution and its other laws clearly prohibit racism. However, believing in egalitarian ideals, even having them enshrined in state policies does not mean that they are acted on. The weaknesses of the legal and legislative framework have hampered their translation into effective **anti-racism** practice.

Discrimination Is a Problem Faced by Everyone from Time to Time.

Statements like this devalue the distinctive racial elements of racism issues by assuming that everyone is a victim. They imply that there is nothing distinctive or special about **racial minority** concerns. Such statements deny the fact that for people of colour it is precisely the fact that they are non-White that makes the crucial difference. In a society that uses racial characteristics as a basis for discrimination, people of colour inherently provide a cue for discriminatory practices. Their skin colour, therefore, is not incidental, but is the central factor in relations with White society.

White European Immigrants Also Experienced Discrimination.

This statement assumes that the historical experiences of White European immigrants and the contemporary situation of people of colour are similar, that the social system is open but that all immigrant groups must expect to start at the bottom of the social and economic ladder. It is only through their own initiative that they can expect to achieve upward mobility and thereby receive full and equal treatment.

This assumption is based on the traditional view that race, ethnicity, and the immigrant experience are one and the same phenomenon. It does not recognize that genetic racial features such as skin colour do not simply disappear in time. It ignores the fact that second- and third-generation Canadian people of colour continue to experience the same prejudiced attitudes and discriminatory behaviour as their parents and grandparents. They continue to be severely hampered in their opportunities for upward mobility.

As long as skin colour is used as a basis for social differentiation, discrimination against people of colour will continue. Equating racial **disadvantage** and discrimination against White European immigrants ignores the importance of the history of colonization, subjugation, and **oppression** of people of colour by Canadians of European origin.

Racism Is a Result of Immigration; Racial Conflict Occurs Because of Racial Diversity in Society.

The argument here is that if immigration is curbed, racism will decrease. However, even before the large-scale immigration of people of colour into

Canada, racism was practised systematically by Canadians in the relation-ship between White colonizers and **Aboriginal peoples**. It has been institu-tionalized at all levels of society and has been integrated into Canada's social and economic systems, including its immigration practices and policies.

Since the 1980s the majority of immigrants to Canada have come from Asia, Africa, Latin America, and the Caribbean. Anti-immigration attitudes are reflected, not in obvious racial terms, but in a collection of myths such as:

- Immigrants take jobs away from Canadians
- Immigrants are a drain on the economy
- Immigrants are unskilled, uneducated, and live in poverty
- Immigrants exploit the welfare system
- Immigrants commit more crimes

These statements are clearly fallacious. Numerous studies (e.g., Economic Council of Canada, 1991) have concluded that immigrants make more jobs than they take. These studies have found that immigrants are more likely to be self-employed, and that they bring a significant degree of skill, education, self-reliance, and innovative flair to the Canadian economy. Immigrants do not displace Canadian residents from jobs; they tend to take jobs that residents do not want. Since 1971, immigrants have paid more in taxes than they have used in services. Finally, immigrant rates of criminality are lower than those of the native-born population (Samuel, 1984).

Anti-immigration sentiment also views racism as the inevitable result of different cultures being brought into close proximity with each other, prompting cultural jealousies and conflicts. Racism, however, is not made inevitable by cultural differences. It is not a matter of inevitable tension between people who are different. Racial conflict exists only when one group has power over another. The White majority in Canada has politi-cal, economic, and social control over most Canadian institutions. When **racial discrimination** is entrenched in a society's institutions and value systems, the social and economic exclusion of people of colour is to be expected.

Minority Groups Refuse to Fit in and Adapt to Canadian Society.

Some people believe that recalcitrant minority groups simply refuse to adapt to Canadian society. Racial inequality is attributed to inadequate efforts by minority groups to adopt the values of the host society. This notion is part of the "blame the victim" syndrome.

Minority Groups Cannot Fit into Canadian Society— They Change the National Identity of the Country.

Another way of explaining the above myth is not that people of colour have difficulties adapting to Canadian Society, it is more a matter of them being unable to adapt to "traditional" Canadian values and traditions. Because of different cultures—differing family structures, belief systems, and so forth—they are by definition outside the cultural integrity of the nation, and therefore, somehow outside the social and political life of the country. It can be said that the problem of racism does not exist within the Canadian consciousness but people of colour get excluded from the Canadian national identity. The position of people of colour is therefore explained not by racism, but in the group itself, by its "deviant" cultural patterns.

This "myth" is related to an issue which has a long history in Canadian society, the search for a national identity (Mathews, 1988; Mandel and Taras, 1987). In more recent times it has exhibited itself in a particular form relating especially to the notion of democratic racism. The idea that is evident today is that the new diverse population groups, especially those who are racially and culturally different from **mainstream** Anglo Canadians (however that mainstream is defined), are threatening the identity of the nation. When the results of a poll were analyzed, it was found that 44 percent of Canadians believe that too many immigrants of colour are being accepted into the country; the pollster noted that Canadians are more apprehensive about "cultural insecurity" than economic issues.

> People from what has traditionally been a White, Anglo-Saxon country are feeling that their way of life is under pressure, either real or imagined, from immigration and an increasingly ethnically plural society. The insecurity is part of a larger resurgence of concern over national identity. (*The Toronto Star*, 1994)

The concept of nation is introduced in order to suggest that Canadian society is a unified cultural community in which different cultures are incompatible. This kind of cultural nationalism defends the image of Canada as being a homogeneous national culture that is constantly under attack from "alien" cultures. The core values which bind this nation together are therefore being challenged and changed, according to this view, and new values and standards of behaviour are increasingly being legitimized, especially by public-sector agencies.

This way of thinking characterizes the ideology and behaviour of right wing White supremacist groups such as the Heritage Front. While such groups can, to a certain extent, be ignored because of their small numbers, such thinking is also evident in the doctrines of the Reform Party, who won a substantial number of votes in the federal election of 1993 and who hold 52 seats in Parliament (Sharpe, 1992).

In Great Britain, the conservative right wing have articulated such views for many years (Parekh, 1986). They view the State as "a community bound together by a deep sense of kinship...[which] is the highest unit of moral and political life" (Parekh, 1986:35). This form of nationalism, based on deeply held notions of kinship, commands authority, respect, and unconditional loyalty from its citizens. Black West Indians, Asians, and other groups cannot share in these commitments to the State, because they are racially and culturally alien. Moreover, they bring with them cultural values and behaviours which do not fit into this view of nationhood. Parekh argues, however, that such notions of the State are anachronistic. The modern state, has little to do with nationalism:

> The United States of America is composed of many nations and nationalities, and yet distinguished by a strong, perhaps too strong a sense of unity. This is also true of almost all modern European states which consist of diverse religious, cultural and ethnic peoples. The modern State is historically unique in that...it has developed an autonomous principle of unity...one located in the very structure of the State rather than something lying outside or beyond it. (Parekh, 1986:39)

The modern State is therefore to be understood as a formal institution; one which is not dependent on substantive identity, or a common race or ethnicity. "It is therefore able to tolerate diversity in a way its predecessors could not" (Parekh, 1986:40).

People fail to understand that future generations of Blacks, Asians, or any other group, will be socialized to the values and standards of the society that they are born and raised into and that, in fact, they have no other home. The belief that minorities will continue to threaten the national identity of the country and its values is another subtle form of democratic racism. Such nationalistic racism, evident also in Britain and other countries in Europe, can be understood in part as a response to the social, economic, and political turbulence of the times; it has been described as the "new moral panic" (Husbands, 1994).

People of Colour Have Cultural Problems. Race Is Not the Issue.

By using the vocabulary of culture, any overt reference to race is avoided. It then becomes possible to argue for curbs on immigration and to focus on certain minorities' predispositions toward anti-social or criminal behaviour.

Non-Whites Lack the Skills and Motivation to Succeed.

The argument here is that people of colour remain at the bottom of the social ladder because they lack the skills, education, and motivation to succeed in Canada. Myths that sustain this belief include the ideas that other races are not as intelligent as the White race, that they come from culturally inferior backgrounds, and that the only reason they come to Canada is to benefit from its social advantages.

This belief flies in the face of the evidence. Immigrants of colour are more highly educated and have higher levels of skills and qualifications than do most other immigrant groups (Richmond, 1992). In the past two decades, only a very small percentage of immigrants of colour in the "independent immigrant" category could be described as unskilled or uneducated, because Canada's immigration system is based on a point scale in which education and job skills are highly rated.

In addition, a significant proportion of immigrants of colour originate from major urban centres. They have already experienced **acculturation** to a postindustrial, cosmopolitan society and have the values and social skills required to succeed in an urban environment.

Multicultural Policies are Sufficient.

Many have suggested that government **multiculturalism** policies are sufficient to address the problems of racism. However, racial inequality and discrimination have political and economic roots in Canada. Multicultural programs and policies are inadequate in eradicating the deeply rooted and complex problems of racism. Cultural solutions cannot solve non-cultural problems.

It is an illusion to expect programs that support cultural retention to also achieve racial equality. Racial justice cannot be attained in Canada without making some fundamental changes to its institutional structures.

Racism Comes from Ignorance. Therefore, Education about Other People Will Eradicate It.

This statement assumes that racism is only an attitudinal problem. As a result, many public policies and programs address racism by supporting educational activities that focus on changing attitudes. By increasing public awareness of Canada's racial diversity, by accepting or trying to understand "the people next door," governments maintain the illusion that Canada is essentially a just, harmonious cultural mosaic. This approach, however, ignores the hidden dimension of discrimination—its systemic exclusion of certain groups from the mainstream of society.

In addition, the assumption that "sensitization" programs will lead to changes in attitudes, which, in turn, will lead to changes in behaviour is questionable. While there is some value in educational initiatives, they fall short of the mark when they concentrate on changing attitudes rather than systems and structures.

Racism Is a Problem for Non-Whites to Solve.

A common perception of non-Whites is that they create racism, they "have a chip on their shoulder," and they can solve it. Implicit also is the view that the oversensitivity of people of colour makes them look for racism when it is not intended—they define a situation as racist when, in reality, racism is not a factor.

As Salman Rushdie has remarked: "...the worst and most insidious stereotype...is the characterization of black people as a problem. You can talk about the *race problem*, the *immigration problem*, all sorts of problems. If you are a liberal, you say that black people have problems. If you aren't, you say that they are the problem" (Rushdie, 1991:138).

All We Need to Do Is Treat Everybody Equally.

This "solution" is no more than an acceptance of the status quo and a denial of the many forms in which racism exists in Canada. Many people are against **equity** and affirmative action programs because they view these programs as a form of "reverse discrimination" in which target group members are given preference in employment and promotion. They maintain that the problems of inequity can be solved by being "colour blind" and pretending that socially constructed differences do not damage the life chances of individuals.

The notion that racism can be eliminated from society by treating everyone equally ignores the historical development of racism. Employment equity programs are designed to counter the effects of past overt discrimination. Lyndon Johnson justified affirmative action programs in the United States on this ground: "You do not take a person who, for years, has been hobbled by chains, liberate him, bring him to the starting point of a race and then say, 'You are free to compete with the others' and still believe that you have been completely fair" (Johnson, 1978).

Employment equity and affirmative action programs have been developed to change historic patterns of racial discrimination in a rational way. They do so by eliminating the structural forms of discrimination that continue to exist today.

Although Racism Exists, Individuals Have the Right to Freedom of Speech.

This statement contends that no matter how strong the evidence of racism may be, the freedoms of individual thought, choice, and action upon which western democracy is founded cannot be interfered with. It rests on the notion that any restriction on individual thought or expression puts Canada on the slippery slope toward **censorship** and totalitarianism. It is therefore more harmful to society to prevent hate propaganda than it is to be harmed by such propaganda (Rausch, 1993).

Particularly vociferous in their support of this principle are those who espouse economic liberalism. Primarily concerned with the freeing of market forces, they argue for the withdrawal of state intervention in any area of social and economic life. Promoting a greater role for the market clearly fits uneasily with strategies of racial equity that enlarge the legislative, judicial, and administrative responsibilities of the state. Strategies such as employment equity and **contract compliance** are therefore seen as constraining personal freedoms and overriding the primacy of individual rights. Such arguments, however,

> can be seen as freedom of the affluent and the powerful, who have the means of access to—and therefore control over—which speech is heard, what ideas are expressed, which money goes to support which projects or investigations, and ultimately, therefore, who gets to communicate what and gets to hear what in this society. So freedom of speech, though

it sounds like the panacea, can simply be a method by which the rich and the powerful and those already in control remain in control. (London, 1993)

Again, while the facts of racism may be acknowledged, the proposed solutions are regarded as even worse, not only because they threaten individual freedom (i.e., they are undemocratic), but because they undermine traditional Canadian values and culture (i.e., they are unpatriotic).

Strategies for societal change, if they are to be acceptable, must originate from the mainstream of society. Strategies that originate from and reflect the concerns of marginalized groups are considered unreasonable and lack credibility. The primary example of such thinking is opposition to employment equity. Rather than being understood as a strategy for redressing past imbalances, employment equity is criticized not only as constraining individual freedom, but as subverting the Canadian way of doing things. Thus, opponents

> say they are only opposed to the unfair and indiscriminate indulgences of this frightening world of empowerment for women and minorities. What they stand for is what they have always stood for; exclusion, entrenchment of their own superiority, and the right to set the agenda. (Dimanno, 1993)

Anti-Racism Is Racism in Reverse.

Opposition to the remedies for racism is frequently characterized by intellectual sloppiness, dishonesty, fabrication, smear, and innuendo. Public discourse on such topics as employment equity and dealing with hate propaganda often uses ridicule and derisive language. For example, the editor of the *Financial Post*, in commenting on the efforts of the British Columbia government to combat hate activity, wrote:

> Commissar Harcourt has streaked ahead by deputizing his citizenry as secret police. Harcourt's Hate Commission will be comprised of N.D.P. hacks and hangers-on who will investigate and prosecute anyone who bad-mouths ethnic, religious, gender, disabled or sexual individuals or groups. This will be a Star Chamber against perceived, imagined and unproven "bigots" and a dandy way to destroy, using public money, political or capitalist rivals. (Francis, 1993)

Another example can be found in a *Globe and Mail* editorial on employment equity: "We are told, on the basis of a pile of government bumph and the sighs of a few oriented consultants...'Well now, do you have to be blind to suffer from a "persistent visual impairment"'?...[If Japanese], how Japanese? A half? A quarter?" (*The Globe and Mail*, 1993a).

Another editorial lambastes Canada's human rights commissions and human rights in general with such comments as "It is either uproariously funny or maddeningly tragic to think of the number of individuals who will be needlessly dragged before the Captain Kangaroo court.... The commission is already mightily predisposed to take even the most outlandish and clearly baseless complaints seriously" (*The Globe and Mail*, 1993b). Referring to a report on the handling of race complaints at the Ontario Human Rights Commission, the editorial queries the age, credentials, and fee paid to the author and suggests the only future for the report was "as bird-cage liner."

Rather than contributing to an objective and critical body of knowledge that might help in developing appropriate strategies to address racism, such shrill diatribes clearly indicate a disinclination to pursue any strategy and a desire to dismantle present efforts.

Anti-Racism Initiatives Are Racism in Reverse.

Another form of criticizing efforts to combat racism is to suggest that those who oppose racism are themselves racists. Anti-racism initiatives are thus discredited by suggesting in strong, emotive language that they are nothing more than, "apartheid in reverse," a "new inquisition," or "McCarthyite witch-hunts."

Anti-racism efforts are thus aligned with creeping totalitarianism and accused of using the anti-democratic, authoritarian methods of the extreme right. "These are fertile times for hate-mongers and reactionaries.... The defenders of the status quo...have discovered a wonderful refuge in their opposition to the excessess of political correctness" (Dimanno, 1993).

Those concerned with addressing racial inequalities have frequently been accused of belonging to fascist, extremist groups. The implication of the accusations is that the issue of race is being used as a cover for promoting conflict in pursuit of other questionable political ends. Those concerned with racial injustice have been labelled as extremists who are using the anti-racism flag to subvert Canada's fundamental institutions, values, and beliefs.

The argument is put forward that by publicizing the facts of racism, it will be exacerbated, and if solutions are pursued that begin to categorize people by race, then there will be greater danger that society will be further polarized by race: "A society that uses inequitable means to try to become more equitable is a society that is going to tear itself apart" (Gwyn, 1993). In response to the Ontario government's financial support to a Black credit union, *The Globe and Mail* commented: "For the government to be actively funding an institution where they check your ancestry before they check your credit shows how far we have gone down the path from multiculturalism to racial separation" (*The Globe and Mail*, 1993a).

Ignored in these views is the "peaceful violence" of racism, which has permeated every facet of the lives of people of colour in Canada for generations. The preference, it seems, is for a "negative peace" of non-confrontation, where the "peaceful" and therefore invisible violence of racism can continue to fester. Undisturbed by government interference, "we should put more faith in Canadians, and less in the social engineers" (Gwyn, 1993). The pursuit of a positive peace, which requires the pursuit of justice, is not allowed to take precedence over the need for order.

SUMMARY

The preceding myths, stereotypes, and erroneous beliefs reflect and reinforce the ideology of democratic racism and become firmly entrenched as racist attitudes. They provide an array of defences in support of entrenched racial inequality. They also provide a climate hostile to race equity initiatives. They are the attitudes of democratic racism.

The remainder of this book presents the evidence of individual, institutional, and cultural forms of racism in Canada and shows how democratic racism has become the prevalent ideology for sustaining racism in Canadian society.

REFERENCES

Althusser, L. (1971). "Ideology and Ideological State Apparatuses." In *Lenin and Philosophy and Other Essays*. London: Monthly Review.

Ball, W., and J. Solomos, (1990). *Race and Local Politics*. London: Macmillan

Billig, M., et al. (1988). *Ideological Dilemmas: A Social Psychology of Everyday Thinking*. London: Sage.

Brandt, G. (1986). *The Realization of Anti-Racist Education*. London: Falmer Press.

CCCS (Centre for Contemporary Cultural Studies). (1982). "The Organic Crisis of British Capitalism and Race." In CCCS, *The Empire Strikes Back: Race and Racism in 70's Britain*. London: Hutchinson.

Dimanno, R. (1993). *The Toronto Star* (September 6).

Economic Council of Canada. (1991). *Changing Faces in the Crowd*. Ottawa: Minister of Supply and Services Canada.

Essed, P. (1990). *Everyday Racism*. CA: Hunter House.

Fleras, A., and J. Elliot. (1992). *Multiculturalism in Canada*. Scarborough, ON: Nelson.

Francis, D. (1993). *Financial Post* (July 3).

Gaertner, S.L. (1976). "Nonreactive Measures in Racial Attitude Research: A Focus on Liberals." In P. Katz (ed.), *Towards the Elimination of Racism*. New York: Pergamon Press.

Gaertner, S.L., and J.F. Dovidio. "Racism Among the Well Intentioned." (1981). In E.G. Clausen and J. Bermingham (eds.), *Pluralism, Racism and Public Policy*. Boston: G.K. Hall.

_____. (1986). "The Aversive Forms of Racism." In S.L. Gaertner and J.F. Dovidio (eds.), *Prejudice, Discrimination and Racism*. New York: Academic Press.

Gilroy, P. (1987). *There Ain't No Black in the Union Jack*. Chicago: University of Chicago Press.

The Globe and Mail. (1993a). "Editorial" (June 18).

The Globe and Mail. (1993b). (July 19).

The Globe and Mail. (1993c). (July 22).

Goldberg, D.S. (ed.). (1990). *The Anatomy of Racism*. Minneapolis: University of Minnesota Press.

Gwyn, R. (1993). *The Toronto Star* (July 18).

Hall, S. (1978). "Racism and Reaction." In *Five Views of Multi-Racial Britain*. London: Commission for Racial Equality.

_____, et al. (1978). *Policing the Crisis*. London: Macmillan.

_____. (1983). "The Great Moving Show" In S. Hall and M. Jacques (eds.), *The Politics of Thatcherism*. London: Lawrence and Wishart.

Henry, F. (1978). *Dynamics of Racism in Toronto*. North York, ON: York University.

Husbands, C. (Jan. 1994). "Crisis of National Identity as the 'New Moral Panics': Political Agenda-Setting About Definitions of Nationhood." *New Community* (Warwick) 20 (2):191–206.

Katz, P.A. (ed.). (1976). *Towards the Elimination of Racism.* New York & Toronto: Pergamon Press.

Kovel, J. (1970). *White Racism: A Psychohistory.* New York: Pantheon.

Lawrence, E. (1982). "Just Plain Common Sense: The 'Roots' of Racism." In CCCS, *The Empire Strikes Back.* London: Hutchinson.

London, J. (1993). "Word for Word." Toronto: CBC Radio (July 18).

Mandel, E., and D. Taras. (1987). *A Passion for Identity: Introduction to Canadian Studies.* Toronto: Methuen.

Mathews, R. (1988). *Canadian Identity: Major Forces Shaping the Life of a People.* Ottawa: Steel Rail.

McConahay, J.B., and J.C. Hough, Jr. (1976). "Symbolic Racism." *Journal of Social Issues* 32 (2):23–45.

Parekh, B. (1986). "The 'New Right' and the Politics of Nationhood." In *The New Right Image and Reality.* London: Runnymede Trust.

Rausch, S. (1993). *Kindly Inquisitors.* Chicago: University of Chicago Press.

Richmond, A.H. (1992). "Education and Qualifications of Caribbean Migrants in Metropolitan Toronto." *New Community* (London) 19 (2).

Rushdie, S. (ed.) (1991). "The New Empire Within Britian." *Imaginary Homelands: Essays and Criticism, 1981–1991*:129–38. London: Granta.

Samuel, J. (1984). *Current: Readings in Race Relations* 5 (2) (April).

Sears, D., and J. McConahay, Jr. (1973). *The Politics of Violence: The New Urban Blacks and the Watts Riot.* Boston: Houghton Mifflin.

Sharpe, S. (1992). *Storming Babylon: Preston Manning and the Rise of the Reform Party.* Toronto: Key Porter.

Sidanus, J., E. Devereux, and F. Pratto (1992). "A Comparison of Symbolic Racism Theory and Social Dominance Theory as Explanations for Racial Policy Attitudes." *Journal of Social Psychology* 132 (3):377–95.

The Toronto Star. (1994). (March 22):A19.

Urban Alliance on Race Relations. (1978). "Why Affirmative Action?" Toronto: Johnson.

Wellman, D. (1977). *Portraits of White Racism.* Cambridge, UK: Cambridge University Press.

Chapter 2
▼▼▼▼▼▼▼▼▼▼▼

Theoretical Perspectives

Today, the theory of race has been utterly transformed. The socially constructed status of the concept of race...is widely recognized, so much so that it is now often conservatives who argue that race is an illusion.... Our central work is to focus attention on the *continuing significance and changing meaning of race.* (Omi and Winant, 1993)

This chapter reviews the theoretical literature on the subject of race and racism, which is substantial. It begins with theories of biological and cultural superiority and ends with sophisticated societal paradigms. A brief review of some of the critical developments in the history of racial theory is presented in the first section of this chapter. To expedite the review, the theories are presented chronologically and identify the major trends in the United Kingdom, United States, and Canada. The various forms of racism—individual, systemic, and ideological—are briefly defined. The chapter concludes by examining some of the methodological and measurement problems in the study of racism.

INTRODUCTION

As they have done in other areas of human behaviour, social scientists have attempted to explain racist behaviour by constructing theories. It is by constructing general as well as specific theories that human behaviour can be understood. Sociological and psychological theories, especially those focussing on White superiority, were heavily influenced by the emergence of racial classifications.

FROM THE NINETEENTH CENTURY TO THE MID-TWENTIETH CENTURY: RACE AND RACIAL CLASSIFICATION

Race as a biological classification has a long history, but in the nineteenth century the biological classification of human beings into "races" became prominent. When social theorists such as Herbert Spencer began to apply the concept of race to social categories, a new school, Social Darwinism, was created. Although Social Darwinists did not intend their work to be racist, others such as Joseph Arthur de Gobineau and Houston Stewart Chamberlain applied the theory to construct a school of social racism in which the supremacy of the white race and European civilization was dramatically featured (Banton, 1983).

Throughout the nineteenth century and most of the twentieth century, the term "race" was used not only to distinguish between groups but also to establish a hierarchical division of races. Physical appearances were thought to correlate with social, psychological, intellectual, moral, and cultural differences. Characteristics such as skin colour were used to establish a racial classification system. This racial order and discourse was then used to rationalize and legitimize the exploitation and oppression of racial minorities.

Not until the mid twentieth century was the concept of the inferiority of people of colour fundamentally altered. In the 1950s and 1960s, many biologists and social scientists met to produce new theoretical models to explain "race." In addition, a number of conferences were organized by the United Nations Educational, Scientific and Cultural Organization to address the issue (UNESCO, 1972). Clear messages and definitive statements emerged from these forums to challenge popular myths about race. There was a consensus among scientists that all humans belonged to a single species, that is, one race.

The concepts of race and racial classification can be rejected as unnecessary and unscientific because they add nothing to the understanding of the human species. Humanity cannot be divided into discrete portions distinguished by biological properties (Rex, 1983). All races are mixtures of populations, and "the term 'pure' race is an absurdity" (Mayr, 1963). In fact, some social scientists have suggested that "race" should be removed from the vocabulary of the field (Banton, 1977). It has been called "man's most dangerous myth" (Montagu, 1964).

However, the consequences of the discourse on race and the social relations within which it has been embedded for the last two centuries cannot be ignored. Human societies continue to function as if races do exist. Racial differentiation continues to affect all areas of social interaction. For all practical purposes, then, race is not so much a biological phenomenon as a social myth that has had devastating consequences (Li and Bolaria, 1988).

Thus, while the concept of race as such may be irrelevant, racism is one of the most important causes of human inequality.

THE 1950s AND 1960s: ASSIMILATION AND INTEGRATION

"**Race relations**" have a long history in the United States. Park (1950) and his associates at the University of Chicago developed the concept of "a race relations cycle" in which **assimilation** into mainstream society was the final stage for ethnic and racial groups. The theory was largely based on the study of the adaptation of **ethnic groups** of European origin. It was also applied to racial groups, primarily "American negroes."

The assimilationist perspective, which conceptualized the **integration** of all groups into mainstream society, was popular for many years. An earlier important work in the assimilationist tradition was *An American Dilemma,* by the Swedish scholar Gunnar Myrdal (1944). He propounded the view that prejudice and racial conflict was a "White problem" which could only be resolved by changing the attitudes and behaviours of Whites toward Blacks. The "dilemma" had occurred, according to this pioneering work, because America had allowed a series of racial discriminatory practices and policies to develop that were in direct conflict with the "American Creed," which emphasized freedom, equality, and justice. Myrdal was the first to call attention to this fundamental value conflict.

In another important theoretical development stemming from the discipline of social psychology, the distinction between prejudice—the attitudes held by individuals—and discrimination—the behaviour prompted by these prejudices—was examined by Gordon Allport's seminal work, *The Nature of Prejudice* (Allport, 1954).

The psychological nature of prejudice as defined by Allport was reviewed by Black scholars such as Jones (1972), who in *Prejudice and Racism* takes the view that attitudes are less important than unequal power relations and institutional practices. However, other social psychologists, such as Gaertner and Dovidio, Katz, and McConahay and Hough, moved beyond the study of prejudice and began to develop theories of racism (see Chapter 1).

Another earlier development of some theoretical importance was the work of Frantz Fanon, who, influenced by Marxian, Freudian, and existential philosophy, in 1952 published *Black Skin, White Masks* (Fanon, 1967). In this work, he called attention to the symbolic analysis of racism and dealt with the duality between Blacks and Whites as expressed in real and symbolic terms. As well, Fanon called attention to the oppressive role of colonization in structuring relations between racial groups.

THE LATE 1960s AND 1970s: FROM RACE RELATIONS TO RACISM

In the 1960s, Black scholars in the United States were instrumental in changing the focus away from "race relations," with its assimilationist, value-conflict approach in which attitudinal prejudice was stressed, to "racism." This shift in perspective resulted in a focus on power relations, in which social, economic, and political inequalities between groups become the centre of attention. It examined in greater depth the role of institutions in both the public and private sectors.

A landmark in the understanding of structural racism was the publication of *Black Power*, by Stokely Carmichael and Charles Hamilton, in 1967.

The authors defined racism as "the predication of decisions and policies on considerations of race for purposes of subordinating a racial group" (Drake, 1991:33). They also drew an important distinction between individual and institutional racism. While the former related to individual attitudes and behaviours, the latter drew attention to the importance of institutions in creating and maintaining policies and practices that, even inadvertently, may exclude a group and result in unequal distributions of economic, social, and political power. Later, the term "systemic" racism came to mean any form of discriminatory policy or practice in a system, whether advertent or inadvertent.

The impetus for the development of institutional or systematic racism came from the mercantilist expansion of European countries into Asia, Africa, and the Americas.

> The empirical evidence…supports the view that prejudice and discrimination based upon skin colour existed [before European expansion] but were not accompanied by any systematic doctrines of racial inferiority or superiority, that is, "racism."… Nor were colour prejudice and discrimination institutionalized as structural principles defining systems of slavery, caste, or class. Slavery is a phenomenon that has existed in many times and places without any connection with either skin colour prejudice or racism. (Drake, 1991:7)

MARXIST ORIENTATIONS: CLASS PRIMACY THEORIES

During the 1950s, writings on racism, especially in the United Kingdom, tended to focus on race relations. Assimilationists were, however, increasingly challenged by a number of theorists who applied Marxian perspectives to their analysis of race relations. Since neither Karl Marx nor Friedrich Engels wrote about race (or gender, for that matter), most neo-Marxists subsumed issues of race and racism into the more traditional class analysis. A prominent Marxist writing in the 1950s argued that modern racism was a product of capitalism and provided European countries with a rationale for exploiting "native people" and their resources (Cox, 1976).

More recently, however, several important theoretical developments in the United Kingdom have inspired considerable controversy. Partially in reaction to the traditional functionalist,[1] assimilationist "race relations" approach, there is a strong neo-Marxist thrust apparent in the writings of Miles and Phizacklea (1984) and others. Neo-Marxists in the United Kingdom, the United States, and Canada have explored the links between immigrant workers and racism by highlighting the exploitation of wage labour, capital accumulation, and resultant class division. Rex (1983), one of the pioneers in the field in Britain, has attempted to bridge functionalism with a neo-Marxist approach, and Marxist-inspired writers such as Hall (1978) have gained prominence. There is a continuing controversy in the U.K. literature with respect to the primacy of class versus the autonomy of race in the analysis of racism.

Another recent important perspective, largely stimulated by the work of Solomos (1993, 1987) and Black scholars associated with the Centre for Contemporary Studies in Birmingham, emphasizes the role of the state in developing a "politics of racism." This analysis of the state's role in producing and reproducing racism has been stimulated by the increasing association of the British state with the doctrines of Thatcherism.[2]

While traditional Marxists give primacy to class and the means of production, neo-Marxists focus on the process of racialization that occurs in capitalist systems. Thus Canadian scholars such as Li and Bolaria (1988:7) note that "race problems begin as labour problems." Racism as an ideology therefore emerged particularly in earlier periods of history in colonial societies. This analysis of racism argues that because capitalist employers needed large pools of labour to maximize their profits, racism served as a rationale for labour exploitation.

Satzewich (1989), writing about racism in Canadian immigration practices, argues that racism is "an ideology imposed from above by those who own the means of production on those who do not: racism acts to mystify social reality, justifies the exploitation of certain groups of peoples' labour power, and contributes to the maintenance of the status quo." He stresses the relationship between racism and immigrant labour in industrial societies, including Canada. According to this view, racist ideology is preserved in order to maintain a cheap labour supply. Racism is something imposed from above, from the privileged members of society, and received by the lower orders.

There are a number of weaknesses in this approach; the main weakness is that it does not apply to all situations. For example, racism can work to the disadvantage of employers, particularly with respect to workforce disruptions and workforce harassment based on race. It says little, if anything, about racism and other divisions in the working class.

Neo-Marxist approaches are also popular in the United States. The debate about race and class, in particular, is still an important issue. For example, Franklin (1991:xiii) poses the question:

> Is the subordinate position of the Black population ultimately derived from the stigma of color, or is it due to the Black population's inferior class or economic position?

He argues that the choice of emphasis influences Blacks' status as well as the nature of discrimination in the United States. Moreover, choosing one or the other of the race–class dichotomy influences the policies and strategies for overcoming racial inequity. Franklin believes that only by creating equality in income and job allocations will the "dominant–subordinate" patterns that maintain racism be eliminated. He looks to the revitalization of American cities, where most African Americans live, to bring this about.

In the United Kingdom, Miles and Phizacklea (1984) attempted to refine some of these earlier notions while maintaining that race and race relations emerge from class—as an epiphenomenon of class and its relation to the means of production. They note that a high demand for labour characterized the British economy during the 1970s and 1980s. People of colour from the Commonwealth provided the necessary labour, but they were relegated to lower-level semiskilled and unskilled jobs. Thus, part of the working class became racialized. Race, in this model, is an ideological construction rather than an analytical category. The primary focus should be on the capitalist relations of production, which become more important than race (Ben-Tovim and Gabriel, 1986).

A more recent Marxist-influenced approach considers racism and other forms of oppression as part of the hegemonic order. This approach has been particularly well received in the United Kingdom, most notably by Stuart Hall (1991). Although Hall considers race a construct, he argues that racism cannot be reduced to classism or any other phenomenon but must be understood as part of the broad socioeconomic and political context within which it flourishes: race and class have an interactive relationship.

In attempting to bridge several neo-Marxian approaches, Rex focussed on "race relations situations," which he defined as:

> situations in which two or more groups with distinct identities and recognisable characteristics are forced by economic and political circumstances to live together in society.... There is a high degree of conflict between the groups and...ascriptive criteria are used to mark out the members of each group in order that one group may pursue one of a number of hostile policies against the other.... [T]he ascriptive allocation of roles and rights referred to are justified in terms of some kind of deterministic theory...scientific, religious, historical, ideological or sociological. (Rex, 1983:159–60)

Rex and his colleagues attempted to analyze racism by specifying the situations in which it occurs, which include those in which race is not a factor. For example, the conflict in Ireland, largely one based on ethnicity rather than race, would nevertheless qualify as a "race relations situation" according to this view. Rex's primary aim was to call attention to the unequal access of Black migrants in the United Kingdom to goods and services as well as to examine the consequences of inequality among both the White and Black working classes (Rex and Moore, 1967; Rex and Tomlinson, 1979).

In summary, a basic change in perspective occurred in the late 1960s and 1970s—from the assimilationist race relations approach in both the United States and then United Kingdom to an emphasis on racism.[3] Analysts concluded that

> it was not black people who should be examined but white society; it was not a question of educating blacks and whites for integration, but of fighting institutional racism; it was not race relations that was the field of study, but racism. (Bourne and Sivanandan, 1980:339)

THE 1980s: FROM RACISM TO ANTI-RACISM

Another important shift in the study of race relations occured in the 1980s. Although many still use the term "racism" to describe the social construction of the biological concept of race, the designation "anti-racism" has taken on some currency.

The word "race"—however positively used, (for example, in "multi-racial education")—validates the basic ideas upon which racism is built (Brandt, l986). Its use negatively influences the development of both policy and practices. Therefore, a more appropriate vocabulary would use "anti-racism," which counters the notion of "races."

"Anti-racism" suggests, in the first instance, that racist institutional policies and practices are the locus of the problem of racism in contemporary society. Thus, in a general sense, anti-racism refers to measures and mechanisms designed—by the state, institutions, organizations, groups, and individuals—to counteract racism. Some social scientists point out that the aims of anti-racism are, by definition, oppositional: its intention is to oppose any organizational or institutional policy or practice that oppresses, represses, or disenfranchises members of a racial group (Brandt, 1986).

Anti-racism is a strong trend in both the United Kingdom and the United States, and more recently in Canada. For example, anti-racism education in these jurisdictions is aimed primarily at dismantling structures and systems that have generated and perpetuated racial barriers and inequities in the policies, programs, and practices of the educational system. Anti-racism also targets administrative procedures that exclude racial-minority educators from full and equal participation in educational institutions. It assumes that a system of inequality exists and that legislation, policy-making, program implementation, and monitoring is required to dismantle it.

SOCIAL RESEARCH IN CANADA: ETHNICITY, MULTICULTURALISM, AND RACISM

The field of race relations and its recent emphasis on racism and anti-racist approaches are often combined with studies of ethnicity and multiculturalism (Frideres, l989). In North American universities, for example, "Race and Ethnic Relations" has been a popular course in sociology. This approach assumes that race and ethnicity are closely related and that a racial group is simply another kind of ethnic group.

Thus a textbook in this field may include the study of Greeks, Italians, Scots, Germans, Blacks, and Chinese. Its assimilationist perspective suggests that the experiences of all groups are similar. In Canada, the experiences of European immigrants who arrived here after 1945 and who suffered discrimination are often cited. It is implied that they overcame discrimination because they were industrious and worked hard, and that this eased their eventual adaptation to Canadian society. This view suggests that, in the long run, race and colour will become unimportant in much the same way that ethnic origins become less important as time goes on and generations change.

The study of race and ethnic relations gradually began to give way to the study of ethnicity. American scholars in particular noticed that people whose ancestors had migrated to the United States in the last part of the nineteenth century and in the early twentieth century, were reclaiming their origins. Ethnicity, it was discovered, is not totally lost as generations change. Third- and fourth-generation immigrants who had successfully integrated experienced a renewed interest in their origins (Reitz, 1980). Moreover, some ethnic cultural patterns, particularly food habits, had carried over to successive generations. Meanwhile, the United States was receiving migrants from countries such as Mexico, Puerto Rico, and other Hispanic countries. These groups continued to value their ethnic origins and culture in the face of racism directed against them and their relative exclusion from American institutions.

An important work establishing the credibility of the study of ethnicity was Glazer and Moynihan's *Ethnicity: Theory and Experience* (1975), which defined the field of study as "all the groups of a society characterized by a distinctive sense of difference owing to culture and descent." Ethnicity was a central concept in understanding the many subgroups in society and was as important as social class as a segmenting variable. In this formulation, race and colour were not considered important factors in maintaining ethnicity. It essentially ignored the differential treatment that racial minorities would continue to experience. In response, Black scholars took the view that emphasizing ethnicity was simply another way of not dealing with the central issue of racism.

Race and ethnicity are often considered to be closely related because both variables differentiate groups in plural or heterogeneous societies. However, considering the two concepts as equal partners, or tagging race onto ethnicity, subsumes race under ethnicity. Ethnicity involves a notion of blood, kinship, a common sense of belonging, and often a common geographic or national origin. It refers to the social origins of groups, whereas race refers to the biological status of groups and the social construction of racism, which often follows.

Race and ethnicity do overlap at times, particularly in areas in which Blacks and Whites are members of the same ethnic group. The most obvious example occurs in the United States, where both racial groups are ethnically American yet do not share equally in the distribution of wealth, power, and privilege. It is not surprising, therefore, that those who have a strong commitment to the elimination of racism perceive ethnicity studies as drawing attention away from racism. This belief has affected Black studies programs at American universities:

> There was pressure on some campuses to transform [Black Studies programs] into Ethnic Studies programs. In some instances, Black Studies publications were reconceived as Ethnic Studies publications.... One response to the Black Consciousness and Black Power movements in the United States was to try to deracialize them, to argue that the Black Experience was similar to that of European ethnic groups and that the passage of time would make race and colour increasingly irrelevant. (Drake, 1991:59)

In the United Kingdom, a similar movement toward multiculturalism has taken place, particularly in schools where multicultural education consists of learning about the heritages and cultures of people rather than dealing with structural racism. One of the most powerful critics of that movement notes that

> anti-racism in the seventies was only fought and resisted in the community, in the localities, behind the slogan of a Black politics and the Black experience. In that moment, the enemy was ethnicity. The enemy had to be what we called "multiculturalism." Because multiculturalism was precisely what I called…the exotic. The exotica of difference. Nobody would talk about racism but they were prepared to have "international evenings" when we would all come and cook our native dishes, sing our own native songs and appear in our own native costumes. (Hall, 1991:56)

In describing the situation in the United Kingdom, Hall equates the concepts of ethnicity and multiculturalism. In Canadian studies, however, multiculturalism has a more applied meaning because its main impetus came from the state, in the form of federal legislation. There has been some work on ethnicity in Canada (e.g., Anderson and Frideres, 1981), but more attention has been paid to multiculturalism (e.g., Elliott and Fleras, 1992).

THE 1990s: DISCOURSE ANALYSIS

Largely in reaction to the economic reductionism of neo-Marxian structuralist analysis and the difficulties inherent in measuring the correlation between attitudes and behaviour, a new perspective on racism—discourse analysis—has developed. Its theorists are influenced by philosophy, semiotics, and linguistic analyses.

Discourse analysis poses the questions: In what ways does the language used to express racist attitudes and make accusations and denials of racism change over time? How do these changes in expression determine changes in the forms of racist attitudes and behaviour, and in responses and resistance? (Goldberg, 1990:xii). Discourse analysis examines everyday conversation as well as the media. Van Dijk (1991) uses a discourse analysis of newspapers and other media to show how social, economic, and political power structures influence the reporting and analysis of news and reinforce their power. Reportage using racial discourse falls into this category of analysis.

MULTICULTURALISM, ETHNICITY, AND RACISM IN CANADA

In view of the considerable evidence of racism in Canadian society, how has the research community in Canada responded to race as a field of inquiry? Several trends can be identified. One of the most comon responses has been neglect. The academic establishment, particularly in the social sciences, has been singularly remiss in undertaking research on racism. A notable exception is the work of social scientists on discrimination against Aboriginal peoples. Anthropologists, in particular, have been in the forefront of research concerning Aboriginal rights to resources and land.

There are many reasons for the lack of attention to racism, but one factor of importance is that studies that concentrated solely on racism did not appear until the late 1970s.[4] Growth in the field was slow, and the literature on race and racism in Canada remains limited. Another important factor is that race as a variable of differentiation is still considered part of ethnicity and ethnic relations. Thus, courses, books, and studies on "race and ethnic relations" remain popular. Race and ethnicity are not distinguished for the purposes of applied policy-oriented research.

One of the first research trends in the study of race and social racism in Canada was the demonstration of the existence of racism in Canadian society. Examples include Henry and Ginzberg's (1985) study of employment discrimination; studies of racism in education, such as those of Ramcharan (1974) and Adair and Rosenstock (1976); and studies of racial discrimination, such as Jain's and the beginning work of Li.[5] Much of the work published in the 1970s was undertaken by academics using traditional scholarly perspectives and methods. Its primary purpose was to influence public policy.

Another trend was to consider race in studies of ethnic groups, particularly those of colour. Important work on the Chinese in British Columbia, Haitians in Montreal, and South Asians in Canada was done in the 1970s and continues to the present. These works reveal that it is not only culture and ethnicity that influence integration into a new host society, but also the forces of racism.[6]

More recently, scholarly research on racism has increased, perhaps because more racial-minority scholars have been hired by universities.[7] Two discernible trends can be identified in the current literature. The first is the use of a neo-Marxian political economy model in which the role of labour migration and labour exploitation is highlighted. Strongly influenced by the theoretical work of Miles (1989), this approach is best exemplified in Satzewich (1993), which brings together the results of a conference held on the subject of immigration, racism, and multiculturalism, sponsored by the Social Research Unit of the University of Saskatchewan.

The second trend, also neo-Marxian, is research that uses a race, gender, or class paradigm to highlight the many factors involved in unequal power relations in societies such as Canada. Feminist scholars, especially feminist scholars of colour, are in the forefront of this approach.[8] In Canada as elsewhere, they have disputed the dynamics of the relationships of ethnicity and class, ethnicity and race, and all three as they relate to gender (Ng, 1984, 1993).

One of the major reasons for the preponderance of attention paid to ethnicity and multiculturalism is Canada's immigration policies and demographic patterns. The aftermath of World War II influenced substantial numbers of Europeans to migrate to Canada. Not until the liberalization of immigration legislation in 1967 did substantial numbers of people of colour arrive in Canada. Thus, late-twentieth-century Canadian society was first diversified by the arrival of White Europeans. A focus on ethnicity and the beginnings of multiculturalism became evident. Even today, "ethnic revitalization" is occurring in Canada (Herberg, 1989; Driedger, 1989; Breton et al.,

1990). In addition to creating a substantial literature on ethnicity, Canadian scholarship has paid considerable attention to multiculturalism (e.g., Elliott and Fleras, 1992).

The policy of the present federal government is to include the dynamics of racism in the context of multiculturalism. Multiculturalism, however, must be distinguished from racism and strategies to promote anti-racism. The essential question is, if federal legislation and policies recognize and legitimize cultural diversity, should

> multicultural initiatives focus on the perpetuation of culture or the enhancement of ethnoracial equality? If the latter, multiculturalism must accentuate the needs and aspirations of *racial* minorities.... However, does this mean that folkloric multiculturalism is obsolete, and in danger of being replaced by an "instrumental" multiculturalism, with its commitment to race relations, social equality, and institutional accommodation? (Fleras and Elliott, l992:6)

An emphasis on the needs of racial minorities in Canada is viewed with caution because of the government's fear that it would be perceived negatively by White mainstream and ethnic communities. It is unlikely, therefore, that the present government will ignore the celebration of cultural diversity in Canada.[9]

It must be admitted that considerable amount of good work has been done under the rubric of multiculturalism and that a legitimate case can be made for its benefits (Elliott and Fleras, l992). However, racial inequalities and the social construction of racism should have pride of place at the level of the state, in public- and private-sector institutions, in teaching curricula and educational institutions, and in scholarly research.

RACE, GENDER, AND CLASS PARADIGMS IN CANADA

In Canada, as in other complex societies with heterogeneous populations, social relations are influenced by such factors as class, gender, and race. While the totality of social life can only be explained in terms of the interactions of these and other distinguishing characteristics, one of them is usually given prominence. The choice of factor is largely determined by the theoretical orientation of the analyst (Stasiulis, 1990).

While racism is an important segmenter of Canadian (and other) societies, class and gender also create significant inequities. Many modern paradigms of society include the "interlocking nature of relevant systems of domination and the varieties of consciousness that flow from them, with a view to understanding how they affect collective action" (Morris, l992:361).

The interrelationships of class, race and/or ethnicity, and gender have especially been re-examined from the perspective of feminist neo-Marxism. (Smith, l987). They have criticized the ethnicity and class perspectives of sociology, in which the issues of gender and race are usually ignored. While

Ng maintains that race and ethnicity can be taken together because of their constructed character, she concludes that

> gender, race/ethnicity, and class are not fixed entities. They are socially constructed in and through the productive and reproductive relations in which we all participate. Thus, what constitutes sexism, racism, as well as class oppression, changes over time as productive relations change. (Ng, 1993:195)

Another Canadian approach to this area is represented by Calliste, whose studies of Caribbean immigrant women show that they have been used as cheap domestic labour (Calliste, 1989, 1992). In this paradigm, it is assumed that all three factors oppress and equally impinge on people's life chances. The combination of the three factors put these women of colour in an especially vulnerable position.

THE FORMS OF RACISM

Because it is an exceedingly complex manifestation of human behaviour, racism takes many forms. The context within which it occurs largely determines the form it takes. In its simplest form, racism has three components: individual, systemic, and cultural or ideological. In individual racism, a further distinction must be made between an individual's attitudes and her or his behaviour. An individual might hold a set of attitudes about Black people—for example, they are lazy, unmotivated, or slow. These attitudes may remain at the level of thought, or they may result in a certain form of behaviour, such as "everyday racism," which includes small acts like not shaking a Black person's hand or not sitting next to a person of colour on a bus.

Another form of racism occurs in collectivities or organizations that have developed policies and practices that are, intentionally or unintentionally, discriminatory. Within police organizations, for example, the former policy requiring officers to be of a certain height and weight was discriminatory towards certain groups of people.

The overarching form of racism resides in cultural symbols and is expressed through language, religion, and art. "Cultural racism" refers to collective and mass beliefs about race that are woven into the fabric of the dominant culture. The use of the word "black" to denote something negative or evil (as in "blackmail") is an example of cultural racism.

At each of these three levels, the racism may be overtly expressed or take on a covert, subtle, or hidden form.

INDIVIDUAL RACISM

Individual racism involves both the attitudes held by an individual and the overt behaviour prompted by those attitudes. The attitudes are often obvious: extremely intolerant, bigoted individuals tend to be proud of their attitudes

Table 2.1

THE FORMS OF RACISM

Type	Manifestations
Individual	Attitudes; everyday behaviour
Institutional/systemic	Policies and practices of an organization; rules woven into a social system
Cultural/ideological	Values embedded in dominant culture

and articulate them overtly and publicly. In a society such as Canada's, however, most people are uncomfortable about expressing their attitudes openly because these attitudes run counter to the prevailing norms. They may show their attitudes by practising racial discrimination.

Individual racism has been defined as the attitude, belief, or opinion that one's own racial group has superior values, customs, and norms and, conversely, that other racial groups possess inferior traits and attributes. Individual racist beliefs provide a lens through which one sees, interprets, and interacts with the world. Because it is rooted in the individual's belief system, racism is a form of prejudice,

> an emotionally rigid attitude...toward a group of people. It involves not only prejudgment but...misjudgment as well. It is categorical thinking that systematically misinterprets the facts. (Wellman, 1972:24)

Prejudiced attitudes are largely unconscious and, as such, unnoticed by most people. They are strongly connected to the ways in which social relations are structured:

> Racist attitudes are largely derivative in nature.... They do not spring up or survive in a vacuum...but grow out of and are continually sustained by the structure of social relations of which they are largely a psychological reflection. (Parekh, 1987:viii)

Implicit in this notion is a rejection of earlier social psychology theories that suggest that racist thinking, **intolerance**, or prejudiced beliefs are rooted in certain deviant personality types (e.g., the authoritarian personality) or related to low socioeconomic status. Wellman (1977) and others argue that middle-class Whites are trained to subscribe to "liberal" ideas of equality and therefore tend to verbalize tolerance, while holding ambivalent and sometimes conflicting attitudes.

In this view, prejudice needs to be placed in a broader sociological context because attitudinal manifestations of racial inequality are related to social, political, and economic stratifications that form social structures and arrangements. This approach shifts the focus on misconceptions that White people might have about "others" to an emphasis on measuring interpersonal, interracial animosity. It views the basis of racism as being the dominant position of White people in Western society, and the benefits that result from this position. This analysis concludes that "personal prejudice is really a disguised way to defend privilege" (Wellman, 1977:39).

A central question about individual racism is: Do racist beliefs necessarily result in discriminatory behaviour and, if so, under what conditions? While there is some debate in the literature regarding the causal relationship between prejudice and discrimination, a body of research demonstrates a clear link (Howitt and McCabe, 1978). Researchers found that in circumstances in which behaviour has no observable victim, there was a clear correspondence between attitudes and behaviour. However, Howitt and Owusu-Bempah (1990) drew an important distinction: racism is not something done only by racists; it is a sociocultural system that achieves specific objectives. It is therefore important to move the conception of racism beyond the an analysis that focusses on interpersonal animosity.

Utilizing a similar analysis, it can be argued that the racist ideology of individuals, like sexist attitudes, is only a symptom of the more serious malaise in the relationships between racial groups. Social and psychological considerations should be examined within the sociocultural context that produces and reproduces inequality and injustice (Howitt and Owusu-Bempah, 1987).

> Personal attitudes far from exhaust the catalogue of discriminatory behaviour.... Discrimination remains so pervasive and entrenched because it is not solely personal.... It permeates both power and private relationships....
> The racist, sexist or homophobe is not an aberrational figure in our culture.... It is the collective culture as much as individual citizens. (Hutchinson, 1992)

Racial beliefs and attitudes of individuals can also be considered as a continuum of weak to strong. A weak attitude merely uses and identifies racial classifications without necessarily prescribing any action. Reeves (1983) identifies weak racism to include beliefs:

- that races of human beings exist;
- that these races differ from one another;
- that the differences are deeply rooted and enduring;
- that the differences are significant, possibly because they appear in themselves to be explanatory, or because explanations of other social features may be inferred from them, and
- that the differences have social consequences, for example, for social policy.

There is no moral evaluation of differences, nor does any form of prescriptive action flow from them.

A medium attitude accords more favourable treatment to the alleged superior race while denying goods and services to the alleged inferior races. Medium racist belief systems may include:

- precise details of how and in what way the races differ;
- an explanation for the continuing existence of races and racial differences;

- reasons for the assumptions being thought significant in terms of social consequences that result or have resulted from racial differences; and
- the belief that differences between races make certain races superior or inferior and that races can be placed in some sort of rank order.

Finally, strong racist beliefs include a prescription for action that follows from all of the above beliefs: that the superior race is entitled to more favourable treatment than the inferior race.

EVERYDAY RACISM

Everyday racism involves the many and sometimes small ways in which racism is experienced by peoples of colour in their interactions with the dominant White group. It expresses itself in glances, gestures, forms of speech, and physical movements. Sometimes it is not even consciously experienced by its perpetrators, but it is immediately and painfully felt by its victims—the empty seat next to a person of colour, which is the last to be occupied in a crowded bus; the slight movement away from a person of colour in an elevator; the overattention to the Black customer in the shop; the inability to make direct eye contact with a person of colour; the racist joke told at a meeting; and the ubiquitous question "Where did you come from?"

From a research perspective, these incidents are difficult to quantify because they are only revealed in the thoughts, feelings, and articulations of victims:

> It is very difficult to determine "objectively" the nature of everyday interaction between Whites and Blacks.... A variety of studies have shown that those who are discriminated against appear to have more insight into discrimination mechanisms than those who discriminate.... Blacks have a certain amount of expertise about racism through extensive experience with Whites. The latter, conversely, are often hardly aware of the racism in their own attitudes and behaviour. (Essed, 1990)

And, although peoples of colour are often sensitive to everyday racism, it may be so subtle that they are unaware of it. Research on racism has therefore tended to focus on what is more immediately visible and measurable. Thus racial discrimination in employment, in the media, and other more visible manifestations of racism have been studied.

In analyzing everyday racism, a further important distinction can be made between active and passive racism. Active racism includes

> all acts that—consciously or unconsciously—emerge directly from the motivation to exclude or to inferiorize Blacks because they are Black. Passive racism is complicity with someone else's racism. Laughing at a humiliating joke...and "not hearing" others' racist comments are passively racist acts. (Essed, 1990)

INSTITUTIONAL AND SYSTEMIC RACISM

Institutional racism is manifested in the policies, practices, and procedures of various institutions, which may, directly or indirectly, consciously or unwittingly, promote, sustain, or entrench differential advantage or privilege for people of certain races. An example of institutional racism is the common practice of "word-of-mouth recruitment," which generally excludes racial minorities from the process.

Institutional racism generally encompasses overt individual acts of racism to which there is no serious organizational response, such as discriminatory hiring decisions based on the employer's **bias**. It also includes organizational policies and practices that, regardless of intent, are directly or indirectly disadvantageous to racial minorities, for example, the lack of recognition of foreign credentials, or inflated educational requirements for a position. According to J.J. Jones,

> Institutional racism can be defined as those established laws, customs and practices which systematically reflect and produce racial inequalities in American society. If racist consequences accrue to institutional laws, customs or practices the institution is racist whether or not the individuals maintaining those practices have racist intentions. (Williams, 1985:131)

Systemic racism, although similar to institutional racism, refers more broadly to the laws, rules, and norms woven into the social system that result in an unequal distribution of economic, political, and social resources and rewards among various racial groups. It is the denial of access, participation, and equity to racial minorities for services such as education, employment, and housing.

CULTURAL AND IDEOLOGICAL RACISM

Cultural racism is sometimes difficult to isolate because it is deeply embedded in the society's value system. It consists of the tacit network of beliefs and values that encourage and justify discriminatory practices. Writers such as Lawrence (1982) are very specific in their connotation of cultural racism and cite the misunderstanding of the cultural patterns of some groups as a basis for it. He writes specifically about the perception of the Black, particularly Caribbean, family, which differs from the type of family considered "normal" by the dominant culture. If the family does not contain a male breadwinner, a financially dependent wife, and their offspring, it is thought to be pathological or deviant. British politicians, for example, routinely display cultural racism when they claim that the "race problem" is caused by pathological cultural patterns (Lawrence, 1982). Some writers prefer the use of the term "ideological racism" (e.g., Reeves, 1983), but both terms refer to racism formulated as a set of values and ideas.

Essed (1990) argues that cultural racism precedes other forms of racism in society. It is reflected in everyday language—whiteness is associated with overwhelmingly positive connotations, while blackness, in *Roget's Thesaurus*, has no fewer than 60 distinctively negative synonyms, 20 of which are related to race. It is reflected in the images generated by the mass media (racial minorities are often portrayed as problems) and by the arts (literature, poetry, and visual art). It is also manifested in religious doctrines, ideologies, and practices.

Cultural racism creates a "we and they" mentality, that is, one's own racial group is considered to be better than other groups. This ubiquitous tendency to view all peoples and cultures in terms of one's own cultural standards and values is known as **ethnocentrism** and plays a central role in racism.

Cultural racism is maintained through the socialization of the new generation. Children learn the cultural beliefs and values of their society at an early age. Ideas and beliefs about races and racism are included in this early learning (Ijaz and Ijaz, 1986; Milner, 1983).

Finally, an important component of ideological racism that has been identified as the "new or modern racism" (Elliott and Fleras, 1992) provides the conceptual framework of this book. "Democratic racism" provides an important insight into why, in a democratic society, many forms of racism exist. As the title of this book indicates, the paradox is that both a liberal democratic value system *and* racist beliefs and behaviours—belief systems that should be in conflict with each other—nevertheless coexist.

Although the various forms of racism can be isolated for discussion purposes, in reality they form a complex dynamic of interrelated attitudes, feelings, and behaviours that are linked to the collective belief system and are expressed in institutional policies and practices. While institutional racism is for many theorists the focus of attention—because the very real discrimination that people of colour face often emanates from institutions—these institutions are composed of individuals who make the policies and implement the actions. Institutional and systemic racism is therefore the result of a series of interactions between the individuals who function within the system and the forces of the system itself.

This approach to racism is strongly influenced by Hall (1991) and others in viewing racism as a social construction of difference. It is based on the idea that minor physical and genetic differences between people can be used as a basis of social differentiation. Thus, social, cultural, and intellectual values are ascribed to these minute differences. These ascriptions lead to racial discrimination and inequality. Racism functions in society to maintain the power and privilege of certain groups at the expense of others. People of colour living as minorities in White-dominated societies are often treated as less than full citizens so that the balance of power relations will not be upset.

Racism takes many forms. At the individual level, prejudiced attitudes may be expressed in the many slights characteristic of everyday racism. It is demonstrated at the cultural and ideological level by the myths and stereotypes that circulate about the inferiority of certain kinds of people. And it is embedded in the policies and practices that regulate social, economic, political, and cultural institutions.

THE MEASUREMENT OF RACISM

One of the most problematic aspects of racism is measuring its many manifestations. What is acceptable as evidence that racism has occurred, and how can this evidence be quantified?

Figure 2.1
THE DIMENSIONS OF RACISM

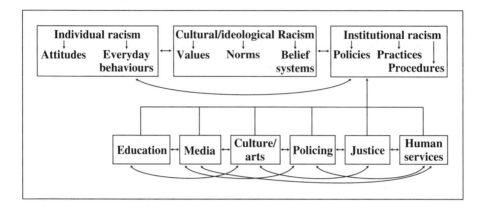

Little research has been conducted in Canada on the issue of measurement. Much evidence of racism must be culled from other indicators. As Weinfeld notes, data of adequate reliability and validity, transformed into recognized indicators and disseminated appropriately, are not available. Thus, most attempts to answer such questions [To what extent is Canada a racist society?] are based on partial snapshots, hunches, or predispositions of the analyst (Weinfeld, 1990).

Since racism and its many manifestations are now issues of central concern to contemporary social policy and practice, the question of measurement is a critical issue. Moreover, the media spend a great deal of time reporting, analyzing, and editorializing about racism. This attention leads people at all levels to pontificate on it, often with little knowledge of the subject. The alleged increase or decrease in racism are frequently cited. These public comments may be motivated by the political agendas of the speakers and writers who have a stake in this field.

Public spokespersons use different criteria to measure racism. Some cite poll results that show changes in attitudes, others cite economic criteria such as differences in income or employment, examples of discrimination in employment, or the number of cases brought to human rights commissions. Using different criteria to document racism leads to confusion about the meaning of the term and the ways in which it can be measured.

Clearly, a multidimensional approach to the measurement of racism is required, but even researchers in the field have relied on various approaches (Weinfeld, 1990). Neither the various spokespersons nor the academic researchers necessarily project an accurate picture. But what is an accurate picture?

How do we know, first, what racism is? Second, how can it be quantified not only for research purposes but for the development and implementation of anti-racist policies and practices? A review of the Ontario Human Rights Commission's disposition of complaints involving racism has shown that racial inequality is difficult to prove because of its hidden nature (Frideres and Reeves, 1989). If it is hard to demonstrate, how can it be measured?

In the first instance, it is again necessary to distinguish between overt individual forms of racism, such as the articulation of prejudicial attitudes, and the commonplace events and incidents that racial minorities confront daily. Attitudes can be studied and measured in a variety of ways. For example, a number of attitude studies undertaken in Canada show that from 12 to 16 percent of the population hold bigoted and intolerant attitudes (Henry, 1978). But how accurate are attitude surveys and polls as a measurement of racism?

In Canada, as elsewhere, studies of racism first focussed on prejudicial attitudes on the assumption that racism was caused solely by individuals acting on their negative feelings. More recently, a number of polls and surveys have considered the issues of racism and ethnicity. Polls have also been taken on matters relating to immigration. However, Gallup and similar polls are crude indicators, and their interpretation is often open to question. Questions asking for a perception of the increase in racism can be interpreted in many ways: a positive response can mean that the respondents have seen a greater number of racist incidents; it can also mean that a larger number of incidents are considered racist today, whereas formerly the respondents considered the incidents related to factors other than racism.

The first interpretation may mean that racism is on the rise, but the second may mean that a concern about racism and its negative effects is on the rise. Similarly, questions about the numbers of people who should be admitted to Canada give rise to various interpretations. People who respond negatively may simply be reflecting the view that Canada has more people than its economy can handle, which is not the same as the view that racial-minority immigration should be controlled.

Conversely, many Canadians pride themselves on their tolerance and respect for diversity and profess belief in the traditional democratic values of fairness and equality. Thus, their answers to pollsters' questions are unconsciously skewed to correspond to what they think a "liberal" response should be. Their ambivalent views are filtered out of the answers. The result is that a more positive response is projected. This is an example of ambivalent or aversive racism, in which people hold two opposing and contradictory attitudes—one friendly, the other hostile (Gaertner and Dovidio, 1986).

A further problem in measuring racism exists in relation to the results of polls and surveys. Since racial attitudes are frequently unconscious, unarticulated, and non-deliberate (Barrett, 1987; Wellman, 1977; Essed, 1990), "self-reports" of racial attitudes do not necessarily conform to behaviour (Phillips, 1971). A gap exists between attitude and behaviour, belief and action, prejudice and discrimination. But the extent of this divergence is not very clear (Barrett, 1984).

Several critical dimensions of the measurement conundrum, particularly with respect to polls and surveys, were revealed in an analysis of anti-Semitism in the United States (Goldberg, 1993). When representatives of major Jewish organizations met to draft a statement about anti-Semitism, a number of facts and figures were presented that seemed to indicate that anti-Semitism was greatly on the increase. One in five Americans, according to one poll, held strong anti-Semitic views; the number of bias crimes against Jews, ranging from graffiti to murder, seemed to have increased; and a number of constitutional challenges against hate-crime laws had been introduced in several states. The American Jewish Committee released a poll showing that 47 percent of New Yorkers, including 63 percent of Blacks, believed that "Jews have too much influence." A national poll revealed that 20 percent of Americans and 37 percent of Black Americans were anti-Semitic.

Although these poll results showed alarming numbers, other indicators of anti-Semitism presented a different picture. For example, overt discrimination against Jews in housing, jobs, and education had all but disappeared in the United States. Moreover, poll questions about Jews having too much influence are not necessarily indicators of anti-Semitism. Is perceived influence a measure of anti-Semitism or anti-Black prejudice? Increasingly, poll questions that allegedly test for negative stereotypes, such as the notion that "Jews stick together," are considered positive rather than negative traits.

In addition to challenging poll questions, this analysis also revealed that little attention is paid to longitudinal comparisons with earlier polling results. For example, the figure of 20 percent of Americans being anti-Semitic represents a drop of nearly one third from a 1964 result of 29 percent. The only indicator of anti-Semitism that does show an increase is the number of actual incidents—a total of 1879 in 1991, which consisted primarily of epithets and swastika daubings. This still amounts to five incidents per day in a total population of 250 million.

Although most poll and survey results do not appear to indicate any massive increase in prejudice, the vast majority of U.S. Jews (85 percent compared with 45 percent in 1983) believe that "anti-Semitism is a serious problem in America today." This disparity is blamed by some on Jewish agencies who use anxiety about anti-Semitism as a means of fundraising. ("People don't give if you tell them everything's okay.") Goldberg (1993) concludes by noting that "the masses are driving the leadership.... Maybe it's time for the leadership to start leading, and tell their public the truth."

Although polls and attitude surveys present considerable obstacles to understanding the manifestations of racism, it is even more difficult to study everyday racism. Everyday racism must be studied from the perspective of the victims who experience it in looks, gestures, and forms of speech. Part of the problem may be that most researchers are White and have not themselves experienced these daily slights. However, the problem of measuring the hidden, innermost feelings and experiences of victims also plays a significant role in limiting research (Silvera, 1989).[10]

An additional, important factor is that evidence based on the everyday experiences of victims—"victim testimony"—is not the kind of evidence that authorities and decision-makers trust. Victims are believed to have "chips on their shoulders" and therefore not to be objective. Victim testimony has been collected by some task forces and commissions investigating aspects of racism in Canadian society. Although their reports have used public consultation to elicit data, they are not considered reliable studies of overt racism.

Some racial-minority leaders maintain that the denial of victim testimony is in itself a form of subtle racism. On the other hand, some minority leaders in responsible positions argue against research of any kind and for a reliance on victim testimony as the only acceptable documentation of racism. Clearly, there is a danger here of "throwing out the baby with the bath water," and a balanced perspective that includes both testimonials and research on measurement must be established.

MEASURING INSTITUTIONAL AND SYSTEMIC RACISM

It is difficult to study and measure covert racism in its institutional or systemic form. What is usually considered evidence is the consequences of alleged discrimination, rather than the intent to discriminate. One of the main problems with the concept of institutional racism is that it does not differentiate the structural features of institutions in society from the actions of groups of individuals. To what extent is racism embodied in institutions, and how can its institutional manifestation be measured?

Weinfeld (1990) has listed a large number of indicators of racism in all its forms. With respect to institutional racism, his list includes socioeconomic measures such as:

- *education*: level of attainment and areas of specialization
- *occupation*: income; mobility; measures of unemployment, underemployment, labour-force participation, and poverty; workplace measures such as racial harassment
- *representation rates*: in upper and middle levels of firms and organizations; degree of racial segregation in work settings and sectors, job **ghettoization**
- *housing data*: residential segregation and quality of housing; incidents of discrimination by landlords and realtors

It is almost impossible to answer the question: "Is racism on the increase?" because the answer largely depends on which of its many facets is being considered and by what method it is being measured. When public figures discuss the alarming increase in racism, they usually rely on a snapshot of attitudes—polls or surveys. Such studies are often enough only crude indicators at best, and "remarkably uninformative; for the most part, they tell us about the relative readiness of sections of the population to subscribe to one set of verbal formula rather than another" (Zubaida, 1972).

Institutional, cultural, and individual racism feature in many of the incidents that occur in institutional contexts. The confluence of individual attitudes and cultural ideologies in institutional contexts result in innumerable examples of both intended and unintended racism. Although the three major forms of racism outlined in this chapter can be isolated for historical analyses, it is often difficult to identify the forms of racism that occur in everyday life. The ways in which racism is manifested are "so much a part of each other that they are often inseparable.... To see how white people do racism...we cannot compartmentalize their thoughts and actions; to see the full picture, the three distinct concepts need to be combined" (Wellman, 1977:39).

SUMMARY

This chapter has reviewed the main theoretical formulations devised by social scientists in the United States, the United Kingdom, and Canada to explain the phenomenon of racism in modern society. There are essentially three main themes in the theoretical literature:

- *assimilation models*, developed earlier in this century, in which race is assumed to be part of ethnicity, and members of racial groups are therefore expected to assimilate into mainstream society with the same ease as did members of White ethnic groups;
- *race relations models*, in which race and racism are considered variables that segment or fractionalize groups in society; and
- *anti-racist approaches*, in which society in general and institutions in particular are expected to challenge racism.

Assimilation approaches generally assume consensus and homogeneity in society, whereas the later theories, especially those that are Marxian-derived, generally consider racism as a manifestation of class-derived conflict. The most recent theoretical themes in the literature stress the manner in which racism is embedded in the language, text, and cultural symbols of modern societies.

This chapter also defined three major forms of racism: *individual racism*, which can be considered in its attitudinal and behavioral dimensions; *institutional or systemic racism* and *cultural or ideological racism*. The chapter concluded with a discussion of the difficulties and complexities of racism.

REFERENCES

Allport, G. (1954). *The Nature of Prejudice*. New York: Doubleday.

Adair, J., and D. Rosenstock. (1976). *Multiracialism in the Classroom": A Survey of Interracial Attitudes in the Schools*. Ottawa: Secretary of State.

Anderson, A., and J. Frideres. (1981). *Ethnicity in Canada: Theoretical Perspectives*. Toronto: Butterworths.

Bannerji, H. (ed.) (1993). *Returning the Gaze: Essays on Racism, Feminism and Politics*. Toronto: Sister Vision, Black Women and Women of Colour Press.

Banton, M. (1977). *The Idea of Race*. London: Tavistock.

_____. (1983). *Racial and Ethnic Competition*. Cambridge and New York: Cambridge University Press.

Barrett, S. (1987). *Is God a Racist? The Right Wing in Canada*. Toronto: University of Toronto Press.

Ben Tovin, G., and G. Gabriel. (1986). *The Local Politics of Race*. London: Macmillan.

Bourne, J., and A. Sivanandan. (1974). "Cheerleaders and Ombudsmen: The Sociology of Race Relations in Britain." In *Race and Class*, vol. xxi(4).

_____. (1980). *Canadian Journal of Women and the Law*.

Brandt, G. (1986). *The Realization of Anti-Racist Teaching*. London: Falmer Press.

Breton, R., et al. (1990). *Ethnic Identity and Equality:Varieties of Experience in a Canadian City*. Toronto: University of Toronto Press.

Calliste, A. (1989). "Canada's Immigration Policy and Domestics from the Caribbean: The Second Domestic Scheme." *Race, Class, Gender: Bonds and Barriers: Socialist Studies*, 5:133–165.

_____. (1992). "Women of Exceptional Merit: Immigration of Caribbean Nurses to Canada", *Canadian Journal of Women and the Law*, 6:85–102.

Carmichael, S., and C. Hamilton. (1967). *Black Power: The Politics of Liberation in America*. New York: Random House.

CCCS (Centre for Contemporary Cultural Studies). (1982). *The Empire Strikes Back*. London: Hutchinson.

Cox, O. (1976). *Race Relations: Elements and Social Dynamics*. Detroit: Wayne State University Press.

Dimanno, R. (1993). "Hostile Reaction to Police Board Official Unfair." *The Toronto Star* (Sept. 6):A7.

Drake, St. Clair. (1991). *Black Folk Here and There*. 2 vols. Los Angeles: Centre for Afro-American Studies and University of California Press.

Driedger, L. (ed.). 1989. *The Ethnic Factor: Identity in Diversity*. Toronto: McGraw-Hill Ryerson.

Elliott, J., and A. Fleras. (1992a). *Unequal Relations*. Toronto: Prentice-Hall.

_____. (1992b). *Multiculturalism*. Scarborough: Nelson Canada.

Essed, P. (1990). *Everyday Racism: Reports from Women of Two Cultures*. Claremont, CA: Hunter House.

Fanon, F. (1967). *Black Skin, White Masks*. New York: Grove Press.

Franklin, R.S. (1991). *Shadows of Race and Class*. Minneapolis: University of Minnesota Press.

Frideres, J. (ed.). (1989). *Multiculturalism and Intergroup Relations*. New York: Greenwood Press.

_____, and W.J. Reeves. (1989). "The Ability to Implement Human Rights Legislation in Canada: A Research Note." *Canadian Review of Sociology and Anthropology* 26 (May):311–332.

Gaertner S.L., and J.F. Dovidio. (1986). "The Aversive Forms of Racism." In S.L. Gaertner and J.F. Dovidio (eds.), *Prejudice, Discrimination and Racism*. New York: Academic Press.

Glazer, N., and D. Moynihan. (1975). *Ethnicity: Theory and Experience*. Cambridge, MA: Harvard University Press.

The Globe and Mail. (1993). "How Did We Wind Up Aboard This Train?" (July 19): A12.

Goldberg, D. (1990). *The Anatomy of Racism*. Minneapolis: University of Minnesota Press.

Goldberg, J.J. (1993). "Overanxious about Anti-Semitism," *The Globe and Mail* (May 24).

Hall, S. (1991). "Old and New Identities: Old and New Ethnicities." In A. King (ed.), *Culture, Globalization and the World System*. Binghampton, NY: Department of Art History, State University of New York.

_____, et al. (1978). *Policing the Crisis*. London: Macmillan.

Henry, F. (1978). *The Dynamics of Racism in Toronto*. North York, ON: York University.

_____, and E. Ginzberg. *Who Gets the Work? A Test of Racial Discrimination in Employment*. Toronto: Urban Alliance on Race Relations.

Herberg, E. (1989). *Ethnic Groups in Canada: Adaptations and Transitions*. Scarborough, ON: Nelson Canada.

Howitt, D., and J. McCabe. (1978). "Attitudes To Predict Behaviour in Males." *British Journal of Social and Clinical Psychology* 17:285–86.

_____, and J. Owusu-Bempah. (1990). "The Pragmatics of Institutional Racism: Beyond Words." *Human Relations* 43(9):885–899

Hutchinson, A. (1992). *The Toronto Star* (March 5).

Ijaz, A., and Ijaz, H. (1986). "Ethnic Prejudice in Children." *Guidance and Counselling*. 2(1) (September).

Jain, H. (1985). *Anti-Discrimination Staffing Policies: Implications of Human Rights Legislation for Employers and Trade Unions*. Ottawa: Secretary of State.

James, C. (1989). *Seeing Ourselves: Exploring Race, Ethnicity and Culture*. Toronto: Sheridan College.

Jones, J.J. (1972). *Prejudice and Racism*. Reading, MA: Addison Wesley.

Kobayashi, A. (1990). "Racism and the Law." *Urban Geography* 11(5):447–473.

Lawrence, E. (1982). "Just Plain Common Sense: The Roots of Racism." In CCCS, *The Empire Strikes Back*. London: Hutchinson.

Li, P. (1988). *The Chinese in Canada*. Toronto: Oxford University Press.

_____, (ed.). (1990). *Race and Ethnic Relations in Canada*. Toronto: Oxford University Press.

_____, and S. Bolaria. (eds.). (1985). *Racial Oppression in Canada*. Toronto: Garamond.

Mayr, E. (1963). *Animal Species and Evolution*. Cambridge, MA: Harvard University Press.

Miles, R. (1989). *Racism*. London: Routledge

_____, and A. Phizacklea. (1984). *White Man's Country: Racism in British Politics*. London: Pluto Press.

Milner, D. (1983). *Children and Race: Ten Years Later*. London: Alan Sutton.

Montagu, A. (1964). *Man's Most Dangerous Myth: The Fallacy of Race*. Cleveland: World Publishing.

Morris, A. (1992). "Political Consciousness and Collective Action." In A. Morris and C. Mueller (eds.) *Frontiers in Social Movement Theory*. New Haven, CT: Yale University Press.

Myrdal, G. (1944). *An American Dilemma*. New York: McGraw-Hill.

Ng, R. (1984). "Sex, Ethnicity or Class: Some Methodological Considerations." *Studies in Sexual Politics* 1.

_____. (1993). "Sexism, Racism, Canadian Nationalism." In H. Bannerji (ed.), *Returning the Gaze: Essays on Racism, Feminism and Politics*. Toronto: Sister Vision Press.

_____, and J. Ramirez. (1981). *Immigrant Housewives in Canada*. Toronto: Immigrant Women's Centre.

Omi, M., and H. Winant. (1993). "On the Theoretical Concept of Race," In C. McCarthy and W. Crichlow (eds.), *Race, Identity and Representation in Education*. New York and London: Routledge.

Parekh, B. (1987). "Preface." In J. Shaw, et al. (eds.), *Strategies for Improving Race Relations: The Anglo-American Experience*." Manchester: Manchester University Press.

Park, R.E. (1950). *Race and Culture*. New York: Free Press.

Phillips, D. (1971). *Knowledge from What*. Chicago: Rand McNally.

Ramcharan, S. (1974). *Adaptation of West Indians in Canada*. Thesis. York University, Department of Sociology.

_____. (1982). *Racism: NonWhites in Canada*. Toronto: Butterworths.

Reeves, F. (1983). *British Racial Discourse*. Cambridge, UK: Cambridge University Press.

Reitz, J. (1980). *The Survival of Ethnic Groups*. Toronto: McGraw-Hill Ryerson.

Rex, J. (1983). *Race Relations in Sociological Theory*. London: Routledge and Kegan Paul.

_____. (1988). *The Ghetto and the Underclass*. Aldershot, UK, and Brookfield, VT: Avebury.

_____, and R. Moore. (1967). *Race, Community and Conflict*. London: Oxford University Press.

_____, and S. Tomlinson. (1979). *Colonial Immigrants in a British City: A Class Analysis*. London: Routledge and Kegan Paul.

Satzewich, V. (1989). "Racism and Canadian Immigration Policy: The Government's View of Caribbean Migration, 1962–66." *Canadian Ethnic Studies* 30(1).

_____. (1993). *Deconstructing a Nation: Immigration, Multiculturalism and Racism in 90s Canada*. Halifax: Fernwood.

Silvera, M. (1989). *Silenced*. Toronto: Sistren Press.

Smith, D. (1987). *The Everyday World as Problematic: A Feminist Sociology*. Toronto: University of Toronto Press.

Stasiulus, D. (1990). "Theorizing Connections: Gender, Race, Ethnicity and Class." In P. Li (ed.), *Race and Ethnic Relations in Canada*. Toronto: Oxford University Press.

Solomos, J. (1987). *The Roots of Urban Unrest*. Oxford and New York: Pergamon Press.

_____. (1993). *Race and Racism in Britain*. London: Macmillan

Weinfeld, M. (1990). "Racism in Canada: A Multi-Dimensional Approach to Measurement." Paper prepared for Conference on Race Relations in the United Kingdom and Canada. North York, ON: York University (June).

Wellman, D. (1977). *Portraits of White Racism*. Cambridge, UK: Cambridge University Press.

Williams. J. (1985). "Redefining Institutional Racism." *Ethnic and Racial Studies* 8(3)(July):323–347.

UNESCO. (1972). *Statement on Race* (Ashley Montague). New York: Oxford University Press.

Van Dijk, T. (1987). *Communicating Racism: Ethnic Prejudice in Thought and Talk*. Newbury, CA: Sage.

_____. (1991). *Racism and the Press*. London: Routledge.

Yon, D. (1991). "Schooling and the Politics of Identity: A Study of Caribbean Students in a Toronto High School." In H. Diaz (ed.), *Forging Identities and Patterns of Development*. Toronto: Canadian Scholars Press.

Zubaida, S. (1972). "Sociologists and Race Relations." In *Proceedings of a Seminar: Problems and Prospects of Socio-legal Research*. Oxford: Nuffield College, 1972.

NOTES

1. "Functionalist" in this context refers to the idea that society is composed of institutions, beliefs, and values, all of which function together to form a whole. Theories that emphasize the assimilation of ethnic and racial groups assume that these groups will ultimately fit into and become part of the larger society.

2. "Thatcherism" refers to the neoconservative approach of Prime Minister Margaret Thatcher's government in the United Kingdom in the 1980s.

3. Canadian scholars have written relatively little on racism, compared with their counterparts in the United States and United Kingdom. The dominant concern in Canadian scholarship, until very recently, has been ethnicity and multicultural studies. Notable exceptions were the publication of Li and Bolaria's *Racial Oppression in Canada* (1985) and Ramcharan's *Racism* (1982). Canadian scholars have now started to research and write more in this area.

4. Frances Henry's *Dynamics of Racism in Toronto* (North York, ON: York University, 1978), was one of the first attitude surveys published on this subject. Other factors responsible for the neglect in this field include the fact that racial minority communities in the first instance expressed their concerns about racism to government; the absence of racial minority researchers and faculty members; and the inability to obtain research funds for studies on racism in Canada because racism was considered an American problem.

5. Others include F. Henry and E. Ginzberg, *Who Gets the Work? A Test of Racial Discrimination in Employment.* (Toronto: Urban Alliance on Racism, 1984); S. Ramcharan, *Racism in Canada* (Toronto: Butterworths, 1983); J. Adair and D. Rosenstock, *Multiracialism in the Classroom: A Survey of Interracial Attitudes in Ontario Schools* (Ottawa: Secretary of State, 1976); W. Anderson and R. Grant, *The Newcomers: Problems of Adjustment of West Indian Immigrant Children in Metro Toronto Schools* (North York: York University, 1975); H. Jain, *Race and Sex Discrimination in the Workplace: An Analysis of Theory and Research and Public Policy in Canada*" (Ottawa: Employment and Immigration, 1981); D. Hughes and E. Kallen, *The Anatomy of Racism: Canadian Dimensions* (Montreal: Harvest House, 1974).

6. M. Labelle, S. LaRose, and V. Piche, "Emigration et Immigration: Les Haitians au Québec," *Sociologie et Société* 15 (1983):73–88, M. LaFerrière, "Blacks in Quebec: Minorities Among Minorities" in C. Marrett and C. Leggon, (eds.), *Research in Race and Ethnic Relations* (1983); V. Ujimoto and G. Hirabayashi, *Visible Minorities and Multiculturalism: Asians in Canada* (Toronto: Butterworths, 1980); R. Warburton, "Neglected Aspects of Political Economy of Asian Racialization in British Columbia," in V. Satzewich (ed.), *Deconstructing a Nation: Immigration, Multiculturalism and Racism in 90's Canada* (Halifax: Fernwood, 1992); K. Anderson, *Vancouver's Chinatown: Racial Discourse in Canada, 1875–1980.* (Montreal and Kingston: McGill-Queen's University Press); N. Buchnigani and D. Indra, *Continuous Journey: A Social History of South Asians in Canada* (McClelland and Stewart, 1986); C. James, *Making It: Black Youth* (1990); K. Adachi, *The Enemy That Never Was: A History of the Japanese Canadians* (Toronto: McClelland and Stewart, 1976).

7. An even more recent trend in Canadian scholarship is the acceptance of a social construct model of racism, such as that taken in this book. This perspective is demonstrated in the recent work of Peter Li, whose study of housing and the racialization of the Chinese community in Vancouver is an important example of this approach. Another significant example is Audrey Kobayashi's (1990) work on the racialization of the law.

8. Ng (1982, 1984); Ng and Ramirez (1981); and Calliste (1989, 1992).

9. Inshad Manji, writing in the *The Toronto Star*, July 5, 1992, noted that "last year, the federal Department of Multiculturalism spent nearly as much on promoting heritage cultures as it did on fighting racism. Yet pursuing both goals at the same time, and with almost equal amounts of money is stupid: racism makes the benefits of promoting heritage cultures null and void. Racism reduces culture to bright outfits, cute accents and tongue-burning foods. It also limits the audiences of ethnic celebrations to those who'd come out and see Ukrainians dancing anyway. *Racism makes multiculturalism premature.*"

10. In the Canadian literature, Makeda Silvera's *Silenced* (1989), which describes the experiences of Black domestics, comes closest to this kind of study.

Chapter 3

▼▼▼▼▼▼▼▼▼▼▼

Racism in Canadian History

It always amazes me when people express surprise that there might be a "race problem" in Canada, or when they attribute the "problem" to a minority of prejudiced individuals. Racism is, and always has been, one of the bedrock institutions of Canadian society, embedded in the very fabric of our thinking, our personality. (Shadd, 1989)

The historical overview in this chapter focusses on the relationship between the dominant White majority group and people of colour. It begins by considering Aboriginal peoples and then examines four racial minority groups—Blacks, Chinese, Japanese, and South Asians—that are the primary targets of racial bias and discrimination in Canada. The chapter goes on to identify racism in the immigration policies and practices of the Government of Canada over the last 100 years. It then explores the evidence of racism in contemporary society, drawing on some of the studies and surveys conducted over the past fifteen years, identifying evidence of overt racism, which are manifested in racist attitudes, assumptions, and practices. The more extreme expressions of beliefs and actions of right-wing "hate groups" are also discussed. Finally, the chapter focusses on discrimination in employment and housing, strong indices of racial discrimination in Canadian society.

INTRODUCTION

Racism in Canada is generally considered a contemporary phenomenon linked to the recent arrival of people of colour. However, the legacy of racial prejudice, discrimination, and disadvantage has its origins in the earliest period of Canadian history. Since more detailed historical accounts of racism exist in other sources, this chapter examines only some of the most telling examples and evidence.

MANIFESTATIONS OF RACISM

THE ABORIGINAL PEOPLES OF CANADA

As in most other western, industrialized societies, racism has been pervasive in Canada. Through the well-documented processes of Christianization, subjugation, segregation, and in some cases, extermination, European colonists denied Canada's Aboriginal peoples their history, language, culture, land, livelihood, and dignity (Richardson, 1993; Fleras and Elliot, 1992; Bienvenue and Goldstein, 1985; Frideres, 1983; Berger, 1982).

The European involvement in Canada began in the seventeenth century, when first French and later British interests focussed their attention on the development of agriculture, the expansion of the fur trade, and the establishment of military posts. The early contacts between French and British explorers, traders, and missionaries and Aboriginal peoples could be described as relatively harmonious and co-operative throughout most of the eighteenth century but, by the nineteenth century, the interaction and relationship dramatically changed (Purich, 1986). As the fur trade declined and Aboriginal peoples were no longer required as sources of labour, patterns of exclusion begin to emerge. European colonizers shifted their economic interests from fur trading to agriculture and the exploitation of other natural resources. This change resulted in a period of relatively "peaceful penetration" and signalled the beginning of a new relationship based on discrimination and exploitation (Bienvenue and Goldstein, 1985).

The Canadian government, through the Indian Act of 1876 and subsequent legislation and treaties, introduced institutionalized racism in the relationship between Canada and its Aboriginal peoples that continues to flourish today (Frideres, 1988; Bolaria and Li, 1988). The Indian Act provided a means of removing political sovereignty from indigenous people by introducing a system of indirect rule and segregation (Fleras and Elliot, 1992). The sweeping regulations under the act included prohibitions against owning land. As well, no Aboriginal peoples could develop land without the agent's consent (Bolaria and Li, 1988). Early clauses, which have in recent years been eliminated, controlled every aspect of the lives and lifestyles of Aboriginal peoples, denying them the right to vote and prohibiting them from purchasing and consuming alcohol (Bievenue and Goldstein, 1985). Later provisions prevented people from leaving reserves without permission and a ticket from the agent (Bolaria and Li, 1988).

The Indian Act was designed to promote coercive assimilation, in which Aboriginal peoples were expected to adopt the cultural attitudes and norms of the dominant culture and give up their own cultural traditions, histories, values, customs, and language (Richardson, 1993; Bolaria and Li, 1988). Aboriginal social and political institutions were systematically dismantled. For example, in 1884 the Indian Act was amended to outlaw the Potlatch ceremony, a political and social institution of West Coast Aboriginals. Using ritual, ceremony, and celebration, the Potlatch provided a central organizing framework in which new leaders were installed, wealth was distributed, names were given and recorded, political councils were held and decisions made, history instruction was provided, and spiritual guidance was given. The Aboriginal peoples were not only denied an opportunity to participate in an important ceremonial festival, but lost control over their political life (Ponting and Gibbins, 1980).

The Indian Act also set out to define "who was an Indian." Yet, as Daniel Raunet points out, "to ask the question in legal terms is in itself discriminatory.... People do not need legislation to know their origin or place on this earth" (in Ducharme, 1986). For the White lawgiver, the Indian was a person registered in an "Indian Register." Indian women who married non-status Indian men simply lost their status. These legal definitions relating to identity totally ignored the fact that Aboriginal peoples were not a monolithic group but represented extraordinarily diverse and distinct populations with different customs, traditions, histories, cultures, and languages (Ducharme, 1986).

From the moment that the federal government assumed jurisdiction over the Aboriginal peoples, Canada's relationship to Aboriginal peoples has been based on cultural, social, economic, and political oppression. It has been characterized by an endless struggle against cultural annihilation and poverty (Duclos, 1990). Aboriginal peoples were displaced from the land that formed the basis of their culture, their way of life, and their livelihood. They were placed on reserves to provide land for newly arrived European immigrants and settlers from the United States.

Although the reserves were located in areas that the various tribes had long occupied, the reserves were much smaller than their previous territories. Land on the reserves could not be disposed of without the permission of the federal government. Native people were expected to survive on the reserves and not to rely on the resources or services available in settler communities. Traditional Native governments were supplemented by band councils that had little power or influence (Bienvenue, 1985). The reserve system created a sharp social, physical, and political separation between colonizer and colonized. The development of this system ensured the isolation of Aboriginal peoples from the White settlers (Bienvenue, 1985).

The economic motive was the major force in the development of the reserve system and the most significant factor in its maintenance and preservation (Bolaria and Li, 1988). Aboriginal lands with valuable resources were often expropriated when provincial and federal government agencies required them for the building of railroads, roads, and dams (Bienvenue, 1985). The Métis in Saskatchewan, the Cree along James Bay, and many other Aboriginal groups were uprooted and relocated at the whim and convenience and for the economic gain of the various Canadian governments (Ducharme, 1986). In Manitoba and Saskatchewan, band councils claim to have lost over a million acres as a result of government expropriation and sale of reserve lands (Kellough, 1980).

Aboriginal peoples were also denied participation in the Canadian political system. Status Indians living on reserves could not vote in federal elections until 1960. Aboriginal people who wished to have the franchise were forced to give up their status and lose all the benefits conferred by the Indian Act, including rights to land, homes, and community (Sharzer, 1985).

The important role of the Christian church in supporting the systematic annihilation of Aboriginal values, norms, religious beliefs and practices, and language has been well documented (Berger, 1992). The Jesuits and other missionaries believed that Aboriginal peoples should not be left in their "inferior" natural state and considered it their mission to replace Aboriginal culture with Christian beliefs, values, rituals, and practices (Bolaria and Li, 1988). The role of the churches was to "civilize and educate Native people," and the churches were given Native land to encourage this (Powless, 1985).

In keeping with this ideology, Aboriginal children were educated in schools established by Protestant and Roman Catholic missionaries on the reserves. Later, the children were sent to residential boarding schools off the reserves. This practice lasted from the late nineteenth century to the 1960s, when the federal government assumed control of Aboriginal education. In both the church and government educational systems, Native children were subjected to systematic oppression and brutality. Many were sexually, physically, and emotionally abused. They were not allowed to speak their language or engage in any of their traditional practices. The coercive and oppressive nature of their educational experience is one of the most blatant examples of systemic racism.

Only recently has the full extent of this abuse been documented, as growing numbers of Aboriginal peoples speak out about their experiences (Richardson, 1993). According to Stanley McKay, a Cree–Ojibwa from Manitoba who is the first Aboriginal moderator of the United Church of Canada, residential schools collaborated in the cultural **genocide** of Aboriginal peoples. He considers his experiences in residential school as a form of incarceration: "My spirit was not broken but my anger is there. It is something that should not have happened. Some people were desperately scarred and wounded" (Roberts, 1993:A1).

European ethnocentrism and racism also affected patterns of Aboriginal socialization. Since most Whites viewed all aspects of tribal life and organization to be culturally and morally inferior, missionaries made efforts to eliminate the matrilineal customs of Aboriginal societies and to promote the norms of the dominant European patrilineal society (Ng, 1993; Bienvenue, 1985). The perceived differences between men and women

> were used by nineteenth-century missionaries to organize Indians into White-approved male and female roles. For example, a man's place was to be in the economic food production world, while a woman's was in the domestic food preparation world. This moved the prime economic unit from the tribe to the European version of the family, the nuclear family. (Clubine, 1991:16)

This process led to

> de-constructing traditional male/female relations among the Native people, and re-constructing and socializing them into male/female roles appropriate to and approved by English colonial society. (Ng, 1993:54)

More recent examples of racism against Aboriginal peoples exist in the relationship between child welfare agencies and Aboriginal families. Since the late 1970s, when provincial welfare programs were first extended to Aboriginal people living on reserves, the system has had the effect of removing many Aboriginal children from their natural parents, their extended families, and their communities. Children were routinely placed in non-Aboriginal foster homes or given for adoption to non-Aboriginal families, with devastating emotional and psychological effects on the children, the parents, and the Aboriginal community (Kline, 1992). Social workers, using middle-class norms to assess Aboriginal families, took significant numbers of children into "care" and placed them for adoption, ignoring the child adoption practices of the Native extended family (Johnston, 1983).

A study conducted by the Canadian Bar Association (1988) revealed that Aboriginal children in British Columbia and Ontario were eight times more likely to be apprehended by the child welfare system than were non-Aboriginal children. Aboriginal children represent 30 percent of the children in care in Alberta and over 60 percent in Manitoba; similar figures exist in other parts of Canada.

Aboriginal women are the most victimized group in Canadian society. From birth, the Aboriginal woman has had to confront all forms of discrimination—gender, race, and class. Her very identity has been determined by a law established by White men. She is frequently the victim of systematic emotional, sexual, and physical abuse, perpetrated since childhood by fathers, foster and adoptive parents, husbands, teachers, priests, social workers, and police (Elizabeth Fry Society, 1992). Submissions to the Canadian Panel on Violence Against Women documented the endemic violence against Aboriginal women. Briefs documented the high levels of sexual, physical, and psychological abuse of Aboriginal women and the lack of transition homes or services in most of the communities in which they live (Canadian Panel on Violence Against Women, 1993). Economically, they are more vulnerable than both non-Aboriginal women and Aboriginal men in relation to levels of income and employment opportunities (Fleras and Elliot, 1992).

The struggles, injustices, prejudice, and discrimination that have plagued Aboriginal peoples for more than three centuries are still grim realities today. The failures of Canada's racist policies toward Aboriginal peoples are reflected in high levels of unemployment: the jobless rate averages nearly 70 percent, and 62 percent of Aboriginal peoples living on reserves receive social assistance. Aboriginal peoples' income averages little more than half of non-Aboriginal income. Aboriginal infant-mortality rates are more than double the Canadian rate. The functional illiteracy of Aboriginal peoples is 45 percent compared with the Canadian rate of 17 percent. The Aboriginal suicide rate is three times the national rate; for young people aged 17–24, the rate is seven times (Canadian Labour Congress, 1992).

Numerous government task forces and reports have documented systemic racism against Aboriginal peoples in the justice system, including the reports of the Donald Marshall Inquiry in Nova Scotia (1989), the Task Force on the Criminal Justice System and Its Impact on the Indian and Métis People of Alberta (1991), the Aboriginal Justice Inquiry of Manitoba (1991), the Saskatchewan Indian Justice Review Committee (1991), the Saskatchewan Métis Justice Review Committee (1991), and the Law Reform Commission of Canada on Aboriginal Peoples and Criminal Justice (1988).

The Aboriginal population of all provincial prisons in 1989 was 57 percent of all inmates (Report of the Aboriginal Justice Inquiry of Manitoba, 1991). The following statistics pertain to Aboriginal peoples in prison in 1988:

> Aboriginal people represent perhaps as many as one million Canadians (or 4 percent of the national population), yet they constitute 10 percent of the federal penitentiary population. They make up almost all of the inmates in certain women's prisons in Yukon and Labrador, and over 70 percent in the Northwest Territories, Manitoba and Saskatchewan. They account for 52 percent of all admissions to Manitoba, Saskatchewan– 61 percent, Alberta–25 percent, and British Columbia–17 percent. (Canadian Bar Association, 1988)

What can be concluded from this brief overview is that the legacy of centuries of dispossession, oppression, and exploitation directed at the Aboriginal peoples of Canada is the direct result of pervasive and intractable racism. This history and its consequences have led Aboriginal peoples to demand self-government, self-determination, and the negotiation and settlement of land claims.

BLACK CANADIANS

The enslavement of Africans and the racial segregation of and discrimination against "free" Black people is also part of the history of Canada. Black slavery was introduced into Canada by the French as early as 1608, and the first slave brought directly into New France from Africa came from Madagascar in 1629. In the St. Lawrence and Niagara regions of Upper Canada, slaves were brought by United Empire Loyalists during and after the American Revolution, and at least six of the sixteen legislators in the first Parliament of Upper Canada owned slaves (Hill, 1981; Lampert and Curtis, 1989). Although slavery did not reach major proportions in Upper Canada, primarily because the land did not lend itself to monocrop agriculture, it was nevertheless actively practised (Walker, 1980).

Contrary to popular belief, until the early nineteenth century—throughout the founding of the present Quebec, New Brunswick, Nova Scotia, and Ontario—there was never a time when Blacks were not held as slaves in Canada (Walker, 1980).

For even the three thousand Black Loyalists who had been emancipated in the American colonies in exchange for supporting the British and who entered Canada in 1783 as "free" persons, there was blatant discrimination. Although they had been promised treatment equal to the White Loyalists in the granting of land contracts, they were bitterly disappointed. While the British promised all Black and White Loyalists settling in Canada 100-acre lots, Blacks either received no land at all or were given barren 1-acre lots on the fringes of White Loyalist townships.

Deprived of the rights of British subjects, Black Loyalists found themselves desperate and destitute. Many were compelled to work as hired or indentured servants to White settlers. Because they were paid about one quarter the wages of White workers, they were deeply resented by unemployed Whites (Winks, 1971). The hostility led to Canada's first race riot in Shelburne and Birchtown, Nova Scotia, in 1784. A mob destroyed Black property and drove Blacks out of the townships (Shepard, 1991).

The precariousness and vulnerability of their lives in Canada convinced about 1200 disillusioned Nova Scotian Blacks to accept an offer by the Sierra Leone Company to sail for West Africa in 1792. The loss to the Black community was significant; many of those who chose to leave were teachers, preachers, and community leaders (Walker, 1980).

After the passage of the U.S. Abolition Act in 1793, which classified any runaway slaves as free, many fugitives from the United States entered Upper Canada. Several thousand Black slaves escaping slavery found their way into Canada via the "Underground Railroad." Many of these early fugitives settled close to the border in the southwestern part of Ontario. Some chose to go to New Brunswick, and smaller numbers went to Montreal.

The passage of the second Fugitive Slave Act in the United States in 1850 brought a significant increase in the Black population of Canada. There may have been 60 000 Blacks in Canada by 1860 (Bolaria and Li, 1988). Their life in Canada was marked by overt prejudice and discrimination. In the 1850s, they were restricted in their ownership of property and were unable to secure education for their children because many White people were opposed to Black children in their schools. Blacks were exposed to ridicule and derision in the local newspapers. Throughout British North America, Blacks were thought, by some, to be responsible for "all the outrageous crimes, and two thirds of the minor ones" (Winks, 1971:248).

With the outbreak of the American Civil War and the Emancipation Proclamation of 1863, many Canadian Blacks chose to return to the United States, recognizing that the value attributed to the colour of one's skin would continue to marginalize them in Canada. The discrimination and exploitation they experienced in almost every aspect of their lives led them to feel that Canada was an inhospitable environment for people of colour (Henry, 1974).

In the early 1900s, the Canadian government sought ways of denying access to Black Americans without directly antagonizing American officials. Although the government had undertaken an extensive advertising campaign to attract farmers from the United States, the Immigration Branch of the federal Department of the Interior informed its American agents that: "the Canadian Government is not particularly desirous of encouraging the immigration of negroes" (Shepard, 1991:17). So, instead of placing an explicit ban on immigration, officials engaged in a campaign to discourage

Black American applicants from settling on the Canadian prairies, and rejected them on medical or other grounds rather than race. A 1910 editorial in the *Edmonton Capitol* summarizes the attitude of the White community toward Black immigration:

> The Board of Trade has done well to call attention to the amount of negro immigration which is taking place into this district. It has already attained such proportions as to discourage White settlers from going into certain sections. The immigration department has no excuse for encouraging it at all.... We prefer to have the southern race problem left behind. The task of assimilating all the White people who enter our borders is quite a heavy enough one without the colour proposition being added. (Shepard, 1991:19)

J.S. Woodsworth, superintendent of the People's Mission in Winnipeg and later one of the founders of the Co-operative Commonwealth Federation (CCF), had the same general attitude toward people of colour in 1903: the "very qualities of intelligence and manliness which are the essentials for citizens in a democracy were systematically expunged from the Negro race." He argued that the American Black was still "cursed with the burden of his African ancestry.... All travellers speak of their impulsiveness, strong sexual passion and lack of willpower.... Hardly a desirable settler" (Troper, 1972:121).

Blacks who remained in Canada lived in largely segregated communities in Nova Scotia, New Brunswick, and Ontario (Winks, 1971). Racial disparity continued to be evident in the schools, government, the workplace, residential housing, and elsewhere. The Ontario legislature established segregated schools, legal challenges to this segregation failed, and separate schools continued. The legislation remained on the statute books until 1964, after Professor Harry Arthurs drew attention to it in a note in the *Canadian Bar Review* (Arthurs, 1963). Segregated schools were also a part of Black education in Nova Scotia, and to a lesser extent (because of a smaller population of Blacks) in New Brunswick. Segregated schools continued in Nova Scotia until the 1960s (Winks, 1978).

Residential segregation was widespread and legally enforced through the use of racially restrictive covenants attached to deeds and leases. Separation and refusal of service was commonplace in restaurants, theatres, and recreational facilities. Several court challenges were launched against these practices by Black Canadians; in one challenge, in 1919, a Quebec court ruled that racial discrimination was not contrary to public order or morality in Canada. The most celebrated case began with a refusal to serve a Black customer in a Montreal tavern in 1931. It ended in the Supreme Court of Canada in 1939, when the nation's highest tribunal concluded that racial discrimination was legally enforceable (Walker, 1985).

The racist attitudes of Whites in Canada were probably reinforced by the pseudo-scientific concept of race popular in Western Europe, Britain and the United States in the late nineteenth century. The concept of White cultural, intellectual, and moral superiority over the Black race was widely held then and continued to flourish well into the twentieth century.

As the study of race was "scientifically" organized, as stereotypes of the "Negro" became more widely known in Canada, as the forces gathered under the rubrics of nationalism and racism began to have their effect, the "Negro" in Canada found himself sliding down an inclined plane from mere neglect to active dislike. (Winks, 1971:292)

CHINESE CANADIANS

The first wave of Chinese to settle in Canada arrived in the 1850s in search of gold. By 1860, however, most of the mines were depleted and those who did not return to China turned to other forms of labour. Chinese were hired for various projects in British Columbia, including the building of railways, bridges, and roads, and work in coal mines and mills (Baureiss, 1985).

In the 1880s, over 1500 labourers were recruited to help lay the track for the Canadian Pacific Railway (CPR) in British Columbia. The emigration was in the form of "Coolie-trade" in which companies advanced the passage ticket and a small sum of money to the Chinese, who, before leaving their country, would give bonds, contracting to work for a period of 5 to 10 years. The companies would hold all the Chinese workers' earnings and were obligated only to provide the workers with the bare essentials (Creese, 1991).

The work assigned to the Chinese contract workers was brutally hard and dangerous. Accidents were frequent, with far more Chinese than Whites as victims. Many workers died from exhaustion and rock explosions and were buried in collapsed tunnels. Their living conditions were appalling. Food and shelter were in insufficient supply, and malnutrition was widespread. There was almost no medical attention, contributing to a high fatality rate from diseases such as scurvy and smallpox. It is estimated that there were six hundred deaths in British Columbia of Chinese labourers working on the construction of the railway (Lampkin, 1985).

After the CPR was completed, new industries, such as mining, fishing, and sawmills, required additional labourers. As the supply of manual labour from Europe and the United States began to dwindle, the Canadian government reluctantly permitted Chinese labourers to fill the demand for largely contract labour required by these industries. From 1881 to 1883, 13 245 Chinese male labourers were recruited to compensate for the shortage of White workers (Bolaria and Li, 1988). These immigrants were not permitted to bring their wives and children with them or to have sexual relations with White women, for fear of spreading the "yellow menace" (Chan, 1983).

Chinese workers were paid one quarter to one half less than their White counterparts. The conditions were appalling, and from 1881 to 1885 hundreds of Chinese died from disease, malnutrition, and exhaustion (Lampkin, 1985). Bolaria and Li (1988) argue that the Chinese immigration during this period was encouraged solely for the purpose of labour exploitation. Immigrants were "welcomed" only as long as there was a shortage of White workers. As soon as there was a labour surplus, the Chinese immigrants were considered a threat to Canadian society and were subjected to intense racial bias and discrimination.

By the mid 1880s, governments were feeling pressure from the White population to limit further Chinese immigration. The federal government passed the first anti-Chinese bill in 1885. In addition, British Columbia passed several anti-Chinese bills to curtail the political and civil rights of the Chinese in the province. The Coal Mines Act of 1890, for example, prevented Chinese from working underground and from performing skilled jobs in coal mines.

Other legislation, introduced as early as 1875, disenfranchised the Chinese so that they were prohibited from voting in provincial and municipal elections (S.B.C. 1875, c. 2). Disenfranchisement was applied to *citizens* as well (Tarnopolsky, 1991). The Chinese were further subjected to a number of discriminatory acts that made it difficult for them to acquire Crown lands, work in skilled jobs in the mines, and obtain liquor licenses. They could not serve in public office; they could not serve on juries or work in the public service; they were barred from the professions of law and pharmacy and excluded from White labour unions (Li, 1988).

Differential wage rates were entrenched in union agreements that allowed lower minimum wages for "orientals" than for "occidental" workers. Differential Asian and White rates were legitimized by assumptions that different wages reflected the inherently different "value" of the labour. In a perverse form of contract compliance, private contractors working with the British Columbia government on federal projects were required by the government not to hire "orientals" (Creese, 1991).

As anti-Chinese sentiment and discrimination grew, Chinese Canadians found that almost the only areas of the labour market open to them were certain sectors of the service industry and of business. Thus, throughout the early twentieth century, Chinese were forced to give up their position in the core labour market and move into domestic service, laundries, and restaurants, where there was less likely to be competition from White workers and employers (Bolaria and Li, 1988). Even so, their presence sufficiently threatened the White community that, in 1907, the latent hostility erupted into brutal violence when large numbers of Whites in Vancouver invaded Chinatown and the Japanese quarter, smashing and destroying property.

One of the most bizarre discriminatory labour policies in Canada was a series of provincial laws preventing "oriental" males from hiring White females. The intent of the Saskatchewan Female Employment Act of 1912, for example, was to "protect" White women from the alleged danger of working for "orientals" (Tarnopolsky, 1991).

The refusal to accept the Chinese, as well as other racial groups, as full citizens manifested itself in yet another way. For the first two years of World War I, racial minorities and Aboriginal people were rejected for military service. Although the militia headquarters did not actually establish a colour-bar, local commanders were encouraged to turn away volunteers on the grounds of the inferiority of their race. Only as the war progressed and shortages began to impede Canada's war effort were racial-minority recruits admitted. Again, in World War II, Black volunteers, along with Chinese, Japanese, and East Indians, were at first not accepted. These barriers were also removed in face of military requirements for more soldiers (Creese, 1991).

A further manifestation of racist ideology translated into racist practice was the concerted effort on the part of British Columbia school boards to keep "Asians" (Chinese and Japanese children) out of the public schools.

JAPANESE CANADIANS

Japanese Canadians experienced similar discriminatory treatment from the time they first settled in British Columbia in the 1870s. They were subjected to economic exploitation, paid lower wages than White labourers, barred from both the federal and provincial franchise, subjected to discriminatory housing covenants, and segregated in schools and public places (Lampkin, 1985).

In 1907, largely as a result of a significant increase in the number of Japanese entering Canada, and as well as the existing populations of Chinese and East Indians in Vancouver, an organization known as the Asiatic Exclusion League was formed. Its goal was to restrict Asians from admission into Canada. The league was a forerunner to the right-wing extremist organizations that would become widespread in Canada in the 1920s and 1930s. Following the arrival of a ship carrying over a thousand Japanese and a few hundred Sikhs, the Asiatic Exclusion League carried out a major demonstration, which culminated in the worst race riot in British Columbia history (Adachi, 1976; Bolaria and Li, 1988).

After the riot, the Canadian government entered into negotiations with the Japanese government, ending with the "Gentlemen's Agreement" of 1908. Under this agreement, the Japanese government agreed to permit entry to only certain categories of persons. These included returning immigrants, their wives and children, immigrants engaged for personal or domestic service, and labourers under specific Canadian government contracts or contracts with Japanese Canadian farmers. A quota was fixed for all but the first group (Adachi, 1976).

Another example of the racial discrimination targeting Japanese was the efforts of the provincial legislature of British Columbia to press the federal government to restrict fishing licences to Japanese Canadians in the 1920s. The ultimate intention of this pressure was to drive them out of the fisheries (Adachi, 1976).

In the late 1930s, anti-Asian sentiment, which had been dormant for about a decade, was inflamed by Japan's invasion of China. Anti-Japanese feelings swept across North America and became virulent once again in British Columbia. The bombing of Pearl Harbor by Japan in 1941 brought it into war against the Allies, and the Canadian government took an unprecedented action (Adachi, 1976). Rejecting the counsel of Canada's senior police and military officers, the Cabinet amended the Defence of Canada Regulations (Order in Council, P.C. 1486, February 24, 1942) to give the minister of justice the authority to remove "any and all persons" from any "protected" area in Canada and to detain such persons without trial (Sunahara, 1981).

Canadians of Japanese origin, including Canadian-born and naturalized citizens—men, women, and children—were expelled from the West Coast of British Columbia and their civil rights were suspended. Twenty-three thousand people of Japanese ancestry, 13 300 of them Canadian-born, were sent to relocation and detention camps in isolated areas in the interior of British Columbia, southern Alberta, and Manitoba.

They were relieved of their property, and 1200 fishing boats owned by Japanese Canadians and naturalized citizens were impounded. Japanese-language schools were closed. Houses, automobiles, and businesses were sold, and savings were impounded. For example, a disabled Japanese Canadian veteran of World War I was given $39.32 for 19 acres of fertile land in the Fraser Valley, a two-storey house, four chicken houses, an electric incubator, and 2500 hens and roosters. He later received an additional $2209.70, after an appeal to the 1947 royal commission, which was established to deal with Japanese Canadian claims for compensation. The settlement clearly did not approach the value of the confiscated property (Lampkin, 1985).

Men were incarcerated in jails and internment camps, and were sent to work on road construction projects in British Columbia, Alberta, and Ontario. They were assigned to sugar-beet farms in Alberta, Manitoba, and Ontario. Abandoned mining towns were reopened to house the evacuees, who were forced to live in abysmal living conditions (Adachi, 1976).

For several years, conditions of virtual apartheid existed for Japanese Canadians (Adachi, 1976; Sunahara, 1981; Kobayashi, 1987). The reason given for this mass denial of rights was wartime security, but no Japanese Canadian was ever charged with sabotage or any other kind of disloyalty before, during, or after the war. The Canadian government did not release the Japanese Canadians until 1947, and it took another two years before they were able to resettle on the West Coast. It is now agreed that the prime factor in their internment was the latent racist feelings harboured by Canadian officials against the Japanese (Ujimoto, 1988).

Sunahara (1980) summarizes the major factors leading to this unprecedented act of racism, including the powerful anti-Asian lobby in British Columbia and a federal Cabinet and civil service predisposed to basing its policy on the views of that lobby. However, underlying these considerations were the racist attitudes prevalent among politicians, bureaucrats, and the public: the manifest superiority of the Caucasian race and its "natural" obligation to rule "inferior," less endowed, non-White peoples (Sunahara, 1980). Not until 1988 was "justice" finally achieved for those Japanese Canadians who were still living, when 12 000 Japanese Canadians were paid $20 000 each as compensation for their internment. As well, they were given a formal apology by Parliament (Ujimoto, 1988).

SOUTH ASIAN CANADIANS

South Asians are people who were born or whose ancestors were born in the Indian subcontinent, and include people from India, Pakistan, Sri Lanka,

Bhutan, and Bangladesh. It also includes people with roots in South Asia who have immigrated from Kenya, Tanzania, Uganda, the Caribbean nations, and other countries.

The first South Asians to enter Canada were Sikhs, who came to British Columbia in the late nineteenth century. By the early twentieth century, the small numbers of South Asians (approximately 5000 in 1908) were viewed with the same racial bias, hostility, and resentment as was directed at other minority racial groups (Buchnigani and Indra, 1985).

As was the case with Chinese and Japanese immigrants, Whites reacted antagonistically to any sign that the non-White population was increasing. The South Asian presence in British Columbia was viewed as a "Hindu invasion." Articles and editorials appearing in British Columbia newspapers expressed the same message: the importance of maintaining Anglo-Saxon superiority (Raj, 1980). The *Daily Colonist* issued the call:

> To prepare ourselves for the irrepressible conflict, Canada must remain a White Man's country. On this western frontier of the Empire will be the forefront of the coming struggle.... Therefore we ought to maintain this country for the Anglo-Saxon and those races which are able to assimilate themselves to them. If this is done, we believe that history will repeat itself and the supremacy of our race will continue. (Ward, 1974:259–260)

To ensure Anglo-Saxon supremacy, legislation was enacted to controle the economic and social mobility of South Asians and to prevent more from coming. Even though citizens of India were British subjects, British Columbia in 1907 disenfranchised them. The government feared that the South Asians might participate in the provincial elections that year. Again, the message communicated by the press was designed to engender fear and prejudice, that the White population needed to be protected against "Hindus." The effect of this paranoia was an amendment to the B.C. Election Act that added "Hindus" to other "Asian undesirables" (Raj, 1980).

The denial of the franchise had serious economic consequences for the South Asian community in British Columbia. Since the voters' list was the basis for both provincial and municipal contracts, South Asians were prevented from bidding on them. As also was the case with Chinese and Japanese, the denial of political rights meant that South Asians were unable to enter professions such as education, law, and pharmacy, and they could not engage in the sale of Crown timber.

They also experienced overt prejudice in the form of racial stereotyping and physical abuse. They were called "ragheads." They could not go to a movie in their native dress. People refused to sit next to them on trains. They could not own property in some sections of Vancouver. Discrimination in housing resulted in many South Asians living in very poor conditions (Bolaria and Li, 1988).

During the 1920s and 1930s, the size of the South Asian community remained static; at the outbreak of World War II it was estimated that only a small community of South Asians remained in British Columbia. However, they continued to press for a repeal of the discriminatory clause in the

Elections Act and in 1947 finally won the right to vote in federal and provincial elections. In 1948, the right was extended to municipal elections
(Lampkin, 1985).

In each of these brief summaries of prejudice and discrimination—against
Aboriginal peoples, Canadian Blacks, Canadian Chinese, Canadian Japanese,
Canadian South Asians—there is a common thread. Racism in Canada is, in
large measure, related to the dominant group's need for cheap labour. It can
be attributed to the division of labour under capitalism (Ng, 1986; Bolaria
and Li, 1988); it is a function of social organization and power differences
(Creese, 1993). Racism is deeply rooted in the legacy and ideology of "White
settler" **colonialism**, which reinforces patterns of power and privilege based
on racial distinctions (Creese, 1993).

IMMIGRATION POLICIES AND PRACTICES

FROM THE 1880S TO THE 1960S

Immigration first became a major issue in Canada in the late 1880s. By the
late nineteenth century the labour needs of the country required large numbers of workers from abroad, so the federal government actively encouraged
White immigrants to settle and farm the vast areas of the country recently
brought under Canadian control. As a result, most immigrants came from
Britain and the United States, but thousands of Italians, Finns, Ukrainians,
and other Europeans also arrived. More workers, however, were still
required, and many thousands of Chinese workers were recruited in the
1880s.

The White population was openly antagonistic toward the newcomers.
As soon as the completion of the CPR was in sight, the federal government
passed a highly discriminatory piece of legislation, entrenching racism for
the first time into laws of the land. The first anti-Chinese law, the Chinese
Immigration Act, was passed in 1885.

A head tax was established on all Chinese males arriving in Canada
(women and children were excluded from admission), partly in response to
the demands of White workers who wanted to eliminate job competition. It
was set at $50 in 1888, and by 1903 it was $500. Under increasing pressure
to "stem the flood" of Chinese immigration, the Canadian government
passed the Chinese Exclusion Act (S.C. 1923, c. 38), which banned Chinese
immigration from 1923 to 1947 (Bolaria and Li, 1988).

Additional restrictive immigration policies were imposed on other racial
minorities. In 1907, British Columbia disenfranchised South Asians and the
federal government passed an order-in-council requiring South Asians to
have $200 in their possession upon arrival in Canada. Canada pressed the
British and Indian governments to pass regulations and legislation to stop
Indian immigration to Canada. These efforts failed, and as a result Canada
passed an order-in-council restricting Indian immigration.

In 1908 the federal government passed the Continuous Passage Act, which stipulated that all immigrants must arrive by an uninterrupted journey, on through tickets, from their country of origin. Indians, as citizens of the British Empire, should have had access to Canada but immigration was made almost impossible by the act (Buchignani and Indra, 1985). Mackenzie King, in presenting a defence of the policy to British authorities, argued that:

> Canada should desire to restrict immigration from the orient is natural; that Canada should remain a White man's country is believed to be not only desirable for economic and social reasons, but highly necessary on political and national grounds. (Report of W.L. Mackenzie King, C.M.G.,1908).

The government was careful not to explicitly bar a particular group from landing, for this might have jeopardized Canada's relations with the rest of the British Empire. Instead, the Continuous Passage Act amended the Immigration Act to allow the government to control East Indian immigration without having the appearance of doing so (Cohen, 1987). In addition, the policy also effectively barred Japanese and other "undesirables" from entry into Canada (Sampat-Mehta, l984). The Chinese Exclusion Act, the Continuous Passage Act, and various regulations to restrict immigration were effective mechanisms for ensuring that almost no Asians or East Indians emigrated to Canada until after World War II.

The 1910 Immigration Act enshrined the government's discriminatory policies in law by creating an excluded class of immigrants deemed undesirable because of Canada's climate or its social, educational, labour, or other requirements—or because their customs or habits were deemed to result in a probable inability to become readily assimilated (Malarek, 1987). The legislation did not specify the countries that had sufficiently different customs or habits to be excluded. Thus it gave immigration officials wide discretion to exclude almost any prospective immigrant on the basis of race, national or ethnic origin, and creed.

Differential treatment based on race and ethnicity was firmly established as government policy. A list of preferred and non-preferred countries was established, and selection was carried out on the basis of whether applicants were from those countries on the "preferred" list: those with affinities to the United Kingdom and United States. Next in preference came immigrants from northern and western Europe, followed by those from central and eastern Europe, and then those from southern Europe. A special permit class included immigrants from Greece, Syria, and Turkey, and European Jews (Bolaria and Li, 1988).

When, in 1914, a shipload of 400 would-be immigrants from India sailed directly from Calcutta and arrived in the Vancouver harbour aboard the Japanese freighter the *Komagata Maru*, they were denied entry. The passengers were held aboard the ship for nearly three months before it was forced to return to India (Buchignani, 1985).

Throughout the history of Canadian immigration, overt and covert policies have excluded racial-minority women immigrants in the hope that excluding women would keep the total numbers of minority-group immigrants down. A 1927 report on oriental activities in British Columbia showed that between 1906 and 1925, 45 women and 41 children had entered Canada, compared with 4909 men (Lampkin, 1985).

The Great Depression, beginning in 1929, prompted the government to invoke a series of restrictive measures to further limit new immigrants to those from the preferred groups. Canadian immigration policy continued to be racist in the 1930s. The dominant and pervasive mindset underlying the policy and the administrative and political framework was "Whites only." White immigrants from Britain were bestowed preferential treatment, followed by White immigrants from the United States and France. Only if these traditional sources of immigration proved insufficient would the government consider admitting White Europeans from countries other than France and Britain.

In l942, when Adolf Hitler activated his "final solution" to eliminate the Jewish people, Canada closed its doors to refugees fleeing Europe. The ship *St. Louis*, carrying Jewish refugees from Europe, attempted to land in Halifax as well as many other ports in North and South America and was denied entrance to all ports. Of all Western countries, Canada admitted the fewest Jewish refugees (Abella and Troper, 1982).

The federal government did not, however, pass any legislation specifically restricting Jews. As was the case in restricting Black, East Indian, and Chinese immigrants, the government chose a more insidious approach by developing informal administrative measures to accomplish its goals. The informality of the practices that had such a devastating impact on Jewish immigration is exemplified in a memo to Prime Minister Mackenzie King prepared by the Department of External Affairs and Immigration in 1938:

> We do not want too many Jews, but in the present circumstances we do not want to say so. We do not want to legitimize the Aryan mythology by introducing any formal distinction for immigration purposes between Jews and non-Jews. The practical distinction, however, has to be made and should be drawn with discretion and sympathy by the competent authorities, without the need to lay down a formal policy. (Dirks, 1977:58)

Jews who were fortunate to have come in earlier waves of immigration did, however, experience widespread discrimination in employment, business, and education; for example, universities maintained restrictive entrance quotas. Other signs of anti-Semitism included restrictions on where Jews could live and buy property. Signs posted along the Toronto beaches warned "No Dogs or Jews Allowed." Many hotels and resorts had policies prohibiting Jews as guests (Abella and Troper, 1982).

As soon as the war ended, there was pressure for a liberalization of immigration policy. In 1947, in a House of Commons debate on immigration policy, Mackenzie King affirmed Canada's need for a larger population and a "pro-active" immigration policy. However, he cautioned his colleagues about the importance of selecting "desirable" immigrants, stating that the people of Canada do not wish, as a result of mass immigration, to make any fundamental alteration in the character of our population. Large-scale immigration from the Orient would change the fundamental composition of the Canadian population. Any considerable Oriental immigration would, moreover, be certain to give rise to social and economic problems of a character that might lead to serious difficulties in the field of international relations. (Malarek, 1987:15)

In 1952, s.61 of the new Immigration Act gave the government the power to limit or prohibit the entry of immigrants for reasons of "nationality, citizenship, ethnic group, class or geographic area of origin, peculiar customs, habits, modes of life…or probable inability to become readily assimilated." The act gave clear preferential status to all White immigrants.

In summarizing Canada's immigration policy until 1967, one can say that the policy divided the world's population into two parts: preferred immigrants, who were of British and European stock and White; and the rest of the world, largely composed of people of colour. The Canadian government's discriminatory policy of immigration was based on the premise that Asians and other people of colour were "unassimilable," that is, they had genetic, cultural, and social traits that made them both inferior and unadaptable (Bolaria and Li, 1988).

The year 1967 marked the beginning of a series of radical reforms in immigration policy, largely as a result of changing demographics and economic pressure to replenish the labour supply. The traditional sources of labour were no longer producing sufficient numbers of immigrants as postwar Europe began to prosper. New labour needs were emerging in Canada; rapid industrialization and expanding new technologies required workers with high levels of skills and education. In response, Canada dropped its racially discriminatory immigration policies. Yet, despite reforms, in a 1975 brief to Parliament the Canadian Civil Liberties Association stated that during a 26-month period, approximately 2000 persons were allowed to enter Canada subject to the posting of cash bonds. All of them were non-Europeans, mostly Asians, South Americans, and West Indians. In no instance were such requirements made of Europeans (Mattis, 1990).

During the 1960s, a new Immigration Act introduced a point system whereby immigrants, regardless of origin or colour, were given points based on job training, experience, skills, level of education, knowledge of English or French, degree of demand for the applicant's occupation, and job offers. The new act opened the doors to immigration from previously excluded countries. While the act allowed for a more open immigration process, some argue that it maintained some of the racist administrative practices of earlier immigration policies (Cohen, 1987; Bolaria and Li, 1988).

FROM THE 1970S TO THE 1990S

New immigration policies opened the door to immigrants from areas that for the past 200 years had been largely excluded—Asia, the Caribbean, Latin America, and Africa. The point system uses nine criteria to assess an applicant's chances of successful integration: age, occupational demand, vocational preparation, arranged employment, location, education, relatives in Canada, official-language competence, and personal suitability. Prospective immigrants are placed in three broad categories: economic, social, and humanitarian. From these categories, they are classified as independent immigrants, family class immigrants, or convention refugees.

The changes incorporated into the 1978 Immigration Act are a result of a number of factors. First was internal pressure, in the form of a multicultural policy that recognized racial and cultural diversity as a fact of life in Canada. The policy affirmed the contributions of racial and ethnic minorities to the economic, social, and cultural development of Canada. Second, the increasing politicization and mobilization of minority groups led to new demands for a more accessible, non-discriminatory immigration policy. Third, pressure was exerted by human rights activists and lawyers (e.g., the Canadian Civil Liberties Association).

A fourth factor was pressure from the international community to eradicate overt racism. Canada's international reputation was badly tarnished by its treatment of Japanese Canadians and Jewish refugees during World War II. Both the formal and informal methods of exclusion that had shaped Canada's immigration policy for over a hundred years were viewed as a contravention of international conventions.

Finally, and probably the most significant force for change, was the economic factor. Immigration from traditional source countries had declined in the 1960s. The postwar recovery of Europe and the establishment of the European Economic Community (EEC) gave Europeans freer access to economic opportunities in Europe and a sense of greater optimism: there was no longer a need to emigrate in order to find work. Also, the labour needs of Canada in the 1960s changed from a dependence on unskilled, manual labour toward a more highly educated and skilled workforce. This fundamental alteration benefited people from developing countries because Europe was unable to supply these workers in sufficient numbers.

The result of all the above factors was a dramatic change in the characteristics of immigrants to Canada in the past two decades. However, as Cohen (1988) and others point out, discrimination did not disappear from Canada's immigration policy. Despite the more universal system and the commitment to non-discrimination in the Act's policy objectives, discrimination was still possible in the immigration process. Under the guise of a universal selection process, a myriad of seemingly neutral administrative procedures had an **adverse impact** on racial-minority immigrants and constituted differential treatment and racial discrimination.

In the first instance, visa offices were unevenly distributed in developing countries, and few resources were committed to them. Until 1990, there was only one visa office in India and one in China. Moreover, there were differences in processing time for assisted relatives (those sponsored by family members who are Canadian citizens) from developing regions, such as Pakistan, as compared with the United Kingdom. Although visitors from the United States were exempt from visa requirements, countries such as India and Jamaica, originally exempt, now required visas.

Immigration officers were given wide latitude and discretion, which allowed for individual prejudices and even overt racism in their decisions. For example, the point system's "personal suitability" category requires immigration officials to assess an immigrant's "adaptability, motivation, initiative, resourcefulness and other similar qualities" and entitles the officer to evaluate the applicant's cultural background and personal style. The officials, however, lacked an objective method to assess the qualifications that potential immigrants had acquired in other jurisdictions, especially developing countries (Malarek, 1987).

Domestic Workers

Canada's domestic workers' program was established in 1955 to deal with the chronic shortage of workers prepared to accept low wages and undesirable working conditions. Initially the program targeted Black women from the Caribbean region, and later it focussed on women from the Philippines. Many of these women who entered Canada as "domestics" were in fact qualified teachers, nurses, and secretaries who were unable to immigrate to Canada because of racist immigration practices. Although they were able to seek other employment after a year's service, they generally faced significant discrimination in the labour market (Ng., 1992; Henry, 1968).

In 1973 their status changed, and the majority of workers came in on "work authorizations" as temporary workers. Their stay in Canada was entirely dependent on maintaining their jobs as domestics. By 1981, 87.9 percent of domestic workers had temporary work permits, and many of them could expect at some point to be asked to return to their country of origin. Securing permanent resident status from within Canada was discretionary (Task Force on Immigration Practices and Procedures, 1981). The government's immigrant domestic program was structured to allow domestic workers who had worked in Canada continuously for at least two years to apply for landed-immigrant status. But, in order to qualify, workers must demonstrate "self-sufficiency" or the potential to achieve "self-sufficiency." These decisions appear to be based on subjective criteria (Cohen, 1987).

The conditions in which many of the domestic workers are compelled to work underline their **marginal** status in the Canadian workforce. Although unemployment-insurance premiums and Canada Pension Plan deductions are made from their paycheques, they are unlikely to secure benefits from their contributions (Silvera, 1993:204). They are denied the right to organize into a trade union and therefore lack the power to bargain collectively for better wages or working conditions. In Ontario, they are not covered by the province's health and safety legislation. "In 1987 the Ontario government amended the Employment Standards Act to provide greater protection for domestic workers. Among other things, the amendments required domestic workers to be paid minimum wage and stipulated the work week. The provincial government's regulatory changes coexisted with Canada Employment and Immigration Guidelines. As late as 1992 Employment and Immigration established certain minimum requirements. The worker should receive $710 per month in Ontario with a deduction of $210 per month for room and board." However, as Silvera (1989) demonstrates in her book on Caribbean domestic workers, these entitlements are seen as bureaucratic jargon. The reality remains the same: the domestics remain intimidated; complaints are rarely laid. Their tenuous legal status in Canada leads many women to fear reporting employers who fail to comply with the regulations.

Finally, recent changes in the program are viewed as another example of racism. The federal government in February 1992 implemented a new requirement for prospective domestic workers (nannies) that they have a Grade 12 education and at least 6 months' professional child-care experience. Critics suggest that this requirement places workers from Third World countries at a disadvantage. While most European workers would be able to meet the new criteria, countries such as the Philippines, India, and Jamaica (where most domestic workers currently come from) have no such training programs; and those with Grade 12 equivalency would be unlikely to want to work for minimum wage (Hernandez, 1992; Ng, 1992).

CONTEMPORARY RACISM

THE CHANGING NATURE OF CANADIAN SOCIETY

Despite the continuing residue of racial discrimination in Canada's immigration policies, a significant shift has occurred in the composition of Canadian society. This changing demographic pattern is largely the result of the ending of the most overt forms of racism in immigration policies and the opening up of immigration to Third World countries.[1]

Canada's population has become increasingly racially diverse. From what was a country largely inhabited by Whites and Aboriginal peoples, the population has changed to include people from more than 70 countries. In addition, the source countries from which immigrants come have dramatically altered. In 1961, 90 percent of Canada's immigrants came from European countries; between 1981 and 1991, this figure declined to 25 percent. Almost half of all immigrants who came to Canada between 1981 and 1991 were Asian-born.

By 1986, 38 percent of Canadians had at least one ancestor who was neither French nor English. In the same year, racial minorities accounted for 6.3 percent, or 1.6 million, of Canada's population. In 1991, the figure had increased to 9.6 percent, or 2.6 million. Recent projections indicate that the racial minority population will rise to 17.7 percent—5.7 million people—in the year 2001.

More than two thirds of racial-minority immigrants to Canada come from Asia. Chinese comprise the most numerous group, with 1.3 million people, followed by South Asians (East Indians, Pakistanis, Sri Lankans, and Bangladeshis) and Blacks, with 1.1 million each. The next most numerous groups are West Asians and Arabs, Filipinos, Southeast Asians (Indochinese), and Latin Americans. The number of Latin American immigrants is expected to grow fourfold by the turn of the century.

Figure 3.1

RACIAL MINORITIES BY PROVINCE, 1986–2001

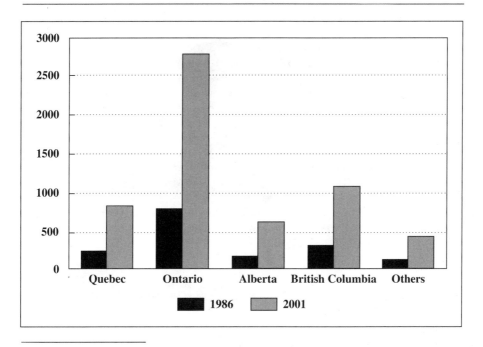

Source: T.J. Samuals, *Visible Minorities in Canada: A Projection*. Toronto: Race Relations Advisory
Council on Advertising, Canadian Advertising Foundation, 1992.

Table 3.1

PROVINCIAL DISTRIBUTION OF RACIAL MINORITIES, 1986–2001

Provinces/Territories	1991	2001
Newfoundland	5 200	11 400
Prince Edward Island	2 600	5 700
Nova Scotia	38 800	85 200
New Brunswick	12 900	28 400
Quebec	367 300	806 800
Ontario	1 270 300	2 789 900
Manitoba	90 500	198 900
Saskatchewan	38 800	85 200
Alberta	274 200	602 300
British Columbia	483 800	1 062 500
Yukon & Northwest Territories	2 600	5 700
Total	2 587 000	5 682 000

Source: T.J. Samuals, *Visible Minorities in Canada: A Projection*. Toronto: Race Relations Advisory
Council on Advertising, Canadian Advertising Foundation, 1992.

Figure 3.2

ETHNICITY OF RACIAL MINORITIES, 1986

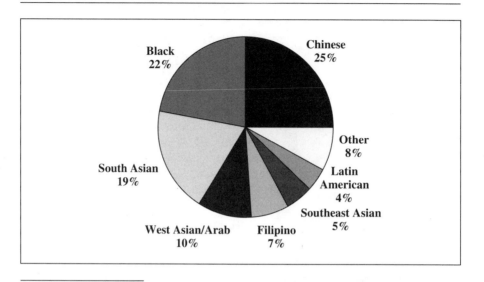

Source: T.J. Samuals, *Visible Minorities in Canada: A Projection*. Toronto: Race Relations Advisory Council on Advertising, Canadian Advertising Foundation, 1992.

Figure 3.3

ETHNICITY OF RACIAL MINORITIES, 1991

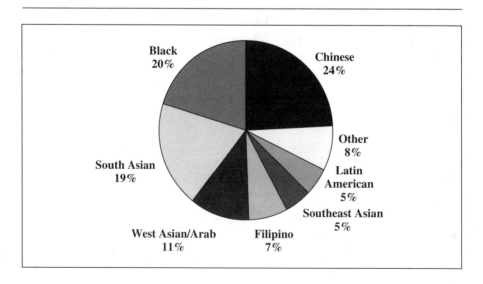

Source: T.J. Samuals, *Visible Minorities in Canada: A Projection*. Toronto: Race Relations Advisory Council on Advertising, Canadian Advertising Foundation, 1992.

Figure 3.4
ETHNICITY OF RACIAL MINORITIES, 2001

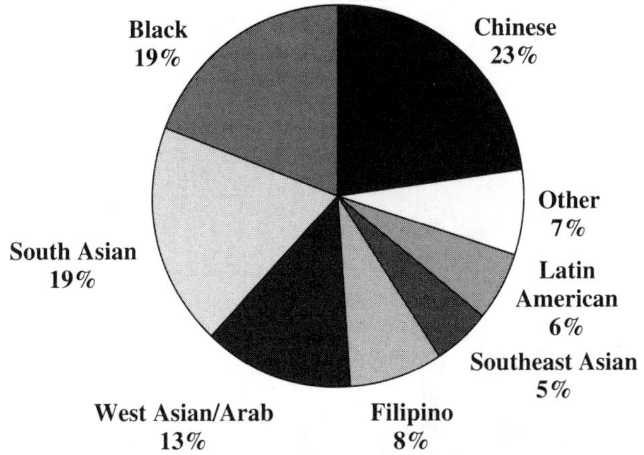

Source: T.J. Samuals, *Visible Minorities in Canada: A Projection*. Toronto: Race Relations Advisory Council on Advertising, Canadian Advertising Foundation, 1992.

By 2001, about half the population of Toronto and two fifths of the population of Vancouver are expected to be racial minorities. About one quarter of the populations of Montreal, Edmonton, Calgary, and Winnipeg are expected to be racial minorities. In Ottawa–Hull and Windsor, one sixth of the populations will consist of racial minorities. Halifax, Kichener, Hamilton, Victoria, and Regina will have 10–14 percent.

There are many kinds of data one can turn to in assessing the impact of these changes in the composition and complexion of immigrants to Canada. One of the most important and reliable sources of data on racism is the direct experiences of the victims. This evidence is found in the numerous reports of task forces, commissions, and surveys, often conducted by academics, public authorities, and ad hoc advisory committees. It is also found in the oral histories of people of colour. A growing body of literature documents the experiences of racial minorities. Although these kinds of data are sometimes dismissed as being too subjective, they are critical to the understanding of racism.

Another source of data is the polls and surveys that seek to measure racist attitudes among individuals or groups. In the past two decades, many such surveys have been initiated by government agencies, politicians, the media, and academics.

A third source is the research findings of academics and commissioned studies by universities and other public sector agencies.

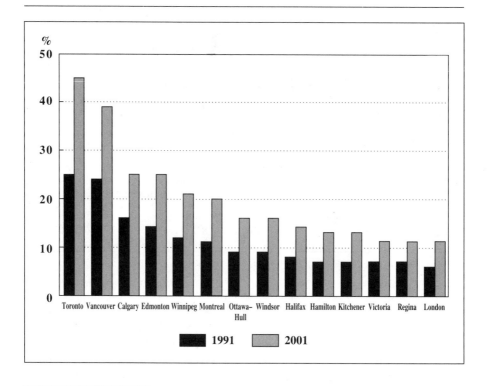

Figure 3.5

**RACIAL MINORITIES IN SELECTED CMA,
1991 and 2001 (PROJECTED)**

Source: T.J. Samuals, *Visible Minorities in Canada: A Projection*. Toronto: Race Relations Advisory Council on Advertising, Canadian Advertising Foundation, 1992.

The final sections of this chapter examine the evidence of employment and housing discrimination. Employment discrimination has been singled out for special attention because it is perhaps the single most important arena in which racism flourishes. Barriers to access and equity in the workplace ultimately affect all other areas of social functioning. With respect to discrimination in housing, only limited research has been done.

VICTIMS' MANIFESTATIONS

Evidence of racism in Canada, particularly over the past two decades, can be found in a number of government-sponsored inquiries, task forces, and commissions, which have usually been established after a series of highly publicized events or incidents involving members of racial-minority communities. For example, in 1975, the Nova Scotia Human Rights Commission received more than 800 complaints of racial discrimination in the educational system. Most were from Black residents in several largely segregated Black communities.

In l977, Walter Pitman, then President of Ryerson Polytechnical Institute, was appointed by the Municipality of Metropolitan Toronto to lead an inquiry into the reasons for an increase in the number of racial-minority persons being assaulted in Metropolitan Toronto.

The Pitman Task Force found sufficient evidence of racism in the city to warrant action. While subway attacks were the most obvious examples of racial violence, the task force found that there were numerous instances of racial violence in parks and recreation areas, in public housing complexes, in school playgrounds, on the streets, and in shopping plazas.

Its report described the vicious and continuous harassment of South Asian businesspeople, the verbal and physical harassment of children, and repeated attacks on the homes of racial-minority members and houses of worship belonging to the South Asian community. The task force found that a substantial number of Toronto's citizens lived in fear, were unwilling to use the subway, and felt uncomfortable and threatened in their own neighbourhoods. While the report dealt with individual racist attacks, it also pointed to the failure of a number of institutions to respond to the problem, including municipal governments, the police, schools, the media, and social agencies.

In the same year, the Ontario Human Rights Commission Annual Report raised concerns about the dramatic increase in reported incidents of assaults and verbal abuse against racial minorities. Another report that year, documenting a series of case histories of **racial incidents** as related by South Asian victims, indicated that the individuals responsible belonged to all groups and socioeconomic categories and even included police and immigration officers. Like Pitman, Ubale identified racism as the root cause and suggested that it was linked to the racial bias and discrimination of Canadian institutions (Ubale, 1977).

Wilson Head (1981) conducted a study on the adaptation of racial-minority immigrants in Canadian society by analyzing their perceptions of discriminatory treatment in the areas of housing, employment, and access to community services. He identified a number of barriers that prevented racial minorities from gaining suitable employment, such as the requirement for "Canadian experience." More than half of the respondents indicated that their present employment was not the type of work they were seeking or trained for.

In terms of community services, both respondents and community agency staff reported that the services were inadequate. The problem areas included the lack of training for staff; the need to hire staff from Black, South Asian, and other immigrant groups; and the need for more ethno-specific agencies. Several staff workers noted that although their Black clients were usually reluctant to talk about racial problems, this was a major concern for many clients.

When respondents were asked about their perceptions of the extent of racial discrimination in Metropolitan Toronto, almost 90 percent of Blacks and 72.2 percent of South Asians felt "some" or a "great deal" of discrimination. In contrast, only 35.3 percent of European respondents felt "some" or "a great deal" of discrimination. Most Blacks (63.7 percent and South

Asians (67.7 percent) reported having been subjected to racial discrimination in Toronto, while only 27.6 percent of the European-born respondents reported that they had experienced some form of ethnic discrimination.

Both Blacks and South Asians thought that racism was increasing. They felt only minimal acceptance by White Canadians and sensed that government agencies were reluctant to deal with racism. These perceptions were consistent with an earlier study carried out by Head (1975), which focussed on the impact of racism on the Black community in Canada.

In 1981, following the killing of a South Asian man in Vancouver, 1800 people demonstrated. The rally was a response to the growing incidence of violent attacks and the widespread racist activities of the Ku Klux Klan. During the rally, several people required hospitalization (Barrett, 1984).

In 1982, the federal government investigation into racial tensions in eleven urban communities across the country found that the racial climate was "tense." The study catalogued expressions of racism that ranged from the subtle acts of "polite racists" to the "sometimes violent" acts of racist zealots in each of these communities (Secretary of State, 1982).

In the same year, the Quebec Human Rights Commission investigated the violence between Haitian-born cabbies and Whites in the taxi industry that resulted from the firing of 20 Black taxi drivers from one company. The inquiry found that customers regularly asked for and were given White drivers only. Moreover, many taxi companies were refusing to hire Blacks. The widespread discrimination against Black taxi drivers was found to be only the latest in a series of racial incidents.

Continuing racial tension in the city of Vancouver resulted in the publication of an important survey documenting racist incidents involving South Asian Canadians in that city (Robson and Breems, 1985). It found that about half of Indo-Canadians (South Asians) had experienced at least one hostile incident in the 2-year time frame of the study. The most frequently cited incidents involved name calling, verbal threats, and physical gestures, which occurred in cars, on the streets, in shopping malls, and in other public places. Graffiti was also frequently mentioned, and property damage was cited by 14 percent of the respondents; damage to cars and other stolen and damaged possessions were most often cited. Seven percent reported having suffered physical harm, and some of these respondents were in the company of young children when attacked.

Of particular interest in this study is the fact that over 70 percent of the South Asian respondents who reported incidents did nothing in response. The authors suggest that one reason for this is that there is no recourse or reporting mechanism in place for many of the more frequently experienced incidents, such as verbal harassment and graffiti. Another important finding of the study was that close contact between South Asians and members of the dominant culture had little impact. Members of the dominant culture who had the most racist attitudes were those living in areas with high concentrations of South Asian Canadians.

In the mid 1980s, the federal government established a parliamentary task force to examine the nature and extent of racism in Canadian society.

The catalyst for the task force was the cumulative effect of "racist incidents," which could no longer be ignored by the government. The report, *Equality Now,* was published in 1984. Authors of the briefs and witnesses who appeared before the task force described the devastating experiences and debilitating effects of racial prejudice and discrimination on the then approximately two million people of colour living in Canada in 1984. The racial barriers identified include both the intentional discriminatory behaviour of racist individuals and the systematic and systemic barriers created by the major institutions in Canadian society, including education, employment, media, justice and law enforcement.

The invisibility of racial minorities was one of the reccurring themes of the briefs, which repeatedly argued that people of colour are excluded from participation in political, social, and economic institutions. They are invisible in the official history of Canada. Racial bias is demonstrated by the recurring questions regarding who is really a Canadian. Participants argued that racism in Canada is unyielding; it does not disappear in one or two or even three generations. Dozens of witnesses argued that racist ideology is woven into Canada's public policies, entrenched in programs, and built into the systems and cultural networks of the whole society. The briefs not only focussed on individual racism, but also identified the important role of education, policing, justice, the media, and the human service delivery system in contributing to racism (*Equality Now*, 1984).

In the late 1980s, evidence of the growing intolerance and acts of discrimination were also documented in the annual reports of the Canadian Human Rights Commission. The 1989 report, for example, raised concerns about the nature of the controversy over whether Sikhs should be allowed to wear turbans in the Royal Canadian Mounted Police (RCMP). The issue resulted in petitions tabled in the Commons carrying the names of as many as 250 000 Canadians who supported the proposition "that a handful of Sikhs wearing turbans would 'crack up the RCMP'" (Camp, 1990). Racist pins and calendars with depictions of turban-clad Mounties appeared across Canada.

The commissioner of the RCMP warned Canadians that "racial violence will cut to the heart of the Canadian soul unless something is done quickly to stop intolerance.... Violence in some form seems inevitable without a concerted effort to combat racism" (Watson, 1990). He also said that he wasn't as worried about the "few dedicated racists" as about the "significant population of well-meaning, intelligent and educated people who are among the opponents of the changes that a multi-racial society inevitably brings" (Watson, 1990).

In 1991, two major incidents in Nova Scotia drew attention to the racism directed at its Black community. In Cole Harbour, a community east of Dartmouth, a fight between a Black and a White youth attending a high school led to a larger confrontation involving about 50 Black and White students and non-students. The RCMP were called in to investigate, and charges were laid against eighteen people, ten of whom were Black. The parents unanimously protested the arrest of the students from these communities and decided to unite to ease racial tensions. Eventually the charges were dropped, except those against five Black plaintiffs.

Reactions to the incidents led to the mobilization of the Black community, and a series of studies and reports were commissioned to examine educational opportunities and labour participation rates among the residents of the three surrounding communities where Blacks lived. The findings of the studies led to the conclusion that the Black residents of the three areas were "significantly disadvantaged" compared with their White neighbours. A report of the Nova Scotia Advisory Group on Race Relations found that racism was rampant in the province and in all levels of the school system. The report also focussed on the racial implications of unemployment among Blacks (*Nova Scotia Advisory Group on Race Relations*, 1991).

In 1991, another incident in Nova Scotia escalated into a series of racial disturbances. After Black youths were refused entrance to a downtown Halifax bar, a brawl ensued in which a Black youth was stabbed. More than a thousand people participated in a march and rally following the incident, to demand action to combat racism in Nova Scotia. In July 1991, the federal, provincial, and municipal governments and representatives from the Black community agreed to form an advisory group on race relations to deal with racism and racial discrimination in education, employment, media policing, justice, and services.

The *Report of the Nova Scotia Advisory Group on Race Relations* (1991) provided the context for these incidents. It suggested that Blacks in the province had been excluded from all areas of mainstream life in communities in which they, their parents, grandparents, and great grandparents were born. Racist attitudes converged with racist policies and practices to deprive Blacks and other minorities from access to housing, education, employment, and other services that most White Canadians take for granted, such as access to bars and restaurants. Bridgal Pachai, executive director of the Nova Scotia Human Rights Commission, suggested that "the story of Nova Scotia is a story of denial of opportunity and broken promises to minorities...who just happen to be Blacks, Aboriginal people and Acadians" (Murray, 1991).

The responses of the White and Black communities to incidents of racial unrest underscore how the two groups (one with power and privilege, the other deprived of fundamental rights) understand racism. Many Blacks readily speak of the explosion of racial tension as inevitable in a racist society, whereas White individuals express shock and anger at the threat of increased racial violence.

In the summer of 1992, the premier of Ontario, Bob Rae, appointed a former Canadian ambassador to the United Nations, Stephen Lewis, to lead a special inquiry on race relations following a disturbance in Toronto a few weeks before. A night of violence and looting followed a peaceful protest by a mixed-race crowd of more than two thousand people decrying the acquittal of Los Angeles police officers whose beating of a Black man was caught on videotape. While the rioters were of all races, the provincial government saw it as a symptom of racial unrest and called for an investigation.

Lewis consulted widely with individuals and groups from racial minorities, particularly the Black community, across the province. He concluded in his report that the root of the problem was anti-Black racism:

> While it is obviously true that every visible minority community experiences the indignities and wounds of systemic discrimination throughout Ontario, it is the Black community which is the focus. It is Blacks who are being shot, it is Black youth that is unemployed in excessive numbers, it is Black students who are being disproportionately streamed in schools, it is Black kids who are disproportionately dropping out.... It is Black employees, professional and non-professional, on whom the doors of upward equity slam shut. (Lewis, 1992:2)

POLLS AND SURVEYS

One of the first surveys of racist attitudes in Canada contained 57 attitudinal items pertaining to racial prejudice (Henry, 1978). The findings revealed that 16 percent of the White mainstream population was extremely intolerant and 35 percent somewhat racist. At least 18 percent had very liberal views about race, and a further 30 percent were somewhat liberal.

The attitudinal survey literature has been remarkably consistent over the 15 years since that first survey was done. Most of the surveys show that between 10 and 20 percent of Canadians are extremely intolerant of racial minorities. Another 20–35 percent are somewhat racist. Combining these two findings suggests that a majority of the population could be characterized as racist.

A decade after the Henry study, another survey found that between 7 and 20 percent of Canadians could be described as strongly racist in their views (Environics, 1988). Evidence of "hard core" racism included the following findings: 19 percent of Canadians agreed with "research findings" that Orientals were superior to Whites who were, in turn, superior to Blacks. Moreover, 13 percent of Canadians would exclude non-White groups from immigrating to Canada, 7 percent would not vote for a Black political candidate, and 9 percent would not vote for a Chinese candidate.

A 1989 survey, conducted by researchers at the University of Toronto and York University, was designed to determine whether there was a significant difference between the racial attitudes of decision-makers—legislators, lawyers, administrators, and police officers—and those of the general population. The survey found that 23 percent of the "elite" Canadians thought minority groups needed to get rid of "harmful and irritating faults," compared with 39 percent of the general population who held the same view. Half of the decision-makers and 70 percent of the general population felt that immigrants often bring discrimination upon themselves; 16 percent of the "elites" and almost one third of the general citizenry believed that "races are naturally unequal" (Gould, 1990).

A 1989 poll in British Columbia, which receives most racial-minority immigrants settling in the West, indicated that many residents believed that immigration does not bring economic advantages to the province. These perceptions were held despite the fact that shortly before, a highly publicized report by Employment and Immigration Canada found exactly the opposite to be the case. The report demonstrated that after 10 years in Canada, Third World immigrants paid more taxes per capita than did western European immigrants. These perceptions were also not shaken by the well-reported findings of the the province's central statistics bureau, which showed that Asian entrepreneurial immigrants contributed $122.9 million into the B.C. economy and $5.4 million into the Alberta economy in 1988. Although entrepreneurial immigrants from Asia created 15 000 jobs in Canada in 1988, nearly half of B.C.'s population thought there were too many immigrants of colour moving into the province.

In a Toronto survey in 1992, when asked how well their racial or cultural group was accepted, 80 percent of those surveyed in the Black Canadian community, 63 percent in the Chinese Canadian community, and 62 percent of the East Indian–Pakistani Canadian community felt there was some prejudice toward them in Toronto. 73 percent of Blacks, 48 percent of Chinese, and 47 percent of East Indians–Pakistanis felt discriminated against in obtaining work, compared with 31 percent of Jews, 16 percent of Portuguese, and 15 percent of Italians. In terms of discrimination in the legal or court system, the survey found that 49 percent of Blacks felt they were discriminated against. Twenty-one percent of East-Indian–Pakistanis felt this way and 9 percent of Chinese (*The Toronto Star*, 1992).

A report by the Economic Council of Canada (1991) attempted to measure the changing attitudes toward prejudice over time by analyzing the results of 62 surveys taken from 1975 to 1990 by Gallup, Decima, Environics, and other polling organizations. The report found that respondents from communities with greater proportions of visible-minority immigrants were "likely to be more tolerant of racial and ethnic differences." The report also concluded that over time there were "diminishing levels of prejudice." However, the results should be approached with some caution, considering the unreliability and validity of the many data sources as well as the kind of statistical analysis performed, which tends to obscure important variables, such as the unit of analysis, the nature of the questions, age distribution of the sample, socioeconomic status of the respondents, age, educational background, gender, and the like.

A survey by the federal immigration department of 1800 adults and fourteen focus groups showed a "growing acceptance" of attitudes and practices that show a dislike for "foreigners." One third of the respondents agreed it was important to "keep out people who are different from most Canadians," while more than half were "really worried that they may become a minority if immigration is unchecked." Almost half admitted there were too many immigrants, even though most actually underestimated how many people were admitted (*The Globe and Mail,* 1992).

Given the extent of ethnocentrism in Canadian society, it is not surprising that these concerns are expressed. However, the number of people who hold these negative attitudes but are not expressing them far exceed those who do, for "fear of being stamped racists" (Samuel, 1988; Wellman, 1978).

In a national survey undertaken by Decima Research in October 1993 for the Canadian Council of Christian and Jews, many of the myths identified in Chapter 1 of this book are reflected in the responses of 1200 respondents. Nearly three quarters of respondents rejected the concept of Canada as a multicultural mosaic, and 72 percent believed that different racial and ethnic groups should try to adapt to Canadian society rather than preserve their original cultures. The survey found that 41 percent of respondents thought that Canada's immigration policy "allows too many people of different cultures and races to come to Canada," and 53 percent agreed with the statement that "some racial and ethnic groups don't make enough of an effort to fit into Canada." Half agreed with the statement: "I am sick and tired of some groups complaining about racism being directed at them," and 41 percent agreed they are "tired of ethnic minorities being given special treatment."

The findings demonstrated some of the paradoxes of racism in Canadian society. For example, while Canadians generally saw themselves as tolerant of other cultures and racism, three quarters believed that racism was a serious problem in Canada. These findings correspond with the central premise of this book: although many White people profess to be liberal, fair minded, and unbiased, they have two opposing and contradictory set of racial attitudes—one expressed in positive terms, the other reflecting negative perceptions, attitudes, and assumptions.

HATE GROUPS

An ideology of White supremacy has long been considered within the bounds of respectable, defensible opinion in Canada. In the colonial era, Aboriginal peoples were portrayed by church and state as "heathens" and "savages" and somehow less than human. These images provided justification for the extermination, segregation, and subjugation of Aboriginal peoples. The dehumanizing impact of such blatant propaganda is clearly evident today in the conditions of many Aboriginal communities (Frideres, 1983).

The 1920s and the 1930s saw the development of racist organizations such as the Ku Klux Klan (KKK), which openly promoted hatred against Catholics, Jews, Blacks, and other minorities. The original Klan was founded in Tennessee in 1866. It established bases in Alberta, Manitoba, Saskatchewan, British Columbia, and Ontario, feeding on Canadian anti-Semitism and the fear of Blacks and southern Europeans. While the KKK in Canada today appears to have only a handful of members, a network of other groups peddle hate propaganda, including the Heritage Front, the Liberty Lobby, the Church of the Creator, the Church of Jesus Christ–Aryan Nation, the Aryan Resistance Movement, and the Western Guard. All these groups share an ideology that supports the view that the Aryan, or White, race is superior to all others morally, intellectually, and culturally and that it is Whites' manifest destiny to dominate society.

Barrett (1987) has made a significant contribution to understanding the recent activities of the extreme right in Canada. He found 130 organizations but under 600 members, many of whom belonged to more than one organization. Hate groups are usually coteries centred on a leader with a mailing list. Aside from holding meetings, they promote their ideology through distributing their literature widely. They hold rallies and parades, distribute buttons, paint slogans, establish dial-a-message telephone lines, demonstrate, and hold counter-demonstrations at the rallies of others. They may engage in paramilitary training, hold church services, or engage in political canvassing.

A recent strategy used by these groups is to defend their activities by presenting themselves as defenders of free expression. Since they consider themselves to be promoting the principles of civil libertarianism, any attempts to curb their activities are portrayed as censorship and therefore anti-democratic.

The extreme right wing in Canada today consists of three main groups: the Ku Klux Klan, the Western Guard, and a third group that includes a number of smaller organizations, such as the Canadian National Socialist Party. Barrett (1987) suggests that the main elements of White supremacist ideology are anti-communism, anti-liberalism, racism, and anti-Semitism. White Supremacists perceive themselves as the "saviours of the White race and Western Christian civilization" (Barrett, 1987:90). They believe that the survival of White society in Canada is in jeopardy because of the practice of allowing "non-Aryans" into the country. The Ku Klux Klan suggests that one alternative to the problem of too many racial minorities in Canada is for the government to give "$35 000 to each coloured family as inducement to return to Pakistan, Africa, and elsewhere in the Third World" (Barrett, 1987). Jews too should be included in this form of "ethnic cleansing." The expansion of the White race should be encouraged by providing financial incentives for White parents to have more children.

Barrett concludes that the ideology of the radical right does, to some extent, reflect "what the majority of people think and feel privately, albeit often unconsciously." While hate groups and hate propaganda may be regarded as marginal phenomena, the impact of such extremists is, according to Barrett, disproportionate to their numbers. They gain notoriety and apparent influence by combining strong stances on sensitive policies (such as immigration), which are controversial and have a substantial popular base, with continuous racist appeals couched in emotional, inflammatory rhetoric and threats of violence.

Barrett suggests that most White Canadians hold racist attitudes, reflected in their comments about Blacks in the workplace, the peculiarity of Jews, or their choice of jokes. The main elements of the White supremacist ideology are anti-communism, anti-liberalism, racism, and anti-Semitism. A relationship exists between many White supremacist beliefs and those of other White Canadians. "The two sets of beliefs…constitute a continuum rather than a dichotomy" (Barrett, 1987:97).

However, according to Barrett, it is important to distinguish between public and private beliefs. While a sizable portion of Whites may, in fact, share many of the less fanatical but nevertheless racist attitudes of the extreme right wing, they may never publicly express those views. This is consistent with the notion of "passive racism." The radical right is articulating what a significant proportion of the dominant community is thinking and feeling, albeit sometimes unconsciously.

Since the publication of Barrett's pioneering work, the numbers of right-wing groups have proliferated in Canada. KKK branches are active in all of Canada's major cities. Offshoot groups such as the Heritage Front, the Church of the Creator, the Knights for White Rights, and the Aryan Nation are flourishing. Their presence is felt in the many telephone "hot lines" established throughout the country that spew forth hate messages, many of which are directed at Aboriginal peoples and racial minorities. Multiculturalism and immigration policies are also frequently criticized. The messages hammer home the theme, "Keep Canada White."

In the past decade, the League for Human Rights of B'nai B'rith (1992) has monitored the number and types of anti-Semitic incidents that have occurred in all regions of Canada. The data file includes a large variety of incidents, ranging from non-violent ones—such as anti-Semitic graffiti—to more violent incidents that involve damage to persons or property and the desecration of synagogues. A recent analysis of this file showed a "significant increase...in the numbers of incidents of all kinds." The report noted that this may merely reflect a "growing tendency of intolerance." But, since longitudinal studies of intolerance are non-existent in Canada, it is not possible to determine whether either intolerance or racist behaviour has increased (Economic Council of Canada, 1991).

These racist incidents target not only the Jewish community. Hate-group activity and hate propaganda is directed at members of the Black, Chinese, and South Asian communities. Reports from various multicultural and anti-racist organizations and networks, as well as the cases in the human rights commissions and courts, support the findings of the League for Human Rights of B'nai B'rith (BCOFR Report,1992; Mock, 1992).

In the early 1990s, the Canadian Human Rights Commission began launching actions to prohibit telephone hate lines. In Vancouver, its action resulted in a tribunal ordering a telephone hate line off the air. Similarly, in Toronto, the Heritage Front was issued with an injunction to stop producing hate messages. In Winnipeg, a human rights tribunal ordered the Manitoba Knights of the KKK to cease airing its messages. The tribunal found that "there is overwhelming uncontradicted evidence that the messages were likely to expose the persons involved to hatred and contempt by reason of their race, religion, national or ethnic origin, colour or sexual orientation." This decision included not only the Manitoba chapter of the KKK, but also "any other individuals who are member of or act in the name of the Knights of the Ku Klux Klan."

By 1992, racist violence was seen to be increasing in many Canadian urban centres. For example, over a period of a few weeks in 1993 three Tamil refugees were beaten in Toronto. One died as the result of the injuries inflicted by his White assailants, and one was paralyzed. These incidents must be studied in the context of a long history of racist attitudes toward immigrants and refugees (or those perceived to be "foreigners" by virtue of the colour of their skin). In 1987, Canadians vehemently reacted to the arrival of a few boatloads of Tamil and Sikh refugees who entered Canada without following the normal procedures, while at the same time expressing little concern about the equally unorthodox arrival of significant numbers of Polish refugees.

CASE STUDY 3.1

EMPLOYMENT DISCRIMINATION

One of the clearest demonstrations of racism in a society is the lack of access and equity experienced by people of colour in the workplace. A number of studies over the past two decades have documented the nature and extent of racial bias and discrimination in employment. One study, *Who Gets the Work?* (Henry, 1984), examined access to employment. In this field research, matched Black and White job seekers were sent to apply for entry positions advertised in a major newspaper. An analysis of the results of several hundred applications and interviews revealed that Whites received job offers three times more often than did Black job applicants. In addition, telephone callers with accents, particularly those from South Asia and the Caribbean, were more often screened out when they phoned to inquire about a job vacancy.

A follow-up study to *Who Gets the Work?* focussed on the attitude, hiring, and management practices of large businesses and corporations in Toronto. *No Discrimination Here* documented the perceptions of employers and personnel managers in these organizations. In personnel interviews, recruitment, hiring, promotion, training, and termination practices, a high level of both racial prejudice and discrimination was demonstrated; 28 percent of the respondents felt that racial minorities did not have the ability to meet performance criteria as well as Whites (Billingsley and Muszynski, 1985).

Thus, racist behaviour stretches along a wide continuum. At one end are the overt and covert daily acts of discrimination involving a significant proportion of the mainstream community. At the other end of the continuum, one finds far more explicit and extreme racist activity in the form of hate propaganda and racial violence perpetrated by a small minority of the population.

DISCRIMINATION IN THE WORKPLACE

Concern over employment discrimination against people of colour, women, persons with disabilities, and Aboriginal peoples led the federal government to establish a royal commission on equality in employment (Abella, 1984). Its task was to inquire into the employment practices of eleven designated Crown and government-owned corporations and to explore the most effective means of promoting equality in employment for four groups: women, Native peoples, disabled persons, and racial minorities. Its findings echoed the conclusions of the report *Equality Now* (1984) that racial bias and discrimination were a pervasive reality in the employment system. The commissioner, Judge Rosalie Abella, observed that "strong measures were needed to remedy the impact discriminatory attitudes and behaviour." The remedy she recommended was employment equity legislation (Abella, 1984).

An analysis of the 1991 and 1992 annual reports of Employment and Immigration Canada shows that few gains have resulted from employment equity legislation. Of the four targeted groups, women made slightly more advances than the others. Aboriginal peoples and people with disabilities made the fewest gains. Although members of racial minorities had higher levels of education than the Canadian population and very high labour-force participation rates, they continued to be concentrated in certain occupational groups.

In the clerical categories, for example, more than 70 percent of racial-minority women were in this category, compared with 61.8 percent of all women; 24.9 percent of racial-minority men worked as clericals, compared with 14.6 percent of all men. In the banking sector, more than 40 percent of racial-minority men were employed in the clerical category, compared with only 19 percent of all men. More racial-minority men, however, were categorized as professionals (16 percent), compared with 6.3 percent of all men. This reflects the point system of immigration in which education and skills are rewarded.

Members of racial-minority groups have higher levels of education than do other Canadians. For example, 23 percent had university degrees, compared to 14 percent of other Canadians. Moreover, racial minorities had consistently higher levels of education than did other workers in the lower-paying occupations. In the category of "semi-professionals and technicians," for instance, 32.3 percent had university degrees, compared with 18.3 percent of others.

Despite higher levels of education, members of racial-minority groups were paid lower salaries than were other Canadians. In an important study, Reitz, et al. (1981) demonstrated that there were considerable income disparities among various ethno–racial groups. People of colour, such as West Indians, and more recently arrived groups such as Portuguese, ranked lowest.

A decade later, the average salary for all levels of education for a member of a racial-minority in both the upper level and middle and other management occupations was approximately 18 percent lower than that of the total population (Annual Report, 1992, Employment Equity Act: 57). Even in the "other manual workers" category, including all levels of education, members of racial minorities earned nearly 10 percent less than all other manual workers. With respect to the industries regulated by employment equity legislation, racial minorities made some gains. Their share of total hiring in the banking, transportation, and communications industries was 11.1 percent but their share of promotions was lower at only 9.5 percent. Promotions were highest in two groups—clerical and professional workers—both of which showed high visible-minority concentrations.

The overall representation of minorities was highest in the banking sector, where nearly two thirds were clustered in the lower ranks and only 12.4 percent were in middle or upper management positions. Despite some slight improvement in the overall position of racial minorities in the employment regulated by the federal act, they are still concentrated in certain sectors; and despite higher levels of education, their earnings are lower than those of other Canadians. As the report notes, "the representation of members of visible minorities in the work force under the Act was lower than their representation in the Canadian labour force in seven of the 12 occupational groups including upper level managers, semi-professionals,...sales workers, service workers,...other manual workers."

One of the key barriers preventing immigrants of colour from access and equity in the labour market is credentialism. Studies in the Ontario (Ontario Ministry of Citizenship, 1989) and British Columbia (Fernando and Prasad, 1986) showed that there is little recognition in Canada of the professional qualifications, credentials, and experience of immigrants. Thousands of individuals find their university degrees and trade diplomas of little value in Canada. These barriers affect doctors, teachers, social workers, nurses, engineers, and others.

Public sector agencies also show a lack of representation of racial minorities. An audit done for the Ontario public service in 1986 showed that 77 percent of civil servants were White and only 11.9 percent were racial minorities, most of whom were clustered in lower-level positions. In 1989, racial minorities formed only 4 percent of the Metropolitan Toronto Police Force. Almost all of them were cadets, constables, or in training; only three had the rank of inspector (Small, 1992). Around the late 1980s, at the Toronto Board of Education, only 5 percent of the teaching staff were from racial minorities, but this figure increased to 8.5 percent with the inclusion of non-teaching staff. Only 6 percent were classified as managers. The Ontario Human Rights Commission has only one racial-minority director. The Metropolitan Toronto Housing Authority, which deals with large numbers of minority clients, has a minority contingent of only 16.7 percent, of whom 11 percent are at a middle or senior management level.

A survey of 672 corporate recruiters (*Currents*, 1989), hiring managers, and agency recruiters across Canada conducted by the Canadian Recruiters Guild concluded that there were gross deficiencies in Canada's recruitment and selection practices. It revealed that the moral, legal, and economic impact of recruitment was either not understood or simply ignored by recruiters.

A study undertaken by the Maritime School of Social Work at Dalhousie University in Halifax (Brambrough, Bowden, and Wein, 1992) tracked its racial-minority and Aboriginal graduates and found that minorities experienced considerable difficulty in obtaining employment after graduation. Acadian and Black graduates took several more weeks to find their first job, and Blacks had to apply to many more employers and undertake many more interviews to get a job offer. (In this respect, the study mirrors the results of *Who Gets the Work?*, which also found that Blacks and others had to make many more telephone calls than Whites to obtain an interview.)

The study also found that upon graduation, Blacks found less desirable jobs than others, including limited or term positions and more part-time jobs. Of particular interest was the fact that Blacks were more often in jobs in which the chances for advancement were relatively low, as were salaries. The report concluded that "Black graduates have been less successful than the Majority group in accessing the more prestigious social work jobs, such as those to be found in family counselling, hospital social work and in administrative/supervisory positions."

Harish Jain, who has done extensive research on employment discrimination in Canada, suggests that racial minorities, as well as women, Aboriginal peoples and people with disabilities, encounter both entry-level and post-employment discrimination in the workplace. He argues that the existence of human rights statutes across Canada have been ineffective in ensuring **equality of opportunity** in the workplace. Jain identifies numerous job barriers in the employment system, including narrow recruitment channels and procedures (e.g., word of mouth recruitment; inflated educational qualifications; biased testing; prejudice and stereotyping in the job interview process; poor performance evaluation; lack of promotions, transfers, and/or salary increases, job ghettoization (Jain, 1985)). Unions are identified as another potential source of both racism and sexism (Leah, 1989).

Non–English-speaking and racial-minority immigrant women are part of a segregated and marginalized workforce and are employed mainly in three areas of work: private domestic service, service industries, and light manufacturing. Many immigrant racial-minority women working in the public sector are employed as cleaners, cafeteria workers, nurses' aides, and lower-level clerical workers (Vorst et al., 1987). Brand (1987) observes that most Black women work at low-status jobs in homes and institutions and do "Black women's work."

An ongoing research project on Caribbean communities in Toronto (Henry, in press) has yielded some interesting results with respect to the continuing impact of racial discrimination on employment. More than one hundred in-depth interviews and many hundreds of hours of participant observation among persons of Caribbean origin in Toronto indicated that the community shows a fairly high level of institutional completeness, considering the recency of Caribbean migration to Canada. Although there are no financial institutions within the community, most service and retail sectors have developed to the extent that goods and services of many kinds can be obtained from Caribbean-owned and -managed businesses.

One of the main reasons for private entrepreneurship among the community was the racial discrimination experienced by job seekers and workers employed in mainstream-owned and -managed firms. Difficulty in obtaining employment was often cited as a major reason for dissatisfaction with living in Canada. In addition, racial harassment on the job and the inability to advance in the company was cited as a contributory factor to private entrepreneurship. Restaurateurs, clothiers, and variety-shop owners said they were "fed up" with racial harassment.

Employment Agencies

Allegations of racial discrimination in the operations of employment agencies in accepting and referring certain clients have been a concern for almost two decades. In 1975, the Canadian Civil Liberties Association (CCLA) conducted a survey of employment agencies. It randomly selected agencies, told their representatives that it represented an out-of-town firm planning to locate in their community, and asked whether, among the services provided, the agencies would agree to refer only White people for the jobs that had to be filled. Of the fifteen employment agencies in Metro Toronto that received discriminatory requests, eleven said they would screen out persons of colour.

The study was repeated in 1976, surveying employment agencies in Hamilton, Ottawa, and London. Again, eleven of the fifteen agencies indicated their willingness to fulfil discriminatory requests. In 1980, the CCLA surveyed ten agencies in Toronto, seven of whom expressed a willingness to abide by a "Whites only" restriction. In 1991, the CCLA repeated the survey for the fourth time, and of the fifteen agencies surveyed in four cities in Ontario, only three declared their unwillingness to accept discriminatory job orders.

Following are some examples of the agencies' responses.

> It is discrimination, but it can be done discreetly without anyone knowing. No problem with that.

> That's no problem, it's between you and me. I don't tell anyone; you don't tell anyone.

> You are paying to see the people you want to see.

> Absolutely—definitely…that request is pretty standard here.

> That's not a problem. Appearance means a lot, whether it's colour or overweight people."(Rees, 1991)

While the role of employment agencies in colluding with discriminatory employers has long been known to those who monitor race relations in Canada, the publicity surrounding a complaint laid with the Ontario Human Rights Commission against two employment agencies in Toronto brought this issue into the public arena. Although the commission found discriminatory information about job applicants in some files, it maintained that the agencies did not have a deliberate policy of discriminating against job applicants. Accordingly, a settlement was reached in which the agencies agreed to develop written policies against accepting discriminatory job requests from employers and to provide training for their employees in race relations and employment equity.

Both agencies also said they would establish 3-year employment equity plans, with goals and timetables that provided for the elimination of barriers in recruiting, referral, and placement services. The chief commissioner of the human rights commission was quoted as saying that this settlement "will provide a blueprint for all employment agencies in the province." A number of critics, however, noted that the settlement was fairly limited and did not adequately encompass all the aspects of this complex issue.

CASE STUDY 3-2

DISCRIMINATION IN HOUSING

Housing provides another example of the how racial discrimination restricts people's choices with respect to accommodation. Although the evidence in Canada is scanty, racial discrimination in rental housing occurs in cities, especially in Toronto and Montreal, where the issue has been studied. Discrimination in Canadian rental accommodation would not be surprising, since the evidence from both the United Kingdom and the United States is overwhelming (Rex and Moore, 1967; Flett, 1979; Ward, 1978; Bristow, 1979).

LANDLORD EXCLUSIONARY PRACTICES

A study by the Canadian Council on Social Development has shown that two types of individual prejudice on the part of landlords lead to housing discrimination. In the first case, landlords hold negative stereotypes about certain groups and believe that such people will make bad tenants. In the second, landlords restrict occupancy on the grounds that their existing tenants would threaten to move out if members of a particular minority group were allowed in (Quann, 1979).

These and other types of prejudice restrict the chances of minority groups to live where they choose. Various methods are then used by rental agents and landlords to prevent members of minority groups from renting or purchasing property. Quann (1979) noted that discrimination may arise as an immediate response to the applicant's manner of speaking over the telephone. Others, who do not have a discernible accent, encounter discrimination when they arrive to see the apartment.

Discrimination appears to be more common in certain kinds of rental accommodation than in others. Owners of rooming houses seem to discriminate most frequently. In private homes, where the owner lives in the building, there is also a high level of discrimination. Most cases referred to human rights commissions concern these types of accommodation (Quann, 1979). While relatively few minority families are ready to purchase houses, the real estate industry also contains some potential elements of racial discrimination. For example, it was alleged that some companies and agents steered racial-minority clients away from certain areas and toward those already inhabited by minority groups. Although some minority-group members want to live in areas already inhabited by their group, if potential buyers are steered toward some areas and away from others, overconcentration may result.

Two significant research studies of racial discrimination in housing have been undertaken in Quebec. In 1981, Black and other racial-minority immigrants living in two sections of Montreal were sampled by census tracts and questioned about their experience with racial discrimination in housing (Teitlebaum and Berube, 1983). Twenty-two percent of respondents had personal experiences of discrimination, and many more had heard of the experiences of others. More than three quarters of those sampled had experienced the typical situation of being told that an apartment was "just rented." The study concluded that racial discrimination in housing in Montreal was severe and that it was not a temporary problem likely to disappear once the groups got to know each other. Housing segregation was on the increase in Montreal, it was concluded, largely as a result of the inability of racial-minority people to exercise free choice in their living arrangements.

A 1988 study undertaken by the Quebec Human Rights Commission used the methodology of field testing developed by Henry and E. Ginzberg (1984) in their study, *Who Gets the Work?* Matched pairs of White and Black actors, pretending that they were in search of accommodation, applied for apartments advertised in the newspaper. The study controlled for sex, age, and social class and found that Black working-class applicants were the most often rejected as tenants.

This methodology was also used in a pilot study undertaken in the mid 1980s to test racial discrimination against single professional women seeking accommodation in Toronto (Henry, 1989). The two women researchers represented themselves as having the same income, same age, and same occupational group. Of the 73 cases tested, 31 showed blatant or overt discrimination. Discrimination was defined as occurring when the Black woman was told there was no vacancy while immediately afterwards the White woman was told there were vacancies. Discrimination was also revealed when different rental fees were quoted for the same accommodation.

Another method of discrimination was to offer different availability dates. In some instances the Black woman was told nothing would be available for five or six months, whereas the White woman was told that something would become available "next month." Clearly, it was hoped that the Black woman would be discouraged and not return.

In ten of the 73 cases, it was difficult to determine with any degree of accuracy whether some evidence of discrimination or differential treatment had taken place. In only 32 of the 73 cases was there no difference in the treatment of or information offered to the researchers.

The results of this small study as well as the Quebec studies clearly indicate that there is a significant amount of housing discrimination. The methodology also reveals that most applicants do not know when they have been the victims of discrimination. When landlords or rental agents act pleasantly but say that they have no vacancies, most applicants will readily accept that explanation. This is especially true in a city such as Toronto, which has gone through periods of extremely low vacancy rates.

Only when a White applicant applies to the same contact person and is shown an apartment, or told that a vacancy will come up in a month's time, or given an application form, or quoted a lower rental rate for the same apartment does a racial-minority person realize that unequal treatment has occurred. Housing discrimination is even more subtle than employment discrimination, since in the latter case it can always be alleged that a job applicant's credentials were not adequate. When seeking accommodation, however, all one usually needs is the first and sometimes last month's rent.

Finally, another manifestation of racism in housing has occurred in recent years in Vancouver. The arrival of large numbers of Hong Kong Chinese, many of whom are relatively wealthy, has created a situation in which they have been blamed for the increase in house prices. In fact, the increase in housing prices is a reflection of a number of social and demographic trends (Li, forthcoming). Moreover, their building of alleged "monster" homes has reinforced the perception of Chinese as alien and unlike Canadians in their tastes and values. A study of this issue has demonstrated that a group can become racialized because of supposed social characteristics. "The controversy over 'unneighborly' and the battle to preserve what some Caucasian Canadians consider to be a 'Canadian heritage' promotes a negative racial connotation for Chinese immigrant (Li, forthcoming). Li argues that attempts by local residents to create zoning regulations against the building of such houses is an example of racism against the Chinese.

SUMMARY

This chapter has provided an overview of the historical and contemporary evidence of racism in Canada. The examples cited demonstrate both the highly complex nature of racism and the diverse forms it takes. There is a brief examination of how racial bias and discrimination have affected specific minority communities, including Aboriginal peoples, Black Canadians, Chinese Canadians, Japanese Canadians, East Indian Canadians, and Canadian Jews.

One sees repeated examples of individual racism when individuals, acting on racial prejudice and stereotypes, translate their negative attitudes into racist and discriminatory behaviour.

Racist ideology strongly influences the development of public policies and legislative enactments. The historical evidence demonstrates how racial bias and discriminatory practices have limited access to education, housing, and employment and have resulted in the denial of the fundamental civil rights to Aboriginal peoples and racial minorities in Canada. The development of restrictive and racist immigration policies lasting over one hundred years represents one of the most compelling forms of evidence of racism in Canada.

The last section of this chapter has documented some of the extensive data on employment and housing discrimination, further illustrating the extent to which racial bias and discrimination function and flourish in Canadian society. The history of racism in Canada can be said to be characterized by the development and maintenance of policies and practices based on the marginalization, exclusion, segregation, and domination of Aboriginal peoples and racial minorities.

REFERENCES

Abella, I., and H. Troper. (1982). *None Is Too Many*. Toronto: Lester and Orpen Dennys.

Abella, R. (1984). *Report of the Commission on Equality in Employment*. Ottawa: Supply and Services Canada.

Adachi, K. (1976). *The Enemy That Never Was: A History of the Japanese Canadians*. Toronto: McClelland and Stewart.

Advisory Group on Race Relations. (1991). *Report*. Halifax.

Arthurs, H. (1963). "Civil Liberties and Public Schools: Segregation of Negro Students." *Canadian Bar Review*, vol. 4:453–57.

BC Organization to Fight Racism. (1993). Canada 125, Surrey: BCOFR.

Bambrough, J., W. Bowden, and F. Wien. (1992). *Preliminary Results from the Survey of Graduates from the Maritime School of Social Work*. Halifax: Maritime School of Social Work, Dalhouse University.

Barrett, S. (1984). "White Supremists and Neo Fascists: Laboratories for the Analysis of Racism in Wider Society." O. McKague (ed.), *Racism in Canada*. Saskatoon: Fifth House, 85–99.

———. (1987). *Is God a Racist? The Right Wing in Canada*. Toronto: University of Toronto Press.

Baureiss, G. (1985). "Discrimination and Response: The Chinese in Canada." In R. Bienvenue and J. Goldstein (eds.), *Ethnicity and Ethnic Relations in Canada* (2nd ed.). Toronto: Butterworths.

Berger, T. (1981). *Fragile Freedoms: Human Rights and Dissent in Canada*. Toronto: Clarke Irwin.

_____. (1992). *A Long and Terrible Shadow: White Values, Native Rights in the Americas 1492–1992*. Vancouver: Douglas McIntyre.

Bienvenue, R., and J. Goldstein (eds.). (1985). *Ethnicity and Ethnic Relations in Canada*. Toronto: Butterworths.

Billingsley, B., and L. Musynski. (1985). *No Discrimination Here*. Toronto: Social Planning Council of Metro Toronto and the Urban Alliance on Race Relations.

Bolaria, S., and P. Li. (1988). *Racial Oppression in Canada* (2nd ed.). Toronto: Garamond Press.

Brand, D. (1987). "Black Women and Work: The Impact of Racially Constructed Gender Roles on the Sexual Division of Labour." *Fireweed* (25):35.

_____. (1993). "A Working Paper on Black Women in Toronto: Gender, Race and Class." In H. Bannerji (ed.), *Returning the Gaze: Essays on Racism, Feminism and Politics*. Toronto: Sister Vision Press.

Bristow, M. (1979). "Ugandan Asians, Racial Disadvantage and Housing Markets in Manchester and Birmingham." *New Community*, 7(2):203–216

Buchnigani, N., and D. Indra. (1985). *Continuous Journey: A Social History of South Asians in Canada*. Toronto: McClelland and Stewart.

Camp, D. (1990). "Diefenbaker Would Have Backed Turbans in the RCMP." *The Toronto Star* (March 21):A25.

Canada. (1922). *Hansard* 2:1509–1572.

Canada Employment and Immigration. (1992). *Annual Report, Employment Equity*. Hull: Minister of Supply and Services.

Canadian Bar Association. (1988). *Aboriginal Rights in Canada: An Agenda for Action*. Special Committee Report. Ottawa.

Canadian Civil Liberties Association. (1991). *Survey of Employment Agencies*. Toronto: CCLA.

Canadian Council of Christian and Jews. (1993). *Survey of Canadian Attitudes towards Ethnic and Race Relations in Canada*. Toronto: Decima Research.

Canadian Recruiters Guild. (1989). Canada's Employment Discriminators. *Currents: Readings in Race Relations*. 5(2), Toronto: Urban Alliance on Race Relations.

Canadian Labour Congress. (1992). *19th Constitutional Convention: Aboriginal Rights Policy Statement*. Ottawa: CLC.

Canadian Panel Violence Against Women. (1993). *Changing the Landscape: Ending Violence: Achieving Equality: Final Report*. Ottawa: The Panel.

Chan, A. (1983). *The Gold Mountain: The Chinese in the New World*. Vancouver: New Star.

Clairmont, D., and D. Magille. (1974). *Africville: The Life and Death of a Canadian Black Community*. Toronto: McClelland and Stewart.

Clubine, C. (1991). *Racism, Assimilation and Indian Education in Upper Canada*. Unpublished manuscript. Ontario Institute of Education, Department of Sociology, University of Toronto.

Cohen, T. (1987). *Race Relations and the Law*. Toronto: Canadian Jewish Congress.

_____. (1988). *Race Relations and the Law*. Montreal: Canadian Jewish Congress.

Creese, G. (1991). "Organizing Against Racism in the Workplace: Chinese Workers in Vancouver Before the Second World War." In O. McKague (ed.), *Racism in Canada*. Saskatoon: Fifth House.

_____. (1993). "The Sociology of British Columbia." *BC Studies* 100 (Winter 1993–94).

Dirks, G. (1977). "Memorandum to Mackenzie King." In *Canada's Refugee Policy: Indifference or Opportunities?* Montreal and London: McGill–Queen's University Press.

Ducharme, M. (1986). "The Segregation of Native People in Canada: Voluntary or Compulsory?" *Currents Readings in Race Relations* 3(4):3–4.

Duclos, N. (1990). "Lessons of Difference: Feminist Theory on Cultural Diversity." *Buffalo Law Review* 38:325.

Economic Council of Canada. (1991). *Report*. Ottawa.

Employment and Immigration Canada. *Annual Reports, Employment Equity Act: l990 and 1992*. Ottawa.

Environics. (1988). *Focus Canada Survey*.

Equality Now: Report of the Parliamentary Task Force on the Participation of Visible Minorities in Canada. (1984). Ottawa: Queen's Printer.

Fernanado, T., and K. Prasad. (1986). *Multiculturalism and Employment Equity: Problems Facing Foreign-Trained Professionals and Tradespeople in British Columbia*. Vancouver: Affiliation of Multicultural Societies and Service Agencies of British Columbia.

Fleras, A., and J. Elliot. (1992). *The Nations Within: Aboriginal–State Relations in Canada, United States and New Zealand*. Toronto: Oxford University Press.

Flett, H. (l979). "Dispersal Policies in Council Housing: Arguments and Evidence." *New Community* 7(2):184–194.

Elizabeth Fry Society of Saskatchewan. (1992). *Aboriginal Women in the Criminal Justice System*, In Western Judical Education Centre on Racial, Ethnic, and Cultural Equity. Saskatoon: WJEC.

Frideres, J. (1983). *Native People in Canada: Contemporary Conflicts* (2nd ed.). Scarborough, ON: Prentice-Hall.

———. (1988). "Institutional Structures and Economic Deprivation: Native People in Canada." In *Racial Oppression In Canada*. S. Bolaria and P. Li (eds.), Toronto: Garamond Press.

Garon, M. (ed.). (l988). *Une Expérience de testing de la discrimination raciale dans le logement à Montréal*. Montreal: Quebec Human Rights Commission.

The Globe and Mail. (1992). (October 14).

Gould, T. (1990). "Who Do You Hate." *Toronto Life* (October).

Head, W. (1981). *Adaptation of Immigrants: Perceptions of Ethnic and Racial Discrimination*. North York, ON: York University.

Henry, F. (In press). *Caribbean Communities in Canada: A Study in Culture and Conflict*. Toronto: University of Toronto Press.

———. (l968). "The West Indian Domestic Scheme in Canada." In *Social and Economic Studies*. Mona, Jamaica: University of the West Indies.

———. (1974). *The Forgotten Canadians: The Blacks of Nova Scotia*. Don Mills, ON: Longmans.

———. (1978) *Dynamics of Racism*. Ottawa: Secretary of State.

———. (l989). *Housing and Racial Discrimination in Canada: A Preliminary Assessment*. Ottawa: Ministry of Multiculturalism and Citizenship.

———, and E. Ginzberg. (1984). *Who Gets the Work? A Test of Racial Discrimination in Employment*. Toronto: Urban Alliance on Race Relations and the Social Planning Council of Toronto.

Hernandez, C. (1992). "Nanny Rule Will Have Racist Outcome." *The Toronto Star* (February 15).

Hill, D. (1981). *The Freedom Seekers: Blacks in Early Canada*. Agincourt, ON: Book Society of Canada.

HRT (Human Rights Tribunal). (1992). *The Canadian Human Rights Commission (and five other complainants) and Manitoba Knights of the Ku Klux Klan and William (Bill) James Harcus*. (December 16). Ottawa: HRT.

Jain, H. (1985). *Anti-Discrimination Staffing Policies: Implications of Human Rights Legislation for Employers and Trade Unions*. Ottawa: Secretary of State.

———. (1988). "Affirmative Action/Employment Equity Programmes and Visible Minorities in Canada." *Currents Readings in Race Relations* 5(1)(4):3–7.

———. and R. Hackett (1989). "Measuring Effectiveness of Employment Equity Programmes in Canada: Public Policy and a Survey." *Canadian Public Policy* 15(2):189–204.

Johnson, P. (1983). *Native Children and the Child Welfare System.* Toronto: James Lorimer and Co.

Kellough, G. (1980). *From Colonialism to Economic Imperialism: The Experience of the Canadian Indian.* In J. Harp and J. Hofley (eds.), *Structural Inequality in Canada.* Scarborough, ON: Prentice-Hall.

Kline, M. (1992). "Best Interests Ideology in First Nations Child Welfare Cases." *Osgoode Hall Law Journal* vol. 30:375–425.

Kobayashi, A. (1987). "From Tyranny to Justice: The Uprooting of the Japanese Canadians in 1941." *Tribune Juive* 5:28–35.

Lampkin, L. (1985). "Visible Minorities in Canada." Research paper for the Abella Royal Commission: Equality in Employment. Ottawa: Minister of Supplies and Services Canada.

Lampert, R., and J. Curtis. (1989). "The Racial Attitudes of Canadians." In *Readings in Sociology.* Tepperman and J. Curtis (eds.), Toronto: McGraw-Hill Ryerson.

League for Human Rights of B'nai B'rith. (1992). *Annual Audit of Anti-Semitic Incidents.* Toronto.

Leah, R. (1991). "Linking the Struggles: Racism, Sexism and the Union Movement." In Vorst et al.(eds.), *Race, Class, Gender: Bonds and Barriers.*

Lewis, S. (1992). *Report on Race Relations to Premier Bob Rae.* Toronto. The quote on page 87 is reprinted wih permission from the Queen's Printer for Ontario.

Li, P. (1988). *The Chinese in Canada.* Toronto: Oxford University Press.

_____. (forthcoming). "Unneighbourly Houses or Unwelcome Chinese: The Social Construction of Race in the Battle over 'Monster Homes' in Vancouver." *International Journal of Race and Ethnicity.*

_____, and S. Bolaria (eds.). (1983). *Racial Minorities in Multicultural Canada.* Toronto: Garamond Press.

Malarek, V. (1987). *Heaven's Gate: Canada's Immigration Fiasco.* Toronto: Macmillan of Canada.

Mattis, W. (1990). "Canadian Immigration Policy 1867-1990: More of the Same." Unpublished manuscript. Toronto.

Mazurek, K.(1987). "Multiculturalism, Education and the Ideology of Meritocracy." In T. Wotherspoon (ed.), *The Political Economy of Canadian Schooling.* Toronto: Methuen.

Mock, K. (1992). *Combatting Hate: Canadian Realities and Remedies.* Toronto: League for Human Rights, B'nai B'rith Canada.

Murray, M. (1991). *The Toronto Star* (June 23).

Ontario Human Rights Commission. (1977). *Annual Report.* Toronto.

Ontario Ministry of Citizenship. (1989). *Access: Task Force on Access to Professions and Trades in Ontario.* Toronto: Ministry of Supply and Services.

Ng, R. (1992). "Managing Female Immigration: A Case of Institutionalized Sexism and Racism." *Canadian Women Studies* 12(3):20–23.

_____. (1993). "Racism, Sexism and Nation Building." In C. McCarthy and W. Critchlow (eds.), *Race, Identity and Representation in Education.* New York and London: Routledge.

Pitman, W. (1977). *Now Is Not too Late: Report on Race Relations in Metro Toronto.* Toronto: Council of Metropolitan Toronto.

Ponting, R., and R. Gibbons. (1980). *Out of Irrelevance.* Toronto: Butterworths.

Powless, D. (1985). "Native People and Employment. A National Tragedy." In *Research Studies of the Commission on Equality in Employment.* Ottawa: Minister of Supply and Services Canada.

Purich, D. (1986). *Our Land: Native Peoples in Canada.* Toronto: James Lorimer.

Quann, D. (l979). *Racial Discrimination in Housing.* Ottawa: Canadian Council on Social Development.

Raj, S. (1980). "Some Aspects of East Indian Struggle in Canada, 1905–1947." In *Visible Minorities and Multiculturalism: Asians in Canada*, K. Ujimoto and G. Hirabagashi (eds.), Toronto: Butterworths.

Ramcharan, S. (1982). *Racism: NonWhites in Canada.* Toronto: Butterworths.

Raunet, D. (1984). *Without Surrender, Without Consent: A History of Nishga Land Claims.* Vancouver: Douglas and McIntyre.

Rees, T. (1991). "Racial Discrimination and Employment Agencies." *Currents: Readings in Race Relations* (Toronto) 7(2):16–19.

Reitz, J., L. Calzavara, and D. Dasko. (1981). *Ethnic Inequality and Segregation in Jobs.* Toronto: Centre for Urban and Community Studies, University of Toronto.

Report of the Aboriginal Justice Inquiry of Manitoba. (1991).

Report of the Donald Marshall Inquiry in Nova Scotia. (1989).

Report of W.L. Mackenzie King, C.M.G., *Commissioner Appointed to Enquire into the Methods by Which Oriental Labourers have been Induced to come to Canada.* Ottawa: King's Printer, 1908.

Report of the Task Force on the Criminal Justice System and Its Impact on the Indian and Métis People of Alberta. (1991).

Report of the Saskatchewan Métis Justice Review Committee. (1991).

Report of the Special Committee, Canadian Bar Association. (1988). "Aboriginal Rights in Canada: An Agenda for Action."

Report of the Nova Scotia Advisory Group on Race Relations. (1991). Halifax.

Rex, J., and J. Moore. (1967). *Race, Community and Conflict.* London: Oxford University Press.

Richardson, B. (1993). *People of Terra Nullius: Betrayal and Rebirth in Aboriginal Canada.* Vancouver and Toronto: Douglas and McIntyre.

Robson, R., and B. Breems. (1985). *Ethnic Conflict in Vancouver.* Vancouver: B.C. Civil Liberties Association.

Roberts, D. (1993). "A Stranger in God's House." *The Globe and Mail* (December 1):A1.

Sampat-Mehta, R. (1984). "The First Fifty Years of South Asian Immigration: A Historical Perspective." In R. Ranungo (ed.), *South Asians in the Canadian Mosaic.* Montreal: Kala Bharati.

Samual, J. (1988). *Immigration and Visible Minorities in the Year 2001: A Projection.* Ottawa: Centre for Immigration and Ethnocultural Studies.

Satzewich, V. (1989). "Racisms: The Reactions to Chinese Migrants in Canada at the Turn of the Century." *International Sociology* 4(3):311-327.

Secretary of State. (1982). *Study of Racial Tensions in 11 Major Cities in Canada.* Ottawa: Secretary of State.

Shadd, A.S. (1989). "Institutionalized Racism and Canadian History: Note of a Black Canadian." Appendix in C. James (ed.), *Seeing Ourselves: Exploring Race, Ethnicity and Culture.* Toronto: Sheridan College.

Sharzer, S. (1985). "Native People: Some Issues." In *Research Studies of the Commission on Equality in Employment.* Ottawa: Ministry of Supply and Services Canada.

Shepard, B. (1991). "Plain Racism: The Reaction Against Oklahoma Black Immigration to the Canadian Plains." In O. McKague (ed.), *Racism in Canada.* Saskatoon: Fifth House.

Silvera, M. (1989). *Silenced* (2nd ed.) Toronto: Sister Vision Press.

———. (1993). "Speaking of Women's Lives and Imperialist Economics: Two Introductions from Silenced." In H. Bannerji (ed.) *The Glaze: Essays on Racism, Feminism and Politics.* Toronto: Sister Vision Press.

Small, P. (1992). "Promote Minorities, Report Tells Police." *The Toronto Star* (September 11):A6.

Sunahara, A. (1981). *The Politics of Racism: The Uprooting of Japanese Canadians during the Second World War.* Toronto: James Lorimer

Tarnopolsky, W. (1991). "Discrimination and the Law in Canada." In *Seminar on Race, Ethnic and Cultural Equity.* Vancouver: Western Judicial Centre.

Task Force on Immigration Practices and Procedures. (1981). *Domestic Workers on Employment Authorizations: A Report.* Ottawa.

Task Force on Access to Trades and Professions. (1989). *Access!* Toronto: Ontario Ministry of Citizenship.

Teitlebaum, B., and L. Berube. (l983). "La Discrimination raciale dans le logement à Montréal." *Collectiv Paroles* (Montreal) 22.

The Toronto Star. (1990). (October). "Who Do You Hate?"

The Toronto Star. (1992). "Minority Community Survey."

Troper, A. (1972). *Only Farmers Need Apply*. Toronto: Griffin House.

Ubale, B. (1977). *Equal Opportunity and Public Policy: A Report on Concerns of the South Asian Community Regarding their Place in the Canadian Mosaic*. Toronto: Ontario Ministry of the Attorney General.

Ujimoto, K. (1988). "Racial Discrimination and Internment: Japanese in Canada." In S. Bolaria and P. Li (eds.), *Racial Oppression in Canada*. Toronto: Garamond Press.

Vorst, J., et al. (1989). *Race, Class, Gender: Bonds and Barriers*. Toronto: Between the Lines.

Walker, J. (1980). *The History of Blacks in Canada: A Study Guide for Teachers and Students*. Ottawa: Minister of State for Multiculturalism.

_____. (1985). *Race and the Historian: Some Lessons from Canadian Public Policy*, Waterloo.

_____. (1987). *Race and the Historian: Some Lessons From Canadian Policy*. Paper presented at the Canada 2000 Conference, Ottawa.

Ward, P. (1978). *White Canadian Forever*. Kingston: McGill–Queen's University Press.

Ward, R. (l984). *Race and Housing in Britain: Approaches to Differential Treatment in Housing*. Monographs on Ethnic Relations, no. 2. Birmingham, U.K.: University of Aston.

Watson, P. (1990). "RCMP Chief Fears Violence if Racism Continues to Grow." *The Toronto Star* (March 4):A 1.

Wellman, D. (1978). *Portraits of White Racism*. Cambridge: Cambridge University Press.

Winks, R. (1971). *Blacks in Canada*. New Haven, CT: Yale University Press.

_____. (1978). *Blacks in Canada*. New Haven, CT: Yale University Press.

NOTES

1. This section is drawn from the projections of T. J. Samuals, *Visible Minorities in Canada: A Projection*. (Toronto: Race Relations Advisory Council on Advertising, Canadian Advertising Foundation, 1992).

PART
TWO

▼▼▼▼▼▼▼▼▼▼▼▼▼▼▼▼▼▼▼▼▼▼▼▼▼▼▼▼▼▼▼▼▼▼▼▼

Racism in
Canadian
Public-Sector
and Voluntary
Organizations

▼▼▼▼▼▼▼▼▼▼▼▼▼▼▼▼▼▼▼▼▼▼▼▼▼▼▼▼▼▼▼

*This part examines a number of key institutions in Canadian society,
particularly those that provide services to the public. The analysis
of racism in policing, the justice system, and human services shows how
the policies, programs, procedures and delivery systems of these
major insititutions discriminate against people of colour.
The discussions in these chapters illuminate the nature of racism
in Canada as articulated in its organizational life.*

▼▼▼▼▼▼▼▼▼▼▼▼▼▼▼▼▼▼▼▼▼▼▼▼▼▼▼▼▼▼▼▼▼▼▼▼▼▼▼

Chapter 4

▼▼▼▼▼▼▼▼▼▼▼▼

Racism and Policing

I must tell you, I don't think there's any Black that was born and raised in Toronto that doesn't know someone personally or hasn't personally experienced police harassment in some form or another. (Al Mercury, quoted in Lewis 1989)

This chapter explores racism in policing institutions. It begins by examining racist attitudes and behaviours and shows how they lead to both the overpolicing and the underpolicing of minority communities. The chapter then discusses the racialization of crime and discusses the criminalization of minorities. Police accountability, response to pressures from minority groups, professional competence, and its relationship to the representation of people of colour on police forces are also discussed. A brief overview of some of the issues relating to police culture and the public complaints process is presented.

The second part of the chapter examines the responses of police services across the country. It concludes with a discussion of policies, training, employment equity, community relations, community-based policing, and use of force guidelines.

INTRODUCTION

Policing institutions derive their authority from a Police Services Act or analogous legislation. In general, policing is a provincial responsibility that is often delegated to a municipality.

Police forces are mandated to enforce infractions against federal laws, including the Criminal Code, the Narcotic Control Act, and the Food and Drug Act. As well, police forces enforce provincial laws and municipal by-laws. Under police force legislation, police officers are given broad discretionary powers in enforcing laws.

It is the duty of Royal Canadian Mounted Police, for example,

> to perform all duties that are assigned to peace officers in relation to the preservation of the peace, the prevention of crime, and of offences against

the laws of Canada and the laws in force in any province in which they may be employed, and the apprehension of criminals and offenders and others who may be lawfully taken into custody." (Royal Canadian Mounted Police Act, s.c. 1986, c. r–9, s. 181(a))

This example clearly stresses the law and other duties of the police. On the other hand, the police function in society incorporates other concepts. In incorporating the need for community policing, the Ontario Police Services Act (1990) requires that policing in Ontario be provided in accordance with the following principles:

- the need to ensure the safety and security of all persons and property in Ontario;
- the importance of safeguarding the fundamental rights guaranteed by the Canadian Charter of Rights and Freedoms and the Ontario Human Rights Code.
- the need for co-operation between the providers of police services and the communities they serve;
- the importance of respect for victims of crime and understanding of their needs;
- the need for sensitivity to the pluralistic, multiracial, and multicultural character of Ontario; and
- the need to ensure that police forces are representative of the communities they serve.

From such concepts as the preservation of peace and order, the prevention of crime, and the pursuit and apprehension of criminals to the concepts of representativeness, sensitivity to victims and the multiracial character of society, and the participation of the community in policing, it is understandable that a certain amount of ambiguity exists in the sometimes conflicting roles that police play in modern society. This ambiguity is particularly salient in the context of racism and policing institutions.

No single area of Canadian life has perhaps caused more concern and more persistent tension and conflict than the relationships between the police and people of colour. For many years, people of colour have strongly indicated that policing in Canada was not carried out with an even hand and that they were singled out for particularly close attention and unnecessary violence.

With respect to the treatment of Aboriginal peoples by police forces across Canada, a number of government reports, such as the *Report of the Nova Scotia Royal Commission on the Donald Marshall Jr. Prosecution* (1990), *The Report of the Task Force on the Criminal Justice System and Its impact on the Indian and Métis People of Alberta* (1991), *the Report on Aboriginal Peoples and Criminal Justice by the Law Reform Commission of Canada* (1991), and the *Report of Aboriginal Justice Inquiry of Manitoba* (1991), have presented evidence of racism. The last study concluded that the "justice system has failed Manitoba's Aboriginal people on a massive scale."

A report to the Metropolitan Toronto Police Services Board on perceptions of policing in Metropolitan Toronto's Aboriginal community concluded:

> One thing that all Native people agree on is that there is a serious problem with policing in the Aboriginal community. There is a perception that the police are guilty of brutality, racism, false arrests, and numerous other offences against Native people. Compounding this is a great sense of helplessness—that there is no recourse for the Native community. There is no place to make a complaint and nobody will listen away. (Mukwe Ode First Nations Consulting, 1992)

Throughout the 1980s and 1990s, a number of government reports in Ontario were initiated in response to incidents involving racial minorities and police. Similarly, in Quebec, the task force report by J. Bellemare, *Investigation into Relations Between the Police Forces, Visible and Other Ethnic Minorities* (1988) was in response to the serious injury and death of members of the Black community at the hands of the police.

The relationship between the police and people of colour will always, it seems, be a sensitive matter. In many ways, relations between the police and the racial-minority communities can be seen as the flashpoint, the means to gauge the general temper of race relations in Canada. As Ungerleider (1992b) points out, considering not only the racial diversity of Canadian society but also inequalities in the distribution of wealth and power, the relations between the police and people of colour will always be extremely fragile because the police are the most visible embodiment of the dominant group's power.

Clearly, if one were to succeed in eliminating racism in the wider society, it would be much easier to attain a much more positive police–race relations climate. The policing of Canada's racial-minority communities cannot be divorced from the way in which society at large views those communities. The attitudes of the police are a reflection not only of the current social views of people of colour, but also of the historical attitudes of the White majority. The consequence of this, as Ungerleider argues, is that the police are more likely to mistreat individuals who are stigmatized by the dominant society. These individuals are more likely to be subjected to small or gross indignities and mistreatment at the hands of the police. The behaviour leads to accusations of "overpolicing" and "underprotecting" minorities.

MANIFESTATIONS OF RACISM IN POLICING

Overpolicing	Racialization of crime
Underpolicing	Police culture
Lack of representation	Poor police-community relations
Use of force	

THE MANIFESTATIONS OF RACISM

People of colour have been complaining for a number of years of a constant pattern of police harassment and police insensitivity to their lifestyles and needs. Police have been perceived by many members of racial minorities as aloof from those they serve, possessing far-reaching and oppressive powers against which minorities had no redress.

Police forces make many discretionary decisions about who they hire, what is to be done, the priorities assigned to activities, and the ways in which to carry out these activities. It is generally accepted that such decisions should be related to societal conditions and needs. However, recent royal commissions and public inquiries have confirmed minority-group and Aboriginal concerns that these decisions have been biased in a manner that reflects selectivity based on race. Their reports have highlighted many of the inherently unfair and racist practices of police forces across the country.

RACIST ATTITUDES AND BEHAVIOUR

Although extensive racism among the police is often alleged and anecdotal evidence of significant specific incidents has been offered, documented research evidence for this assertion is relatively slim. Most studies relate to police "personality" traits such as authoritarianism, dogmatism, and conservatism. The only study in Canada on this subject was undertaken by Ungerleider, who sampled 251 uniformed officers in two major municipalities in Canada. His study examined the judgements that police officers made about others. It found that 25 percent of the officers were either confused in their judgement of others or irrationally negative, and concludes that "the existence of a large number of Canadian police officers who make irrational judgements about others is disquieting" (Ungerleider, 1992b).

Another perspective on this sensitive issue as to whether police officers are more likely to betray racist tendencies, above and beyond the occasional "bad apple" incident, has been put forward in a study of the Metropolitan Toronto Police Force that found no evidence of organized, intentional prejudice or bias against racial minorities (Andrews, 1992). While acknowledging that the force had done a reasonable job of ensuring that those who are recruited did not display an overt bias, Andrews found

> that a change occurs after joining the Force. There was significant evidence that many police officers who are constantly in contact with the public develop strong feelings and beliefs as to attributes of individuals, based on factors such as appearance and racial background. These officers would no doubt be offended if their attitudes were described as potentially racist. Nevertheless, the same attitudes can and do produce a bias in behaviour which results in unequal treatment of individuals of different cultural or racial backgrounds.

What is evident here is not so much a symptom of personal belief as evidence of a developed culture and value system within the organization.

As a result of work experience whereby police officers are exposed to an extremely selective cross-section of the population, an attitudinal bias toward people of colour may creep in.

OVERPOLICING

Policing priorities can be both formal and informal. Formal priorities are those that are specifically identified as priorities of a police force. Informal priorities are peculiar to an officer or a set of officers.

There is little disagreement that policing activities and resources ought to be focussed on those areas of high risk, having a high probability of criminal activity or requiring high levels of service. But what constitutes "high risk" or a "higher level of service"? For example, recent newspaper reports claim that frauds and white-collar crimes are on the increase. These cases have overloaded the system. The police advise that many of these crimes will go uninvestigated and that an affected company should do the preliminary investigation before going to the police. In other words, the police state that white-collar crimes can go unchecked, relative to other crimes. Most white-collar crimes are committed by White people who occupy positions of power, rank, and confidence in an organization (Reiman, 1984). Thus, by choosing not to make white-collar crimes a priority, the police simultaneously remove a large segment of the community from potential criminal liability. The segment of the community largely responsible for white-collar crime is underpoliced.

Who defines what is "high risk" or a "higher level of service"? This is not an objective exercise. As already noted, police–race relations are influenced by the structural features of a society in which opportunity, rewards, and constraints are unequally and unfairly distributed.

Canadian society is hierarchically stratified along a number of dimensions, including ascribed attributes such as skin colour, ethnicity, sex, and religion, as well as along such lines as economic and political power. As Ungerleider argues:

> The categorization of people in this way can provide a shared sense of identity as well as distinctive perceptual, normative and behavioural patterns. These differences are injected into society's policy process including affecting criminal justice—creating disputes about what behaviours are to be considered criminal and how seriously particular criminal violations are to be regarded.

The criminal justice system reflects and promotes the interests of the more powerful members of society. These members, in turn, exert influence to diminish the priority and resources given by the police to those criminal activities in which they themselves are more likely to engage (for example, white-collar crime) and to increase the priority given to "street" crimes, which are committed by less advantaged people.

"Overpolicing" refers to the extent to which police use discretion in the surveillance of a community and the apprehension of people within that community. Are police cruisers seen more frequently, for example, in communities that are densely populated by people of colour? Is the police presence more clearly noticeable at any event involving people of colour? Are business establishments such as restaurants and clubs that are owned, managed, or patronized by Black people under more frequent police surveillance? Sometimes such police presence may be obvious and visible; at other times, unmarked cars and plain clothes hide their surveillance. One notable result of overpolicing is that charges tend to be more frequently laid against Blacks.

One of the reasons given in Metropolitan Toronto for the number of accused Blacks being totally out of proportion to their numbers in the total population is that it is the direct result of police priorities and actions. The "war on drugs," for example, and the consequent drug sweeps in poor and Black areas involve police techniques that entail significant numbers of people being arrested and charged when, in fact, only a few may be guilty. Drugs, both hard and soft, have been viewed by police as an excuse for raids using overwhelming manpower and resources. As more and more Blacks crowd into the courtrooms, it is inevitable that the perception is encouraged that Blacks are more prone to criminal behaviour.

The overpolicing of racial minorities can be understood, therefore, within the larger sociopolitical context, in which the police contribute to the criminalization of marginalized individuals and groups by selecting what is "high risk" criminal behaviour. It can also be seen in the methods chosen to address that deviant behaviour.

Overpolicing can be seen, as well, in the discretionary decisions and behaviour of individual police officers. For example, the Race Relations and Policing Task Force (Government of Ontario, April 1989) heard numerous examples of the active harassment of racial minorities by police. For example, the Task Force quotes one presenter: "Harassment is being released from prison, finding a job, to have a police officer come to your job and ask your employer, 'Why have you hired him, don't you know he's a criminal'?" This presenter went on to tell of racial-minority young people constantly being stopped by police on the street, especially after dark. She told the task force: "The questions are always being asked [by police]: 'Where are you going'? 'Where you coming from'?"

The Task Force found that Black youth in particular tended to view police with distrust and fear, feelings said to be rooted in confrontations involving physical and verbal abuse by some police officers. In Toronto, the task force was told by several Black youths of police using racial slurs and exercising their right to use force in excessive or humiliating ways:

> We will talk about jay-walking. There are situations in Windsor where five people will walk across a street on a red light, which is jay-walking. If one or two of them are Black, they are the ones that will get the jay-walking ticket. If a Black is out going to work in the wee hours of the morning...and most people working in the Big Three are out there at 5:30, 6:00 o'clock in the morning waiting for a bus...he is apt to be harassed there. [The police] will go so far as to look in your lunch bag, and things of this nature.

This kind of anecdotal evidence, received by the Race Relations and Policing Task Force and other forums like it across Canada, make it abundantly clear that people of colour believe they are treated quite differently from the majority community by the police. Black people, it seems, are far more likely to be stopped and searched by the police and far less likely to be cautioned than are their White counterparts.

Other anecdotal evidence suggests that racial minorities are often charged and accused of crimes they did not commit. The police may arrest a racial-minority member who, they say, resembles someone they are searching for in connection with a crime committed. Blacks allege that identities are not carefully checked, and that to White police officers "all Blacks look alike." This tendency appears to be especially true for younger members of the Black community, who are more vulnerable and easily harassed. While these reports certainly acknowledge that the majority of police conduct themselves professionally, there continues to be ample evidence of improper and, sometimes, discriminatory behaviour by some police officers.

Racially prejudiced police behaviour has not been clearly defined in Canada, and as a result it is generally not seen as a disciplinary offence by police forces. In addition, because the impartiality of the complaints procedure is generally seen as being severely compromised (it entails the police investigating the police), few complaints of racial discrimination and harassment by police are actually made. Consequently, the seriousness of the nature and extent of the issues of overpolicing and the harassment of people of colour are difficult to quantify and largely dependent on the kinds of anecdotal evidence presented to such government-appointed task forces as the ones cited above.

THE RACIALIZATION OF CRIME

Overpolicing clearly contributes to the notion that certain racial groups, particularly Blacks, are more disposed to commit crimes than are Whites and other races. Because of their interactions with the Black community, police and some members of the justice system commonly believe that Blacks are responsible for more crimes and that Blacks come from a crime-prone culture, notably Jamaica.

In the United Kingdom, the racialization of crime has been evident since the early 1970s, and it reached a high point in the early 1980s (Gilroy, 1987:72–109). "The idea that Blacks are a high crime group and the related notion that their criminality is an expression of their distinctive culture have become integral to British racism in the period since the "rivers of blood" speech. These comments were made in a speech by a member of Parliament, Enoch Powell, in objecting to Black emigration to Britain and suggesting the repatriation of existing citizens in 1968.

Gilroy argues that, as earlier notions about the volume of Black immigration and the diseases and sexuality of such emigrants gave way to concerns about their distinctive cultural expressions, the focus of the new racism became their criminality. Crime—specifically the criminal acts of "mugging," robbery, drug charges, and street rioting—were understood to be the natural expressions of Black culture, which was defined as "a cycle in which the negative effects of black matriarchy and family pathology wrought destructive changes on the inner city by literally breeding deviancy out of deprivation and discrimination" (Gilroy, 1987:109–10).

In recent work, Cashmore and McLaughlin argue that in the United Kingdom the police began to suggest the ideas of Black criminality following the disturbances of the early 1980s:

> the police, aided by a hyperbolic mass media, were able to nail down their problem more precisely. Blacks, particularly young Blacks, were a new force in British society and one which, unless checked, could undermine the nation's stability. A rush of lurid editorials, academic theses and television documentaries tended to confirm the police's premise: Blacks were a problem. (Cashmore and McLaughlin, 1991:3)

Similar patterns may be emerging in Canadian cities, particularly with respect to police interactions with the Black communities in Toronto and Montreal. As happened in an earlier period in the United Kingdom, Black crime appears to be becoming the central focus of police activity that leads directly to the reinforcement of a racist ideology. Such ideology directed at the Black community means that Black life, in a more general sense, is being examined and understood or misunderstood through the "lens which criminal signs and imagery provide" (Gilroy, 1987:76).

Thus, the racialization of crime, in which Blacks are increasingly identified with criminal behaviour, reinforces the need for "overpolicing" and helps to explain and legitimize the differential behaviour of police officers toward members of these communities.

UNDERPOLICING

Minority experiences and perceptions relate not only to situations of overpolicing. Members of racial minorities have consistently alleged that police often underpolice them—that is, police fail to protect them adequately or to respond to their requests for assistance. The Lewis Task Force on Race Relations and Policing in Ontario found, for example, that racial-minority battered women believed that they received less sensitivity from police than did White females who had been abused. They alleged that police were particularly slow in responding to their calls and that many police seemed to believe they somehow liked or deserved abuse from men.

Another example of the potential of underpolicing is the length of time that police take to respond to hate activity directed at people of colour. Again, anecdotal evidence has suggested long delays before the police have appeared. The result is that eyewitnesses may have forgotten details or, even worse, can no longer be contacted. In some instances, the attitude and manner of the police have left victims feeling that they were to blame for the harassment they had suffered.

One of the more blatant and appalling examples of underpolicing is the Betty Osborne case in Manitoba. In November 1971, several white youths gang-raped and murdered Helen Betty Osborne, a Cree teenager in The Pas, Manitoba. Not until a reinvestigation in 1987 was one youth sentenced to life imprisonment, one companion acquitted, and a third granted immunity from prosecution for testifying. A subsequent inquiry revealed details of complicity between the RCMP and "respectable" white townspeople so that details of the original case were not investigated or made known (Report of the Aboriginal Justice Inquiry of Manitoba, 1991).

ACCOUNTABILITY

An underlying tenet of Canadian democracy is the obligation of its public institutions to explain and justify their activities in public. This account-ability provides legitimacy to the democratic state. With regard to policing, it requires of police forces the acceptance of the notion of community con-trol and participation in the decision-making processes of policing.

One of the major problems that has been identified inhibiting improved police–race relations and more equitable policing services is the concern that people of colour do not have access to, and are not able to participate in and influence, the decision-making processes of policing institutions. If the police are not directly accountable to the racially diverse communities they serve, then it follows that they are less likely to reflect and respond to the needs and concerns of those communities.

It has been said that most Canadians unfortunately know little about the operation of their police forces. Policing is still in many ways, for many Canadians, a "closed" public institution, surrounded by mystery and secrecy. The isolation of the police from the racially diverse community they suppos-edly serve exists in part because relatively few members of the public have taken an active interest in the police. Many Canadians also feel that public order is the responsibility of the police alone. This attitude also diminishes the sense of police community accountability—they are encouraged to perceive themselves as the only organization of social control, as the sole protectors and guardians of society.

The police, however, have also been criticized for not wishing to con-form to this democratic obligation of accountability. The police have diffi-culties with, if not antagonism toward, meeting this obligation. It has been suggested that the notion of a democratically accountable police force is a contradiction in terms, when the police are empowered to infringe on the liberties of citizens and are legally entitled to use force and violence to uphold law and order. The police deal in and with conflict and are empow-ered by the state to do so (Cashmore and McLaughlin, 1992:110).

It has been suggested that rather than having a democratic notion of accountability—to a political process and to the community—the police tend to view their accountability in different terms. Within this policing ide-ology, an obligation to the political process—which is portrayed as parti-san—is seen in negative terms. The police are seen as preferring to derive

their legitimacy and authority from a general acceptance of the laws and regulations they enforce, the values they stand for, the morality they are supposed to support, and the order they maintain. It is toward this process of
upholding community standards that the police feel they are accountable. At
the same time, it is within this broader framework that they feel they directly represent the "common good."

By further capitalizing on societal tensions, they have been criticized for
further mobilizing their legitimacy through their role as society's crisis managers. The police, in wanting greater authority and resources as the sole protectors of order, have at the same time been promoting and feeding a societal
fear of disintegration into disorder, uncertainty, and anarchy.

In order to cope with increasing crime rates and public disorder, the
police tend to demand even greater organizational and professional autonomy. The issue of democratic accountability is inevitably regarded by the
police with some apprehension and resistance. It is resisted as an unnecessary
and dangerous intrusion on their ability to do their increasingly difficult job.
They are seen as promoting what has been called the crisis conspiracy, in
which urban centres are on the verge of collapsing into disorder and anarchy
(McLaughlin, 1992).

The idea of chaos and crisis in every area of society, and the image of the
police vainly trying to cope with the overwhelming demands of a society in
turmoil, is a self-serving image the police are likely to support in their
requests for more resources and greater autonomy. They tend to substanti-
ate these fears and continue to push the moral panic button by releasing
crime statistics that focus on the explosion of violent crime. The imprecise
manner in which people of colour have been linked to crime and disorder
contributes to the image of certain racial minorities as being a major cause
of this turmoil and therefore as subversive and unwanted elements in
society.

The need for more democratic accountability and the reduction of police
powers in this "urban battlefield" scenario are therefore seen by the police
as a wholly irrelevant, badly timed, and unnecessary intrusion. They believe
they need to be released from all the controls of government—all the political, legislative, bureaucratic, and financial fetters—so that they can better
contain the explosion of violent crime.

The police feel, as the Metropolitan Toronto Police Association states,
that they "are probably the most regulated group of working people in
Ontario" (Metropolitan Police Association, November 11, 1992). They see
recent government initiatives as "additional controls." These "arbitrary"
actions have "engendered a growing sense of frustration and anger among
the police, especially front-line officers confronting increasing crime."

The protest against the Ontario government by the Metropolitan Toronto
and provincial police associations in the fall of 1992 was in large part symptomatic of this police outrage at what was perceived as "political intervention." Attempts to introduce some mechanisms for greater democratic
accountability were viewed as something that should be discouraged and nul-
lified. Such intervention is either invalidated by the police as some socialist

conspiracy or marginalized as resulting from the unreasonable demands of vociferous special-interest groups.

This job action was in part launched to protest what the Metropolitan Toronto Police Association termed "the disproportionate representation of self-interest groups on government-appointed committees reviewing the police." The demands for greater democratic accountability tend to be seen as opposing the police and are therefore painted as somehow subverting the democratic process. It is frequently considered by the police as challenging the maintenance of law and order, and therefore akin to being a threat to the state.

The demands for increasing police empowerment and greater professional autonomy are further promoted by the notion that policing is so specialized that nobody outside policing can be expected to comprehend its distinct and peculiar complexities. In this type of thinking, the police feel that any errancy or irregularities by police officers should be handled internally. That is why one of the demands made by the police associations in Ontario to the provincial government (in their protest of 1992) was for a review of the need for the Special Investigations Unit, a semi-autonomous unit under provincial jurisdiction that was established to investigate police shootings.

In the crisis–conspiracy scenario, more often than not, racial minorities are depicted as principal protagonists. Suppressing drug dealers is easily translated to mean the suppression of racial minorities. Such a focus legitimizes the police role for the majority of Canadians. Race has become a causal factor in the increase of violence and disorder. In the maintenance of law and order, the police have also been able at the same time to identify culpable villains.

This interconnectedness appears to be reinforced by a survey of Canadian police officers about their greatest fears regarding the future. Police officials reported that they are fearful about two issues: "drug abuse and the likelihood of collective violence from disadvantaged visible minorities" (Bayeley in Ungerleider, 1992b). When asked about the basis of their fears, police officials justified their fears with reference to "increased militancy in the pursuit of political goals, manifest in obstructive and deliberate law-breaking, as well as open disrespect for policing carrying out their duties," though they were unable to provide any concrete evidence in support of their claims.

If the policing ideology of accountability outlined above, and as reflected in the statements of the Metropolitan Toronto Police Association, is allowed to dictate police decision-making it will clearly not require police to negotiate their presence in neighbourhoods, to cultivate the consent of the community, or to take into account the needs of the community. This tendency will inevitably encourage people of colour to perceive police forces as exclusionary. The police will need to be less responsive to changing expectations of policing and less responsive to the changing needs and concerns of the population.

PROFESSIONAL COMPETENCE

One of the major criticisms of the police is that they are inadequately trained to respond appropriately and sensitively to the needs and concerns of racial-minority communities. When there is antipathy between the police and racial-minority communities, mutual stereotypes, reinforced by ignorance, misunderstanding, and serious incidents of conflict, can develop that are unfavourable and un-helpful to both groups.

In their submissions to the Ontario Task Force on Race Relations and Policing (Lewis, 1989), "Ontario's police made it exceedingly clear that they consider themselves to be professionals. Members of the public, for their part, were no less adamant in demanding that police behave professionally." Although, as the task force noted, what each considered this to mean was an open question, the equitable treatment of the public they serve must be accepted as one of the basic yardsticks of professional conduct.

The police are constantly required to deal with an increasingly diverse public in situations in which the enormous need for communication is matched only by manifold possibilities for confusion and insensitivity. In commenting on the gross deficiencies of police–race relations training in Ontario, Stephen Lewis, in his report to the premier of Ontario following the Yonge Street disturbances on May 4, 1992, stated:

> The situation, it seems to me, is grossly unfair to the police and to new recruits in particular. We have a society of immense diversity, with a complex proliferation of multiracial and multicultural sensibilities, and we don't prepare our police for dealing with it. These are areas where the exercise of judgement, and the development of skills for conflict resolution become every bit as important as the grasp of sophisticated technology. If we really believe in investing in our justice system, then the people who are on the front-lines deserve the best training possible. It is ultimately a test of management. The management of a police force in the 1990's requires qualitative shifts in training, and without those shifts, things go wrong. (Lewis, 1992)

Source: © Reproduced with permission from the Queen's Printer for Ontario

REPRESENTATION

Although there is widespread agreement that the composition of police forces should reflect the make-up of the general population, it clearly does not. Less than 2 percent of police officers in Canada are people of colour. While there are significant variations across the country, the greatest representation is in the Metropolitan Toronto Police Force, with just over 4 percent. However, in this city, people of colour represent over 26 percent of the available labour pool. Police forces are clearly out of step with the general labour market. No police force in Canada has a complement of racial-minority employees close to parity with any reasonable community population or workforce criteria.

By the late 1970s, there was a general recognition that many police recruitment and hiring criteria and practices were inherently discriminatory. Height and weight restrictions, for example, that had no direct relationship to effective job performance unfairly discriminated against people of colour who were smaller in stature than other groups. Many tests and other entry criteria heavily favoured White, middle-class, Canadian-born and -educated applicants. Even the advertising of careers in police work was carried out in media that did not reach large segments of the racial-minority audience.

Accordingly, a number of police forces have undertaken special efforts to attract people of colour to police work, and the rate of recruitment has improved. By the late 1970s, the Metropolitan Toronto Police, for example, began to advertise career opportunities in the ethnic media. Many aspects of assessment tests and entry criteria for acceptance were adjusted. Minority police officers were given a higher profile.

Despite these efforts, minority-group representation in police forces continues to be disproportionately low, especially in the upper ranks. And, while obvious attention must be spent on the recruitment and hiring of minority police officers, an important corollary is retaining them in the force once they have been hired.

An issue that has not received systematic study in Canada is whether minority officers leave police forces at the same rate as their White counterparts. A report from the United States suggested that they do not (National Urban League, 1980). It also indicated that Whites might be drawn away from the police force by attractive alternatives, whereas Blacks would be pushed out by negative experiences.

POLICE CULTURE

Impediments continue to exist that make recruiting (and retaining) minority officers difficult. Some of these impediments are found in the attitudes of individual police officers that are revealed in overt manifestations of racism such as verbal slurs or discriminatory acts by supervisors.

Other impediments to racial-minority recruitment reside in negative perceptions of policing among many racial-minority communities, which may make police work an unattractive career choice for them. Many racial-minority communities have a very different notion of the nature of policing from that generally understood by the police in Canada. For example, a study of police recruitment of minorities conducted in New York City (Hunt, 1971) found fundamental differences in the perceptions of the police role between Whites and racial minorities. Minorities found the service aspects of police work more important than the pay, fringe benefits, or job security, compared with Whites. Whites, on the other hand, were attracted to police work by the concepts of law and order; minorities found this work repugnant. Minorities saw policing as the opportunity to help and serve others rather than simply to enforce the law.

Within this context, Andrews (1992) found no evidence of organized, intentional prejudice or bias against racial minorities. What this review did find, however, is that, over time, officers develop strong feelings and beliefs about the attributes of individuals, based on factors such as appearance and racial background. The review concluded that these attitudes, when taken collectively, can and do produce a bias in behaviour that produces unequal treatment of individuals of different cultural or racial background.

From their initial consideration of policing as a career to their assign-ment as officers on patrol, police personnel are subjected to pressures that encourage their acceptance of a set of beliefs and values that may present an obstacle to better relations between them and the communities they serve. Ungerleider (1992b) identifies the following beliefs and values that influence the outlook of police officers toward the conduct of their work:

- a sincere commitment to a broadly based police role in society, centred on the enforcement of criminal law, the protection of the public, and the maintenance of order;
- a concern for the maintenance of police authority and control, and respect for that authority on the part of the public;
- a general belief that society and the court system are too lenient;
- a general belief that the press is unfair in its coverage of police matters;
- a strong action orientation; a belief that police must take action to resolve anxiety, uncertainty, and disorder;
- a tendency to respond to all public calls and to attempt to find solutions or at least to reassure the persons involved;
- a belief in the mutual support and backup, accompanied by non-interfer-ence and secrecy as far as the actions of other line officers are concerned;
- a general trust in the validity or appropriateness of police action, accom-panied by a limited concern for the abuse of authority;
- among operational officers, a general distrust both of top management's understanding of the complexities and priorities of the operational role, and the likelihood that top management will protect an officer who is falsely accused by the public;
- a limited tolerance for deviance from broadly accepted social values and beliefs;
- a relatively rigid definition of what is "right" and "wrong" behaviour;
- a tendency to stereotype as hostile those people who question police authority; and
- a tendency to simplify events and to fit people and incidents into cate-gories that can be dealt with through police action.

Chief among the factors identified by Ungerleider that help to sustain the beliefs and values of the police and to impede addressing the problems between the police and the citizens they serve is the part that "life on the street" plays in their experience. The "street" is exalted as a *raison d'être* of policing, and "street experience" is asserted to be the foundation of police knowledge.

However, police officers are inadequately prepared for the social realities they confront and the range of tasks they are called upon to perform "on the street," including mediating disputes between landlords and tenants or among family members, locating runaway children and missing persons, maintaining order during or following public events such as labour disputes or sporting contests, enforcing traffic regulations, and comforting the bereaved and victims of accidents and crime. Although the social realities that police officers face often require the knowledge and disposition of social workers, labour mediators, and counsellors, much of their preparation involves recipe-oriented information, largely devoted to understanding and applying the law.

As Andrews (1992) notes in his audit of the Metropolitan Toronto Police Force,

> the culture of police forces in general tends to produce a "we and they" philosophy. Part of this is probably necessary, related to the need to maintain a detached view of the world being policed; part is brought about over time by virtue of the high level of contact with people who break the law; part is undoubtedly due to the image of policing as portrayed on television and in other media.

Police forces in Canada have generally followed a policing model primarily concerned with maintaining a well-trained and disciplined force. Crime fighting is seen as the principle activity of policing. This notion of policing tends to increase the isolation of police officers from members of the public through its excessive emphasis on crime control and solution. This isolation can also lay the foundation for a more selective isolation from various minority groups.

COMPLAINTS PROCESS

There has been a persistent community demand for independent civilian review investigative boards to investigate complaints against the police. Not only should there be an impartial and fair complaints procedure in which citizens can feel free to voice their grievances, but in incidents involving serious injury or death, the police force should not be placed in the untenable position of investigating itself.

The lack of an effective, impartial, and independent complaints procedure is viewed by many racial minorities as a major stumbling block in ensuring not only that police treat all members of the community in a non-discriminatory manner, but that there are also credible avenues of recourse available when individuals are unfairly treated. When this doesn't exist, there is considerable distrust and suspicion on the part of minorities of the integrity and openness of the process.

USE OF FORCE

Given the recent series of police shootings of Blacks, the use of police firearms is of concern. The Lewis Task Force in Ontario recommended that police officers be limited to the use of deadly weapons in a "fleeing offender" situation, and that the use of deadly force should be limited to situations in which the person fleeing poses an immediate threat of death to police officers or others.

Police shootings of Blacks in major urban centres such as Montreal and Toronto in recent years have brought the entire policing system under increasing suspicion by the Black community. For example, six of fifteen victims of police shootings between 1988 and 1991 in Metropolitan Toronto were Black. Five of those six were youth, all of whom were unarmed. The fear within a growing sector of the Black community is that these shootings are part of a systemic pattern. Since 1987, the Montreal Urban Community police have shot to death eight men, including four Blacks and three Hispanics.

Since the late 1970s police shootings of Buddy Evans and Albert Johnson, members of the Black community in Metropolitan Toronto and other communities have continued to advocate for legislative changes in policing, particularly the requirement that police report on the unholstering of their guns.

CASE STUDY 4.1

THE POLICE SHOOTING OF TREVOR KELLY

Trevor Kelly, 43, was a Black man shot by a Montreal Urban Community Police officer during a confrontation that began during a routine police patrol. The Jamaican-born man had a lengthy criminal record and was scheduled to appear in court on a charge of assaulting a peace officer.

Constable Gerard Carrier, of the Quebec provincial police, said Mr. Kelly "approached the cruiser during a routine patrol and uttered threats toward the MUC officers." According to Constable Carrier, when the two uniformed officers left the car, Mr. Kelly lunged at one of them with a knife and was shot with a single bullet.

The names of the officers involved were not revealed to the media, but according to police officials they were being treated for shock. In Quebec, shootings by police must be investigated by another force.

DISCUSSION

According to a *Globe and Mail* report, Dan Phillip, president of the Black Coalition of Quebec, would not categorize the shootings as racially motivated, but said there are grave problems in police treatment of non-Whites that lead to this sort of tragic incident. "Every time a police officer approaches a member of the Black community, he draws his gun and he is ready to shoot," Mr. Phillip said. "There is a racist assumption that there will be trouble."

Noel Alexander, president of the Jamaican Association of Montreal, said he had similar concerns that police overreact when dealing with Blacks. He said Mr. Kelly, regardless of the verbal threats he was making, could have been disarmed or, at worst, shot in the leg. "He didn't have to be shot to death—that's really not acceptable," Mr. Alexander said.

CASE STUDY 4.2

THE POLICE SHOOTING OF MICHAEL "WADE" LAWSON

On December 8, 1988, Michael "Wade" Lawson, 17 years of age and a student at Erindale Secondary School, was shot and killed by Peel, Ontario, police officers while he and a 16-year-old friend were driving a stolen car.

The officers involved said they attempted to stop the vehicle and fired only after the driver tried to run them over. Lawson was shot in the back of the head, and the rear window of the car he was driving was shot out. The officers were part of an "old clothes" undercover unit, which meant they were not only out of uniform, but wearing old clothes. They did not identify themselves and did not try to stop the car, which was heading away from them when they fired.

EVENTS

A number of community rallies and public demonstrations were held to protest the shooting. They were spearheaded by the Black Action Defence Committee, whose principal spokespersons were Charles Roach and Dudley Laws. On December 12, four days after the shooting, two Ontario Cabinet ministers, the solicitor general and the minister of citizenship, called a meeting with representatives of the Black community. Some leaders boycotted the meeting, and the tone of the discussions was angry.

A month after the shooting, in January 1989, one police constable was charged with manslaughter and his partner was charged with aggravated assault. Community representatives denounced the inadequacy of these lesser charges. The charge of manslaughter, for example, does not allow the issue of the motive of the police officer to be laid open to public scrutiny.

Five thousand buttons were distributed by the Peel Police Association, reading "We support 1191 and 1139"—the badge numbers of the two police constables charged.

On November 21, 1989, preliminary court hearings were held with regard to the charges against police constables Anthony Malaragni and Darren Longpre. The judge noted that he was considering more severe charges, including second-degree murder. The case was adjourned until December 21, 1989.

On December 21, 1989, the police constables were both charged with manslaughter. Police staged a work-to-rule in protest against these new charges.

A preliminary hearing was held on May 16, 1990, and as of this writing the case is still before the courts.

CONCLUSION

The Lawson shooting demonstrated that, when suspected of a crime, police officers are treated differently by the criminal justice system than ordinary citizens. Ordinary citizens are charged with the most serious crime possible, frequently well before the police have completed their gathering of evidence. The court process determines whether the charge is justified and whether it should be dismissed or diminished.

Police officers, on the other hand, are not charged until all the evidence has been gathered and analyzed. They are seldom charged with the worst offence available, and prosecutors, when deciding whether charges should be laid, give special consideration to any possible defence.

This situation in the Lawson shooting created the perception that police officers have additional rights under the law, that they are shielded from the application of the law they have sworn to uphold. The procedure followed in the wake of the Lawson shooting created a crisis of confidence in the police for a significant proportion of Toronto's population.

The distribution of buttons by the local police association supporting the two police officers charged, as well as the work-to-rule to protest the new charges, indicates a police position suggesting that police officers should not be charged in such circumstances. It argues that the reputation, liberty, livelihood, and position of police officers should not be jeopardized by prosecuting them.

The investigation into the fatal shooting of Lawson was further prolonged after an experienced Crown attorney was asked to review the case. A month after the shooting, charges were laid against the two police officers. On December 21, 1989, over a year after the shooting, both officers were charged with manslaughter. Preliminary hearings were set 18 months after the shooting, and the case is still before the courts. Community respect for the criminal justice system further suffers as a result of these delays.

The community demand that murder charges be laid against the two police officers was not satisfied. The changes in the charges laid against the accused police officers indicate the inadequacy of the criminal justice system to charge police officers promptly and appropriately. The laying of lesser charges against the officers also meant that the issues of racism and the officers' motives could not be pursued in court. This indicates a denial by the criminal justice system of any potential of racial motivation.

The second major demand from the community was that the investigation of the shooting be undertaken by an independent civilian inquiry. The community did not consider the process of "police investigating police" as the basis for an impartial and objective review. The practice of a police force investigating itself, or of another force determining whether criminal charges should be laid, has been strongly criticized for not being independent or legitimate.

In response to this criticism, the Ontario Ministry of the Solicitor General created the Special Investigations Unit to investigate "the circumstances of serious injuries and deaths that may have resulted from criminal offences committed by police officers." In the latter part of 1992, the unit was transferred from the Ministry of the Solicitor General to the Ministry of the Attorney General as an arm's-length agency. It is, however, still receiving criticism for being underresourced and for relying on ex–police officers as investigators.

The establishment of an independent civilian board of inquiry was not undertaken, nor is such a board mentioned in the new Police Services Act in Ontario. The unwillingness to implement this concept continues to be seen by a broad section of the community as a major barrier to improved police race-relations.

Another strategy used to justify police behaviour in the shootings of Black people is to blame the victims for being in situations they should not have been in, such as an automobile theft. They may, in addition, be portrayed as big, crazy, and dangerous, or as requiring more aggressive treatment because they commit more crimes.

RESPONSES

The disproportionately high number of Blacks who have been the victims of police shootings in major urban centres such as Toronto and Montreal over the past decade have provided the major impetus for changes in the policing system. It is a truism that many of these shootings could have been avoided if the police had been better prepared to deal with the realities of serving a multiracial population. Racial minority hostility toward the police continues not only because of the shootings themselves, but even more because of the apparent lack of any clear strategy or response by the police and the criminal justice system as a whole to deal appropriately with such shootings. In too many instances the criminal justice system has reacted slowly and inappropriately, and in some cases has initiated actions that further exacerbate police–community tensions.

RACE RELATIONS POLICIES

Notwithstanding their sometimes inappropriate responses to crisis situations, police forces across Canada have implemented many of the recommendations contained in the numerous studies and reports produced over the past two decades that have addressed the issue of police–race relations. The major areas in which efforts have been made include policy, the training of police officers, the improvement of ethno-racial representation in police forces, community relations, the complaints process, and the use of force.

Policy statements are important in providing a foundation for policy and program development and as a reference point for service delivery. They also provide a clear public message of a corporate commitment to improving racial equity.

The Metropolitan Toronto Police Services Board's Race Relations Policy emerged from Standing Order No. 24, "Declaration of Concern and Intent," which was first developed in 1979 and whose key statement is that "every member of the Force must avoid any expression or display of prejudice, bigotry, discrimination, and sexual or racial harassment," and that any violation of this order will result in disciplinary action.

In 1990, the Standing Order was reaffirmed, together with a broader race relations policy that addressed community relations, employment equity, staff development and training, media relations, and public complaints. Published in booklet form, it has been widely distributed.

In Ontario, a race relations policy for police services was adopted in 1993. This was in direct response to the recommendation of the Lewis Task Force on Race Relations and Policing for a policy to assist police services in Ontario with race relations initiatives and to enhance community policing. Lewis also recommended that the policy be credible to all partner groups, clearly oppose racism and discrimination in the practice of policing, and promote a service orientation to policing (Lewis, 1992).

The Ontario Race Relations Policy for Police Services contains an introduction, a statement of principles, a statement of policy, specific objectives, and a glossary. The first statement of the policy defines the essence of the document: "The right of all Ontarians to equal rights and opportunities is enshrined in federal and provincial law." It goes on to articulate key principles of racial equality and fairness, community service and community policing, and accountability. More particularly, the policy commits Ontario's police services to:

- provide the fullest possible services in a fair and equitable manner to all segments of the public, without discrimination on the basis of race, ancestry, place of origin, colour, or ethnic origin;
- extend fair and equal treatment under the law to every community and individual in its jurisdiction, without discrimination on the basis of race, ancestry, place of origin, colour, or ethnic origin;
- maintain a respectful and co-operative relationship with all communities that recognizes their racial, cultural, and linguistic diversity, thereby fostering the kind of community support that is essential to effective, secure policing; and,
- maintain a discrimination-free workplace for all personnel, to ensure that the organization is bias-free and that it reflects the racial diversity of the community.

In fulfilling these commitments, the policy further commits Ontario's police service to implement the following objectives:

- Personnel at all levels, uniformed and civilian, must clearly understand that racially discriminatory behaviour, such as racial harassment, racial name-calling, racist graffiti, racial jokes, or racially biased hiring, is not tolerated and is considered grounds for disciplinary measures consistent with the Police Services Act.
- Police procedures and practices in every area of operations and administration—such as response to calls, investigation and arrest, crowd control, recruiting, hiring and promotion—must be free of discriminatory elements.
- The workforce at all levels, whether uniformed or civilian, should reflect the racial diversity of the community.
- Personnel at all levels, both uniformed and civilian, must:
  – understand racism in all its forms—overt, covert, systemic—and have the skills to ensure that it is not manifested in their behaviour or any systems they manage;
  – understand, be sensitive to, and work positively with racial and cultural differences among people in the community and within the police service itself; and,
  – understand the principles of community policing and have the skills to implement them in their areas of responsibility.
- Mechanisms must be in place to promote and facilitate active, meaningful participation by the community, including racial minorities and Aboriginal peoples, in the planning of police services and the implementation and monitoring of this policy.
- Mechanisms for addressing racial complaints within the workplace or by members of the public against police personnel should be in place, known and accessible to citizens and police service personnel.

- All segments of the community and all police service personnel must be informed about this policy and its implementation.

In commenting on the police officers' familiarity with the race relations policy of the Metropolitan Toronto Police Force, Andrews (1992) found "a surprising variation in the level of familiarity.... Many police constables at the Divisional level were not familiar with the contents or intent of the total Policy.... There are no operating standards specified for the Policy so that compliance depended more on common sense situational application than it did upon statements of procedures."

Andrews also noted with surprise that among community groups there was not as much familiarity with the policy as one might expect. He suggested that while it may be important to have statements of policy or intent, it is the impact of these statements on police behaviour that is more important to the community.

This cautionary attitude toward the value of policy statements is perhaps reinforced by the conclusion of the 1992 report of the Ontario Task Force on Race Relations and Policing, which noted that "race relations and policing matters may still not be seen by some senior civil servants, some police services board members, and some senior police officers as real, significant, or worth the commitment of long-term planning and resources." Clearly, a structure and culture that is unable to accept racial diversity will not create policies to deal with it (Hunt and Cohen, 1971).

TRAINING

Training has been viewed as the primary remedy for improved police–race relations in Canada. Notwithstanding the massive human and financial resources being expended on such training programs, they still have not received the kind of rigorous scrutiny that is demanded. As Nadine Peppard has said, "the field of race relations training remains largely unexplored and . . . little thought has been given to what the objectives of such training should be" (Peppard, 1983). These comments are perhaps even truer today than when they were first made in 1983. While there is increasing pressure for much more police–race relations training, there is still no clear answer to the question as to what, if any, effect race relations training has on police officers.

Is it realistic to hope for any meaningful improvements in police–race relations as a result of training? Too many programs have been poorly coordinated, superficial in content, and seem to have little impact. There are many reasons for this. First, there is no clear agreement as to what the goals are, except at the most general levels. Second, training has been provided in an organizational environment that has not always been particularly supportive. With few exceptions, there have not been the kinds of tangible organizational support systems and resources to put race relations and equal opportunity policies into meaningful practices that can reinforce training. Third, there is confusion as to whether attitudes, knowledge, or skills should be taught. Most of the training efforts seem to be dictated by some abstract

notion of the general desirability of providing enlightenment on racial matters, not by the actual work-related requirements of policing.

There appear to be few examples of incorporating into race relations
training the work-related skills to implement, for example, employment equity in training. Race relations training must be seen as part of a process that
will continue long after the training itself finishes. It also needs to be contex-
tualized into the operational requirements of policing and to be planned as a
series of incremental advances, each built upon previous achievement.
Finally, the relationship between training and performance needs to be firmly established, so that clear, measurable objectives for the training can be set.

REPRESENTATION OF MINORITIES

What has been done to ensure that the recruitment and promotional
processes of Canadian police forces will make them more representative of
the multiracial population they serve?

By the late 1970s, police officials had come to recognize that many of
their recruitment criteria and practices were inherently discriminatory. A
number of efforts were made to change these criteria and practices, and special programs were initiated to attract racial minorities to police work. These
efforts have been intensified to the point where the Employment Equity
Plans Regulation of the Ontario Police Services Act (1990) is regarded by
many as the most far-reaching employment equity initiative in any institutional sector in Canada. The objective of the regulation is for every police
force to have the same percentage of the prescribed groups in its workforce
as exists in the community it serves. Police forces are required to establish
composition goals, hiring goals, and position goals.

However, the regulation does not prescribe timelines for the achievement
of these goals. As the report of the Lewis (1992) report notes with concern,
the formula-driven nature of the regulation, combined with the current
absence of hiring opportunities, "will make painfully slow the process of
ensuring police services have a racial-minority representation which approx-
imates the community."

Notwithstanding the considerable resources that the Metropolitan
Toronto Police Force has devoted to minority recruitment for a number of
years, Andrews (1992) found that the representation of people of colour on
the force was about one third the level of their representation in the population as a whole. In addition, minority representation is heavily concentrated
in the entry levels of the force.

Both Andrews and Lewis conclude that even the most advanced employment equity efforts will not significantly improve the racial diversity of
police forces. Long debated and resisted in police circles is the consideration
of such additional options as lateral entry, direct entry, and the application
of innovative career-path plans such as the permanent specialization of uniformed officers, particularly at higher levels. As Andrews (1992) notes,

> other highly structured institutions, such as the military, have dealt
> with the need for and use of different skill sets in a very different way

than police forces. That fact alone makes it very difficult to accept the rationale that there are no alternatives to the present structure.

USE OF FIREARMS

In response to the concern that police officers do not always use only as much force as is necessary to bring a situation under control, recent efforts have been made to provide much clearer guidelines about the use of force, alternatives to lethal force, the filing of a report whenever guns are drawn or used, and the need to amend the "fleeing felon" provision of the Criminal Code.

In 1992, for example, Ontario introduced a new regulation that states that "a member of a police force shall not draw a handgun and discharge a firearm, unless he or she believes, on reasonable grounds, that to do so is necessary to protect against the loss of life or serious bodily harm."

However, part of the present confusion is that police officers are also governed by the Criminal Code, which allows a police officer to draw and discharge a firearm to apprehend a suspect who attempts to escape, unless escape can be prevented by less violent means. Many have urged changes to this section of the Code, which allows the use of lethal force against a fleeing felon who does not present a risk to life. In the Spring of 1994, the government of Canada indicated its commitment to change these provisions of the Criminal Code.

COMMUNITY RELATIONS

The primary thrust of present responses to improve relations between police and minority races is the elimination of racism in existing police services. However, not only are efforts being made to ensure an impartial police service, but mechanisms are being put in place that will attempt to ensure that policing services are more responsive and sensitive to all sectors of the population.

A number of forces across Canada have implemented a variety of programs oriented toward improving relationships with the communities they serve.

Despite the tremendous amount of activity in police forces across Canada to implement various programs to "improve police–community/race relations," the results are somewhat dismaying. Most of the programs have been designed primarily to improve the police image in the community. Many have been dependent on external sources of funding, and very few have been adequately evaluated as to their actual impact on police–minority relations.

Police–community relations has largely been characterized by public criticism of the police, on the one hand, and police efforts to counter that criticism, on the other. As community frustration intensifies, the police have generally responded by making minor adjustments to meet the immediate crisis and have avoided comprehensive plans for change in response to community needs and demands.

In addition, police–community relations programs have traditionally been developed by the police to resolve police–community conflict by changing the community instead of the police. Programs have been designed to change community attitudes, opinions, and perceptions through the provision of information, through "opportunities for positive police–community contact," and through the projection of the appearance of substantive change by the revision of superficial aspects of police operations, deployment modes, or supplemental services, without any change in basic police practices and enforcement policy.

Given the basic intents of most police–community relations programs, the programs have not generally led to direct and meaningful involvement of citizens in police policy-making. Other factors that contribute to this lack of effective public participation are the lack of resources among community groups, the lack of support from police leadership and the rank-and-file for this kind of involvement, and the lack of understanding among police personnel about the benefits of such programs.

SUMMARY

This chapter has explored racism and policing by looking at the attitudes and behaviours of the police as individuals, as well as the ideologies, structures, and practices of law enforcement organizations. Case studies of the shootings of Blacks provide a graphic illustration of the impact and consequences of police racism. The conflictual relationship between police and racial minorities—particularly Aboriginal peoples and Blacks—is also demonstrated by the evidence of several task forces established to examine racism among the police. This chapter has analyzed the many manifestations of racial bias and discrimination and showed how deeply entrenched racism is within all areas of law enforcement. Some of the critical areas discussed include the overpolicing of minority communities, the racialization of crime and the criminalizaiton of racial minorities, the lack of police accountability, the emphasis on law and order rather than provision of service, the use of excessive force, and the professional competence of the police. The last section of the chapter summarized some of the institutional responses by the police, including training, employment equity, and independent complaints systems.

REFERENCES

Andrews A. (1992). *Review of Race Relations Practices of the Metropolitan Toronto Police Force.* Toronto: Municipality of Metropolitan Toronto.

Bellamare, J. (1988). *Investigation into Relations Between the Police Forces, Visible and Other Ethnic Minorities.* Montreal: Commission des Droits de la Personne du Québec.

Cashmore, E., and E. McLaughlin (eds.)., (1991). *Out of Order: Policing Black People.* London and New York: Routledge.

Gilroy, P. (1987). *There Ain't no Black in the Union Jack.* Chicago: University of Chicago Press.

Hodgson, J. (1993). *Police Community Relations: Analysis of the Organizational and Structural Barriers Inhibiting Effective Police–Community Exchanges.* Ph.D. Dissertation, Department of Sociology. North York, ON: York University.

Hunt, I.C., and B. Cohen (1971). *Minority Recruiting in the New York City Police Department.* New York: Rand.

Institute of Race Relations. (1987). *Policing Against Black People.* London.

Jain, H. (1986). *Recruitment and Selection of Visible Minorities in Canadian Police Forces: A Survey of Selected Police Agencies.* Research and Working Paper Series. Hamilton, ON: McMaster University, Faculty of Business.

Jayewardene, C.H.S., and C.J. Talbot. (1990). *Police Recruitment of Ethnic Minorities.* Ottawa: Canadian Police College.

Law Reform Commission of Canada. (1991). *Report on Aboriginal Peoples and Criminal Justice.* Ottawa.

Lewis, C. (1989). *Report of the Task Force on Race Relations and Policing.* Toronto: Government of Ontario.

Lewis, S. (1992). *Report to the Premier on Race Relations.* Toronto.

Metropolitan Police Association, In a Brief to the Solicitor General of Ontario, Nov. 11, 1992.

Mukwe Ode First Nations Consulting. (1992). *As We Were Told.* Toronto: Metropolitan Toronto Police Services Board.

National Urban League. (1980). *Staying Power: Keeping Minority Police Officers in the Force.* New York.

Peppard, N. (1983). *Currents: Readings in Race Relations* (Toronto) 1(3):6–11.

Province of Alberta. (1991). *Report of the Task Force on the Criminal Justice System and its Impact on the Indian and Métis People of Alberta.* Main Report, vol. 1. Edmonton.

Province of Manitoba. (1991). Manitoba Attorney General Submission to the Aboriginal Enquiry. Winnipeg.

Province of Nova Scotia. (1989). *Report of the Royal Commission on the Donald Marshall Jr. Prosecution: Findings and Recommendations*, vol. 1. Halifax.

Reiman, J. (1984). *The Rich Get Richer and the Poor Get Prison.* New York: Macmillan.

Ungerlieider, C. (1992a). "Intercultural Awareness and Sensitivity of Canadian Police Officers." *Canadian Public Administration* 32(4)(Winter):612–622.

_____. (1992b). "Issues in Police Intercultural and Race Relations Training in Canada." Ottawa: Solicitor General of Canada.

Chapter 5

▼▼▼▼▼▼▼▼▼▼▼

Racism and the Justice System

A Black youth faces a White-dominated system with White police, White lawyers and White Judge, and a White Crown attorney. (A Black youth at the Jamaican Canadian Association Conference, 1990)

This chapter examines the justice system[1] from the perspective of differential treatment and racism. The evidence from studies and the various official inquiries into the justice system will be discussed. Specific issues of concern include differential treatment in the courts, such as in the granting of bail and sentencing disparities, and the attitudes of justice system officials. The lack of minority representation in the justice system will also be highlighted. The chapter concludes with a case study of two views of racism in the justice system.

INTRODUCTION

In addressing the topic of racism in the justice system and particularly in the courts, Pomerant outlined a persistent problem with respect to the identification and validation of racism:

> Minority persons and groups often allege that discrimination is regularly encountered by them in their contacts with the Canadian criminal process. Unfortunately, its incidence is difficult to objectively verify. . . . A court can readily justify matters such as credibility findings, detention orders and harsh sentences by articulation of "legitimate factors." (Pomerant, 1992:6)

Racial discrimination in Canada's justice system has not been extensively or systematically studied. Objective research evidence of differential treatment in the courts is confined to a very small number of studies. Part of the problem stems from the fact that the study of racial discrimination in the justice system in Canada is beset by a wide range of methodological constraints. The most problematic is the absence of systematic and comprehensive forms of data collection and analysis. Only recently has there been any attempt to identify and document the effects of bias and discrimination in the institutional structures of Canadian society and in the justice system in particular.

ABORIGINAL PEOPLES
AND THE JUSTICE SYSTEM

Research accompanying the several commissions of inquiry on Aboriginal peoples and the justice system has thus far provided the best source of information on inequity in this institution.

For example, in 1991, the Manitoba Justice Inquiry found that 22 percent of Aboriginal persons appearing in the provincial court faced four or more charges, compared with 13 percent of non-Aboriginal persons. The data showed that Aboriginal persons who were charged with the same offence faced 2.72 charges per person, compared with 2.19 for non-Aboriginal persons—almost 25 percent more charges per Aboriginal person.[2]

With respect to bail, the inquiry found that charged Aboriginal persons were 1.34 times more likely to be held in pre-detention, adult male (18–34) Aboriginal persons spent approximately 1.5 times longer in pre-trial detention, and Aboriginal women from the same age group were 2.4 times likely to be held in pre-trial detention. Aboriginal youths in pre-trial detention were detained an average of 29.3 days, compared with 10.8 days for non-Aboriginal youths.

It was also found that while 61 percent of Aboriginal respondents to a survey said they saw their lawyer three or fewer times, 63 percent of non-Aboriginal respondents saw their lawyers four or more times. Forty-eight percent of Aboriginal respondents spent less than an hour in total with their lawyers, compared with 46 percent of non-Aboriginal inmates who saw their lawyers for three or more hours. Guilty pleas among Aboriginal persons were 10 percent greater than for non-Aboriginals. Twenty-five percent of Aboriginal persons received a sentence that involved some form of incarceration. The inquiry found that 79 percent of Aboriginal offenders received full sentences compared with 69 percent of non-Aboriginal offenders. Forty-two percent of Aboriginal accused received the minimum sentence, compared with 58 percent of non-Aboriginal persons (Sinclair, 1992).

The Saskatchewan Indian Justice Review Committee and the Saskatchewan Métis Justice Review Committee found that status Indian, Inuit, non-status Indian, and Métis admissions accounted for 68 percent of all admissions to provincial correctional centres in 1990–91. As well, Aboriginal persons were the majority of those incarcerated for other Criminal Code and provincial or municipal offences (Linn, 1992).

RACIAL MINORITIES
AND THE JUSTICE SYSTEM

Given the findings of these commissions and reports, racism appears to be widespread in the administration of justice. Moreover, racism in the Canadian justice system is not restricted to the inequitable treatment of Aboriginal peoples but also applies to racial minorities. While there is little objective research in this area, the issue has been examined from the perspective of the minority perceptions of the justice system. If the perceptions even moderately reflect the nature extent of the problem, it can be concluded that racism is a major problem in the justice system.

In acknowledging the existence of racism in the justice system, the Minister of State for Multiculturalism and Citizenship noted:

> Can we really be surprised that prosecutors and judges and Crown attorneys should discount eyewitness testimony and disbelieve evidence given under oath? Or that law enforcement officers should approach Native Canadians from the point of view of scepticism and conclude their investigation at the first convenient moment, whether or not all the ends are tied up neatly?...But injustice before the court does exist and, perhaps no less important, confidence in the justice system to eliminate that injustice does not. (Wiener, 1990)

Several task forces, such as those in Nova Scotia, Alberta, and Manitoba, have produced substantive documentation and evidence that racism exists in the justice system. The Donald Marshall, Jr., Commission, for example, concluded that being Native was a factor in Marshall's wrongful conviction and imprisonment (Royal Commission, 1989). The commission also found that "the court's decision amounted to defence of the criminal justice system at the expense of Donald Marshall in spite of the overwhelming evidence that the system itself had failed" (Royal Commission, 1989:7).

With respect to racial minorities in other parts of Canada, Lewis (1992) described the relationship between the justice system and minorities as "two solitudes in life."[3] Lewis went on to recommend that a comprehensive review be conducted of Ontario's criminal justice process with a broad mandate inclusive of the judiciary. The expression of racism in Quebec's system of justice mirrors that in other parts of the country. This "unwritten law" takes away the rights that have been democratically granted to all people, including racial minorities, and:

> By some unspoken societal consensus, a generalized negativity towards Blackness persistently links Black skin to criminality. All too frequently Black skin colour becomes the initiating catalytic factor which jettisons Black people into the criminal justice system. It is also Black pigmentation that colours and preconditions and plots the quality of our trajectory through a system seemingly inimical to our interests. (Thornhill, 1988:68)

The problem of racism in the justice system was also acknowledged by the Law Reform Commission of Canada (1992), when it noted that "racism in the justice system is a consistently expressed and central concern to Canada's minorities." It is exemplified in the lack of jobs and positions of power and influence in the justice institutions. It is also evident in the lack of access to police protection and legal aid, police harassment, and differential treatment in sentencing. The commission went on to acknowledge that "the racism of which these groups speak mirrors attitudes and behaviour found in Canadian society as a whole" (Law Reform Commission of Canada, 1992:10).

While the report *Equality Now* (1984) did not focus on the manifestations of racism in the justice system, it did provide some information on the weaknesses in Canadian law in dealing with and awarding remedies for hate-motivated crimes. In this respect, the report provided additional information on how the justice system inadvertently upholds racist action through a weak legislative framework.

The differential treatment of minorities in Canada's criminal justice system has been documented by few objective studies. It is evident largely through the perceptions of victims of discrimination in the justice system. The findings of the studies indicate that minorities are treated differently at every stage of the process of dispensing justice. Differential treatment is found with the police, in the courts, and in the correctional system. Growing evidence confirms the claim that differential assessments of racial minorities leading to differential decisions start at the point of entry into the system and continue up to the point of exit from it.

THE MANIFESTATIONS OF RACISM

It has been be argued that the law that is the foundation of the practices and policies exercised by the courts is itself racist, in that principles germane to its interpretation were developed during an era in which peoples of colour and other disadvantaged groups were barred from participating in society and the justice system.

Many people understand law as being neutral. The fallacy of this approach becomes obvious when it is understood that laws maintained slavery and made it illegal for Blacks to learn to read and write and participate in public life. Laws also were used to restrict the entry of racial minorities into Canada, and law was used to intern Japanese Canadians. Laws were also used to rob Aboriginal peoples of their land, history, and culture. Law cannot therefore be understood as a neutral construct. Both the common law and codified law are inherently political.

Law has ignored or omitted racism in its deliberations. But it is not as innocent of the charge of racism as it would claim. Kobayashi (1990:449) argues that the culpability of the law can be examined in many ways:

> the law has been used through direct action, interpretation, silence and complicity. The law has been wielded as an instrument to create a common sense justification of racial differences, to reinforce common sense notions already deeply embedded within a cultural system of values.

Recent work in critical legal theory posits the need to establish a connection between law and culture "situating legal theory within social, political, and economic conditions, and interpreting juridical procedures according to dominant ideologies" (Kobayashi, 1990:449). Such contexts were not evident in traditional legal discourse because law, like other disciplines, did not "address the meaning of law outside [its] own terms." The study of law in abstraction from the social relations and the social system that it purports

---

MANIFESTATIONS OF RACISM IN THE JUSTICE SYSTEM

Racially biased attitudes and
   practices of judges, jurors, lawyers,
   and other court officials
Jury selection procedures
Sentencing disparities

Lack of representation
Neutrality of law
Perceptions of guilt of
   minority accused
Discretion by crown attorneys

---

to regulate will always be idealistic, artificial, and inherently biased. The legal system produces and reproduces the essential character of law as a means of rationalizing, normalizing, and legitimizing social control on behalf of those who hold power and the interests they represent.

INITIAL CONTACT: THE POLICE[4]

For most individuals, the police are the first point of contact with the justice system. This first contact often influences a case's future developments and the decisions with respect to it.

Racial minorities often complain of overpolicing. Squad cars often cruise through communities that are densely populated by racial minorities. Despite this oversurveillance, racial-minority persons complain that they do not receive equal protection under the law. For example, a frequent complaint is that the response time of police is greater in racial-minority communities than it is for the general population (Jamaican Canadian Association, 1990).

At the Jamaican Canadian Association's 1990 Toronto conference, the concerns of Black youth were specifically examined. The youth stated unequivocally that they felt alienated from the systems that administer justice in Ontario. Conference participants stated publicly that they bore the brunt of police arbitrary stops, searches, charges of resisting arrest, and use of force. Black youth talked extensively about negative stereotyping of members of the community. For example, they said that when a group of them congregated in a public place, they were more likely to gain the attention of police officers than were a group of White youths. They explained that this occurs because of a prevailing stereotype that Black youths are believed to be criminals. When Black youths get together, police are thought to assume that they are plotting a crime.

As a result, the relationship between police and racial-minority communities is extremely tense, especially in urban areas. In Toronto and Montreal especially, several highly publicized shootings of Black youth have added to the tension.

REPRESENTATION

The lack of representation of racial minorities in the justice system contributes to the perpetuation of racial stereotypes in the system (Bickenbach, 1989). It leads racial minorities accused of committing a crime to perceive that justice will not be done when the system itself does not understand them. The fact that the police officer, courthouse personnel, and the judge are all White creates the perception that justice will not be done. Hutchinson (1992) notes that although attempts are being made to address the gender imbalance in the judiciary,

> the general commitment to diversify the legal profession and judiciary is woefully lacking. It is hardly surprising that almost all judges are White, when fewer than 3 percent of lawyers are members of a visible minority and fewer than 1 percent are Native Canadian.

ATTITUDES AND PERCEPTIONS OF JUDGES AND LAWYERS

Many of the respondents interviewed in a study conducted as part of the Marshall inquiry (Head, 1991) voiced significant fears about racial discrimination in the courts. They expressed concern about the attitudes of persons in the system. Several respondents felt that judges pose the problem.

There was criticism that Blacks are usually tried by White judges and White juries. A White legal aid lawyer expressed his concerns:

> There is an unmistakable change in the atmosphere when I enter the courtroom with a Black client. The hostility of court personnel, including judges and others, is unmistakable and is recognized by all including the alleged lawbreaker. It is impossible, under these conditions, for a Black client to receive equal justice. (Head, 1991)

The study, based on a sample of more than 500 individuals, also found that Blacks showed a high level of distrust and hostility towards the criminal justice system. They expressed the view that Blacks were treated more harshly than Whites in "some instances."

In a project undertaken in Toronto, racial minorities' perceptions of the justice system were studied(Equal Opportunity Consultants, 1989). The findings were similar to those of the study conducted as part of the Marshall inquiry. The Toronto study found, for example, that racial minorities criticized the criminal justice system for being unrepresentative of the increasingly diverse population of Ontario. It was repeatedly stressed that the overwhelming majority of judges, crown attorneys, and other legal professionals were White, male, and mainstream Canadians.

Judges were especially criticized for stereotypical attitudes, behaviours, and views of racial minorities. In particular, members of the Black community consistently said that most judges believe that Black people are more prone to criminal behaviour because they see so many of them in their courtrooms.

Minority lawyers interviewed as part of the same project said that some judges make racist comments from the bench. In one case, a lawyer requested a conditional discharge for a youth of 19 whose case had all the elements for a compassionate hearing. The presiding judge said: "I am not accepting that. People like him need to be sent to prison." In another case, a judge, while sentencing a tall, heavily built Black man convicted of trafficking a small amount of cocaine, stated: "I am afraid of you. I'm going to give you a year in prison."

In addition, minority respondents felt that some judges do not believe that racial-minority accused are "innocent until proven guilty." Some racial minorities believe that they must prove their innocence to the court, not the reverse. Moreover, there are many instances in which defence counsel recommend bail at a preliminary hearing, but the judge refuses to grant it for racial-minority offenders. A standard rationalization for the refusal to grant bail is that most racial minorities "can't raise the money." This raises some questions about what is "reasonable bail." For example, a minority lawyer has argued that although the bail may be granted, it appears to be disproportionately high for members of racial-minority groups (Westmoreland Traore, 1982:23).

In Manitoba, a series of complaints against a particularly contentious member of the judiciary has taken place over a period of 20 years. The judge made disparaging remarks about women and Aboriginal peoples. In one instance, he said that it would be a "joyful result if residents of the Long Plains Indian Reserve killed each other off." Although the judge was suspended when the transcript of these remarks was made public, a formal judicial hearing into his conduct has not taken place because such a hearing would stir up "too much publicity; plus it would make the entire profession and system look bad." This excuse was offered by a former chief provincial judge of the province to the Manitoba Judicial Council (*The Globe and Mail*, 1993).

Justices of the peace have also been criticized for their role in perpetuating racism in the justice system. Respondents in the Toronto study described the racist attitudes of many justices of the peace appointed by the system. The issue of bail and the assessment of financial credibility of sponsors was specifically cited. Other examples included the laying of charges. In one case, a justice of the peace refused to lay charges which had been brought by racial-minority persons. In one such case a young, Black, male lawyer was assaulted by a police officer in a legal clinic. He went to a justice of the peace to lay a charge against the police officer without revealing the fact that he was a lawyer. The justice of the peace refused to lay the charge and asked: "Were any of your bones broken?" Eventually, the lawyer was assured that the officer would be charged. He returned to the justice of the peace some days later and found, to his surprise, that the charge had not been laid. When the young man revealed that he was a lawyer by showing his law society membership card, the charge was laid instantly.

Racist attitudes are said to be found among other court personnel such as Crown and defence counsel as well as duty counsel. A frequent complaint is that both the Crown and the defence counsel often have not adequately prepared their cases involving racial minorities. Sometimes, inexperienced Crown counsel are assigned to prosecute high-profile cases involving minorities. Moreover, many Crown and defence counsel are thought to harbour racially biased attitudes.[5] These attitudes are expressed in many ways, including counsel's submissions to the court. A frequent complaint is that counsel often advise racial minorities to plead guilty either because "no one will believe your story" or to expedite a case. Many racial minorities are not aware that a guilty plea guarantees a conviction. They therefore agree with their defence counsel's advice and find themselves with a criminal record for a crime they did not commit.

The consistent omission of information about the racial overtones of a case applies also to Crown attorneys, who have a considerable amount of discretion.[6] Although Crown attorneys do not initiate prosecutions, they play a crucial role in advising the police with respect to whether a *prima facie* case can be made from the accumulated evidence and whether prosecution is justified. They also have the power to withhold evidence until the trial and, as well, to proceed summarily or by indictment. Abusing their power by not recognizing or accepting the racial overtones of a case often leads to situations in which victims of racially motivated crimes find themselves the accused party in the criminal justice system (Westmoreland Traore,1982:18).

Although much criticism is directed toward Crown attorneys and judges, one area in which defence counsel have been sharply criticized is their refusal to believe in the existence of racially motivated attacks. As in any criminal case, defence counsel face the challenge of advising their clients to the best of their ability. However, this task is made more difficult by the nature of the defence and the prevalent scepticism about the existence of racially motivated attacks. In these cases, victims are often dissuaded by their own defence counsel from raising questions of racism by being told that to do so would only make matters worse for them. For the same reason, counter-charges are very infrequent (Westmoreland Traore, 1982:27).

Victims of racially motivated incidents are therefore doubly jeopardized because of the systematic omission or suppression of vital information from the record of the court. Thus, the court is rarely forced to rule on the matter of racial motivation either as part of *mens rea*[7] or as a factor in sentencing. The victim therefore has little opportunity to obtain satisfaction from the court for racially motivated attacks.

CASE STUDY 5.1

THREE VIEWS OF RACISM FROM THE JUSTICE SYSTEM

Frances Henry has had a number of personal experiences in the courts, since she frequently appears as an expert witness on matters relating to challenging the jury on the cause of racial discrimination or with respect to Caribbean immigrants in Toronto. She has encountered several examples of bias among justice officials. Three cases will be described here.

In the first case, elements of racial bias were noted in the attitudes and behaviour of a Crown attorney in one case and a federal judge in another. These examples of bias are, however, somewhat mitigated by a very positive example in which a provincial judge was convinced of the need to challenge a jury on the cause of racial discrimination because the expert-witness testimony readily convinced him that action to combat racism in the system was required.

THE CROWN ATTORNEY

In a case involving a charge of attempted murder against a Black youth from Jamaica, a Crown attorney badgered and harassed 16-year-old defence witnesses, most of whom were of Jamaican origin, and reduced some of them to tears. More importantly, this Crown made some offensive and biased comments that bordered on racism. For example, she referred to the Jamaican Black youth as being "lackadaisical" with respect to their habits, especially with regard to keeping time.

Henry protested the use of this term, whereupon the Crown rolled her eyes and said, "Well, whatever." When a defence witness noted some differences in the cultural behaviour of Jamaicans as compared with Canadians, the Crown seemed to denigrate the important role of culture and instead made a comment to the effect that people have to learn "our ways" when they migrate to Canada.

THE FEDERAL JUDGE

In another case involving a contempt charge against the leader of a right-wing extremist group, Henry and another expert witness, Professor Susan Ehrlich of York University, Department of Linguistics, Language and Literature, were called to testify that the telephone hate-line messages produced by this group contained elements of racism toward racial-minority groups, gays, and other disadvantaged groups. During both the examination-in-chief and cross-examination, the judge frequently interjected with a variety of observations and questions:

- Henry's objectivity as a witness was called into question because the judge labelled her a "militant anti-racist" on the basis of her *curriculum vitae,* which includes not only many research-based books and papers on race relations but also membership in an anti-racist organization.
- In discussing the change from the designation "race relations" to "anti-racism," which Henry said occurred because it was recognized that the latter more accurately stated a position against a negative and destructive force in society, the judge countered by saying that it also suggested moving from a value-free designation to one invoking a value judgement. (Is one to assume therefore that Canadians should not take a stand against racism?)
- In saying that the messages provoked hatred and created the potential for social disruption, the judge went into a long and totally unnecessary diatribe about how he as a French Canadian did not take offense every time someone said something negative about his ethnic group. He pointed to a message about French Canadians that he said did not offend him. He continued by suggesting that perhaps groups maligned by the Heritage Front telephone messages should start their own telephone message lines.
- In questioning Ehrlich on the meaning of the term "minority group" in the context of the racial groups that the Heritage Front demeans, the judge posed a situation involving employment equity. He asked, if ten applicants were applying for a job, and four were White males, would they not constitute a minority group?

THE PROVINCIAL JUDGE

In a very different case, a provincial judge was asked to rule on the applicability of challenging the jury for cause on racial discrimination. The case involved charges against a Black person. Again, Henry, as an expert witness, was asked to testify with respect to racism against Black people in Canadian society in general and in the justice system in particular. Throughout the lengthy testimony, the judge listened attentively, took copious notes, and asked many questions. After the examinations by the defence and the Crown attorney, the judge raised a number of important and substantial issues for the witness to comment upon.

In his decision finding in favour of the need to challenge for cause, the judge stated that he had been convinced by the expert witness testimony. His judgement began with the notion that the Canadian Charter of Rights and Freedoms guarantees a fair and public hearing. He further noted that this Charter guarantee is defeated by bigoted jurors who cannot provide that context: "If one or more jurors are so in the grip of bigoted thinking that the accused's colour outweighs for decisional purposes both the law and the evidence, the trial would be unfair" (Macdonald, 1993).

The judge stated that the Charter's guarantee of independence and impartiality is also challenged by bigoted jurors. Because a jury engages in collective decision-making, "an impartial jury must of necessity be comprised of individuals who are responsive to their oaths, the evidence, and the law and not responsive to some preformed fixed viewpoint" (Macdonald, 1993).

The judge summed up by noting that a significant dimension of racial bias is present in this society such that a juror may not be indifferent and that a jury containing one or more such persons is unlikely to be fair and impartial. Challenges for cause on racial prejudice were therefore "shown to be appropriate in order to ensure that this trial complies with Charter requirements."[8]

The first two cases show that an element of individual bias is apparently present in these officers of justice. While Crown attorneys are known to badger and harass witnesses and this seems to be part of the accepted norms of the courtroom, it becomes inappropriate when the badgering includes language and labels that signify bias. In the second case, the judge appeared to be in some form of conflict between the training and philosophy of the judicial system and his own set of values. His personal values seemed to be shaken by some of the expert-witness testimony and seemed to lead him to make inappropriate comments. The third case is an example of a system working well. An open-minded judge was influenced by expert-witness testimony to use any and all legal means to inhibit contamination by potentially biased jurors. On the important issue of racism, the judge commented that

> quite apart from constitutional requirements which dictate the result in this case, it is appropriate and necessary for the court to respond to these significant concerns [of racism] so that everyone may have confidence that this court is truly everyone's court.

The exercise of discretion is the essence of the enforcement and application of laws. Due to the dominant character of executive and judicial action, which require the exercise of discretion, racism is more difficult to detect and challenge when it is related to executive or judicial action or inaction (Binavince, 1989) Yet, the consistent claims and experiences of minorities suggest that they are treated differently by the courts. This perception is held very strongly, particularly as it relates to sentencing.

SENTENCING DISPARITIES

One aspect of the justice system that has been extensively studied in the United States is differential sentencing. Members of racial-minority communities in Canada as well as in the United States have consistently alleged that disparities between Whites and Blacks with respect to sentencing exist. The U.S. evidence, however, is ambiguous. There is growing evidence to suggest that racial minorities, particularly those of Afro-Caribbean origin in the United States and the United Kingdom, are treated differently and subjected to less favourable decisions than are White people at each stage of the process of dispensing justice. Differential assessments, leading to differential decisions, start at the point of entry and continue to the point of exit from the justice system (Petersilia, 1985; *Harvard Law Review*, 1988; U.K. Race Advisory Committee, 1989).

The differential sentencing of minorities was also identified as a problem in the Toronto study referred to earlier (Equal Opportunity Consultants, 1989). With respect to sentencing, lawyers cited several instances of differential sentencing:

> A young White woman was given 30 days for shoplifting, whereas a Black woman was given 90 days for the same offence, and both were first offenders.

> In another case involving fraud, a group of Black youths each received six months, whereas in a very similar case, two months earlier, a White youth received 90 days.

> In another case five youths, three Whites and two Blacks, were charged with possession of marijuana. The three Whites were fined $40 per joint, whereas the two Blacks were sent to jail for three days. (Equal Opportunity Consultants, 1989)

People working in the courts tend to regard these as isolated incidents. While sentence disparity plagues the entire justice system and has been the subject of much study, differential sentencing is particularly important to racial minorities. Ample anecdotal evidence shows that racial minorities tend to receive harsher sentences than do others charged with similar offences. The very limited research evidence in Canada indicates that such allegations may be true, at least in those jurisdictions studied.

A study in Nova Scotia considered eight defendant variables, one of which was race. Legal information on the charge and on the defendant's prior convictions was obtained for over 1000 people who faced Criminal Code non-driving offences. The presence of counsel and the decisions made by the court were also examined. The study showed that the majority of defendants were young, single, male, and often unemployed. Race was determined by an observer in the courtroom. It was found that Black persons accounted for 15 percent of the defendants but less than 2 percent of the population of the province. Clients represented by legal aid lawyers rather than privately retained counsel were, for the most part, young, unemployed and racial minorities. Of major significance was the finding on sentencing:

Sentencing patterns were significantly associated with the defendant's race, even when restricted to first offenders convicted of summary charges. White defendants received discharges in 23 percent of the cases, while a Black first offender never received a discharge. (Renner and Warner, 1981:72)

Ten or so years later, research conducted under the auspices of the Marshall inquiry showed virtually the same results. Among a sample of 177 cases of convictions for theft, including those of 51 Blacks and 126 non-Blacks, 11.1 percent of the Whites received an absolute discharge, whereas none of the Blacks did. Moreover, 15.7 percent of the Blacks received a conditional discharge, while among Whites the percentage was 27 percent. In addition, Blacks with a lengthy criminal record were more likely to be incarcerated than non-Blacks with a similar record.

The study also showed that factors associated with discharges included having counsel, being employed, and having high levels of education. Since many young Nova Scotian Blacks do not meet these criteria, their low levels of discharges are explainable by the "role of adverse effects discrimination" (Royal Commission, 1989). Thus the traditional factors that influence sentencing cannot be applied to sectors of the population that either cannot or do not meet these criteria.

JURY SELECTION PROCESSES

Jury bias has been identified as a major contributor to the perpetuation of racism in the justice system (Pomerant, 1992; Petersen, 1993). Jury selection is critical to the process of providing justice; in the Toronto study, many Black respondents singled out this issue as extremely important. Having a Black accused tried by a White jury does not, according to the perceptions of racial-minority people, fulfil the criterion of "trial by a jury of peers." The issue of the extent to which a jury is representative of the community raises questions about the appropriateness of the current practice of using voters' lists to select juries. Many minorities are not eligible to vote, so they are underrepresented on voters' lists. The use of these lists to compose a pool has also been called into question because they quickly become inaccurate. They fail to include persons who move into or exclude those who move out of the community after each election. They are also not updated until a new election is called.

Pomerant and others have argued that for equality in jury trials to have meaning, jury selection should provide reasonable and equal opportunities and means for the parties to challenge the selection pool. It is also necessary to challenge the selection of jury panels and exclude from service unqualified, incompetent, or morally biased prospective jurors. In addition, it is argued that minority jurors should have the same opportunities as anyone else to be chosen for service. Their minority status should not prevent them from being chosen.

The use of the peremptory challenge by either the Crown or the defence counsel can further limit the diversity of a jury. In one case, a jury was being selected for the trial of a police officer accused of shooting a Black person. A Black woman, after answering questions with respect to her impartiality, was declared impartial and accepted by the prosecutor. The defence counsel for the police officer promptly rejected her as a juror. The final jury included six men and six women, one of whom was Asian. The racial designation of the jurors became an issue in this case. A pre-trial motion put forward by the Crown argued that the Canadian Charter of Rights and Freedoms, which bans racial discrimination, should apply to jury selection so that lawyers could not reject potential jurors because of their race. The defence argued against the motion, and it was rejected by the judge, who noted that this would open up the selection procedure to too many factors. He noted that a jury should reflect the racial composition of a community but urged lawyers to "be guided by their own conscience" (*The Toronto Star*, 1993(b)).

In this instance, a peremptory challenge was used in the selection process to keep a racial-minority off the jury because the accused was a police officer. The challenge is most frequently used, however, to determine whether jurors hold prejudices or opinions that would bias their objectivity. The factor of race is not usually questioned in the *voir dire*.[9] A number of defence lawyers have attempted to persuade judges that in the case of a Black accused, the *voir dire* should include a challenge on the cause of racial prejudice. If the judge accepts the challenge, a lawyer may ask questions to elicit racial prejudice. Frances Henry has often been called to testify as an expert witness on racism to help lawyers argue for this process. The judge has accepted the challenge in only two cases out of six. In a few instances, judges have accepted the challenge without expert witness testimony. In 1993, the Ontario Court of Appeal, hearing an appeal of Regina versus Parks (appealed because the challenge for cause on racism was not allowed), found that the challenge of racism was legitimate because of the prevalence of racism in the system. The importance of the issue was demonstrated recently in a trial in Hamilton, Ontario, in which challenge to the jury for cause on racism was applied. Almost one quarter of the prospective jurors questioned admitted to some form of bias because the accused was Black (Law Times, 1994).

The issue of jury selection and bias is important because the jury verdict all but binds a trial jury, at least in terms of establishing guilt or innocence. The recent Rodney King case in the United States showed that an impartial jury is a critical factor in ensuring the community's confidence in the justice system. Ensuring that the jury itself does not detract from a fair trial is an important part of the preservation of democracy.

RESPONSES TO RACISM

LACK OF POLITICAL WILL

How has the justice system responded to allegations of inequity and racial bias? One of its agencies—The Law Reform Commission of Canada—in a recent (1992) publication noted that politicians have, for the last 20 years, refused to deal with racism in the criminal justice system due to a lack of political will. Former Supreme Court Judge Bertha Wilson, after calling attention to the issue of gender bias, went on to head an investigation on this aspect of inequity in the system. It is hoped that the recognition of gender bias signals an equal concern with racial bias. Judge B. MacLachlan recently spoke out against racism and stereotyping in all the institutions of Canadian society. One form of response, therefore, has been the recognition of the issue by important agencies and high-profile members of the legal profession.

DENIAL

The above examples have been a few voices in the wilderness, however. There is still persistent and considerable denial of racism in the courts. Judges and Crown counsel on the rare occasions when they do address allegations of racism, invariably deny them. "Crown attorneys have not control over intake and arrest, we deal with everyone equally.... I have never noticed that one group is treated differently. I don't care whether someone is Black, White or green," said Stephen Leggett, head Crown counsel at the court located on Finch Avenue in Toronto (*The Toronto Star*, l992). Others, such as defence counsel Peter Abrahams, believe that race makes a difference in the legal system.

> You find that Black youths are denied bail more often than their young White counterparts. The first question you're asked as a lawyer going into a hearing is whether your client is Black. Everybody knows that there is a racial element to a criminal trial. Police, Crown attorneys and judges are not immune to it. (The Toronto Star, 1992)

The denial of racism in the justice system is not confined to the legal profession. For example, there was considerable criticism of the then attorney general of Ontario, Howard Hampton, for creating a task force to investigate the issue. A Progressive Conservative MPP angrily stated in the legislature that members of the justice system had been "slandered."

> You stated publicly that it was your opinion that the justice system was rife with systemic racism. Statements such as these slander the reputation of every judge, Crown attorney, justice of the peace and police officer who makes up the justice system. (The Toronto Star, l992)

Faced with continuing pressure from minority communities, especially Blacks, the government of Ontario announced some new initiatives for the justice system. A new system of developing jury pools to increase the representation of juries was announced by the attorney general. The announcement was greeted with allegations of reverse racism and fears about the imposition of jury quotas (*The Toronto Star*, l993a). One of the country's most prominent lawyers, Edward Greenspan, said that "there is something fundamentally wrong with the notion that 12 people of one color can't fairly try an accused of a different color." Hutchinson counters this argument tellingly:

In a society that still divides power and opportunity along racial, class and other lines, it is a profound error to imagine that one's race and background does not give one a certain perspective on social values, how society works and what others think.... It is the privilege of the White establishment to pretend that race is not important and that it does not contribute heavily to the kinds of lives that people live.

While recognizing that the views of individuals are as diverse as their backgrounds, Hutchinson argues that there is at least a chance of an accused receiving a fairer and more balanced decision when it reflects "the views of the whole community, not only part of it" (*The Toronto Star*, 1993a).

A task force on systemic racism has been created by the Ontario government to study and make recommendations on this issue. In other provinces, the results of inquiries have already been completed in Nova Scotia, Alberta, and Manitoba.

EMPLOYMENT EQUITY

Again in Ontario, pending employment equity legislation forced a number of hiring and appointment measures to be taken. A concerted effort has been made to hire more minority lawyers in the public service and to appoint more to the judiciary. A Black Legal Aid Clinic was formed to provide services to the Black community; similar services were already available for the Chinese and Aboriginal communities.

TRAINING

Only a limited amount of anti-racist training has been undertaken in the justice system. The Judicial Education Committee in Ontario, which had earlier sponsored gender training, agreed in principle to offer anti-racist training to judges but was constrained by lack of money. Some training was undertaken by Ministry of the Attorney General for staff such as Crown counsels and offices that fell under its jurisdiction, such as the Public Complaints Commission. For the most part, however, practising judges, defence and Crown counsels, and other members of the justice system have not had any comprehensive training in matters relating to the manifestations of racism in public systems.

SUMMARY

While research on racial discrimination in the justice system in Canada is limited, sufficient evidence suggests that it is of grave concern in this country. It is also a serious problem in both the United States and the United Kingdom. Various public inquiries, task forces, and commissions have been conducted over the past decade, and the anecdotal evidence gathered in public consultations with individuals, organizations, and racial-minority communities reflects a growing sense of distrust and fear of the justice system in Canada. There is a fundamental absence of faith in the fairness of the system.

The recent racial unrest in Toronto, Montreal, Halifax, and other Canadian cities has been, in part, a response to the perception among Black people that they are the victims of racial bias and discrimination, which are widespread in law-enforcement agencies as well as the courts. Allegations of police brutality and harassment are widespread. Several Black men have been killed by police in the past few years in Toronto, Montreal, and Ottawa. No police officers have been found guilty. Growing concerns have been expressed about the low numbers of racial minorities and Aboriginal peoples employed in the legal system as well as on juries.

The justice system in Canada is plagued by a systemic bias that results in the overcriminalization of particular groups in society.[10] Blacks (and other racial minorities) face discriminatory practices and procedures at every stage of the administration of justice.

The law is not value-neutral, and the justice system reflects the systemic bias that exists in the broader Canadian society. Therefore, a critique of the legal system cannot be accomplished without recognizing that the law is an institution that enjoys a dialectical relationship with the broader society. As such, systemic racism in the society is reflected in the formal and informal practices of the legal system.

There is some consensus among scholars that racial disparities in the criminal justice system have developed because policies, practices, and procedures have been adopted without systematic efforts being made to find out whether they have a differential effect on members of racial-minority communities.

Racial discrimination is not limited to the justice system; it exists in virtually every other social institution. However, the justice system has a special responsibility to function with fairness and to show that discrimination in any form is a denial of the justice it claims to uphold.

REFERENCES

Bickenbach, J.E. (1989). "Lawyers, Law Professors, and Racism in Ontario." *Queen's Quarterly* 3 (Autumn):585–598.

Binavince, E. (1989). "The Juridical Aspect of Race Relations: A Discussion Paper." In O.P. Dwivedi (ed.), *Canada 2000: Race Relations and Public Policy.* Guelph, ON: Department of Political Science, University of Guelph.

Equality Now. (1984). Report of the Special Committee on Visible Minorities in Canadian Society. Ottawa: House of Commons.

Equal Opportunity Consultants. (1989). *Perceptions of Racial Minorities Related to the Services of the Ministry of the Attorney General.* Toronto: Ontario Ministry of the Attorney General.

The Globe and Mail (June 28). (1993).

Harvard Law Review. (1988). "Race and the Criminal Process." vol. 101:1472–1641.

Head, W. (1991). "The Donald Marshall Prosecution: A Case Study of Racism and the Criminal Justice System." *Currents: Readings in Race Relations* (Toronto) 7(1) (April).

Hutchinson, A.C. (1992). Quoted in *The Globe and Mail* (December 3).

Jamaican Canadian Association. (1990). Conference: "Meeting The Challenge— Police–Black Relations." Toronto, Spring.

Kobayashi, A. (1990). "Racism and the Law." *Urban Geography* 11(5)447–473.

Law Reform Commission of Canada. (1992). "Consultation Document." Ottawa.

Law Times. (1994). February 21–27.

Lewis, S. (1992). *Report to the Premier of Ontario.* (June 9). Toronto.

Linn, P. (1992). "Report of the Saskatchewan Indian Justice Review Committee and the Saskatchewan Métis Justice Review Committee, January 1990." In Western Judicial Education Centre, *Conference Materials on Racial, Ethnic & Cultural Equity.* Vancouver.

Macdonald, J.A. (1993). *Decision on Challenge for Cause in Regina vs. Griffis.* Toronto: Ontario Provincial Court. (August).

Petersen, C. (1993). Institutionalized Racism: The Need for Reform of the Criminal Jury Selection Process." *McGill University Law Journal* 38:147–179.

Petersilia, J. (1985). "Racial Disparities in the Criminal Justice System: A Summary." *Crime and Delinquency*, vol. 31, no. 1, 15–34. (January).

Pomerant, D. (1992). "Jury Selection and Multicultural Issues." Ottawa: Law Reform Commission of Canada.

Province of Manitoba. (1991). *Manitoba Attorney General Submission to the Aboriginal Justice Inquiry.* Winnipeg, Manitoba.

Reiman, J.H. (1979). *The Rich Get Richer and the Poor Get Prison: Ideology, Class, and Criminal Justice.* New York: Wiley.

Renner, K.E., and A.H. Warner. (1981). "The Standard of Social Justice Applied to an Evaluation of Criminal Cases Appearing Before the Halifax Courts." *Windsor Yearbook of Access to Justice.* Windsor: University of Windsor.

Province of Nova Scotia. (1989). *Royal Commission on the Donald Marshall, Jr., Prosecution.* "Digest of Findings and Recommendations." Halifax.

Royal Commission on the Donald Marshall, Jr., Inquiry Report. (1989). Part 4. "The Sentencing Sub-Project." 128–131. Halifax: The Commission.

Second Report of the NACRO Race Issues Advisory Committee: Race and Criminal Justice. (1989). London.

Sinclair, C.M. (1992). "Report of the Aboriginal Justice Inquiry." In *Western Judicial Education Centre, Conference Materials on Racial, Ethnic & Cultural Equity.* Vancouver.

Staples, R. (1975). "White Racism, Black Crime, and American Justice: An Application of the Colonial Model to Explain Crime and Race." *Phylon* 36.

Thornhill, E. (1988). "Presentation to the Donald Marshall Inquiry." In *Proceedings of Consultative Conference on Discrimination Against Natives and Blacks in the Criminal Justice System and the Role of the Attorney General.* Halifax.

Wiener, J. (1990). Speech to the Western Judicial Education Centre, Vancouver (May 13).

(1992). *The Toronto Star* (October 12):24.

(1993a). *The Toronto Star.* Moloney, P. "SIU Arrived Four Hours After Shootings Jury Told.": A17.

(1993b). *The Toronto Star* (May 22): "Should Juries Reflect a Society's Racial Mix?": D4.

Westmoreland Traore, J. (1982). "Race Relations and the Criminal Justice System." Paper presented at a Conference on Justice and Minorities. Vancouver (April).

NOTES

1. "Justice system" here refers to police institutions, the courts, and correctional facilities.

2. It is hoped that the Commission on Systemic Racism in the Justice System will provide statistical information on the extent to which disparaties exist in the justice system. The commission is scheduled to study, among other things, sentencing disparities,

racism in the jury selection process, and racial-minority participation in the policy-making function of the justice system. It is expected to report late in 1994.

3. After the publication of that report, the government of Ontario created a task force to study systemic racism in the justice system. It is expected to report late in 1994.

4. Although this book contains a separate chapter on policing, it is necessary here to briefly review some material on police, who are the first point of contact before individuals reach the courts.

5. See the following case study.

6. For a systematic presentation of the powers of Crown attorneys, consult Morris Manning, "Abuse of Power by Crown Attorneys," *Special Lectures of the Law Society of Upper Canada*. Toronto: 1979.

7. *Mens rea* refers to the conscious intention of a person to commit a crime.

8. The challenge for cause based on racial discrimination was upheld by the Ontario Court of Appeal in Regina versus Parks. Justice Doherty accepted the fact that bias among jury members is possible in a society in which "wide spread anti-Black racism is a grim reality" (*The Toronto Star*, December 15, 1993:25).

   Presumably the way has now been cleared for lawyers to use the challenge whenever appropriate. While this judgement and that of the Provincial Court (Macdonald, 1993) have shown progress in the justice system with respect to the issue of racism, it should also be noted that the Ontario attorney general has appealed the Court of Appeal decision to the Supreme Court of Canada and has asked the court to condone trials in which people of colour are not allowed to question the jury on racism. The Supreme Court of Canada in April 1994 rejected the province's attempt at appeal. (Leave to the Supreme Court was denied.)

9. *Voir dire*: "to speak the truth."

10. A number of Marxist-oriented critiques of the justice system have been undertaken. Reiman (1984), for example, argues that the justice system should be viewed as a functional institution that maintains the status quo in the interests of the dominant class. He argues that the justice system is properly functioning for the dominant elite in society by maintaining their interests under the guise of legitimately controlling for law and order. Reiman asserts that the goal of the justice system is not to reduce crime or achieve justice, but to project to the public a visible image of the threat of crime—e.g., the activities of poor, Black youth. He suggests that society derives benefit from the existence of crime, and thus there is reason to believe that social institutions work to maintain rather than to eliminate crime.

   Reiman's argument is that in order to maintain the image of a functioning justice system, laws are created that prohibit acts of poor youth. These laws would increase the need for "criminals" to engage in secondary crime—for example, the drug addict's need to steal to pay for drugs. At the same time that certain behaviour is classified as criminal and delinquent, many acts of the wealthy are not treated as criminal. He argues that there is an astounding incidence of disease, injury, and death due to hazards in the workplace and that this is the consequence of the refusal of management to pay for safety measures and of government to enforce safety standards. He cites white-collar crime as an example of the selection process in defining criminal activity. His assertion is that the definition of crime benefits the economically advantaged while targeting the disadvantaged.

   Moreover, Reiman argues that the broad discretion given to police, prosecutors, and judges who influence arrests, charges, and sentencing rates facilitates the creation of the public perception of "who is criminal." He asserts further that the demeaning prison experience is meant to create future crime by emasculating prisoners in a violent, unsafe environment. The stigmatization of prisoners ensures that ex-offenders will find difficulty integrating back into society. This, coupled with police harassment, ensures that ex-offenders will be targeted by police and re-criminalized. The justice system is designed to "maintain and encourage the existence of a stable and visible class of criminals."

Staples (1975) uses a colonial model to analyze race and the law. This type of historical analysis identifies the origins of racism that permeate modern racial and economic stratification. He argues that Blacks are not protected by the law because they have no power to enforce the law. The power to define what constitutes a crime is in the hands of the dominant members of society, and this power is a mechanism of racial subordination.

The colonial model assesses the Black community as an underdeveloped colony whose economics and politics are controlled by leaders of the racially dominant group. Staples contends that crime by Blacks and the treatment of Blacks by the legal system is a result of the neocolonialist structure of society.

The central theme of the arguments put forth by these theorists is the importance of ideological control for the maintenance of inequality in society.

Chapter 6

▼▼▼▼▼▼▼▼▼▼▼▼

Racism and Human-Service Delivery

No amount of tinkering can fix the problem. What is required is a massive shift in attitudes, a revolution which would see a multifaceted approach, including full funding for ethnocultural and racial-community agencies and a decision-making process that is controlled by people truly representative of the population. (Minna, 1991)

This chapter examines the dynamics of individual, institutional, and cultural racism as they are reflected in the policies and practices of traditional, mainstream, human-service organizations. Included in the analysis are a wide range of human-services provided by social and health-care agencies such as family- and child-service agencies, mental-health clinics, child-care facilities and child-welfare agencies. Although it does not specifically consider other human services such as hospital and community health clinics and community or recreational centres, the issues are very much the same.

This chapter also looks briefly at the critical challenges confronting ethno-cultural and racial-community-based organizations that are attempting to meet the needs of specific constituencies such as immigrants, refugees, Blacks, Chinese, South Asians, and other communities. Some barriers that affect the delivery of service are analyzed, including lack of representation of people of colour in mainstream human-service organizations; the marginalization and differential treatment experienced by racial-minority practitioners in these agencies; and the racist ideology underpinning the provision of services and modes of treatment. A case study of a women's hostel, Nellie's, provides the reader with a clear illustration of how racism, in its many dimensions, operates in the context of a human-service agency.

INTRODUCTION

As is the case with other Canadian institutions and systems (e.g., education, law enforcement, government agencies, media), a growing body of evidence indicates that racist ideologies and practices affect the administration and operation of human-service organizations, the delivery of services to individual clients and communities, the allocation of resources, training, and education programs, and the access and participation of people of colour as clients or patients, managers, staff, and volunteers.

THE MANIFESTATIONS OF RACISM

Racial and cultural barriers influence the provision of services and the quality and appropriateness of those services. Racial bias and discrimination can be reflected in the allocation of resources by funders, who may ignore the dramatic rise in immigrants and refugees in recent decades and the particular needs of racial-minority groups and the agencies that serve them. An aspect of racism may be reflected in the view of funders that racially specific services are an unnecessary duplication of the programs and services offered by mainstream agencies.

Racist assumptions and practices may also influence the employment opportunities for minority social workers and health-care practitioners. Professional credentials acquired in other countries, for example, may not be recognized in Canada. Professional competency is therefore measured by standards and norms that undervalue the training received by racial minorities.

Racial bias may also be reflected in the modes of treatment and approaches to problem resolution, which may ignore the effects of systemic racism on the client or fail to take into account cultural values, community norms, and indigenous resources. Racism may also influence the common assumption that views racial minorities from a "problem" perspective—either they have problems, or they are the cause of problems. A further example of racism commonly found in human-service organizations is the failure to provide services that are racially sensitive, culturally appropriate, and linguistically accessible.

The disempowering effects of racism in human-service organizations may be further compounded when a person of colour is also an immigrant or refugee. The effect of this double group identification is even greater marginalization and disadvantage. Women of colour who are immigrants are particularly vulnerable, as are the elderly.

MANIFESTATIONS OF RACISM IN HUMAN SERVICES

Lack of access to appropriate programs and services
Ethnocentric values and counselling practices
Devaluing of the skills and credentials of minority practitioners
Inadequate funding for ethno-racial community based agencies
Lack of minority representation in social agencies
Monocultural or ad hoc multicultural model of service delivery

A number of studies have drawn attention to these and other pervasive racial barriers, which exist in almost all the major traditional, mainstream, human-service delivery organizations across Canada (Doyle and Visano, 1987; Sanga, 1987; Chan, 1987; Bambrough et al., 1992; Bergin, 1988).

EDUCATION AND TRAINING

Few undergraduate and postgraduate educational programs provide the skills and knowledge necessary for social workers, doctors, nurses, and other human-service practitioners to confront racism in their professional values, norms, and practices. For example, faculties of social work, medicine, and nursing have resisted incorporating into their curriculum the study of racism. Moreover, the theories, methodologies, and traditional skills taught in these programs bear little relation to the needs of clients from diverse racial and cultural backgrounds (Agard, 1987; Allodi, 1983).

ACCESS TO SERVICES

Additional evidence of the failure of traditional, mainstream social and health-care agencies is provided by the findings of numerous task forces and consultations undertaken to assess the quality and accessibility of care and services provided to racial and ethno-cultural client groups by traditional human-service agencies (Canadian Task Force, 1988; Radford, 1989; British Columbia Task Force on Family Violence, 1992; Bergin 1988; Medeiros, 1991; James and Muhammad, 1992).

In 1987, the Social Planning Council of Metropolitan Toronto publicly reported on a comprehensive study it had commissioned (Doyle and Visano, 1987). The findings suggest that while access to basic social and health services is a form of universal entitlement, mainstream agencies in the human-service delivery system have failed to provide accessible and equitable services. The researchers identified many linguistic, cultural, and racial barriers and discriminatory practices, as well as an absence of strategies to address these obstacles. They found institutional discrimination reflected in indifferent attitudes and a lack of commitment to seek remedies for patterns of exclusion and inaccessibility.

Some of the barriers to health and social services identified by minority-group clients are lack of information about the services provided, the unavailability of service, the service providers' lack of knowledge of the linguistic and cultural needs of different groups, and the inappropriateness of treatment modes and counselling. There was a widespread perception that the difference in racial and cultural backgrounds between clients and White, Anglo human-service professionals frequently resulted in misconceptions and negative judgements being made by service providers. All these problems are made more acute by the general problems that all consumers experience, such as child-care and transportation costs, lengthy delays, and physical distance from agencies (Doyle and Visano, 1987).

Another significant finding of the study was the existence of "two solitudes," in which mainstream agencies and ethno-racial services exist side by side, with little interaction and coordination in planning and delivering services. ("Mainstream" agencies offer services to anyone in the community who meets general eligibility criteria; "ethno-racial" agencies provide services to people on the basis of membership in a particular racial or cultural group.)

Ethno-racial organizations act as brokers and advocates for minority populations by providing settlement and integration services, language interpretation for mainstream agencies, family counselling, and so on. Support services are offered in which practitioners from agencies accompany clients to other organizations, assist in helping interpret their needs, and represent them and their interests. These services exist largely because of the failure of traditional organizations to adequately respond to the changing needs of a multiracial and pluralistic society.

Services provided by many ethno-racial agencies that are often absent in the mainstream agencies include more flexible hours, with evenings and weekend services; drop-in services; locations in accessible, informal settings, such as community centres; home visits; community outreach; advertising of services in the multicultural media; and group counselling (Bridgman, 1993).

REPRESENTATION

One of the most profound barriers to access and equity in human-service agencies is the absence of people of colour at every level including boards of directors. In a recent study (Murray et al., 1992), the boards of some 1200 non-profit organizations in Canada were surveyed. It was found that these boards were predominantly composed of people with British origins; 28 percent were at least three-quarters British. An additional 30 percent were at least half British. The next most common group was those of "other Northern European origins" (German, Dutch, Scandinavian), with 47 percent of boards having at least some representation from this group. French Canadians were well represented, with 47 percent of boards. People of colour, however, were almost entirely absent.

Racial-Minority Professionals in Human-Service Organizations

People of colour who are professionals working in human-service organizations often confront biases, barriers, and conflicts totally unknown to mainstream practitioners. A recent study in Nova Scotia (Bambrough et al., 1992), revealed that Black social work graduates from the Maritime School of Social Work found less desirable jobs than others, including limited or term positions and more part-time jobs. Moreover, once they obtained work, they found that their opportunities for advancement were relatively limited and salary levels low. The report concluded that Black graduate social workers had been less successful than the majority group in accessing the more prestigious social work jobs, including family counselling, hospital social work, and administrative or supervisory positions.

Another formidable manifestation of bias frequently encountered by minority workers is the fact that the knowledge, skills, and experience they have acquired in their home countries may not be recognized or be significantly undervalued. Degrees earned abroad are often not accredited, and foreign-trained graduates have no access to retraining (Access, 1989). In Ontario, five years after the Task Force on Access was concluded—with numerous recommendations and strategies for an effective assessment of the skills and experience of immigrants—there was still no formal implementation of its recommendations.

A related concern is the fragile position of community workers, who play a pivotal role in providing services to racial and ethno-cultural communities but do not have formal degrees or certificates. A private member's bill in the Ontario legislature would prohibit workers without "credentials" from operating as certified social workers. Patricia O'Connor, of Toronto's George Brown College, pointed out that the implications of the regulation limiting certification to university graduates was that funding for publicly funded agencies might be contingent on hiring only those with the right credentials (Webster, in *Now*, 1992).

Social workers and other human-service practitioners from diverse racial and cultural communities may experience serious conflicts between their cultural values and those of the dominant culture, which influences the practices and priorities of their organization. Minority workers commonly function from a dual perspective—they understand the needs and concerns of their own communities and the limitations of the programs of mainstream human-service organizations. On the other hand, mainstream practitioners in social work and health-care practitioners are trained to view their services as having universal applicability and accessibility. There is considerable pressure on racial-minority practitioners to conform with traditional agency practices (Scarborough Mental Health Coordinating Group Report, 1992).

Minority workers are frequently isolated and marginalized in mainstream agencies. They are concentrated at the entry levels or in front-line positions. Their primary role is to serve clients who share the same racial or cultural background, but they tend to have limited power and status in the organization. This practice can result in a kind of ghettoization, especially of staff who are people of colour, where all "problems with Blacks" are referred to the Black worker (Thomas, 1987). Racist attitudes and behaviours are considered a significant barrier to good working relationships between White and minority practitioners.

Head (1986) examined the extent of racial discrimination in some Toronto hospitals. His research findings confirmed the general perception of racial-minority women working in these institutions: racial-minority nurses were underrepresented at the decision-making and supervisory levels. Despite having similar educational qualifications, most minority health-care workers were represented in the lower levels of the hierarchy. White nurses in the sample were twice as successful in gaining promotions as Blacks. A considerable degree of apathy, hopelessness, and fear existed among Black respondents. Many were hesitant about participating in the study, for fear of being reprimanded or fired. More than half the Black respondents indicated they had been harassed by patients.

Clearly, the human-service delivery system has largely failed to adapt its programs and services and administrative and organizational practices to meet the needs of a multiracial society. The result of this neglect is inadequate and inappropriate services to members of racial and ethno-cultural minorities.

Some of the most significant barriers are the staff's lack of knowledge and skills; the system's lack of anti-racism policies, programs, and practices; culturally and racially inappropriate modes of treatment; lack of trained cultural and linguistic interpreters; and overly bureaucratic procedures. All of these factors negatively affect the delivery of services.

FAMILY SERVICES

A study prepared by the Multicultural Coalition for Access to Family Services in Metropolitan Toronto underlined some of the critical issues facing racial and cultural minority communities (Medeiros, 1991). It found an "appalling lack of services" in ten ethno-cultural and racial communities. The report concluded that methods of family-service delivery are based on "certain notions of family structure, values and what is taken as normal behaviour and functioning within society, as defined by White, middle class Judeo-Christian standard" (12).

Fewer than 8 percent of staff at established mainstream agencies spoke a language other than English, and only 14 percent of front-line staff were identified as being from the ten communities studied. While $14.6 million was allocated annually to Metro for family services, only $900 000 went to ethno-cultural agencies. "The issue is not just lack of money, but rather a complacent disregard for the needs and the rights of ethno-cultural and racial communities"—who represent 60 percent of the population of Metro (7). The study indicates that 62 percent of the established family-service agencies had no policies or practices to address the needs of ethno-cultural and racial communities.

One can conclude that the systemic barriers, first identified in the early 1980s, continue to operate in the delivery of family services to ethno-cultural and racial communities. Racial, linguistic, cultural, and geographic barriers significantly affect family counselling from assessment and diagnosis to intervention and treatment. Mainstream family services continue to presume that "immigrants shed their values, religion, language, and colour as they enter Canada and that they pass nothing on to subsequent generations. The reality is that they cannot relinquish their cultural and racial heritage without risking major personality conflicts" (10).

One of the leading authorities in the field of social work, race, and ethnicity in the United Kingdom (Cheetham, 1982) suggests that no amount of asserting the irrelevance of race, colour, and ethnicity alters the fact that racial discrimination and disadvantage chronically influence the circumstances of ethnic and racial minorities. The fact that multicultural or anti-racist policies have been established in many family-service agencies appears to have made little difference because mainstream agencies continue to function without fundamental changes to their service-delivery systems and with dominant cultural values underpinning their organizational practices (Bridgman, 1993).

Clinical models of treatment and intervention offered by mainstream human-services commonly ignore or dismiss the strength and significance of group identity and loyalty. At the same time, they fail to recognize the supportive role that racial and ethno-specific groups play in helping ethno-cultural and racial minorities to confront social, economic, and political disadvantage and discrimination.

Much of the influential literature on family therapy has drawn a boundary around the nuclear family. Solutions to problems have been sought within this internal system, without taking into account the extended family maintained by many clients and the pressures placed on them by their environment. Yet, one cannot consider family dysfunction without considering the context of family life.

As a result of these barriers, many clients underutilize or terminate their involvement with an agency, finding the manner of service-delivery "too institutionalized, fragmented and culturally insensitive" (Agard, 1987). Their reasons for doing so are related to the biased nature of the services: "The services offered are frequently antagonistic or inappropriate to the life experiences of the culturally different client; they lack sensitivity and understanding; they are oppressive and discriminating toward minority clients" (Sue and Sue, 1990:7).

MENTAL HEALTH SERVICES

The findings of a national task force to conduct hearings on access to mental-health services by immigrants indicate that health and social services for immigrants are highly fragmented and unco-ordinated (Canadian Task Force, 1988) and that they have been developed without an overall plan for co-ordination with the mainstream service-delivery system. The task force identified numerous racial, cultural, and linguistic barriers that prevented the effective use of mental-health services. Ethno-cultural and racial groups and service providers agree that the lack of a common language is the barrier that most interferes with assessment and treatment.

A survey conducted by a hospital in Toronto found that the need for more mental-health services among immigrant, refugee, and racial-minority women is greatest for those who have been sexually assaulted (Pilowsky, 1991). The report also found that the common barriers immigrant women face when seeking mental-health services are language, a lack of personnel trained to be sensitive to people of different cultures and races, and a lack of free services and information.

The lack of professional, trained interpreters affects all areas of human-service delivery. In Ontario, some limited efforts were made by the provincial government (Ontario Ministry of Citizenship, 1989) to support the training of cultural and linguistic interpreters. In some of the major hospitals, resources were allocated to hire trained interpreters. However, the majority of social and health-care agencies rely on volunteers, family, or their own unqualified employees to interpret. Consequently, many patients or clients choose not to disclose personal and pertinent information to avoid embarrassment. The translation may provide misleading data because of lack of professional expertise (Canadian Task Force, 1988).

Another significant barrier between minority clients or patients and mainstream human-service delivery is the fact that many groups consider social and health concerns to be a collective problem, affecting others as well as the person seeking help. Members of both the immediate and extended family, especially elders, expect to be involved in the assessment of the problem and to play an active role in the treatment. While the centrality of the individual is an indispensable foundation of social work in Western societies, it is for some minorities an incomprehensible concept (Cheetham, 1982). In many immigrant cultures, independence from the family is not a primary goal. Enormous value is placed on interdependence, co-operation, and loyalty to the family. Each family member is expected to put the family's needs ahead of individual desires (British Columbia Task Force, 1991).

The formal and bureaucratic atmosphere of mental-health facilities and other social and health agencies creates an alienating environment. Sterile reception areas, often staffed by culturally insensitive staff, complex and confusing administrative forms, service-delivery information printed only in English, and a lack of flexible office hours are common features of these clinics (Doyle and Visano, 1987).

Minority professionals have pointed out the profound difference in worldview that typically separates White interviewers from clients of colour (Sisskind, 1978). Racial stereotyping often skews the initial assessment of therapists, who may view traits such as aggressive behaviour as indicative of a personality disorder, when in fact they may be a normal response to living in a racist society. Professional norms as well as class-bound values are used to judge normality or deviance (Dominelli, 1989).

In one study, when therapists interviewed patients, they tended to assign diagnoses of depression to Whites and of schizophrenia to Blacks. When they used a standardized interview form, differences between Blacks and Whites disappeared. Another submission to the task force (Harambee Centres of Canada) identified racial stereotyping as a potential factor in biasing assessments (Canadian Task Force, 1988).

Traditional interviewing techniques in social work and the health sciences commonly emphasize professional distance between the client and the therapist, a non-directive style, and emphasis on verbal, emotional, and behaviourial expressiveness and self-disclosure. They also stress self-responsibility and examining past experiences. These techniques are rooted in a North American value system that may directly conflict with the client's cultural norms. Racial-minority clients whose lives have been marked by racism may well be disinclined to engage in self-disclosure with a White professional. For many minorities, sharing intimate aspects of one's experiences only occurs after a long and intense relationship has been established.

CHILDREN'S SERVICES

Racism in societal institutions has a significant impact on services to children and child-welfare policies and programs. It also has a profound affect on the self-image of racial-minority children.

In a study of African Canadian children (children of African heritage in Canada, regardless of place of birth) under the care of child-welfare agencies in Canada, Louis identified a number of ways in which the cumulative effects of the racism of bigoted peers, teachers, other adults, the media, and fellow African Canadians affects these children.

One of the most important effects of this negative socialization are that the African Canadian child's self-image becomes distorted and that a positive sense of racial identity is undermined before it has a chance to develop (Louis, 1992). Children begin to develop racial awareness at 3 to 5 years of age; they are aware of differences between racial groups and can recognize and label these differences. Children at this early age can also identify themselves in racial terms (Milner, 1975).

Louis (1992) observed that when African Canadian children were removed from their natural families, they entered into an almost exclusively White world (White social workers, lawyers, counsellors, doctors, judges, court officials. Foster families and adoptive parents are also often White). African Canadian children tended to be placed with White families. This uprooting of children from their own family and community and their placement in all-White environments can have a debilitating effect on the self-image and group identity of these children. They often feel insecure and unable to discuss their experiences with racism. Thus, however well intended the caregivers and the agencies, there is a general failure to recognize the unique problems facing these children in care and an absence of programs to address their needs. Numerous studies in the United Kingdom reached similar conclusions (Ahmed, 1981).

Children from oppressed racial and cultural groups tend to have preoccupations different from those of their White peers. In order of concern, they have questions about their own identity; about racism and Whites; and about other groups. For White children, the order seems to be questions about people of colour; comments that reflect stereotypical or negative attitudes; and questions about their own identity (Derman-Sparks et al., 1980). These findings have significant implications for policies and practices involving racial-minority children from day care to child welfare.

BARRIERS AFFECTING WOMEN

Racism and sexism meet in the lives of women of colour and affect their daily experiences as well as their access to services. In cases of sexual assault or family violence, these women may be under even more pressure than Anglo-Canadian women not to report the incident, in order not to breach the solidarity of the community (British Columbia Task Force, 1992). On the other hand, they may be isolated and not have the traditional family-support networks. Immigrant and refugee women are often unaware of their legal rights; they fear that if they report their husbands for abuse, they might lose their landed-immigrant status and be sent back to their home country.

The lack of fluency in English creates another barrier that affects immigrants' access to protection and safety. Their first difficulty is finding out which services are available; the information is mostly available only in English. Linguistic, cultural, and racial barriers make it difficult for these women to seek help from social workers, police, counsellors, doctors, and religious leaders. In an Ontario study, 62.2 percent of the battered immigrant women interviewed cited a fear that they would lose "everything—house, children, reputation—everything I worked for" once they involved the police as an important reason for not calling the police. Also, 42.2 percent of the women cited fear that a husband or partner would be brutalized or victimized by the police as a reason for not calling the police (ARA Consultants, 1985).

Within the service-delivery system, from interactions with the police to experiences in the courts and access to shelters, these women are likely to encounter racial bias and discrimination. Social workers or judges may have mistaken and stereotypical attitudes, leading them to disbelieve the woman of colour, particularly if she is describing the conduct of a White person. For victims of abuse, racism adds another painful dimension to the experience and to the problem of finding help.

These barriers lead some researchers to conclude that victims of family and sexual violence from minority cultures confront not only the trivialization and denial that are the by-products of sexism, but also the denial that stems from the invisibility of racism in Canadian society (British Columbia Task Force, 1992).

CASE STUDY 6.1

NELLIE'S

This case study illustrates some of the major themes and issues identified in this chapter. It shows how human-service professionals and organizations, with established and significant track records in providing diverse critically important services, are often unable to adapt their policies, programs, professional attitudes, and behaviours to control racism in its diverse forms.

Nellie's is a women's hostel in Toronto for battered and homeless women. It was co-founded in 1974 by June Callwood and Vicki Trerise. From 1991 to 1993 it was rocked by controversy, conflict, and internal strife. The focus of the dissension was racism in the organization. At the centre of the controversy was a woman of enormous prestige who, especially in the mainstream community, is viewed with great respect and affection.

Callwood, a journalist, broadcaster, and social activist, is widely revered for her involvement in and commitment to many social justice issues. She was a founding member of the Canadian Civil Liberties Association and several peace and feminist organizations, and the driving force behind Jessie's (a home for unwedded mothers) and Casey House (an AIDS hospice). She was awarded the Order of Canada for her outstanding contributions to Canadian society.

BACKGROUND

Nellie's has provided an important community service in Toronto in the past two decades, serving battered women, homeless women, women in emotional distress, prostitutes, destitute refugees, and incest survivors. As is the case with most human-service organizations, in recent years, the ethno-cultural and racial composition of the clients has changed; more than half the clients are immigrants, refugees, and women of colour. The most recent influx included women from Somalia and Ethiopia. In responding to its changing client population, Nellie's recruited some women of colour as staff and board members. However, the nominal increase in representation did not address the fundamental conflict over race and power that emerged in the organization.

EVENTS

In the early 1990s, Nellie's became the focus of public attention as a result of actions that occurred in the organization. Allegations of racism surfaced and then escalated in the course of several months, and they were extensively reported by the media. The allegation of racism appeared to stem from two issues: a clash of ideologies over service and program-delivery issues, and a power struggle between staff and board members who were White and staff and board members who were women of colour.

It appears that the catalyst for the conflict was a difference of opinion about whether to provide programs and counselling for incest victims. Some staff wanted to provide services for women wanting help for suffering related to past abuses, and others believed that Nellie's current resources were insufficient to handle these clients. Those opposed to introducing this service were mainly women of colour who were relatively new to Nellie's. Those arguing for counselling were White workers who had been at the shelter for a longer period and felt that the agency should provide this service.

In staff meetings and board meetings, racial tension increased. Questions of who had the power to make critical decisions in the organization were raised. Staff members who were women of colour felt the need to coalesce for support and formed a caucus group. In a series of letters, the group expressed its perception that systemic racism was operating at Nellie's and expressed concern about the absence of a grievance mechanism to deal with their views on racial issues.

The Women of Colour Caucus argued that despite the fact that Nellie's was supposedly structured on a feminist collective model, in which all members had equal access to decision-making, it operated on the basis of a subtle hierarchy of power and authority. Women of colour felt marginalized, isolated, and excluded. From their perspective, issues such as client access to culturally and racially appropriate services and equitable participation and representation in the workplace were ignored or deflected. Despite the efforts of the caucus to place the issue of racism on the organizational agenda, many of the White board and staff continued to deny the validity of these perceptions and dismissed the signs of a growing crisis in the organization.

Although June Callwood was not the central issue, she stood at the centre of the struggle. In the highly charged atmosphere of a board meeting at Nellie's. one of the staff read a document prepared by the caucus identifying a wide range of concerns, including racial inequities in the workplace, their colleagues' racist behaviour, and discriminatory barriers in the development and delivery of services. The demands called for improved equity hiring practices, a grievance policy, a strong anti-racism mission statement, and new evaluation and training procedures.

Following the reading of the document, Callwood responded with an angry criticism of the Black woman who had read it and disclosed that the woman had once been a Nellie's client. Callwood implied that the woman should have been grateful for the support and assistance the organization had given her, rather than complaining about racism. The board asked Callwood to apologize for the breach of confidentiality and the inappropriateness of her remarks. Michelle Landsberg quotes Callwood as saying, "I blew it." She began by saying, "I was coerced into this apology.... Only a small part of it is sincere"(Landsberg, 1992). At a subsequent board meeting, there was a call for Callwood's resignation.

In the spring of 1993, Callwood resigned from the board of Nellie's. In a special article in *The Toronto Star*, she suggested that she was the victim of tactics of "intimidation and naked aggression." She observed that "the tactics of intimidation which have been effective at Nellie's are not strategies that anyone can condone.... Such naked aggression only hardens differences and does the cause of racism serious damage" (Landsberg, 1992).

The charges of racial bias and discrimination at Nellie's and Callwood's resignation created a furor in the mainstream community. Several editorials appeared in the press, and numerous articles were written by Callwood's media colleagues and friends, all furiously denouncing the actions of the women of colour at Nellie's and ardently defending Callwood's integrity. Journalists in *The Globe and Mail* (Thorsell, 1992; Dewar, 1993; Marchand, 1993). Pierre Berton (1992) wrote: "If June Callwood is a racist then so are we all."

In an eleven-page *Toronto Life* article about Nellie's, Elaine Dewar insinuated that the charges of racism against Callwood and Nellie's were totally fallacious, purposely contrived by the caucus, and supported by other radicals outside the organization to gain power and control in the agency. She commented, "Anyone planning a run at Nellie's could surmise that if Callwood was pushed on the subject of racism, she might leave" (Dewar, 1993:35)

In far fewer numbers, articles appear in the media analyzing the conflict from the perspective of the women of colour involved in the issue (Landsberg, 1992; Barker and Wright, 1992; Benjamin et al., 1993).

ANALYSIS

Confronting and challenging racism in a human-service organization is fraught with risk and pain for the organization's clients, staff, and board of directors. The backlash effect and resistance often extend well beyond the organization; both the mainstream and the minority communities are implicated in the struggle. In this instance, the media played a critical role in reinforcing the position of the White group in Nellie's and helped mobilize public sentiment against the Women of Colour Caucus. By depicting those who were calling for change as radicals, reverse racists, and aggressive power-seeking individuals, the media further polarized the situation and reinforced the marginalization of people of colour in Canadian society.

The perspective of the White staff of Nellie's and June Callwood was that Nellie's provided important, effective programs and services and used a progressive, egalitarian model of service-delivery that included everyone. Most of the White women in the organization were feminists and saw themselves as unbiased, fair-minded individuals, committed to equality and dedicated to service.

As is the case with most White human-service professionals, they were confident of their professional skills and knowledge and believed that Nellie's current structure, norms, and mode of operation met the needs of the groups it was serving. While they recognized that the changing client group required some organizational adjustments (such as increasing the representation of women of colour in the agency), they saw no need for radical changes in the work environment, service-delivery model, or decision-making and administrative processes.

Thus, they were shocked when they were accused of racism in their attitudes and behaviour and in relation to their organizational policies, practices, and structures. They were unable to identify the subtle and overt ways in which they continued to exercise power and control and thus felt unjustly accused.

For the women of colour, there were significant costs in exposing the racism at Nellie's. Their demands for substantive change were met with a powerful backlash, not only in their own organization, but in the mainstream community. The media were instrumental in devaluing and delegitimizing the concerns of women of colour and reinforced the White-dominated status quo. In analyzing this issue, three prominent anti-racism practitioners observe:

> Anti-racism, like other struggles for social change, brings about division and emotional turmoil. Effective anti-racism work identifies resistance to change and lays bare on the one hand, holders of historic power and privilege that is based on skin colour, however relative that power may be, and on the other hand, powerlessness and internalized oppression of Black women and other women of colour. (Benjamin et al., 1993)

CONCLUSION

This case study demonstrates how racism, in all its diverse dimensions, affected a highly respected human-service agency such as Nellie's. It also provides a graphic illustration of the strategies commonly used to minimize the issue of racism in White-dominated organizations.

RESPONSES TO RACISM

Dominelli (1989:391–403) identifies five strategies used to resist dealing with racism. All of them operate in Case Study 6–1 and in the other examples cited in this chapter.

- *Denial strategies* are based on the idea that there is no such thing as cultural and institutional racism, only personal racism in its crudest form.
- *Colour-blind strategies* focus on the notion that all people are the same, that members of any race have similar problems, needs, and objectives.
- *Patronizing approaches* appear to accept the principle of equality between Whites and people of colour. But when the power and privilege of White

people is challenged, demands for substantive change are met with fierce resistance and the status quo is affirmed.

- *"Dumping" strategies* rely on placing the responsibility for eliminating racism on the shoulders of the victims. Professionals see themselves as neutral players.
- *Decontextualization strategies* acknowledge the presence of racism "out there" in the external environment, but not "in here," in *this* organization.

These responses are characteristic of organizations that operate on an assimilationist model of human-service delivery. This model recognizes that racial and cultural diversity exist in the broader community, but views this reality as irrelevant in determining the role and mandate of the agency, the nature of the service delivered, the constituencies served, the professional staff hired, and the volunteers recruited.

In monocultural organizations, linguistic, cultural, and racial barriers to service-delivery are neither identified nor addressed. Thus, the services provided by them remain inaccessible to multicultural and multiracial communities. The underlying assumption is that, despite the obvious differences in the cultural backgrounds and racial identities of clients, all people share common needs and desires and therefore require similar modes of service and intervention.

Many voluntary social agencies and some health-care organizations have attempted to respond to racial-minority demands for more accessible and equitable services by introducing a multicultural organizational model. The change, however, appears often to be cosmetic. New initiatives include the translation of communication materials, the recruitment of board members and volunteers from minority communities, and the hiring of one or two "ethnic" workers. Multicultural and anti-racism issues, while important, are considered separately from the day-to-day life of the organization. The needs and interests of minorities are dealt with on an ad hoc basis, rather than being integrated into the structure, policies, programs, and practices of the organization.

The responsibility for change is often delegated to the front-line worker, who may function in a totally unsupportive environment. Concrete action to promote change is sometimes deferred as the organization attempts to juggle competing demands and priorities. Racism is perceived to be an issue mainly in terms of minority client–mainstream professional interactions and relationships. Therefore, the primary responsibility of the agency is to provide opportunities for human relations–race relations sensitization-training programs for front-line staff.

Mainstream agencies continue to be ineffective in delivering services to ethno-cultural and racial communities. Despite some modifications in the policies of funding agencies such as the United Way of Metropolitan Toronto, some municipalities in Metropolitan Toronto, and the Ontario government, a significant shift is required in the policies and practices of funding bodies.

The controversy over the production of *Show Boat* (discussed in Chapter 9) provides an interesting insight into the limitations of some organizational responses to racism as it relates to human-services. The United Way of Metropolitan Toronto had attempted to develop a multicultural–anti-racist policy and program to assist its member agencies in becoming "more accessible, responsive and reflective of the total community through a process they have called multicultural/anti-racist organizational development" (Action, Access and Diversity, 1991).

The thrust of the policy was to encourage member agencies to develop more inclusive services and to identify racial and cultural barriers in their organizational structures and programs. The United Way prided itself on its "pro-active" approach in providing anti-racist training to its staff, reaching out to racial-minority communities, establishing advisory committees that included representatives from racial communities, recruiting racially and culturally diverse board members, and establishing what it considered to be a more equitable allocations process.

However, the United Way's decision to sponsor a performance of *Show Boat* as a fundraiser, in conjunction with one of its member agencies, the Canadian Institute for the Blind, created a wave of controversy, particularly among people of colour. The refusal of the organization to withdraw from sponsorship led many in the community and some members of the agency to question its commitment to anti-racism. Some argued that the United Way bowed to the interests of the marketplace and the power elite, who threatened to withdraw their financial support if the United Way cancelled their fundraising event. To protest the organization's position on *Show Boat*, the United Way's recently created Caribbean/Black Advisory Committee and several volunteers resigned from the agency.

ANALYSIS

White, Anglo-Canadian human-service practitioners have generally been unwilling to acknowledge that services developed to help those who are most vulnerable can work against the interests of racial and cultural minorities (Cheetham, 1982). White practitioners in the human services are often oblivious to racism as a powerful social force. They generally lack an understanding of racial minorities' daily struggle with prejudice and discrimination. A preference for homogeneity and assimilation runs deep in the institutions of Canadian society and clearly weaves its way into the human-service delivery system.

Ethno-cultural and racially specific community-based agencies have filled the huge gap in the service-delivery system created by the failure of mainstream institutions to serve the needs of a multiracial, multicultural, immigrant population. These agencies are generally isolated from the mainstream delivery system. They have undertaken the responsibility of providing more effective, responsive, and equitable services to minority communities, with little recognition or remuneration.

While minority communities have great trust in this alternative form of human-service delivery, there has been an overwhelming lack of support from government and other funding bodies for community-based agencies. Generally the funding has been in the form of time-bound projects rather than operational funding.

SUMMARY

White human-service practitioners use a variety of rationales to deny, ignore, and minimize the issue of racism in their organizations, their professional values and practices, and their personal belief systems and relationships. The case study of Nellie's demonstrates how mainstream agencies continue to operate within an assimilationist monocultural model of service delivery that views the **pluralism** of Canadian society as being irrelevant to their mandates, policies, structures, and operations. Despite the growing number of anti-racism policies developed by agencies such as the United Way and municipal and provincial agencies, there is little evidence of a willingness to alter the ideology that shapes traditional human-service delivery.

REFERENCES

Access. (1989). Task Force on Access to Professions and Traders in Ontario. Toronto: Ministry of Citizenship, Government of Ontario.

Agard, R. (1987). "Access to the Social Assistance Delivery System by Various Ethnocultural Groups." In *Social Assistance Review Committee Report*. Ontario Ministry of Community and Social Services.

Ahmed, S. (1981). "Children in Care: The Racial Dimension in Social Work Assessment." In J. Cheetham et al. (eds.), *Social and Community Work in A Multiracial Society*. London: Harper and Row.

Allodi, F. (1983). "The Utilization of Mental Health Services by Immigrant Canadians." *Canada's Mental Health* (Toronto) 3 (March):9–12

ARA Consultants.(1985). *Wife Battering Among Rural, Native and Immigrant Women*. Toronto: ARA Consultants.

Bambrough, J., W. Bowden, and F. Wien. (1992). *Preliminary Results from the Survey of Graduates from the Maritime School of Social Work*. Halifax: Maritime School of Social Work, Dalhousie University.

Barker, D., and C. Wright. (1992). "The Women of Colour on the Nellie's Saga." *The Toronto Star* (September 3).

Benjamin, A., J. Rebick, and A. Go. (1993). "Racist Backlash Takes Subtle Form Among Feminists." *The Toronto Star* (April 30):A23.

Bergin, B. (1988). *Equality is the Issue: A Study of Minority Ethnic Group Access to Health and Social Services in Ottawa–Carleton*. Ottawa: Social Planning Council of Ottawa–Carleton.

Berton, P. (1992). "If Callwood Is a Racist Then So Are We All." *The Toronto Star* (May 23):H3.

British Columbia Task Force on Family Violence. (1992). *Is Anyone Listening*.

Bridgman, G. (1993). *The Place of Mainstream and Ethno-Racial Agencies in the Delivery of Family Services to Ethno-Racial Canadians*. Master of Social Work Thesis submitted to the Faculty of Graduate Studies, Graduate Program in Social Work, York University.

Canadian Task Force on Mental Health Issues Affecting Immigrants and Refugees in Canada (1988). Ottawa: Ministries of Multiculturalism and Citizenship and Health and Welfare.

Chan, K. (1987). "Ethnic Minorities and Accessibility to Services in a Two-Tiered, Social Service System: The Case of Chinese in Montreal." *Currents: Readings in Race Relations*, 4(3) (Summer):6–7.

Cheetham, J. (1982). "Introduction to the Issues." In J. Cheetham (ed.), *Social Work and Ethnicity*. London: George Allen and Unwin.

Cumming, A. (1991). *Identification of Current Needs and Issues Related to the Delivery of Adult ESL Instruction in B.C.* Victoria: British Columbia Ministry of Provinicial Secretary and Ministry Responsible for Multiculturalism and Immigration.

Derman-Sparks, L., C.T. Higa, and W. Sparks. (1980). "Children, Race and Racism: How Race Awareness Develops. *Interracial Books for Children Bulletin* 11 (3 and 4)3–9.

Dewar, E. (l993). "Wrongful Dismissal." *Toronto Life* (March):32–46.

Dominelli, L. (1989). "An Uncaring Profession? An Examination of Racism in Social Work." *New Community* 15(3):391–403.

Doyle, R., and L. Visano. (1987). *Access to Health and Social Services for Members of Diverse Cultural and Racial Groups.* Reports 1 and 2. Toronto: Social Planning Council of Metropolitan Toronto.

Green, J. (1982). *Cultural Awareness in the Human Services.* Englewood Cliffs, NJ: Prentice-Hall.

Head, W. (1986). *Black Women's Work: Racism in the Health System.* Toronto: Ontario Human Rights Commission.

Health and Welfare Canada and Multiculturalism and Citizenship Canada. (1988). *After the Door Has Been Opened: Mental Health Issues Affecting Immigrants and Refugees in Canada.* Ottawa: Canadian Task Force on Mental Health Issues Affecting Immigrants and Refugees in Canada.

Jackson, B.W., and E. Holvino. (1989). *Working with Multicultural Organizations: Matching Theory to Practice.* Proceedings of "A Workshop on Diversity: Implications for Education and Training," Toronto.

James, C., and H. Muhammad. (1992). *Children in Childcare Programs: Perception of Race and Race Related Issues.* Toronto: Multicultural and Race Relations Division and Children's Services of the Municipality of Metropolitan Toronto.

James, A., W. Hay, M. Parry, and R. Ghumra. "Court Welfare Work with Asian Families: Problems in Practice." *New Community* (London) 18(2):265–280.

Knowles, C. (1990). "Black Families and Social Services." In A. Cambridge, S. Feuchtwang, (eds.), *Anti-Racist Strategies, Research and Ethnic Relations Series*, Aldershot, UK: Gower.

Landsberg, M. (l992a). "Callwood Furor Masks Real Racism Struggle at Nellie's." *The Toronto Star* (July 18).

_____. (l992b). "The Nellie's Furor: June Callwood Tells Her Side." *The Toronto Star* (July 23):F1.

Lechy, O. (1992). "Health Care System Must Adapt to Meet Needs of Multicultural Society, MDs Say." *Canadian Medical Association Journal* 146(12):2210–2214.

Louis, C. (1992). "Issues Affecting African-Canadian Children in Alternative Care." *Multiculturalism* (Toronto) 14(2 and 3):58–60.

Marchand, P. (l993). "Callwood Denounces 'Bullying' by Self-Defined Weak." *The Toronto Star* (June 21).

Medeiros, J. (1991). *Family Services for All.* Toronto: Multicultural Coalition for Access to Family Services.

Mental Health Coordinating Group of Scarborough. (1992). *Together for Change.* Scarborough.

Minna, M. (1991). "Social Service System Cheats Metro's Ethnics." *The Toronto Star* (June 5):A23.

Milner, D. (l975). *Children and Race.* London: Penguin.

Murray, V., P. Bradshaw, and J. Wolpin. (1992). "Power in and Around Non-Profit Boards: A Neglected Dimension of Governance." *Non-Profit Management and Leadership*, 3(2):165–82.

Pilowsky, J. (1991). *Community Consultation Report.* Toronto: Doctors Hospital, Multicultural Women's Programme.

Ontario Ministry of Citizenship. (1989). *Access.* Toronto: Task Force on Access to Professions and Traders in Ontario.

Radford, B. (1989). "Mainstream and Ethno-Specific Social Assistance Delivery Systems." *Currents: Readings in Race Relations* (Toronto) 5(3):34–35.

Rees, T. (1987). "Equality of Access." *Currents: Readings in Race Relations* (Toronto) 4(3):1–2.

Sanga, D.(1987). "A Systematic Approach to Discrimination in the Provision of Social Services: South Vancouver." *Currents: Readings in Race Relations* (Toronto) 4(3):8–9.

Sisskind, J. (1978). "Cross-cultural Issues in Mental Health." In *ERIC Reports*. Washington: U.S. Dept. of Education.

Sue, D., and D.W. Sue. (1990). "Issues and Concepts of Cross-Cultural Counselling." In *Counselling the Culturally Different: Theory and Practice*. New York: John Wiley and Son.

Tator, C. (1990). "Strategy for Fostering Participation and Equity in the Human Services Delivery System." In R. Doyle, K. Rahi (eds.), *Organization Change Toward Multiculturalism*. Toronto: Access Action Council.

Thomas, B. (1987). *Multiculturalism at Work*. Toronto: YWCA.

Thorsell, W. (1992). "A Question of the Pot Calling the Kettle White." *The Globe and Mail* (May 23, 1992):D6.

United Way of Greater Toronto (1991). *Action, Access and Diversity: A Guide to Multicultural/Anti-Racist Change for Social Service Agencies*. Toronto: United Way.

Webster, P. "Toronto Social Workers" Skills Buried By New Urban Realities." *Now Magazine* (October 1, 1992). Toronto.

Weissman, H. (1982). "Fantasy and Reality of Staff Involvement in Organizational Change." *Administration of Social Work* 6(1) (Spring):37–45.

PART
THREE

▼▼

Racism in
Educational and
Cultural
Institutions

▼▼▼▼▼▼▼▼▼▼▼▼▼▼▼▼▼▼▼▼▼▼▼▼▼▼▼▼▼▼

Part Three continues examining various institutional structures by analyzing racism in schools and universities, the media, and cultural and arts organizations—the major vehicles by which society's values, beliefs, and norms are developed, strengthened, and protected.

These institutions are the primary sites for the production and reproduction of racist values and ideology. The chapters in this part show how the myths and assumptions of democratic racism are employed to avoid acknowledging the racism in Canada.

▼▼

Chapter 7

▼▼▼▼▼▼▼▼▼▼▼▼

Racism in Canadian Education

Visible-minority students are exposed to discriminatory educational practices which, like a multitude of timeless voices, tells them loudly or softly that they are intellectually, emotionally, physically and morally inferior. (Thornhill, 1984:3)

This chapter analyzes the role of education in producing and reproducing racial bias and inequality. Racism in education mirrors the racist ideology of the dominant culture, and this chapter focusses on the ways in which racism is reflected in the learning environment and forms an intrinsic part of the learning process.

The negative effects of racist ideology and differential treatment on students of colour are examined by referring to government-commissioned reports, a significant body of research, and the testimonies of Aboriginal peoples, students of colour, parents, and others. An analysis of the components of the educational system illustrates how racism is part of the educational environment.

An examination of curriculum, including the hidden curriculum, provides some insight into the ways in which schools marginalize minority students and exclude their experiences, history, and contributions. This marginalization has a significant impact on the identities and self-esteem of racial-minority students. There is an extended discussion of assessment and placement and the contentious issue of streaming Black students into low-level, non-academic programs.

The effect of teachers' attitudes and expectations in influencing and limiting the learning of many racial-minority students is examined by considering how ethnocentric values and biases often lead to a stereotyping, particularly of Black children, that has consequences for students' performance.

Another manifestation of racism examined in this chapter is the dysfunctional relationship between educational institutions, racial-minority parents, and communities. This is followed by a discussion of the overt expression of racism in the form of racial harassment (racial graffiti and physical and verbal abuse) that minority students confront both in the school and out of it. The chapter concludes by reviewing some trends and patterns in educational institutions' responses to racism.

INTRODUCTION

It is a strongly held conviction in Canada and other Western democracies that educational institutions play a central role in providing an environment that fosters the attainment of life opportunities for all students. The educational system is assumed to be the main instrument for acquiring the knowledge and skills that will ensure full participation and integration into Canadian society. A significant body of evidence, however, demonstrates that educational institutions have preserved and perpetuated a system of structured inequality based on race.

In the past two decades, many studies, reports, and surveys have documented the ways in which racial bias and discrimination are woven into educational policies, programs, and practices and are reflected in the attitudes and norms of teachers, principals, and administrators. These studies demonstrate the complex and far-reaching impact of racism on the life chances of racial-minority students. One of the most powerful examples of racist ideology and practices in Canada's educational system was the brutal and oppressive treatment of Aboriginal children in residential schools in many provinces.

THE MANIFESTATIONS OF RACISM

As was pointed out in Chapter 3, a systematic effort was made to annihilate Aboriginal cultural values, norms, and customs in the schools. Aboriginal children were physically and emotionally wrenched from their communities and subjected to extreme physical, psychological, and sexual abuse. Through a process of coercive assimilation, supported by the government agencies and churches that ran the schools, Aboriginal children were forbidden to speak their language, to practice their traditions and customs, and to learn about their history.

Haig-Brown (1988), who documented the experiences of former students in several Aboriginal communities who were forced to attend residential

---

**MANIFESTATIONS OF RACISM IN
THE EDUCATIONAL SYSTEM**

Racially biased attitudes and practices of teachers and administrators
Eurocentric curriculum
Racial harassment and racial incidents
Streaming of minority students (especially Blacks) into non-academic programs
Assimilationist culture of the school
Lack of representation
Devaluing of the role and participation of parents and the community

schools over a period of 60 years, suggested that the cultural oppression and ethnocentric indoctrination of the educational process were a microcosm of the domination of Euro-Canadian culture over all aspects of Aboriginal life. Cummins (1992:3) stated that it is not unreasonable to conclude that one of the central goals of these schools was to "prepare children of subordinated groups for their status in life by rekindling shame from one generation to the next."

First Nations' psychologist Roland Chrisjohn summed up the research he and others have done on residential schools and defined the residential school "as an institution formed to make war on First Nations languages, religions and societies" (*Catholic New Times*, 1993). In extensive interviews conducted with Aboriginal students, he found that those who attended these schools felt that the experience had deeply affected their sexual relations, their ability as parents, and their feelings about their religion and culture and had contributed to alcohol abuse, high levels of suicide, and wife abuse (Wilson, 1991). The legacy of racial disadvantage in education is reflected in the facts that only about 20 percent of Aboriginal students finish secondary school and that very few make it to university (Fleras and Elliot, 1992).

In addition to the many research studies (Ramcharan, 1987; Mendoza, 1987; Solomon, 1992; Samuda and Kong, 1986) documenting racism in education, a growing body of evidence has emerged from government-initiated public inquiries and task forces. These documents provide further data on the ways in which educational institutions have failed to provide accessible and equitable education to racial-minority students.[1]

In Nova Scotia, for example, the Nova Scotia Advisory Group (1992), in identifying racism in the province's educational system, underscored the importance of acquiring an education that ensured the personal, social, economic, and political mobility, independence, and security of all citizens. However, as its report points out, minorities, particularly Black students, have been unable to develop their full potential:

> Unfortunately, the educational history of Black Nova Scotia is characterized by a legacy of institutionalized racism. This continues to be demonstrated by exclusion, insensitivity, cultural genocide, stereotyping, discrimination and segregation....
>
> There remains no provincial race relations policy in the area of education; disproportionately few Black teachers; insufficient references to the Black experience in the curricula; and the undermining of the self-esteem of the Black child. The Black perspective, the Black experience and Black contributions to Nova Scotia society must therefore be institutionalized in the provincial education system. (Report, 1991:5)

Similarly, in Ontario, the Stephen Lewis Report (1992) concluded:

> Everywhere the refrain of the Toronto students, however starkly amended by different schools and different locations, was essentially the refrain of all the students. Where are the courses in Black history? Where are the visible minority teachers? Why are there so few role models? Why do our guidance counsellors know so little of different cultural backgrounds?

Why are the racist incidents and epithets tolerated? Why are minority students streamed? Why do they discourage us from university? Where are we going to find jobs? What's the use of having an education if there's no employment? How long does it take to change the curriculum so that we're part of it? (20)

Source: © Reproduced with permission from the Queen's Printer for Ontario.

In Quebec, the significance and impact of racism in education has been described by Thornhill:

> Pretending to be colour-blind in the face of the hardships encountered by Asian, Native and Black youngsters and professing not to perceive any difference in treatment, is still tantamount to sidestepping the problem.... Visible minority students are exposed to discriminatory educational practices which, like a multitude of timeless voices, tells them loudly or softly that they are intellectually, emotionally, physically and morally inferior. (1984:3)

A recent report of the Four-Level Government/African Canadian Community Working Group found compelling evidence of the negative education experienced by Black youth in Metropolitan Toronto (1992). In a background study for the working group, Daenzer (1992) found that the educational process contributes to the reinforcement of racism in two fundamental, related ways: it assaults Black identity and it negates the right of Blacks to participate as full citizens in Canadian society. Consulting more than 300 students, she found that African Canadian students feel that they have inherited a legacy of social marginalization. They enter the school system as "undesirables":

> For at least one generation, the African Canadian community has been crying out in anguish over the poor performance of its youth in the Ontario school system. The drop-out rate, the truancy rate, the basic-streaming rate: all of these have pointed inexorably to the fact that where Black kids are concerned, something is terribly wrong. (77)

Finally, racism in the school and its consequences have been clearly characterized by Thomas (1984):

> In the school, racism says that more Black, Native and Portuguese children will end up in dead-end streams; that European languages such as French and Spanish are more valuable than Punjabi, Cree, Greek or Jamaican English; that children from Britain, the United States, or European countries are more likely to "fit in" and bring with them knowledge which the school can credit than those who come from Third World countries; that heritage or third language classes interfere with children's ability to learn English; that Black students create trouble by hanging around together and playing loud music; that immigrant parents are either uninformed or expect too much from the school system; that Chinese children are better at and should be encouraged to excel in sciences and maths; that in schools where all children are White, Anglo-Saxon there is no problem of racism

because there are no "visible minorities"—suggesting that it is the presence of minority children which creates racism. (21)

RACIST ATTITUDES IN CHILDREN

By the time children enter school at the age of 5, they already have been exposed to racially constructed images of social relations (Rizvi, 1993; Ijaz and Ijaz, 1986; Milner, 1983). The racist popular culture, which includes racist images and negative stereotypes of people of colour in films, books, and toys, has a strong influence on children's attitudes and perceptions. The portrayal of Blacks as criminals, Arabs as subhuman, Asians as untrustworthy, and South Asians as terrorists, and the absence of people of colour in the stories they read, the pictures they see, and the music they hear, influence children's ideas about racial differences. The social environment and the daily experiences of children communicate both implicit and explicit messages.

Research consistently finds that White children prefer Whites and typically show negative attitudes toward Blacks, Asians, and Aboriginal peoples (Aboud and Skerry, 1984; Ijaz and Ijaz, 1986). It suggests that children become aware of differences in physical characteristics such as skin and hair colour at about the age of 3. At about the same time, they also begin to develop labels for racial groups, often based on oversimplification and misinformation. Between the ages of 4 and 7, children form racial preferences, and by the ages of 8 to 12 they deepen their understanding of the status associated with particular groups. At this stage, overtly prejudicial behaviours may emerge. This form of racism has a significant, enduring impact both on how White children see themselves and on how they perceive "others" (Essed, 1990). As well, it has a negative effect on the development of minority children's self-image and self-esteem (Milner, 1983).

Thus, children do not enter the classroom as blank slates. The first challenge in addressing the effect of cultural racism on children is for the educational system to provide students with the critical skills to challenge racist assertions and practices and develop the tools to create alternative social structures and relations (Rizvi, 1993).

CURRICULUM

Curriculum has two dimensions: the formal curriculum and the hidden curriculum (Cheung, 1987). The formal curriculum consists of content and the processes of instruction, which are shaped by the selection of educational materials such as books and teaching aids. The formal curriculum also embraces teaching practices and evaluation procedures, including assessment and placement practices.

The hidden curriculum includes teachers' personal values, their unquestioned assumptions and expectations, and the physical and social environment of the school. Some key questions about racism in the curriculum are: What counts for knowledge? From what perspective does the teaching take place? What images are drawn upon? What learning materials are used?

How is knowledge transmitted? What kinds of knowledge are absent, ignored, and denied?

Formal Curriculum

Many educational theorists, anti-racism advocates, bureaucratic profession-als, and racial-minority parents and communities believe that the curriculum of the schools is seriously flawed. Efforts to adapt it under the rubric of multiculturalism and cultural diversity, while making some progress in reducing bias, stereotyping, and negative images in textbooks (Pratt, 1984), were largely piecemeal, ad hoc, and lacking in co-ordination. These prob-lems were largely the result of the confusion and lack of clarity on what to do and why (Thomas, 1984; Moodley, 1984; Kowalczewski, 1982; Brandt, 1986).

Eliminating racist curriculum has several dimensions. The first involves a critical appraisal of overtly racist curriculum. This entails identifying racial bias, ethnocentrism, stereotyping, and omissions in curriculum materials. It requires asking questions such as: What subjects are taught? What books are selected for teaching? What books should be withdrawn because they are racist in their images, content, or overt or covert messages (Klein, 1986)? After considering these issues, the Forum for Action on Multicultural Education in British Columbia released a report to the government calling for a provincially mandated anti-racism curriculum from kindergarten to grade 12 (Lucow, 1993).

The issue of bias in the classics is a matter of concern not only in Canada, but also for anti-racist educators and advocates in the United States and Great Britain (Brandt, 1986; Lee, 1985; Council on Interracial Books, 1980). There is increasing evidence that reading "literary classics" such as *Huckleberry Finn* and *The Merchant of Venice* without being prepared to deal with their racism does untold damage to minority children, who are further marginalized by the racist language, images, and concepts in these texts (Lee, 1985).

English teachers often fail to deal with the fact that literary texts do not transcend the contexts in which they are written and in which they are read (Pinar, 1993). The social, cultural, and political contexts of all authors, including William Shakespeare and Mark Twain, should form part of any teaching of literature. Equally important and often ignored are the percep-tions, assumptions, understandings, and experiences that the student brings to the reading of the text.

Bias in the classics and in other texts has an impact on the perceptions, attitudes, and behaviour of both minority and mainstream students. (Council on Interracial Books for Children, 1980; Lee, 1985). For example, in a Kitchener–Waterloo, Ontario, high school classroom in which *The Merchant of Venice* was being studied, a Jewish student came to class one day to find swastikas painted on her desk. The teacher admonished the unknown perpetrators and called the custodian in to remove the offending graffiti. The student commented that the custodian cleaned the swastikas off her desk, "but no one cleaned them off me" (Ferri, 1986).

Daenzer (1992) argues that the assault on racial-minority students' identity is the direct consequence of bias and exclusion in curriculum content. She and other authorities (Kehoe, 1984; Moodley, 1984; Cummins, 1992; Pratt, 1984; Lee, 1985; Solomon, 1992) share the view that the reproduction of knowledge in the classroom perpetuates racist thinking among both White students and their teachers.

Racism in the curriculum manifests itself in subjects such as history, literature, social studies, geography, and science. The perspectives of novelists and poets who reflect the history and experiences of non-Western cultures are generally omitted from the Eurocentric curriculum. The history curriculum often exhibits a dominant-culture bias that expresses itself in the way history texts are written. There is an unwillingness to look beyond the study of British, American, or European history, and multicultural history is often considered as separate and distinct from Canadian history. History in its textbook form is frequently nothing more than a representation of tradition (McGee, 1993); and tradition, as Raymond Williams (1977:115) suggests, is "always selected and thus presents us with a system of values disguised as a natural and transcendent process of cultural development." In other words, history is a reflection of the perceptions of the one who tells the story, describes the events, and interprets them.

A comprehensive analysis of school textbooks shows how Eurocentrism and racism operate through curriculum (Klein, 1985). In the curriculum, the history of people of colour begins when Whites "discover" them. Human civilization is portrayed as an evolutionary process in which Euro-American culture—the Western legal system, democratic forms of government, and a capitalist economy—is considered the best in the world. This perspective is also manifested in the learning resources, which often fail to reflect alternative viewpoints.

Science classes also provide opportunities for fostering racism in the classroom. Bias is reflected in the omission of people of colour from most scientific texts; their images and contributions to scientific development are absent. A more specific example of bias in science curriculum is the study of theories of race that legitimize and provide justification of the superiority of the White "race." Teachers commonly resist critically discussing with their students the recent resurgence of theories of biological or scientific racism, which seek to link race with intelligence and other traits.

The importance of Eurocentric curriculum in reproducing racism in education is stressed in the following observation:

> Until curriculum is studied less as a receptacle of texts than as activity, that is to say, as a vehicle of acquiring and exercising power, descriptions of curricular content in terms of their expression of universal values on the one hand, or pluralistic, secular identifier on the other, are insufficient signifiers of their historical realities. (Viswanathan, 1989:167)

Hidden Curriculum

One of the most difficult aspects of racism to isolate and identify is the hidden curriculum, which embraces the social and cultural environment of the school and is formed by the personal, professional, and organizational assumptions, values, and norms of those working in it. It is often through the school's hidden curriculum that the **hegemony** of racism is experienced and through which Black pupils become marginalized (Brandt, 1986). The hidden curriculum is the tacit teaching of social and economic norms and expectations to students in schools (Kehoe, 1984).

It is manifested, for example, in school calendars (in their choice of which holidays are celebrated and which are ignored), concerts and festivals, bulletin-board and hallway displays, school libraries, school clubs, and the kinds of behaviours tolerated (e.g., racial harassment).

Educators and researchers have developed a clearer picture of how various areas of the hidden curriculum affect the culture of the school and its negative impact on racial-minority students. Solomon (1992) and Yon (1991) provide many examples of how the hidden curriculum contributes to racism and the marginalization of specific groups in the school system. They draw attention to the forging of racial-minority student subcultures that can be understood as defiance and opposition to the closed, dominant, and hierarchial culture of the school. Cummins observes:

> Just as particular forms of identity were being negotiated when Aboriginal children were beaten or starved for speaking their mother tongue, so today the curriculum and patterns of educator–student interaction in school either constrict or expand students' possibilities for identity formation. (1992:3)

The formation of cliques, the use of specific language codes (speaking in dialect), and the setting of social boundaries between themselves and the White students and teachers are part of a perceived need on the part of Black Caribbean students to assert their identity. This subculture is interpreted as a response to the problem of self-esteem in an environment that does not support Black students' needs (Solomon, 1992; Yon, 1991).

PEDAGOGY

The most powerful examples of the hidden curriculum are the attitudes and practices of educators in the classroom. Several researchers have suggested that the learning difficulties of minority students are often pedagogically induced, that is, influenced by how the teaching is done (Cummins, 1988). Kehoe (1984) sums up the problem succinctly: "It is a fact rarely accepted that there is less wrong with the learner than with the process and institutions by which the learner is taught" (64).

The studies demonstrate the complex relationship between teachers' expectations and their conformity to these expectations in terms of their students' academic performance. A teacher who holds stereotypical opinions about a particular racial group is likely to translate these biases into differential teaching techniques and classroom treatment (Shapson, 1990; Verma and Bagley, 1979; Brandt, 1986; Mullard, 1984). Kehoe (1984) views teacher expectations as a significant source of inequality in the classroom. He argues that teachers may make subjective evaluations of the capabilities of their students for the purpose of grouping and that those assessments may be unrelated to academic potential. He cites a study showing that children who spoke in a dialect were about three times as likely not to respond to questions given in standard English as were children in the higher group who spoke standard English. Moreover, membership in these groupings remained unchanged from grade to grade.

To introduce a more egalitarian approach to the education of all children, regardless of ethnic or racial origin, teachers should raise their expectations of Blacks in intellectual spheres and lower them in relation to their sports ability. Teachers should also be aware of the impact of school sport on the consciousness of Black students (Solomon, 1992). It is ironic that the one area of school life that Blacks dominate is marginal. Solomon (1992) suggests that this is an area in which parents must work with teachers to ensure that the latter relinquish the ideology that guides the differential development of Black students for "the dubious world of sports and White students for predictable futures in attainable jobs"(125).

Several studies have suggested that learning difficulties are often pedagogically induced, in that children designated "at risk" frequently receive instruction that confines them to a passive role and induces "learned helplessness" (Cummins 1984). Cummins (1988) adds that instruction that empowers students will encourage them "to become active generators of their own knowledge" (143).

Following a similar perspective, Brandt (1986) suggests that certain pedagogic styles, such as reliance on didactic teaching, are inappropriate to **anti-racist education**. Pedagogic practice must be examined to consider the extent to which it promotes collaborative learning, which involves not only teachers and pupils but the wider community's perspectives and "knowledge," especially that of marginalized groups. The benefits of co-operative, collaborative, group-centred learning as an effective teaching strategy that is consistent with anti-racism goals is supported by a number of educators (Brandt, 1986).

The dynamic of race creates enormous resistance in classrooms that are controlled by teachers who continue to be deeply committed to what Solomon describes as the dominant teaching paradigm of cultural assimilation. He adds that "defensive barricades" are being established to resist any form of anti-racist education (1992:127).

Teacher attitudes toward racial minorities are expressed in statements about "colour blindness," made by teachers who proudly declare that they never see a child's colour and that they treat all children in the same way (Brandt, 1986; Lee, 1985). The refusal of educators to recognize that racism is part of the "baggage" that racial-minority children carry with them and the refusal to recognize racism as part of the daily policies, programs, and practices of the educational system are "part and parcel of a wilful blindness which spurs us on to execute some veritable gymnastic feat of the mind, all aimed at avoiding the problem" (Thornhill, 1984:3).

This denial of the salience of race in the lives and on the life chances of children of colour results from the efforts required by teachers to suppress the negative associations and stereotypical images that pervade the culture of the dominant society. These efforts, although unconscious, affect classroom practices. At the same time, equal opportunity is assumed to exist; thus the lack of success on the part of Black students, for example, is often attributed to dysfunctional cultures, communities, or families (Sleeter, 1993). The position of power and privilege that White educators enjoy in the classroom is rarely acknowledged or understood. Their own racial and cultural identities are generally invisible, as is their resistance challenging and deconstructing racism in the educational system.

The silence that generally pervades the classroom on the subject of racism echoes loudly in the attitudes of students, who daily struggle to affirm their identities in an institutionalized culture that denies their feelings, stories, and experiences. McGee (1993) argues that educators must begin to take responsibility for the effects of their pedagogical and curricular decisions.

ASSESSMENT, PLACEMENT, AND STREAMING

One of the largest barriers to educational equity is the system of assessment and placement. There is a significant body of data indicating that psychological assessment and placement procedures are riddled with racial, cultural, and linguistic biases (Cummins, 1988; Samuda and Kong, 1986).

The consequence of these practices is the streaming of immigrant and racial-minority students. In elementary schools, special-education classes are filled with immigrant and children of colour, who often repeat grades. At the secondary level, the streaming of students consists of separating high school students into three streams: technical and vocational programs, general-level programs, and university-entrance programs. Streaming results in the placement of significant numbers of Black Caribbean students in the lower-level programs.

Critics of streaming suggest that early adolescence is too early an age at which to make such an important educational decision. Studies in North America, the United Kingdom, and Australia show that disproportionate numbers of Black, Aboriginal, and poor students are directed away from programs that lead to higher education. Parents have rebelled against this sorting mechanism, which has the potential to put their children at the bottom of the socioeconomic hierarchy (Cummins, 1992; Tator and Henry, 1991; Samuda and Kong, 1986; *Equality Now*, 1984; Kehoe, 1984; Mendoza 1987). A study done by Economic Council of Canada concluded that 70 percent of high school students who do not go to university are being short-changed by current school practices. It called for more relevant programs for students (Lewington, 1992).

At the centre of the streaming controversy is a deep distrust of assessment procedures that allocate students to different-level programs. This general distrust has led to the parents' reluctance and sometimes refusal to allow formal assessments that may uncover any disability their children may have. They have argued that, historically, giving school authorities permission to assess and place students in certain academic or non-academic streams is tantamount to committing their children to "dead end," low-track school curricula. For example, the overrepresentation of Black students in vocational programs at the secondary level in Metropolitan Toronto's boards of education can be considered a function of the institutionalized racism of streaming (Wright and Tsuji, 1984).

A study of secondary students in the City of Toronto in 1987 concluded that Black Caribbean students born outside of Canada were more likely to be placed in basic-level programs. Even after the socioeconomic status of their parents was taken into account, they had lower marks in English and mathematics and had achieved fewer credits by the age of 15 (Cheng et al., 1987).

Samuda et al. (1980) surveyed the assessment methods used for minority and immigrant children in many Ontario schools and found that the traditional classification was based on the presumption of internal pathology or deficits. In addition, it is now generally accepted that "objective" tests are not as "culture free" or "culture fair" as test manufacturers would have one believe. Test materials are developed to assess children of the mainstream culture and do not accurately reflect the learning potential and achievement of students from minority cultures.

In a study of 400 assessments of students enrolled in English as a second language programs in a western Canadian city, Cummins (1992) found that the psychologists lacked the knowledge to assess the children's academic potential and that the tests were frequently culturally biased. The psychologists were oriented to locate the cause of an academic problem in the minority child, which prevented a critical scrutiny of a variety of other possible contributors to the child's difficulty. The psychologists' training resulted in a "tunnel vision" that did not consider the experiential realities of the children.

Cummins believes that racially biased assessments emanate from psychologists who frequently lack the knowledge base required to assess the student's academic potential. The assessments' Eurocentric orientation and lack of sensitivity to the children's cultural backgrounds and linguistic skills provided results that were significantly different from those of the children upon whom the test was normed. Cummins argues that institutionalized racism is apparent both in the lack of awareness of the educational psychologists and in the failure of the institutions that trained these psychologists to make them aware of the knowledge gaps and their consequences.

Even educators who are genuinely committed to anti-racist and intercultural education may lack important information, which leads them to make poor decisions regarding minority students. For example, a teacher may hold the view that using two languages in the home confuses bilingual children and consequently may advise parents to speak only English.

Cummins' (1988, 1992) research suggests that power and status relations between minority and majority groups exert a major influence on school performance. Minority students are disempowered educationally in very much the same way as their communities are disempowered by interactions with societal institutions. Minority students are "empowered" or "disabled" as a direct result of their interactions with educators in schools.

The streaming of Black students into low-level academic programs and the large numbers of Black students placed in vocational programs have been issues of debate for more than a decade. In consultations with the Stephen Lewis Task Force (1992) and the Four-Level Study (1992), many Black community leaders argued that despite tense relations with the police, many more young Blacks are injured in the classroom than on the streets. High school teacher Lennox Farrell suggested that "this is the only community where our youth has a lower level of education than their parents" (O'Malley, 1992:A19).

The Toronto Board of Education undertook two major studies of the progress of Black students compared with that of Whites and Asians in high school. They found a dramatically higher percentage of Blacks in basic school programs, which emphasize vocational rather than academic training. One out of every 33 Asian students was enrolled in a basic program while the number for Whites was one in ten. For Blacks, it was one in five (O'Malley, 1992:A19).

At a conference on facilitating the academic success of Black children in Canada in the spring of 1992, educators considered supportive alternative models for incorporating Black education into schools. Their concern was expressed in the repeated observation of Black educators that "Black students are not failing school; the school system is failing" (Walker, 1991).

SCHOOL–COMMUNITY RELATIONS

The unequal relationship between educational institutions, parents, and the community is another manifestation of systemic racism. The notion that parents' involvement and responsibilities cease once the child has entered the school gate is a form of disempowerment that continues to be a common feature of school life in Canada. Many racial-minority parents perceive schools as requiring no input and tolerating no interference from outside. Cummins (1988) argues that minority students are empowered in the school context to the extent that parents and communities are themselves empowered through their interactions with the school: "When educators involve minority parents as partners in their children's education, parents appear to develop a sense of efficacy that communicates itself to children with positive academic consequences" (141).

A number of other factors hinder the relationship between the school and the Black community. For example, parents express dissatisfaction with the school's unilateral handling of discipline and curriculum matters. They describe communication with the school as one-way and non-transactional and initiated only when the school is reporting disciplinary problems. In the area of program placement, parents appear to be unaware of and uninvolved in critical decisions affecting their children's educational welfare (Solomon, 1992).

Rather than practising a collaborative approach, school authorities tend to favour a more exclusionary approach to parent and community participation in the school. Many educators (and other professionals) seem to believe that a collaborative relationship with parents will reduce their independence and that their professional competence is being challenged.

Similarly, it has been suggested that racial minorities do not have the opportunity to contribute in a meaningful way to policy planning and implementation. Often their involvement is limited to superficial encounters with the system, in which their suggestions are solicited but then disregarded: "We carry on, business as usual, speculating, diagnosing, examining, studying, implementing and remedying, without once ever consulting the victims" (Thornhill, in Samuda and Kong, 1986:289).

What is required are more visible partnerships with a greater sharing of power. White teachers must recognize that they cannot make crucial educational decisions or carry out initiatives alone; they have a responsibility to enlist the guidance of parents and community members who are knowledgable and competent to provide this help (Buchignani, 1984).

RACIAL INCIDENTS AND HARASSMENT

Racial harassment is one of the most painful manifestations of racism. It is, as well, a common, everyday experience for racial-minority children in and outside of the school. In Canada, there is no accurate assessment of the frequency, nature, or distribution of racial harassment, nor is there any documented analysis of either perpetrators or victims. However, a body of impressionistic evidence is provided by students, parents, minority communities, and in some cases, boards of education reports. Some educators believe that the number of racial incidents in Canada's schools has steadily increased in recent years. Teachers and principals are filing reports about racially motivated occurrences with greater frequency than ever before (Kohane, 1992).

Racial harassment in educational institutions includes racial slurs, ethnic and racial jokes, and racist graffiti. It is expressed in racial conflict and tension between groups and by threats and physical assaults on minority students and teachers. It has become so serious that in Edmonton the police chief stated that his department was contacting various minority groups to defuse potentially violent situations in the city's public schools. In one instance, 40 people arrived at a high school armed with crowbars and baseball bats to avenge an alleged attack on an East Indian student (Oake, 1991).

One of the barriers to dealing with these kinds of incidents is institutional resistance, a general unwillingness to acknowledge and report racial conflict, harassment, or violence. McCaskell (1993) reported that teachers were reluctant to report racist incidents because they didn't want to be seen as lacking control over their classes; department heads did not report it because it "looked bad" for them; principals were reluctant to report it because it reflected negatively on their school; and superintendents did not report it because they were supposed to provide leadership. He concludes that racial incidents and hate activity, although known at an informal level, do not become institutional knowledge, despite a requirement by boards to report such incidents.

The result of this individual and institutional denial is that a range of inappropriate responses have been adopted by boards of education. First, the most common response has been to ignore or redefine the "racial" dimension of these incidents—"There's no problem here." Second, informal policies have emerged as ad hoc responses to individual incidents of harassment. There appear to be significant problems in implementing these policies. Finally, a "multicultural approach" uses the curriculum to emphasize tolerance and respect for other cultures and racial groups.

Hatcher and Troyna (1993) lack confidence in most of these approaches arguing that there is no empirical evidence of their effectiveness. In their discussion of racial harassment and conflict in schools, they provide a multidimensional framework for analyzing a racial incident. They conclude that a constellation of factors and influences contribute to the understanding of any racial confrontation, including structural racism and differential power relations between groups; ideological beliefs and attitudes; cultural values and understandings; institutional values, procedures, and practices; children's subcultures; the specific experiences of the individuals; the context and history of the incident; and the details and nature of the incident (197).

RESPONSES TO RACISM

For most of Canada's history, including the first seven decades of this century, the issue of racism was totally absent from the agendas of educational institutions and totally invisible to White educators. Assimilation—the complete absorption of different ethnic and racial groups into the majority culture—was considered the only appropriate model for educational institutions as well as the broader society.

Although the educational system had no formal policy on monoculturalism, this pervasive and coercive ideology influenced the training of educators, the practice of teaching, the content and context of learning, the hiring and promotion practices of boards, and the cultural values and norms underpinning all areas of school life. Students from diverse backgrounds were expected to leave their cultural, religious, and racial identities at the front door of the school.

The assismilationist approach to education ignored the fact that large numbers of children experienced racial bias and discrimination both outside and inside the school. The monocultural approach to education operated unchallenged until the mid 1970s and continues to influence education today in many Canadian educational institutions (Tator and Henry, 1991; Thomas, 1984; Shapson, 1990; Cummins, 1986; Fleras and Elliot, 1992).

In 1971, largely in response to demographic, social and political pressures, the federal policy of multiculturalism was declared. The government's commitment to preserve and promote Canada's cultural diversity and to overcome barriers to full participation was a catalyst for school systems to begin examining their policies and practices.

MULTICULTURAL EDUCATION

Multiculturalism, as government policy and later as legislation, provided the moral and empirical foundation on which to move away from the monocultural, assimilationist orientation. Many school boards gradually developed policies, programs, and practices intended to create a learning environment that respected the cultures of all students. Initiatives were introduced that focussed on the histories, traditions, and lifestyles of diverse cultures. Cultural pluralism, or multicultural education in its most effective expression, acknowledged the reality of diversity in Canadian society and aimed to produce students who were more tolerant, respectful, and understanding of cultural differences. The major thrust of the multicultural approach was attitudinal change.

An empirical study of multicultural ideologies and programs in six countries in the 1970s concluded that three key assumptions underpinned multicultural education:

- learning about one's culture and ethnic roots will improve one's educational achievement;
- learning about one's culture and its traditions will promote equality of opportunity; and
- learning about other cultures will reduce children's (and adults') prejudice and discrimination toward those from different cultural and ethnic backgrounds. (Bullivant, 1981:236)

However, after almost two decades of multicultural education in Canada, the limitations of this approach have become increasingly apparent. The policies and programs that were developed relied on untested assumptions about culture and its transmission (Kehoe, 1979).

Multicultural education in many educational jurisdictions tended to focus on a "museum" and "monolithic" approach to the study of complex and constantly evolving cultures. Educators taught students about the material and exotic dimensions of culture, such as food, festivals, and folktales, rather than the values and belief systems that underlie cultural diversity. Important factors shaping cultural identity, such as racial, linguistic, religious, regional, socioeconomic, and gender differences, were often ignored (Moodley, 1984). Moreover, the teachers often had very little knowledge or understanding of other cultures, which inadvertently led both teachers and students to trivialize and stereotype different ethnic and racial groups.

Perhaps the most serious weakness of multicultural education was its failure to acknowledge that racism was endemic in Canadian society. While schools attempted to "respond to special needs," to affirm ethnic minority children's background culture and language, to celebrate festivals, and to teach "mother" (heritage) languages, "multicultural" history, and non-Western music, the real problem of racial inequality was ignored. In a growing number of boards of education in the 1980s, many parents and representatives of diverse racial and ethnic groups urged trustees to undertake radical changes to alter an educational system that they believed was disadvantaging their children. They maintained that the fundamental issues were not so much cultural as racial; not lifestyles but life chances; not heritage but competence; not diversity but disparity; not prejudice but discrimination. As one parent expressed it in the foreword to the Toronto Board of Education's *Policy on Race Relations* (1979): "The issues facing the colour of my skin are more pressing than those facing my culture."

The huge body of literature documenting the limitations of multicultural education in Great Britain and the United States (Mullard, 1984; Brandt, 1986; Troyna, 1987) supported the concerns of parents and advocacy groups in Canada. A growing consensus developed that educational policies centred on promoting cultural diversity did little to address racial inequities and were an inadequate vehicle for challenging the racism inherent in the school system.

The basis of multicultural education was a problem paradigm, which in itself was racist. The underlying assumption was that racial- and cultural-minority children in the educational system suffer because they are "socially disadvantaged." According to this perspective, many minority children seem to suffer from a negative self-concept and low esteem, resulting in defective perceptual, cognitive, and linguistic skills that were often exacerbated by the negative, non-supportive values of their social and family background (Kowalczewski, 1982). The duty of the schools (especially those with high concentrations of minority students) therefore was to provide a curriculum relevant to the needs of such disadvantaged groups, in order to enhance their self-image and to promote racial harmony and mutual tolerance.

Both monocultural and multicultural education ignored the role of educational institutions in the generation and reproduction of racism (Cummins, 1992; Moodley, 1984; Thomas, 1984; Wright and Tsuji, 1984). These approaches ignored the reality of racism as a powerful and pervasive force that shaped all of Canada's institutions. Thus, the racial conflicts in the wider society were mirrored in the educational system (Solomon, 1992).

ANTI-RACISM EDUCATION

Anti-racism education as both a theoretical and practical approach to institutional and systemic racism was formulated in both the United States and Great Britain. It first appeared in the Canadian educational context in the late 1980s and is still evolving. The shift to this model was largely the result of the persistence of minority communities, especially Black parents, in drawing attention to the way racism limited the academic progress and circumscribed the life chances of their children.

The central thrust of anti-racism education, is to change institutional and organizational policies and practices that have a discriminatory impact and to change individual attitudes and behaviours that reinforce racial bias and inequality. It has motivated some boards of education to develop new policies and has acted as a catalyst for the gradual introduction of various initiatives, including the training of educators in anti-racism; reviews of personnel practices; an analysis of assessment and placement procedures; the introduction of employment equity strategies; a review of curriculum materials to identify for racial bias, and the development of anti-racism curriculum resources and strategies.

Largely in response to the Stephen Lewis report (1992) and the demands of racial-minority communities for greater racial equity, Ontario introduced two new measures. First, a legislative act required all boards of education in Ontario to develop and implement anti-racism policies in their schools. However, no additional funds would be allocated to the school boards to develop and implement these policies (Lewington, 1993). One positive feature of the new measures were proposed changes in the teacher-selection process at university faculties of education. The faculties were required to develop new admission criteria that would increase the representation of minority groups. These criteria included a recognition of the experience acquired by teachers trained outside of Canada.

The second initiative involved a destreaming process, in which grade 9 students would no longer be separated into academic and vocational streams. The streaming would be delayed until grade 10.

However, as the various task forces and studies cited in this chapter demonstrate, anti-racism has not transformed the educational system, nor has it resulted in the dismantling of racist practices. The concluding chapter of this book will identify some of the critical obstacles to anti-racist education.

BLACK-FOCUSSED SCHOOLS

The failure of the mainstream school system to provide equitable education to Black students has led to the development of another alternative model of education: "Black-focussed" schools. Advocates of Black-focussed schools argue that the current educational structure inhibits the maximum social and intellectual development of many Black students; therefore, a need exists for a more radical approach to racism. In Metropolitan Toronto, government officials and members of the Black community recommended that a Black junior high school be established in each of the area's six municipalities. The proposed separate Black schools would be administered and have a curriculum designed and implemented by skilled Black educators.

SUMMARY

This chapter identified some complex and far-reaching consequences of racism in the educational system. The findings of task forces, surveys, and studies, and the testimonies of students and parents from all parts of Canada, document the impact of racial bias and racist practices on Aboriginal and racial-minority students. The negative educational experience of Black students was highlighted as a powerful example of the failure of educational institutions to dismantle pervasive structural racial inequalities.

Racist ideology in education is reflected in the attitudes, beliefs, assumptions, and interactions between White Anglo-Canadian educators and minority students. It is also demonstrated in the assertion made by many mainstream educators that they are "colour blind" and therefore cannot be racist. Such educators fail to understand their own individual and collective identities as well as the social, cultural, and racial identities of their students.

The manifestations of racism were illustrated by examining the components of the educational system. This chapter showed how racism is woven into the formal curriculum and influences the ways in which knowledge is structured, valued, and transmitted. Examples of bias in curriculum content were provided to show how teaching materials and subject matter can minimize the contributions of racial minorities.

Also noted was the importance of the hidden curriculum in creating a negative and hostile physical and social environment for students of colour. Racism in the schools is reflected in the ethnocentric attitudes, assumptions, and practices of White teachers and other educators who fail to acknowledge their own racial biases. The evidence of racism in educational institutions is demonstrated by the failure of boards and schools to develop an inclusive and equitable relationship with racial-minority parents and communities.

The issue of biased assessment and placement procedures has been high on the agenda of anti-racism advocates. These procedures are some of the most powerful forms of differential treatment in the educational system and affect the educational achievement of racial-minority groups, especially Black students.

The chapter concluded with a description of the institutional responses to racism. It considered assimilationism, examined the multicultural model and its ineffectiveness in addressing racism, and then investigated the anti-racist orientation to education. The concept of separate schools for Black students was put forth as a recent alternative model.

REFERENCES

Aboud, F., and S. Skerry. (1984). "The Development of Ethnic Attitudes." *Journal of Cross-Cultural Psychology* 15:3–34.

Black Community Task Force on Education. (1978). *Final Report on the Aspirations and Expectations of Quebec's Black Community in Respect to Education, Montreal*. Report Submitted to the Superior Council of Education's Committee on Interconfessional and Intercultural Affairs. Montreal.

Brandt, G. (1986). *The Realization of Anti-Racist Education*. London, Falmer Press.

Buchignani, N. (1984). "Educational Strategies to Increase Racial Tolerance." *Currents: Readings in Race Relations* (Toronto) 2(3):13–20.

Bullivant, T. (1981). *The Pluralist Dilemma in Education: Six Case Studies*. Sydney, Australia: George Allen and Unwin.

(1993). "Canim Lake Band Educates Royal Commission." *Catholic New Times* 17(7)(April 4):9.

Cheng, M.G., M.Y. Tsuji, and S Ziegler. (1987). *The Every Student Survey*. Toronto: Research Section, Toronto Board of Education.

Cheung, M. (1987). *Visible Minority Representation in the Toronto Board of Education*. Research Paper 173. Toronto: Information Services Division of the Toronto Board of Education.

Chiang, L. (1986). "Is Our Understanding of the Hidden Curriculum Hidden From Us?" Paper presented at the 1986 Conference of the Philosophy of Education Society of Australia. Armidale, Australia.

Council on Interracial Books for Children. (1980). *Guidelines for Selecting Bias-free Textbooks for Children*. New York: Council on Interracial Books.

Cummins, J. (1984). *Bilingualism and Special Education: Issues in Assessment and Pedagogy*. Clevedon, England: Multilingual Matters, and San Diego: College Hill Press.

_____. (1986). "Empowering Minority Students: A Framework for Intervention." *Harvard Educational Review*, 56(1).

_____. (1988). "From Multicultural to Anti-Racist Education." In T. Suutnabb-Kangas and J Cummins (eds.), *Minority Education: From Shame to Struggle*. Clevedon, U.K.: Multilingual Matters.

_____. (1992). "Lies We Live By: National Identity and Social Justice." *International Journal of the Sociology of Language*.

Daenzer, P. (1992). "Black Youth and Elementary and Secondary Education in Metropolitan Toronto." In *Towards a New Beginning:Report of the Four-Level Government\African Canadian Community Working Group*. Toronto.

D'Oyley, V., and S. Shapson. (1990). *Innovative Multicultural Teaching*. Toronto: Kagan and Woo.

Equality Now. (1984). Report of the Special Committee on Visible Minorities in Canadian Society. Ottawa: the Queen's Printer for Canada.

Essed, P. (1990). *Everyday Racism: Reports from Women of Two Cultures*. Claremont, CA: Hunter House.

Ferri, J. (1986). "Are Teachers to Blame if Play Arouses Racism?" *The Toronto Star* (July 16).

Fleras, A., and J. Elliott. (1992). *Multiculturalism in Canada*. Scarborough: Nelson Canada.

Haig-Brown, C. (1988). *Resistance and Renewal: Surviving the Indian Residential School*. Vancouver: Arsenal Pulp Press.

Hall, S. (1981). "Teaching About Race." In A. James and R. Jeffocate (eds.), *The School in the Multicultural Society*. London: Harper.

Hatcher, R., and B. Troyna. (1993). "Racialization and Children." In C. McCarthy and W. Critchlow (eds.), *Race, Identity, Representation in Education*. New York and London: Routledge.

Kehoe, J. (1979). "Effective Tools for Combating Racism in the Schools." Keynote Address to the Third Annual Human Rights and Liberties Institute. Vancouver.

_____. (1984). *A Handbook for Enhancing the Multicultural Climate of the School*. Vancouver: WEDG.

Klein, G. (1985). *Readings in Racism: Bias in Children's Literature*. London and New York: Routledge & Kegan Paul.

_____. (1986). *Reading into Racism: Bias in Children's Literature and Learning Materials*. London: Routledge & Kegan Paul.

Kohane, J. (1992). "Educator Calls for Racism Education to Begin as Early as Possible." *Canadian Jewish News*. (December 10):42.

Kowalczewski, P.S. (1982). "Race and Education: Racism, Diversity and Inequality, Implications for Multicultural Education." *Oxford Review of Education* 8(2):145–161.

Ijaz, A., and H. Ijaz. (1986). "The Development of Ethnic Prejudice in Children." *Guidance and Counselling* 2(1) (September):28–39.

Lee, E. (1985). *Letters to Marcia: A Teacher's Guide to Anti-Racist Education*. Toronto: Cross-Cultural Communication Centre.

Lewington, J. (1992). "Test Abilities, Students Say." *The Globe and Mail*.

_____. (1993). "Ontario Attacks Racism in the Classroom." *The Globe and Mail* (July 16):A6.

Lewis, S. (1992). *Report on Racism Presented to the Premier of Ontario*. (June). Queen's Printer for Ontario.

Lucow, M. (1993). "Anti-racism Education Urged for B.C. Public School System." Canadian Jewish News (December 16): 17.

McCaskell, T. (1993). Presentation to the Community Forum Sponsored by the Metropolitan Toronto Council Committee to Combat Hate Group Activity.

McCarthy, C. (1993). "After the Canon: Knowledge and Ideological Representation in the Multicultural Discourse on Curriculum Reform." In C. McCarthy and W. Critchlow (eds.), *Race, Identity and Representation in Education*. New York and London: Routledge.

McGee, P. (1993). "Decolonization and the Curriculum of English." In C. McCarthy and W. Critchlow (eds.), *Race, Identity and Representation in Education*. New York and London: Routledge.

Mendoza, A. (1987). *Report on a Teachers' Survey: An Analysis of Teachers' Experiences, Observations and Opinions of Caribbean/Black Students Educational and Social Adjustment in the Metro Toronto School System*. Unpublished manuscript.

Milner, D. (1983). *Children and Race: Ten Years Later*. London: Alan Sutton.

Moodley, K. (1984). "The Ambiguities of Multicultural Education." *Currents: Readings in Race Relations*. (Toronto) 2(3):5–7.

Mullard, C. (1984). *Anti-Racist Education: The Three O's*. Cardiff: National Association for Multiracial Education.

Oake, G. (1991). "Racism Hits Edmonton Schools." *The Toronto Star* (December 12).

O'Malley, S. (1992). "Demand Quality Education, Black Parents Told." *The Globe and Mail* (August 20):A1, A19.

Pinar, W. (1993). "Notes on Understanding the Curriculum as Critical Text." In C. McCarthy and W. Critchlow (eds.), *Race, Identity and Represenation in Education*. New York and London: Routledge.

Pratt, D. (1984). "Bias in Text Books: Progress and Problems." In R.J. Samuda et al. (eds.), *Multiculturalism in Canada: Social and Educational Perspectives*. Toronto, Allyn & Bacon.

Ramcharan, S. (1987). "The Role of Education in Multi-racial Canada." In O. Dwiveldi, R. D'Costa, L. Stanford, and E. Tepper, (eds.), *Canada 2000: Race Relations and Public Policy*. Guelph: University of Guelph.

Report of the Nova Scotia Advisory Group Presented to the Minister Responsible for the Administration of the Human Rights Act, Government of Nova Scotia: (1991).

Richmond, A.H. and A. Mendoza. (1987). "Education and Qualifications of Caribbean Immigrants and their Children in Britain and Canada." In R.W. Palmer (ed.), *In Search of a Better Life: Perspective on Migration from the Caribbean*. New York: Praeger.

_____. (1990). "Education and Qualifications of Caribbean Migrants in Metropolitan Toronto." In R.W. Palmer (ed.), *In Search of a Better Life: Perspective on Migration from the Caribbean*. New York: Praeger.

Rizvi, F. (1993). "Children and the Grammar of Popular Racism." In C. McCarthy and W. Critchlow (eds.), *Race, Identity and Representation in Education*. New York and London: Routledge.

Samuda, R.J., D. Crawford, C. Philip, and W. Tinglen. (1980). *Testing, Assessment, and Counselling of Minority Students: Current Methods in Ontario*. Toronto: Ontario Ministry of Education.

_____, and S.L. Kong. (l986). *Multicultural Education: Programmes and Methods*. Kingston, ON, and Toronto: Intercultural Social Sciences Publications.

Sarick, L. (1993). "Speed of Classroom Reforms Fuels Anxiety." *The Globe and Mail* (January 6):A1.

Shapson, S. (1990). *Multicultural Education: A Research Paper to Inform Policy Development*. Burnaby, B.C.: Faculty of Education, Simon Fraser University, prepared for the BCSTA Education Committee.

Sleeter, C. (1993). "How White Teachers Construct Race." In C. McCarthy and W. Critchlow (eds.), *Race, Identity and Representation in Education*. New York and London: Routledge.

Solomon, P. (1992). *Black Resistance in High School: Forging A Separatist Culture*. Albany: State University of New York Press.

Tator, C., and F. Henry. (l991). *Multicultural Education: Translating Policy into Practice*. Ottawa: Ministry of Multiculturalism and Citizenship.

Thomas, B. (1984). "Principles of Anti-Racist Education." *Currents: Readings in Race Relations* (Toronto) 2(3).

Thornhill, E. (1984). "Fight Racism Starting with the School." *Currents: Readings in Race Relations* (Toronto) 2(3):3–7.

_____. (1986). "Guidelines for Implementing More Visible Partnerships in Schools." In R.J. Samuda and S. Kong (eds.), *Multicultural Education: Programmes and Methods*. Toronto: Intercultural Social Sciences Publications: 287–294.

Toronto Board of Education. (1979). *Policy on Race Relations*.

Toronto Board of Education. (1987). *Consultative Committee on the Education of Black Students in Toronto Schools*. Toronto: Board of Education for the City of Toronto.

Towards a New Beginning: The Report and Action Plan of the Four-Level Government/African Canadian Community Working Group. (November 1992). Toronto.

Troyna, B. (1987). "Race and Education: Two Perspectives for Change." In B. Troyna (ed.), *Racial Inequality in Education*. London: Routledge.

_____, and R. Hatcher. (1992). "Racist Incidents in Schools." In D. Gill, B. Mayor, and M. Blair (eds.), *Racism and Eduction: Structures and Strategies*. London: Sage.

_____, and J. Williams. (1986). *Racism, Education and the State: The Racialization of Education Policy*. London: Croom Helm.

Verma, G., and C. Bagley. (1979). "Measured Changes in Racial Attitudes Following the Use of 3 Different Teaching Methods." In G. Verma and C. Bosley (eds.), *Race, Education and Identity*. London: Macmillan.

Viswanathan, G. (1989). *Masks of Conquest: Literary Study and British Rule in India*. New York: Columbia University Press.

Walker, S. (1991). "Schools Don't Do Enough for Blacks, Educators Say." *The Toronto Star* (April 15).

Wilson, D. (1991). "Native Bands Demand Action on School's Abuse of Children." *The Globe and Mail* (June 19):A4.

Wright, E., and G. Tsuji. (1984). *The Grade 9 Survey*. Research Paper 174. Toronto: Information Services Division of the Toronto Board of Education.

Yon, D. (1990). *Schooling and the Politics of Identity*. MA Thesis, Graduate Programme in Social Anthropology, York University.

_____. (1991) "Schooling and the Politics of Identity: A Study of Caribbean Students in a Toronto High School." In H. Diaz et al. (eds.), *Forging Identities and Patterns of Development*. Toronto: Canadian Scholars Press.

NOTES

1. *Parliamentary Task Force Report; Equality Now* (1984); *Stephen Lewis Inquiry* (1992); *Nova Scotia Advisory Group Report* (1992); *Report of the Four-Level Government/African Canadian Community Working Group* (1992).

Chapter 8

▼ ▼ ▼ ▼ ▼ ▼ ▼ ▼ ▼ ▼ ▼ ▼

Racism in Universities

Including African and non-White scholars in one's intellectual cosmos does not necessarily mean a lowering of standards. When this university finally opens its gates and minds to non-White intellectuals, ideas and personnel, then visiting professors like me will cease to be one-year stands, interesting exotica or simple white elephants. (Lgundipe-Leslie, l991)

This chapter continues the discussion of education by examining the role of universities. Although many believe that higher institutions of learning are free of discrimination and racism, this chapter makes clear that this is not the case. It discusses inequity and racism as they affect the university. The lack of minority representation at faculty and administrative levels continues to be a problem; the teaching of a basically Eurocentric curriculum has also become an issue, and harassment and overt racism continue to plague minority students. The university, like other institutions, has denied and resisted change in the name of academic freedom and the merit principle.

Data gathered from reports and studies carried out by a number of universities in Ontario forms the basis of the discussion. This chapter differs from others in focussing almost entirely on Ontario universities. Thus, its observations do not necessarily apply to universities throughout Canada.

INTRODUCTION

The university has always been considered part and yet not part of society. The term "ivory tower" suggests that the university is removed from the realities of society and that it is above the criticism levelled at other educational institutions. As a result, it is accused of elitism. But like other institutions in society, the university has recently come under another level of attack because it is perceived to be a bastion of male White supremacy. Moreover, its curriculum is alleged to be Eurocentric and patriarchal, and its rules and regulations antiquated. The university was able to maintain its hallowed traditions for many years because it served a basically homogeneous population, few of whose members challenged the values on which it was based or the regulations governing it.

The university is based on values and traditions that have gained legitimacy over the many years of its existence. The foundation of the academic quest for truth and knowledge rests on the values of honest intellectual endeavour, stimulated by adherence to the most valid methods of inquiry; complete dependence on the principle of merit by those who engage in its primary activity of research and teaching; the creation and maintenance of standards of excellence in all of its activities; and the strict adherence to freedom of thought and expression.

Little more than a decade ago, it would have been almost inconceivable to suggest that the university contains elements of racism (or sexism and homophobia) in its structure and organization. It was considered above such common ailments. The realization that the university is like any other institution in society, reflecting the same attitudes, beliefs, rules, and regulations found in the larger society, is relatively new. When it is understood that the university is a microcosm of society, it becomes easier to accept that, despite its venerable pursuit of truth and knowledge, it too can be permeated with racist attitudes and behaviours.

The brunt of criticism directed at the university has come from the academic left wing, now labelled by the conservative right wing as following the principles of "political correctness" or becoming the "thought police." Those who ask for curriculum reviews to diminish Eurocentric biases or more representative hiring practices that would diversify the faculty, staff, and student body are often labelled "PC'ers." Conservatives also criticize the policies adopted by some Canadian universities regarding sexual and racial harassment. The magnitude of these problems has been grossly exaggerated, it is claimed, and their means of resolution waste valuable resources. Moreover, it is believed, these offences are so difficult to define that rules designed to protect "the accuser can be very unfair to the accused" (Sullivan, 1993).

It can be argued, however, that reforms are needed not to promote political correctness but to uphold the broad range of intellectual diversity that is the hallmark of any institution of higher learning. The university is not only a centre for higher learning but its constituents are, in the main, youth. Reforms can therefore play a major role in socializing students to progressive values that stress equality and equity.

THE MANIFESTATIONS OF RACISM

LACK OF REPRESENTATION

Canadian universities, especially those in Ontario, grew rapidly during the 1960s and 1970s and expanded their faculties enormously. Financial constraints increasingly affected universities' ability to hire new faculty and resulted in fewer opportunities to hire women, racial minorities, and other disadvantaged groups. Today, relatively little hiring occurs, except in a few "growth" fields, such as computer studies and management. Thus the demand for representational faculty and staff hiring has come at a time when major growth, except paradoxically in student enrolments, has become severely limited. The universities are, therefore, in a conundrum because racial-minority student enrolments are increasing while financial constraints prevent substantive hiring.

Nevertheless universities, like other institutions (especially in Ontario, where legislated employment equity will soon regulate hiring), are required to review their hiring policies and practices. Many have already done employee workforce audits, and their results with respect to minorities, women, and other disadvantaged groups are less than impressive. For example, at the University of Toronto, the country's largest university, the numbers reveal a pattern of inequity.

Visible-minority student enrolment at the University of Toronto was almost 40 percent, yet less than 10 percent of its faculty were members of racial-minority groups. Even more revealing is the fact that this 10 percent were heavily concentrated in a few fields, such as engineering and computer sciences. Disciplines such as the social sciences had very few minority faculty, and the sociology department did not have a Black faculty member.

At York University, the figures differed only slightly. Even fewer faculty members—6.4 percent from racial-minority groups, and at all academic levels,

Table 8.1

REPRESENTATION OF UNIVERSITY OF TORONTO EMPLOYEE AND STUDENT POPULATIONS BY DESIGNATED GROUP AND STAFF CATEGORY

	Men	Women	Visible Minorities	Aboriginal Peoples	Persons with Disabilities
Canada[3]	56.0%	44.0%	6.3%	2.1%	5.4%
Metropolitan Toronto[3]	53.6%	46.4%	16.4%	0.9%	4.7%
Faculty[1]	76.2%	23.8%	9.5%	0.1%	3.9%
Professional Librarians[1]	21.0%	79.0%	9.7%	0.0%	5.2%
Administrative Non-Unionized Staff[1]	32.4%	67.6%	22.4%	0.4%	4.3%
Administrative Unionized Staff[1]	59.3%	40.7%	19.7%	1.0%	8.3%
Students[2]	40.9%	59.1%	38.7%	1.7%	n/a

Sources: [1]University of Toronto Employment Equity Workforce Survey (updated to April 30, 1993), [2]Race and Ethnicity Survey of Graduate and Undergraduate Enrolment (1991), and [3]Canada Employment and Immigration Commission, Availability Data, 1988.

including graduate assistants, there were more racial-minority men than women. At other employee levels, one third of parking and security personnel were racial minorities, as were 20 percent of unionized staff, 16 percent of teaching assistants, 9 percent of part-time faculty, and 8.8 percent of professional and managerial staff. Moreover, East Asians constituted by far the largest pool of minority employees in all sectors with the exception of the "other manual" category, where Blacks were nearly three quarters of the racial-minority employees (University of Toronto Employment Equity Annual Report 1992–1993). Other university employee audits, including some in other provinces, also reveal an insufficient number of racial-minority faculty.

Universities clearly face a problem of non-representativeness at the academic and senior management levels. While many are now sensitive to the need to increase female representation on faculty and a few have implemented an affirmative action strategy to hire more women, the hiring of minorities and other target-group members has generally received less attention. (The University of Toronto, however, increased its minority hirings significantly in recent years.[1])

PROMOTION AND TENURE DECISIONS

The academic community has, over many years, devised procedures for promotion and tenure in the system. These rules generally relate to the need to establish excellence in research and, to a lesser extent, in teaching and service to the university. In some universities, excellence in teaching is now considered equal to excellence in research. The standards used to assess excellence vary from field to field, but demonstrated excellence, however it is measured, is a requirement for advancement.

What is excellence, and how can it be measured? Traditional measurements of excellence may discriminate against women and minorities. For

Table 8.2

RACIAL-MINORITY FACULTY AT SELECTED CANADIAN UNIVERSITIES (%)

University	Visible-Minority Faculty	Year
British Columbia	9.3	1990
Simon Fraser	7.0	1990
Dalhousie	7.8	1991
Manitoba	7.2	1990
Calgary	11.0	1991
York	6.4	1990
Toronto	9.9	1991

Source: (First six above) Federal Contractors Program, Compliance Review Reports for 1990 and/or 1991; University of Toronto Ethnicity Survey of Graduate and Undergraduate Enrolment.

example, the field of women's studies, only recently added to the curriculum of several universities, is not as highly regarded as other areas of specialization. Since many women scholars are in this area, their specialization, research, and publications are not regarded as highly as other fields. Minority scholars face the same barriers because they are often in fields that relate to the study of race and ethnicity.

The denigration of the fields of specialization of "minority" faculty takes many forms. For example, publishing in peer-assessed 'refereed' journals is an important criterion of academic assessment. Minority scholars may publish in smaller community-oriented or advocacy publications, which are often given less weight in promotion and tenure decisions. Similarly, many minority scholars participate in less prestigious locally organized conferences, which carry less consequence than do the larger national and international disciplinary conferences.[2]

Minority academics also have a heavier burden of student counselling, advising, and graduate-student supervision because there are too few academics to meet the demands of the growing student body. These additional commitments are rarely given the weight they deserve. Minority academics are also required to participate in more university committees and organizations because these bodies now demand the participation of "a woman" and, increasingly, of "a racial-minority." These extra service commitments are not valued in promotion and tenure decisions.[3]

Academics in these specialized fields often also play an advocacy role, and their personal involvement may be said to detract from their research and teaching. Subjective involvement and advocacy are thought to undermine the reasoned objectivity that supposedly is the hallmark of academic excellence.

One of the ways in which these barriers to advancement are being eliminated is that promotion and tenure committees have become more representative. Women members of the committees frequently bring the barriers to the attention of other members, who as a result are being made more sensitive to the extra demands made on minority faculty in a system that is not changing fast enough to meet the needs of an increasingly heterogeneous student body.

STUDENT RECRUITMENT: UNDERGRADUATE AND GRADUATE

Some universities, particularly those in or near large urban areas, have significant numbers of minority students. At the graduate level, many minority students are "visa students," who often must overcome the bias involved in assessing foreign undergraduate credentials. While there is never much doubt about credentials from the University of Edinburgh or other well-known European universities, universities in the Third World are subjected to very careful and sometimes negative scrutiny. This issue has been examined by the Ontario Task Force on Access to Professions and Trades in Ontario (1989), which investigated the "rules and practices affecting entry to professions and trades." The task force found that "large numbers of foreign-trained individuals...were rejected" at the early stages of application (82). It recommended that applicants be re-assessed through tests and other appropriate measures to determine their level of ability and prior training.

Most universities, regardless of where they are situated, should examine their policies and practices with regard to admissions criteria. Queen's University, for example, in its draft report on race relations, recommended that its recruiting be targeted at high schools that had substantial numbers of minority graduates. The universities cannot manage the issue of recruitment alone, however; the barriers that plague minority students at the primary and secondary levels of education must be addressed by the primary and secondary schools.

CURRICULUM

The area of curriculum is usually considered sacrosanct by the more conservative elements in the university environment. "'Nobody can be told what and how to teach" is an oft-repeated sentiment in this community. Yet the Eurocentric nature of much of the current university's offerings cannot be denied. The Queen's University report on race relations identified a number of critical areas:

- the existence of course names that do not reflect their content (e.g., "The History of Political Thought" should be renamed "The History of *Western* Political Thought"
- the prevalence of core courses (required of majors students) that include only Eurocentric issues
- the lack of anti-racist courses in the curriculum and the need to make these mandatory in some curricula
- the need to hire faculty who can teach courses that do not have a Eurocentric focus
- the need to introduce more interdisciplinary studies, such as Black studies and Native studies
- the need to review science curricula to make the important point that even science is not value-free
- the need to develop supplementary programs for minority students that would help them meet academic standards

Curricula and hiring strategies should be reviewed. Innovative hiring strategies, such as recruiting a specialist in Third World or Commonwealth literature for the one new appointment in an English department, instead of hiring another specialist in eighteenth-century literature, would in all likelihood increase the pool of qualified minority applicants.

At the University of Toronto, a presidential advisory committee on race relations and anti-racism initiatives was given the mandate to explore curriculum, student recruitment, hiring and promotions, and other equity-related issues (Memorandum, 1992). It called for more courses reflecting non-European traditions, the inclusion of non-Eurocentric perspectives in current courses, and a greater sensitivity in the ways in which traditional courses are taught. For example, academics who teach literature courses on Shakespeare's tragedies, Renaissance poetry, or American literature have a responsibility to analyze the texts' historical context and to discuss how these writings have become part of the literary canon. As McGee (1993) points out:

> Students should be made aware of the fact that literary texts do not transcend historical contexts (both the contexts in which they are written and the contexts in which they are read) but are the grounds of contention and debate and the site of historical contradictions. (285)

UNIVERSITY CLIMATE: RACIAL INCIDENTS AND ASSAULTS

A further manifestation of racism is the environment in which students learn. Minority students have complained that the campus is often a hostile environment. Many universities have received student complaints of racial harassment from fellow students, technical and administrative staff, and faculty. At York University, a group of Black students, claiming that they had been harassed by security guards, staged a protest at the president's door. (The university responded quickly by agreeing to hire another staff member at its Centre for Race and Ethnic Relations and to provide training for the guards.)

Students at a number of campuses have complained of harassment in the residences, cafeterias, and other public places on campus. Graffiti smeared on washroom walls and other surfaces are often racist. Racial-minority students therefore react to this hostility by forming racially and ethnically based student associations, claiming particular space in public places (such as the "Black table" in the cafeteria), and generally socializing only with each other.

THE SLOW RESPONSE TO RACISM

REASONS FOR THE SLOW RESPONSE

As recently as the 1980s, members of the Canadian university community were denying the existence of racism among them, even though it had been demonstrated in many reports and studies. It could "point to few specific accomplishments" (Meininger, 1990). For example, in 1989, the Association of Universities and Colleges of Canada surveyed the universities about their policies and practices for addressing race relations. Of 37 responding institutions, only a few had developed formal or comprehensive policy statements. The others "relied on a variety of general devices...presidential statements, collective agreements, memoranda of understanding with human rights commissions, and more recently, undertakings on employment equity" (4). Some reported special programs for targeted groups, usually Aboriginal students, and a few others indicated that newly formed committees were studying the issue.

The few universities that recognized the existence of a "racial problem" on campus and the corresponding need for a response were motivated not by institutional introspection but by the occurrence of some nagging racial crisis. At York University, for example, a committee on race and ethnic relations was finally established only because a graduate student in residence was consistently subjected to racial harassment. The student was first told by the manager of the residence that she was too sensitive. When she complained to her department, little was done, other than to give her a hearing. Concluding that the university was not prepared to deal with the issue, she mobilized her fellow students of colour. Student pressure finally led to the creation of a committee to look into the complaint. This committee was split in its view of the issue, and its report—awkwardly split into a majority and a minority section—was rejected. Another committee had to be established. Its detailed report (York, 1989), including many important structural recommendations, has yet to be implemented in more than tokenistic terms.

Dalhousie University instituted a transitional-year program for disadvantaged students as well as a number of other affirmative-action admission policies in some of its academic units. It is somewhat of a leader among universities, yet it initiated a recruitment program in its law school aimed at Black and Aboriginal students only as the result of the Marshall inquiry, which had been established to inquire into the false imprisonment of Donald Marshall, Jr. Among the inquiry's findings was that there were insufficient numbers of Aboriginal lawyers in Nova Scotia.

Universities have also not participated in efforts to influence public policy. They have not made submissions to special government commissions such as *Equality Now*,[4] and they do not usually include the subject of racial minorities in their "regular briefs" to governments. As individual scholars, members of academe rarely respond to such requests. Only four academics made submissions to *Equality Now*.

Until fairly recently, then, racism was not on the public agenda in institutions of higher learning, largely because its existence was denied; and there were few if any champions of the cause. Meininger (1990) suggested a number of reasons for this lack of interest:

- Minority students are generally very concerned about their vulnerability and have usually kept experiences of racism to themselves. In addition, until recently universities did not have complaint or grievance mechanisms that dealt with racial harassment and other forms of racism.
- Few members of the faculty had any expertise in race and ethnic relations. Those who did tended to examine the issue elsewhere in society, rather than in their own back yard.
- Staff associations and unions were busy with bread-and-butter issues, rather than ideological and systemic issues.
- Academic administrators and managers respond primarily as a result of political pressure or evidence of conflict. Since pressure to create equity and equality for racial-minority students did not exist, it was not on the academic administrative agenda.

- The women's movement, which urged equity and curriculum change, had not yet made its mark.
- The general slowness of institutional change, and the *particular slowness of institutional change at universities*, also contributed to the lack of response to racial and other equity-related issues.[5]

Finally, universities have been subject to financial constraints, as have the other institutions that depend largely on public financing. It has therefore been necessary to increase the number of part-time faculty, who are hired to teach specific courses for one to three years. They are not eligible for tenure protection and are not protected by collective agreements. As a result, they do not challenge the status quo because of their feeling of powerlessness: "If people feel vulnerable, you can be sure they won't articulate beliefs that challenge the status quo" (*The Toronto Star*, July 18, l993:B1).

STRUCTURAL RESPONSES[6]

At the structural level, the university response has been inadequate. While it might be expected that an institution of higher learning, in which specialists in many important fields are employed, would develop innovative approaches to change, this has not been the case. The university has generally used the same approach as other liberal institutions: initiating conservative actions that do little to change the status quo.

Three basic approaches have been taken. First, some universities have established a centre or committee, such as York's Centre for Race and Ethnic Relations, the University of Windsor's Office of Race Relations, or the University of Toronto's Advisory Committee on Race Relations and Anti-Racist Initiatives. These units generally lack real power, are constrained by small budgets, and are essentially removed from the main decision-making of the university. They are sometimes required to deal with the grievances of students against professors, fellow students, or staff; to develop public educational procedures for the academic community; and generally to act as a resource for the academic community and to represent the university in the community at large. They have no real role to play in the important decision-making areas of the university, such as hiring, promotion, or curriculum content, and their power is therefore extremely limited.

Second, some universities have appointed special advisors to the president who are often members of racial minorities themselves. They are overworked because they continue some of their teaching activity and are overburdened by the emotional demands of the job. Although constantly faced with the pain of others in the university community, they find themselves powerless to effect real change in the system. They are in high-burnout, tokenistic positions. In one case, an advisor resigned after less than two years, declaring himself totally frustrated. In another, the racial-minority appointee agreed to stay on only after being offered perks such as more sabbatical time.[7] Third, and most recently, some universities have struck special committees whose mandate is to identify barriers to racial-minority members of the academic community and make recommendations. Examples include Queen's University, whose committee created a very comprehensive report, as did a similar group at the University of Toronto. Although some recommendations can be implemented with little effort—such as the hiring of an African studies specialist at the University of Toronto—most have little chance of implementation because of financial and other constraints.

Many universities now have explicit or implicit policies of hiring men only if it can be shown that they are demonstrably superior to a woman candidate (Gruhn, 1991). This area of employment equity has resulted in the greater hiring of women, but the measure has not been applied to racial minorities, Aboriginal peoples, or people with disabilities.

In sum, none of the models of change in universities demonstrate a real commitment to systemic, institutional change. The university has done little more than, and possibly not as much as, other institutions in Canadian society.

SUMMARY

The university, like other institutions, has resisted anti-racist change and until fairly recently has denied that racism could exist in a place of learning. Since the introduction of some moderate policies and change strategies in many Canadian universities, critics have emerged who raise issues of academic freedom of expression and adherence to academic standards of merit. Recent statements by university spokespersons (Kimura, 1993) caution universities about making changes that threaten these traditional values.

The conflict between traditional academic values and the recognition that racism runs counter to these values—the value conflict of democratic racism, in fact—has placed universities in the stressful position of having to carefully negotiate two points of view. The university, "as a site of social reproduction, social change, and counter-hegemonic social resistance," has not fulfilled its mandate (McGee, 1993:285).

Perhaps the words of an Aboriginal Canadian graduate student sum up the concerns about the university and academic freedom:

> I would question how free academe has been in the past. Aboriginal peoples, people of colour, women, lesbians, gays and bisexuals and persons with disabilities have traditionally faced affirmative-action programs and systemic barriers favouring White males. Essentially, the university community has held in place a power structure that has censored the voices of marginalized peoples since the European invasion of Turtle Island [the Aboriginal name for North America].... White men and, increasingly, White women are basking in academic freedom. What about the rest of Canada? (Simpson, 1993)

REFERENCES

Abella, R. (1984). *Equality in Employment: A Royal Commission Report*. Ottawa: Supply and Services Canada.

Access. (1989). Task Force on Access to Trades and Professions. Government of Ontario.

Employment Equity Survey. (1991). North York: Employment Equity Office, York University.

Equality Now: Report of the Parliamentary Task Force on the Participation of Visible Minorities in Canada. (1984). Ottawa: Supply and Services Canada.

Federal Compliance Program. (1990–91). *Compliance Review Reports for UBC, Simon Fraser, Dalhousie, Universities of Manitoba and Calgary.*

Gruhn, R. (1991). "Employment Inequity." Speech presented at meeting of Society for Academic Freedom and Scholarship, Toronto.

Jensen, A. (1968). *Social Class, Race and Psychological Development.* New York: Holt, Rinehart & Winston.

Kimura, D. (1993). "Universities and the Thought Police." *The Globe and Mail* (June 28).

Lgundipe-Leslie, M. (1991). "Forum," *University of Toronto Bulletin* 16 (September 9).

McGee, P. (1993). "Decolonization and the Curriculum of English." In C. McCarthy and W. Critchlow (eds.), *Race, Identity and Representation in Education.* New York: Routledge.

Meininger, T. (1990). "Visible Minorities and the Universities: Some Obstacles and Challenges on the Road to Social Justice." Unpublished paper. York University.

Memorandum. (1992). Presidential Advisory Committee on Race Relations and Anti-Racism Initiatives, University of Toronto.

Moreau, B. (1987). "Adult Education Among Black Nova Scotians." *Journal of Education* (May).

Report of the President's Committee on Race and Ethnic Relations. (1989). North York: Centre for Race and Ethnic Relations, York University.

Simpson, L. (1993). "When Racism Gets Swept Under the Mat of Freedom." *The Globe and Mail* (July 16).

Sullivan, P. (1993). *University of Toronto Bulletin* 9(November 22).

Sweet, L. *The Toronto Star.* (1993). "Academic Angst: the Professional Privilege of Tenure: A Job For Life." (July 18):B1.

The Toronto Star. (1994). "Behaviour Code Called Threat to Free Speech." (February 7):A10.

NOTES

1. Impressionistic evidence suggests, however, that one or two ethno-racial groups such as South and East Asians are disproportionately represented among recently hired faculty in Canadian universities. They are, in the main, hired in mathematics, computer sciences, and engineering. This leads to the anomalous situation in which several Asian professors teach math or computer sciences, but social science departments such as sociology and psychology do not have even one Black professor.

2. For example, Frances Henry often attends Caribbean Studies Association meetings. Each time she applies for travel funds, she must present detailed information on the size and other features of the association. Far less information is required for an applicant planning to attend American Anthropological Association in the United States.

3. Support for these assertions comes from interviews conducted among minority faculty while serving on university committees that deal with equity issues. See, for example, the "Summary Report, Committee on Race and Ethnic Relations, York University," (May 1986). The issues of hiring, promotion and tenure decisions, curriculum reviews, and related concerns as they pertain to racial minorities and other employment equity groups were clearly articulated by participants.

4. *Equality in Employment* (1984) is the report of the Royal Commission (headed by Judge Rosalie Abella) established by the federal government to inquire into the employment opportunities for visible minorities, women, persons with disabilities, and Aboriginal peoples.

5. The most recent example of this is the Ontario Council of Universities' recommendation that the "zero tolerance" policy against sexual and racial harassment and discrimination announced by the government of Ontario be rejected because it contravenes academic freedom and freedom of expression (*The Toronto Star,* February 7, 1994).

6. Many of the following observations result from experience on committees created to deal with equity and change. Many discussions have been held with colleagues at various universities to ascertain the range of activities relevant to instituting anti-racist change. Employment-equity directors and co-ordinators at a number of universities were also consulted. In addition, interviews were held with members of the Council of Ontario Universities and the Canadian Association of University Teachers.

7. Personal communication.

Chapter 9

▼▼▼▼▼▼▼▼▼▼▼▼

Racism in Arts and Culture

> The core of racism in the arts remains constant: the refusal to treat as valid
> cultural experience, knowledge or expertise of an artist of colour—wedded
> to the belief that Eurocentric values are better. (Nourbese Philip,
> 1992:225)

This chapter explores the nature of cultural racism as ideology and practice. Cultural racism provides the context for racist attitudes, beliefs, assumptions, values, and norms. The ways in which this form of racism is expressed in both the production and transmission of culture are examined. The practice of cultural appropriation—the use of another culture's images or experiences by artists from the dominant culture—is then analyzed as an example of racist ideology and practice.

A case study of the Royal Ontario Museum's exhibit, "Into the Heart of Africa," highlights the impact of cultural racism in the context of issues such as cultural appropriation, Eurocentrism, and power relations. A second case study, of the musical *Show Boat*, focusses on representation, stereotyping, marginalization, and censorship. The two case studies and examples demonstrate the power of the dominant culture to create, reproduce, and transmit certain cultural forms while marginalizing the images, voices, and writings of people of colour.

Eurocentric aesthetic values and standards continue to shape all aspects of culture. The chapter identifies barriers to the access, participation, and representation of people of colour in the arts and cultural institutions by reviewing some policies and practices of funding agencies, such as art councils and other cultural organizations.

INTRODUCTION

Culture and cultural expression are the mirror in which racism is both reflected and reproduced. The racism in various aspects of the arts, such as literature, visual art, film, dance, and theatre, emanates from the racism embedded in the dominant culture's values and institutions. Cultural racism finds its expression primarily in the perceptions, attitudes, values, and norms of White males, who have controlled and shaped cultural life in Canada. A Eurocentric bias provides the lens through which the White decision-makers in Canadian cultural organizations and institutions filter their view of the world, establish priorities, assess the quality of art forms, and allocate resources.

Cultural racism is one of the most important frameworks of interpretation and meaning for racial thought in society (Essed, 1990:44). Cultural racism is so deeply ingrained in the symbol systems of a group or society that it is almost always denied. In a sense, cultural racism is the most invisible form of racism, because it is seamlessly woven into the collective belief and value systems of the dominant group.

White culture is an invisible veil that envelops Canadians (Katz, 1978:10). Cultural racism is an ideology that divides society into "in" and "out" groups— "us" and "them." Images of "otherness," conveyed in a wide diversity of art forms, shape perceptions, discourse, and identity (Hall, 1992). The cultural images in the stories, narratives, and photographs created by the media and arts "in group," become the building blocks of social reality (Lubiano, 1992). Culture is the central mechanism through which the dominant group reaffirms itself through image and representation, and it is the vehicle through which marginalized groups are excluded. In this way, arts and cultural organizations play a significant role in the production and reproduction of racism in a society (Nourbese Philip, 1993; Morrison, 1992a; Ferguson, 1990).

Until very recently, cultural forms of racism were largely ignored as an area of study, as an area of advocacy, or as a focus of **anti-racism organizational change**. However, writers, artists, musicians, and filmmakers from the Aboriginal, Black, South Asian, and other communities have begun systematically to challenge the power of mainstream cultural institutions that marginalize and silence them.

MANIFESTATIONS OF RACISM IN THE PRODUCTION OF CULTURAL ART FORMS

Canada's mainstream cultural institutions—museums and art galleries, theatres, film-production houses, publishers, ballet and opera companies, symphonies,

---

MANIFESTATIONS OF RACISM IN CULTURAL INSTITUTIONS

Lack of access to funding
Marginalization of the cultures
   of people of colour
Cultural appropriation
Eurocentric aesthetic values
Negative images and stereotyping

Invisibility of images, narrative,
   and voices of people of colour
Lack of representation on boards,
   art councils, unions, and
   professional organizations

arts councils and artists, and writers' and performers' unions and professional associations—contribute to the marginalization of people of colour.

The power and dominance of White culture is reflected in its definition
of "great works of art," "literary classics," and "world-class music." It is
reflected in decisions about who is selected to direct, produce, or perform in
artistic productions and where they will be presented; which authors are
deemed worthy of publication; which artist's works are given public exhibition space; whose music is played in concert halls; whose music gets recorded and played on mainstream radio; and whose voices and images become
part of television programming. It is reflected in the funding policies and
practices of government agencies and private foundations and in the ethno-
racial representativeness of those who work in cultural organizations in the
public and private sectors. As well, it is manifested in the power relationship
between mainstream cultural organizations, and ethno-racial communities,
and artists of colour.

The extent to which racism is intrinsic in the production of culture and
integral to the role and function of cultural and arts organizations can be
seen in the stereotypical, negative images of people of colour projected on
the screen and from the stage. The casting of actors is frequently based on
assumptions made by casting agents, producers, and directors who believe
that skin colour determines an actor's suitability for a part. The issue of representation lies at the centre of an examination of cultural racism. It raises
questions about "who has the power to define whom, and when, and how"
(McCarthy and Critchlow, 1993:xvi).

CULTURAL APPROPRIATION

At the root of cultural racism in the arts is the marginalization and oblitera-
tion of the cultures of "others," so that the dominant group's cultural images,
symbols, and norms remain intact. Conversely, culturally creative expressions developed by people of colour are appropriated and interpreted by
White visual artists, producers, musicians, and writers. This phenomenon is
called "cultural appropriation."

In recent years the controversy over cultural appropriation has spilled
over into many arenas. Curators, authors, and visual artists incorporate into
their creations images derived from cultures that are not theirs. When members of the dominant culture benefit materially from the production and dissemination of the history, traditions, and experiences of other cultural
groups, it is as if a party were being held in a house that's been in their family as far back as memory serves, and the family is not included in the celebration (Williams, 1992). Furthermore,

> the issue of appropriation has to do with access; it is rooted in the prob-
> lem of access. For 300 years, we, women, we people of colour, have had
> no access to many institutions in this country. (6)

Cultural appropriation is clearly demonstrated in the following case
study. The controversy over an exhibit of African artifacts at the Royal

Ontario Museum in Toronto provides an insight into the broader question of how museums in general have contributed to cultural racism by virtue of the ways in which artifacts are acquired and value is attributed to them, the context and content of the exhibits that display the artifacts, and the nature of the relationship between the artifacts, the institution, and the living cultures and communities for whom these artifacts have special meaning. These kinds of debates raise fundamental questions about "the very status of museums as historical, cultural theatres of memory. Whose memory? For what purposes? (Clifford, 1990:141).

CASE STUDY 9.1

INTO THE HEART OF AFRICA

"Into the Heart of Africa" was an exhibition, mounted by the Royal Ontario Museum (ROM), consisting of about 375 artifacts from central and west Africa that had been stored by the ROM for over 100 years. It opened in November 1989 and closed in August 1990. Ostensibly, the theme of the exhibit was the impact on Africa of colonialism, particularly at the height of the colonial period.

The exhibit included such items as photographs of Canadian missionaries and military stations, reproductions of newspaper articles, scales that had been used to measure gold dust for the colonizers, spears that White soldiers brought home after their battles against Africans, traditional beaded jewellery, and masks. Many of these relics were acquired by Canadian soldiers who participated in Britain's colonial campaign in late-nineteenth-century Africa. Other artifacts had been acquired by Canadian missionaries while attempting to bring "Christianity, civilization and commerce" to Africans. These artifacts, many of which had a significant financial value and all of which had enormous cultural value to those societies from whom they were taken, were eventually donated to the ROM.

The curator, Dr. Jeanne Cannizzo, a specialist in African art, suggested that the show was intended to examine both Canadian and African sensibilities. The objects in the ROM collection were an expression "not only of the world view of those who chose to make and use them, but also of those who chose to collect and exhibit them" (Cannizzo, 1991(b):151). She stressed her desire to illustrate the social history that provided the context of the exhibit and to expose the racist assumptions of Canadians involved in the colonization and Christianization of Africa. Her intent was also to show that White Canada had a somewhat less than perfect understanding of the complexity and richness of African societies.

Despite these positive intentions, the exhibit became the most controversial show in the history of the ROM. From the perspective of those who opposed the exhibit, "Into the Heart of Africa" was a demonstration of cultural racism and appropriation in which the images, stories, and voices of Africans were silenced and the real story of colonization remained misinterpreted and misunderstood.

One of many problems with the exhibit was the strong use of irony to deliver the message (Butler, 1993). For example, the exhibit relied on a liberal use of quotation marks around words and phrases such as "the unknown continent" and "barbarous" people, and the dramatization of a White missionary bringing "light" to a continent "full of Muslims, and animists and fetishists." The quotation marks were meant to inform the viewer about the racist assumptions underlying these labels.

However, what the curator and the ROM failed to recognize was that the irony of the exhibit's texts required a certain degree of shared knowledge between the curator and the observer (Butler, 1993). Many visitors did not understand these subtleties and interpreted the images and phrases such as "barbarous customs" literally. This is reflected in the comment of one visitor who thanked the ROM for the lovely show on "primitive Africa" (Crean, 1991:26).

On the other hand, many members of minority communities in Toronto, as well as visitors from Africa who clearly understood the irony, felt that the exhibit only reinforced racist stereotypes and assumptions. Some of the most controversial objects included an engraving depicting Lord Beresford thrusting his sword into a Zulu man. The engraving was accompanied by its original caption: "Lord Beresford's encounter with a Zulu." Near the engraving was a display of Zulu spears and shields. Beside it was another picture of Zulu soldiers, who were described as "savages." Still another photograph showed a missionary giving African women "a lesson in how to wash clothes." A flyer distributed by members of the Coalition for the Truth about Africa to communicate their concern about the exhibit's racist images posed the question: "Did Africans not know how to wash before the arrival of Europeans?"

An audio-visual slide show in the exhibit, entitled "In Livingstone's Footsteps," provided viewers with a simulation of a lecture that missionaries might have delivered to a congregation of worshippers in the nineteenth and early twentieth centuries, during the missionization of Africa. The lecture contains highly derogatory, culturally racist, and paternalistic language. As Crean (1991) pointed out, although a caption at the entrance to the room and an oral disclaimer by the narrator at the beginning and end of the show explained that this was a fictional re-enactment, most viewers would likely have missed this important piece of information because relatively few of them would have sat through the entire presentation.

A visitor from Uganda noted that

> the show gives an overwhelming colonial impression. If the ROM is trying to say that these are historical facts and we're ashamed of them, that message doesn't come through.

The exhibit's irony was clearly inappropriate for many Blacks. A young student said:

> I look at those spears and shields and all I can think of is how did they get them? By killing Africans, that's how. What am I supposed to feel?

A prominent member of Toronto's Black community, Charles Roach, questioned the ROM's objectives:

> I have to ask what is the ROM's objective in presenting Africa in 1990 from the perspective of the missionaries? Why show the colonials trampling through Africa imposing their lifestyle on the people? To me, it's a form of cultural genocide and I put it in the larger context of what's happening to Black people in Toronto—the police shootings and the discrimination we face." (Roach, 1990)

In glorifying acts like the slaying of the Zulus—the precursor to the apartheid and the enslavement of Africans in South Africa—Roach found the exhibit chilling.

Other members of the Coalition for the Truth about Africa commented on the likelihood of children misreading the irony of the messages. A teacher who visited the exhibit twice with classes analyzed the negative impact of the exhibit. She found the tour guides unable to explain or interpret the exhibits without sharing their racist assumptions and understandings. One guide leading a group of students explained that "the missionaries civilized the pagans of Africa" and that the Zulu were "an extremely vicious tribe" (McMelland, 1990:10). Another guide, on a subsequent visit by this teacher with a grade 5 class, explained that missionaries taught the Africans to carve wood and that a mask had been used to practise "barbaric rituals, vicious, barbaric rituals." Another guide offered her view on how crazy African girls were to put pieces of ivory through their noses.

Susan Crean identifies a related problem with this exhibit:

> By presenting the African collection through the history of its donors, by giving pride of place to the personal stories of the White Canadians who happened to bring them to Canada, Cannizzo creates a context in which that history is claimed rather than criticized and rejected, showcased even while she tut-tuts from between the lines. (1992:121)

Members of the Black community protested against not only the images contained in the exhibit but saw the same marginalization in the exclusionary process used by ROM in developing the exhibit. They criticized the museum for not consulting the community more widely.

After developing promotional materials for the exhibit, the ROM hired a consultant from the Black community to review these materials. The consultant voiced concern about both the stereotypical language and inappropriate images in the brochure. These concerns were expressed by other people who saw the brochure. At this point, educators with the Toronto Board of Education initiated discussions with the ROM because it was intended that students in this board would visit the exhibit. The board identified a number of concerns about the promotion, including stereotyping, the use of irony, and the ethnocentric perspective of many of the displays and captions (Lalla and Myers, 1990:6).

The ROM subsequently created focus groups, who also voiced concern about both the direction of the show and the inappropriate language of the brochure. The ROM agreed to redo the brochure (at a cost of $28 000). The groups were also concerned that there was no contemporary content in the exhibit. In response, an African historian was hired to develop, with the community, programs that included lectures, music and dance performances, workshops, and films, which were presented at the ROM after the exhibit was launched, in February 1990.

At a reception for selected members of the Black community to preview the *completed* exhibit, further concerns were expressed. Some guests felt that they had been invited to simply "rubber stamp" the exhibit, rather than being invited to comment. The previewers, primarily visual artists and writers, objected to words and phrases such as "dark continent" and "mysterious land" (Da Breo, 1989–90(b)).

EVENTS

"Into the Heart of Africa" opened in November 1989. Opinions and feelings among some members of the Black community ran high, and sixteen Black groups in Toronto formed the The Coalition for the Truth about Africa. The coalition began to picket in front of the ROM early in March 1990. It concentrated its efforts on Saturdays, a particularly busy day for the museum. As many as 20 to 50 demonstrators, carrying placards and distributing pamphlets, appeared early in the mornings.

Several of the demonstrators read speeches using a bullhorn to attract the crowds. They called the ROM the "Racist Ontario Museum," and while they did not demand, in the first instance, the closure of the exhibit, they urged the museum to change or clarify the offending explanatory texts. Failing that, however, they demanded that the show be closed. The ROM responded by saying that it had no plans to change the show in any way, that it was historically accurate, and that people were simply reacting to it in different ways. Its director was also quoted as saying that the museum would stand by its curator and the exhibit. Jeanne Cannizzo, in the meantime, kept a low profile and declined to speak about the controversy (Butler, 1993).

On at least two occasions, the demonstrations became violent. In one instance, a few of the demonstrators raised their voices to visitors attempting to enter the museum. Officials called the police, who tried to break up the demonstration. As a result, 35 police officers and 50 demonstrators were involved in a violent confrontation. Two demonstrators were arrested, and two police officers and several demonstrators were hurt. The ROM responded to this incident by applying for and receiving an injunction from the Supreme Court of Ontario to prevent protesters from picketing within 50 feet of the museum's entrance. The following day, more than 75 people, chanting "ROM is Racist Ontario Museum," continued the demonstrations.

As a result of the confrontations, educators from the Toronto Board of Education concluded that "Into the Heart of Africa" had no direct educational value for elementary students, and if secondary students viewed the exhibit, they were to be given extensive preparation (Lalla and Myers, 1990:4).

ANALYSIS

A controversial museum exhibition became the focus for a major ideological and physical confrontation between the Black community of Toronto and one of its leading cultural and educational institutions.

Although the museum took steps to involve a few members of the Black community, in doing so it also apparently made several significant errors. First, the community involvement occurred after the exhibition had been fully mounted and after brochures and flyers describing the exhibition had already been printed. Second, although ROM invited representatives of the Black artistic community to comment, it did not seek the views of a broadly based cross-section of Toronto's Black population. Third, it chose to ignore the concerns of those who were consulted.

Once the coalition had been formed and had begun its demonstrations, the ROM appeared to "dig in its heels" and consistently refused to meet the demonstrators' demands. Neither did ROM show much sensitivity to the perspectives of the Black community and others who shared their concerns. Instead, ROM's officials continued to affirm their support of the exhibit and appeared to take offence at the attempts made to interfere (as they saw it) in their museum and curatorial roles.

After several months, Cannizzo broke her silence and attempted to justify the exhibition. Seven months after the show was launched, she stated that "the exhibition does not promote colonialism or glorify imperialism.... It should help all Canadians to understand the historical roots of racism" (Cannizzo, 1990). Her article did not demonstrate particular sensitivity to the concerns of the Black community.

Exacerbating the tense situation was the media coverage of these events. A number of feature pieces were written, most of which were critical of the protesters, who were characterized as radicals, bullies, blackmailers, terrorists, and revision-ists. An art critic wrote that the "price of popularity must sometimes be paid for at the cost of integrity." He went on to observe that this show "caused a minor uproar here" (Hume, 1989). He observed: "Some members of the Black community considered it racist. It wasn't, of course."

Journalists in most of the mainstream newspapers and magazines dismissed the protest as the work of "radicals." A headline in *The Globe and Mail* reads, "ROM Adds Insult to Injury in Debacle Over African Show," (Drainie, 1991); the *The Toronto Star* accused the "self-righteous left" (Hume, 1991); and the *Toronto Sun* concluded: "Why are we so bloody eager to be held hostage by the ravers from the political left? They won big on this one, you know" (Blatchford,1990).

For the Black community and its representatives, the incident merely confirmed that

> as long as institutions and individuals fail to understand how thoroughly racism permeates the very underpinnings of Western thought, then despite all the good will in the world, catastrophes like "Into the Heart of Africa" will continue to hap-pen. Intentions, particularly the good ones, continue to pave the way to hell. And to Africa (Nourbese Philip, 1992).

CONSEQUENCES

"Into the Heart of Africa" was scheduled to tour several museums in Canada and the United States. The controversy led to the cancellation of the exhibit by the other museums. In response, the director of the ROM, John MacNeill, commented: "the controversy which surrounded this exhibition and led to the cancellation of the tour impinges on the freedom of all museums to maintain intellectual honesty, scientific and historical integrity and academic freedom."

CONCLUSION

This case study crystallizes many of the issues related to cultural racism and cul-tural appropriation. Nourbese Philip (1993) suggests that at the heart of the ROM controversy are changing beliefs about the role and function of museums and other cultural institutions, especially the issue of who should have the power to represent and control images created by "others." The traditional values and practices of institutions such as museums are difficult to change.

One analyst poses an important question about the ROM controversy: Would the institution have supported a more critical approach to the subject? Would it have risked offending its important patrons, some of whom donated artifacts to the collection? (Butler, 1993:57).

The ROM controversy also illustrates how the past converges with the present. The protesters saw a relationship between the symbolic domination, reflected in the colonial images of the exhibit, and the sense of powerlessness experienced daily by Black people in Canada. The linkage between racism in different sectors of society was made by a critic who emphasized the importance of understanding how the struggles with the ROM and the Metropolitan Toronto Police were welded togeth-er: "Inside the ROM is institutional racism and outside is the brutal reality" (Roach, 1990).

This case study also emphasizes the intrinsic link between colonialism and cul-tural racism. The process employed by ROM to conceptualize and develop "Into the Heart of Africa" was based on the colonial model of objectification. Mitchell suggests that the West habitually rends the world as object or, more specifically, "the world as exhibition" (1989:219–222) and argues that this process of organizing and ordering the world is identical to the logic and processes of colonialism. The outcome of this process is the domination of the body, spirit, and soul of the "others."

Objectification is also very much a part of the way in which Africans in the exhibit were depicted. The lens of the camera held by the missionary or colonizer captures the "object" (the women washing clothes), but the "objects" are rendered powerless and silent. They appear not to challenge their oppression. The exhibit was totally "devoid of images and voices of resistance" to colonial subjugation (Butler, 1993:63). There are numerous examples in the history of Africa in which Africans resisted domination both physically and in writing. This should have been included in the narrative.

Crean (1991) summarizes the cultural racism of the exhibit by stating that "Into the Heart of Africa" was "a classic case of a cultural institution unable to see its own bias and unprepared to examine its own cultural assumptions" (127).

Figure 9.1
TWO PROCESSES OF CULTURAL APPROPRIATION

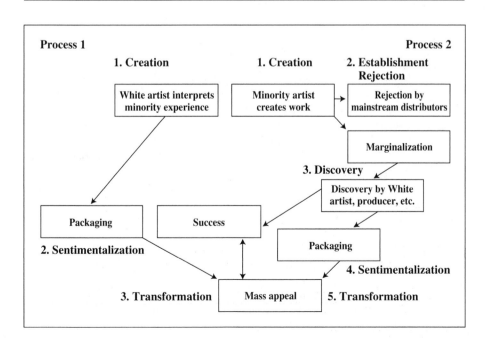

CULTURAL APPROPRIATION IN OTHER ART FORMS

In recent years, cultural appropriation has created controversy concerning White artists who interpret the experiences of the "others," including Asians, Asian Canadians, Africans, Black Canadians, and Aboriginal peoples. Protests against this practice have been countered by cries of censorship from White artists and cultural producers.

For example, many mainstream writers object to the Canada Council's and Women's Press's guidelines on cultural appropriation. They suggest that these policies jeopardize their right of freedom of expression (Paris, 1992). The Writers Union of Canada's commitment to support the rights of racial-minority writers to greater freedom of expression and access has not been well received by many mainstream writers. June Callwood, a co-founder of the union, warned her colleagues of the dangerous emotionalism in the positions and strategies used by writers of colour to assert their own freedom of expression while undermining the freedom of mainstream writers. She referred to these efforts as the acts of the "self-defined weak" that include "bullying and intimidation" (Callwood, 1993).

The defences of freedom of expression and artistic licence are challenged by many artists of colour. In a world dominated by White values, images, and norms, where people of colour are either absent from most cultural production or misrepresented as racial or gender anomalies, it has been observed that:

> it is critical for disenfranchised racial minorities to maintain possession and control over the telling of "her stories and histories.... Any representation of ourselves and our cultural experiences done by an outsider would be from a comparatively superficial perspective, simply because he/she hasn't had the experience of surviving racial oppression—complete with all its complications, consequences, and contradictions." (Browning, 1992:33)

Thus, Browning (1992) concludes that White artists\writers who attempt to speak on behalf of the "others" or who believe that they can interpret their experiences are perpetuating their own positions of privilege and dominance.

Building on this analysis, Nourbese Philip (1992) draws attention to one of the central paradoxes in cultural appropriation. While there is a profound lack of respect for artists of colour and their aesthetics, there is generally a strong approval of the White artist who culturally appropriates those traditions and benefits from them.

Brant (1990) holds the view that the truth is not told by the many White writers who use their hundreds of years of colonial supremacy to speak for Aboriginal peoples.

> I do not say that only Indians can write about Indians. But you can't steal my stories and call them your own. You can't steal my spirit and call it your own. This is the history of North America—stolen property, stolen lives, stolen dreams and stolen spirituality.... If your history is one of cultural domination you must be aware...you have to tell the truth about your role, your history, your internalized domination and supremacy.

MARGINALIZATION OF PEOPLE OF COLOUR IN PUBLIC CULTURE

People of colour confront both subtle and overt barriers as they attempt to move from the margins of mainstream culture into the centre. The title *Out There* (Ferguson, 1990), suggests that the power of the centre depends on the relatively unchallenged authority of the dominant culture. In other words, cultural racism is maintained by silencing artists, writers, and musicians of colour who, having been relegated to a place outside the dominant culture, find it difficult to challenge dominant modes of cultural production and dissemination.

The racism of cultural institutions has been characterized as a form of organizational apartheid that in the past relegated aboriginal art to museums and the category of "anthropology," while White artistic productions went to public galleries and were categorized as "art." This devaluing of the art of Aboriginal peoples and artists of colour is considered by some to be not only cultural domination but cultural genocide (Danzker, 1991).

A further example of cultural racism is the canon of "great works" by White, mainly male, writers and dramatists that is incorporated in the curricula of educational institutions and considered the only material appropriate for mainstream audiences. It is assumed that this body of writing represents the best of human culture and creativity. Cultural racism is reflected in "objective" and "neutral" reviews of literary, arts, and entertainment critics who defend their judgements by maintaining that universal criteria and standards can be applied to all creative arts, thereby ignoring their own cultural and ideological frameworks and biases. Racism is sometimes hidden in efforts to stifle debate about representation, access, and equity. Those who challenge racist attitudes, policies, or practices are often accused of "censorship" and their concerns are dismissed as examples of "political correctness."

The invisibility of people of colour, especially women of colour who are writers, is of prime concern in a collection entitled *Returning the Gaze: Essays on Feminism and Politics* (Bannerji, 1993). The editor maintains that the first task confronting women of colour is to counter existing stereotypes and "to create a critical space." The absence of the voice of non-White women artists, she argues, leads to a misunderstanding about

> our critical abilities… and intensifies the historical and existing common sense which imputes non-intellectuality to Third World peoples in general and women in particular. It matches racist notions about our difference. (x)
>
> As non-White women, our experiences of "difference" need form and expression. For this reason, creative writings or oral histories are crucial.… In Canada, until recently, even the feminist presses and publications were bereft of our presence. (xi)

Canadian poet George Elliot Clarke, in a 1993 symposium entitled "Whose Voice Is It, Anyway?" sponsored by *Books in Canada,* raged against the lack of access experienced by Aboriginal writers and writers of colour, a reflection of dispossession caused by ethnocentrism.

> We must seize the means of cultural propagation; we must fight to achieve the grants, review the public readings, the writer-in-residence-ships, the media invitations, the university chairs.... All Canadians have tales to tell and poems to sing.... Whose literature is it, anyway? (Clarke, 1993)

As suggested earlier, efforts to change or challenge these assumptions are generally met with fierce resistance. For example, when the Art Gallery of Ontario (AGO) established a task force to examine the issue of representation both from the perspective of governance—who sits on the board and who is hired for senior management positions—and in terms of the extent to which the AGO supported artists who reflected the diversity of Ontario, the media argued that the Ontario government had gone too far. It implied that the AGO must "show and publicize the work of current Ontario artists even if the AGO curators think that, at the moment, most of their work is mediocre" (Fulford, 1992). The implicit assumption appeared to be, all art that does not fit within the Euro-American tradition is *ipso facto* inferior.

These assumptions were in evidence in an exhibit at the Vancouver Art Gallery (VAG). In 1991, the Artists' Coalition for Local Colour held a protest outside the gallery. The coalition was formed primarily by South Asian artists and cultural workers in response to the VAG's decision to mount an exhibit of South Asian art imported from the United Kingdom. The coalition argued that this was a blatant example of the systemic racism of the organization and resulted in a lack of access, participation, and equity for local artists of colour. Moreover, the VAG decided that, in light of the controversy, it would celebrate the opening with a private viewing of the collection rather than a formal opening event. No members of the South Asian community were invited to the opening.

REPRESENTATION AND MISREPRESENTATION

The following case study looks closely at the issues of representation, misrepresentation, marginalization, stereotyping, cultural appropriation, freedom of expression, and the power of the dominant culture.

Here, "representation" concerns not only the inclusion or omission of images of people of colour in art. McCarthy and Critchlow (1993) suggest that it is ultimately a question of who holds the power "to define whom, and when, and how" (xvi). Representation indicates who controls the production and transmission of images in art and society.

CASE STUDY 9.2

SHOW BOAT

In the winter of 1993, Live Entertainment Corporation, which had an exclusive contract to manage the new North York Municipal Arts Centre in Ontario, announced that a production of the musical *Show Boat* would launch the opening

---

of this important new institution. The play is based on a 1926 novel by American writer Edna Ferber.

Show Boat chronicles the lives of a White, southern family and the performers who work on a boat that travels on the Mississippi River over four decades, entertaining White audiences in the southern and midwestern regions of the United States. The play begins during the post-emancipation period and continues through the first decades of the twentieth century. In the world depicted in the novel, Blacks exist as backdrop. Almost every reference to them in the novel employs demeaning and derogatory stereotypes:

The cook was a wooly-headed Black with a rolling protuberant eye and the quick temper of his calling.

A simple ignorant soul, the Black man, and…somewhat savage…

One drop of nigger blood makes you a nigger in these parts…

I kind of smell a nigger in the woodpile here in more ways than one.

Eight months of flies and niggers and dirty mud-tracking loafers is enough for me, Captain Hawks. I'm thankful to get back for a few weeks where I can live like a decent white woman.

Long before White-aproned Jo, breakfast bell in hand, emerged head first from the little doorway beneath the stage back of the orchestra pit, like an amiable Black python from its lair… (Ferber, 1926)

The Jamaican Canadian Society, in stating its position on *Show Boat* wrote that it is a musical based on a novel filled with degrading images of Blacks.

The words leap off the page and hit one in the face like a ton of bricks and plant deleterious images in the minds of readers such as 'shiftless Joe'…"teeth gleaming and eyes rolling." There are no redeeming descriptions of Blacks in the novel; throughout they are portrayed as dimwitted, childlike, animalistic, lazy, drunk and irresponsible. Nowhere in the novel or in any of the subsequent plays or films is the horrifying reality of Black peoples' suffering experienced throughout this period (Coalition to Stop Show Boat, 1993).

The musical first appeared in 1927 and was revised and restaged numerous times, with productions in the United States, the United Kingdom, and Canada. Two film versions were also based on the novel. Each version retains the negative and demeaning stereotypes of Blacks happily singing and dancing. Only the character Joe, played by Paul Robeson, laments his plight in the famous song, "Ol' Man River." The opening line of the song, in its earliest rendition, begins: "Niggers all work on the Mississippi." This was later changed to "Darkies" and then "Colored" and finally "We all work." However, in most productions, while he moves White audiences with his music, Joe remains a lazy, good-natured "negro." He displays no rage or resistance. The other Black characters are equally passive figures who never challenge their oppression.

EVENTS

A large and diverse segment of Toronto's Black community launched a protest shortly after learning about the decision to produce *Show Boat*. A coalition was formed to "Stop *Show Boat*." Its concern centred on the ways in which the various productions of the play distorted the memory, history, and experiences of Black people who lived through slavery and the Reconstruction period. Opposition to the play was based, in part, on the fact that it romanticized and trivialized one of the most oppressive periods of Western civilization and misrepresented the deep emotions, conditions, and experiences of Blacks in those horrific times.

Show Boat is seen as an example of both misrepresentation and cultural appropriation. In this instance, White writers, producers, directors, composers, and lyricists assume the right to create and transmit inaccurate and stereotypic images of "others." The music of *Show Boat* is drawn largely from the rich musical traditions of Afro-American culture. The appropriation of this music by the dominant culture for its own use and profit, while at the same time portraying Africans and Afro-Americans as a people bereft of culture, was a common practice in a racist society (Nourbese Philip, 1993).

The Black community, the Coalition to Stop Show Boat, and other groups argued that the decision to mount this controversial musical in a public municipal arts theatre in a municipality in which thousands of Blacks live indicated a staggering lack of sensitivity toward the community. The continued racism and oppression that were an everyday reality for Black Canadians were considered irrelevant by the decision-makers of Live Entertainment Productions as well as the mayor of North York and other politicians who gave absolute freedom to the producers in all aspects of the management of the North York Performing Arts Centre.

The Coalition to Stop Show Boat argued that Blacks in the various versions of *Show Boat* are viewed as backdrops, props, and stage dressing and provide a "colourful" context for the lives of the White people in the story. In every production of the musical, Black characters have functioned as singing caricatures, enhancing the picture of a people who are happy in their condition. Their portrayal is incidental to the story. When they do appear, they are depicted as passive, cheerful, ignorant, singing and dancing stereotypes.

Although recent revisions of the play removed some of the more offensive stereotypes and problematic language, the critics of *Show Boat* argued that the play was designed for White audiences and that all of its productions have perpetuated the same myths and misconceptions about Black people that existed in its first production. The protesters argued that the play reinforced the negative images of Blacks that are part of the mainstream culture and that influence the way in which White people see and interact with Black people daily (Lee, 1993; Auguste, 1993a). The Chair of the African Heritage Educators' Network wrote:

> We Africans in the diaspora define ourselves. When we cry out in anguish over our suffering under the yoke of "artistic license," our pain cannot be trivialized by dominant groups' attempts to define us. (Farrell, 1993)

The Chair of the Coalition to Stop Show Boat expressed a similar view of the musical:

> *Show Boat* has resonated in the Black community.... It is the symbol of systemic and cultural racism. It symbolizes what we suffer in our daily lives, no matter what we have achieved in this society, no matter who we are. (Henry, 1993:54)

However, the producers of *Show Boat* and a significant cross-section of the media, including many editorial writers, journalists, and theatre critics, were unsympathetic. One of Canada's most respected writers suggested that it was "dangerous nonsense" to describe *Show Boat* as racist; he urged the producers not to "scrub *Show Boat* too clean," that is, not to remove the overt racist language and stereotypes (Berton, l993). He meant that the racism of the play belongs there because of the historical context in which the story was written.

THE CENSORSHIP DEBATE

The backlash to the protest against *Show Boat* was linked to the rhetoric of censorship and political correctness. The Black community's call for greater sensitivity and responsibility in the selection of cultural productions in publicly funded institutions was seen as a violation of freedom of expression. The protesters were considered to be undermining one of the fundamental and sacrosanct values underpinning a democratic society. Editorials published in *The Toronto Star*, *The Globe and Mail*, and the *Toronto Sun* were highly critical of the Black community's position on *Show Boat,* suggesting that what was being called for was the rewriting of history as well as the stifling of creative expression.

Some questioned whether the media's strong stand in support of the production—particularly that of the three Toronto newspapers—was influenced by their vested interest in the production. Each of the newspapers received significant revenues from the show's advertisements, which appeared daily for several months. One of the *Toronto Star's* own columnists noted, "Live Entertainment Corporation of Canada are among the *Star's* half-dozen biggest advertisers" (Slinger, 1993). Nourbese Philip (1992) observed that the quantum leap from racism to censorship was "neither random nor unexpected." The issue of censorship is central to the dominant cultures of liberal democracies like Canada. In these cultures, "censorship becomes a significant and talismanic cultural icon around which all debates about the 'individual freedom of man' swirl."

The Coalition to Stop Show Boat argued that calling for a play to be boycotted was not a condonation of censorship. It was, rather, a calling into question of the social responsibility and morality of dedicating a publicly funded building, in one of the most racially diverse cities in the world, with a production that demeaned a large segment of that community. Farrell (1993) suggested that the real and initial concerns about *Show Boat* concerned a hierarchy of rights: the rights of a producer to artistic freedom versus the rights of a community not to be hurt, not to have its children hurt by stereotypes.

The tension between the competing principles of an individual's right to freedom of expression and the right of communities to be protected from forms of speech and expression that do harm was recognized by the most revered of libertarians, John Stuart Mill (l984), who suggested that

> as soon as any part of a person's conduct affects prejudicially the interests of others, society has jurisdiction over it, and the question whether the general welfare will or will not be promoted by interfering with it becomes open to discussion. (41)

> Whenever, in short, there is a definite damage or a definite risk of damage either to an individual or to the public, the case is taken out of the province of liberty and placed in that of moral or law. (49)

The question remains, what constitutes harm and who will make this definition for the purpose of determining what legally may be said or done in the public domain? Many groups, including Jews, have argued powerfully, with respect to hate propaganda, for example, that the risk of not attending to hate groups is greater than the risk of regulating them. In the same way, women's groups and others have vigorously opposed the production and dissemination of pornography. They have argued that pornography has the potential to cause serious harm to women and children. In each of these examples, freedom is not viewed as an absolute right. It is tempered with the notion of justice and the protection of the rights and freedoms of those who are most vulnerable.

Landsberg (1993) posed the question, "Why is it censorship to protest a demeaning and irrelevant theatrical production?" She observed that these protests have provided a valuable form of public education and free speech. Similarly, the director of the Simon Wiesenthal Centre of Canada wrote: "The Black community has every right to protest what it sees as a racist vehicle"(Littman, 1993).

CONSEQUENCES

Three additional factors increased the stakes in this debate and demonstrated the ripple effect of cultural racism into other institutional arenas. First, a North York Board of Education trustee publicly expressed her concern about the play: "Most of the plays that portray Black or any other ethnic groups in a negative way are always done by a White man, and usually always [sic] a Jewish person is doing plays that denigrate us" (Valpy, 1993). Although she soon publicly apologized for her insensitivity to the Jewish community, the spectre of Black anti-Semitism heightened tensions and misunderstanding between the two communities. Members of the Jewish community took exception to editorials and other articles appearing in a Black community newspaper that they felt were indicative of Black anti-Semitism. Similarly, individuals in the Black community spoke about their pain, frustration, and anger at having racism ignored by the Jewish community and others (Auguste, 1993a,b).

A second factor in the controversy was that several voluntary organizations intended to sponsor a performance of *Show Boat* for fundraising purposes. One of them, the United Way of Metropolitan Toronto, had prided itself on its anti-racism position, policy, and practices. When the controversy arose, the board of the United Way, after considerable discussion, chose to proceed with their fundraiser. To protest the United Way action, 19 of the 22 members of its Black and Caribbean Fundraising Committee resigned, as did several other volunteers. The United Way position led to the questioning of the organization's commitment to anti-racism. Further questions were raised by some members of the Black community about whether there were fundamental inequities in the allocations process for funding the Black community's human-service agencies.

The third factor related to the intention of Live Entertainment to bring in 200 000 students to see the production. The corporation indicated that it planned to produce "educational" packages to "enlighten" students about the history of slavery and the Reconstruction period after they had seen the show. The materials were to be developed by an Afro-American academic who had been retained to act as the primary consultant for the educational program. In response to the plan to develop these programs, critics protested both the choice of the play and the development of educational materials based on a racist text. In a letter to Ontario's minister of education, they stated that:

> creating the opportunity for the school-going community to be entertained at the expense of some of its members is not the best strategy for helping eliminate racism. To argue that seeing *Show Boat* would itself be a lesson in racism is to argue that one learns best about radiation by being continually exposed to it.

Likewise the central impetus for the show is entertainment and economic gain. It was never intended to be educational.... Any educational package accompanying the show would therefore be at best inadequate and inappropriate. (Ijaz, 1993)

In a similar way, Black educators argued that

It is inappropriate for the producers of *Show Boat* to use the educational system of Ontario to make a dollar over the objection of the Black community and at the expense of the self-esteem of Black children and youth. To allow *Show Boat* materials into the schools is the systemic racism that says "I have political and financial power over you, even if you object." (Black Educators' Working Group, 1993)

CONCLUSION

This case study demonstrates how cultural racism functions and how pervasive its impact is on both the dominant culture and marginalized groups. It demonstrates how invisible cultural racism can be to White people and how acutely present it is in the lives of people of colour. It also clarifies the links between racism in one sector, such as the arts, and other arenas, such as the media, education, and the marketplace.

The *Show Boat* controversy continues to reverberate with significant consequences for all the protagonists, including the Black community, the Jewish community, the United Way and other agencies that sponsored *Show Boat*, the media, boards of education, municipal and provincial government agencies, and other cultural agencies. *Show Boat* is a clear example of how the cultural power and racist ideology of individuals and institutions converge to further marginalize, exclude, and silence people of colour.

The relationship between White cultural professionals and people of colour in the arts reproduces the symbolic basis of colonial domination (Butler, 1993). In the examples of "Into the Heart of Africa" and *Show Boat*, the conflict between the interests of the producers and the Black and other communities who challenged the power of the dominant culture was constrained by further acts of marginalization and exclusion. This process has been described as

the act of conceptualizing, inscribing, and interacting with "others" on terms not of their choosing; in making them into pliant objects and silenced subjects of our scripts and scenarios; in assuming the capacity to "represent" them. (Comaroff and Comaroff, 1991:15)

ALLOCATION OF GRANTS AND RESOURCES BY FUNDING AGENCIES

Historically, the policies and practices of arts councils—by virtue of their neglect and lack of support of minority artists, artistic organizations, and projects—have been a powerful vehicle for perpetuating racism in the arts. It has been extremely difficult for writers, artists, musicians, directors, producers, and performers of colour to receive grants from arts councils and government agencies because they are perceived to be unable to meet Eurocentric aesthetic standards. They often find themselves relegated to the margins of the arts and labelled as "not professional." Funding organizations have tended to view Black, Asian, and Aboriginal Canadian artists and cultural companies as "exotic" or "folkloric." As a result, it has been thought that they should be supported through multicultural funding agencies rather than expect to share in the limited resources of arts councils.

In essence there are two distinct policies operating providing unequal support structures to arts within the dominant culture, and the art produced by Aboriginal artists and artists of colour. "These two art worlds operate within separate infrastructures and rules and standards; and the source and magnitude of funding are different...and the art works of these two art worlds carry unequal market value and social status" (Li, 1994).

As the 1980s drew to a close, there were escalating demands by Aboriginal, Black/African, and Asian artists and writers for funding agencies to address cultural and racial barriers in their structures. They were urged to identify biases and discrimination in their staffing, composition of juries and panels, and criteria of professionalism, quality, and excellence. Critics of these "relentlessly White" organizations argued that "in a country where a working artist is almost by definition a government funded artist, this situation amounted to cultural apartheid" (Bailey, 1992:22). Nourbese Philip (1992) shares the grave concern about funding agencies: "The divide between the lived reality of the Black artist and the funding policies of arts councils, between the Black artist and the art world in general, is so great as to be almost unbridgeable" (227).

Arts funding is premised on two notions of culture, which are mutually exclusive: one views culture as art, to be funded by arts councils; the other understands culture as an anthropological phenomenon that should be funded primarily by agencies such as multiculturalism and citizenship at the federal level and ministries of culture or citizenship at provincial levels (Wong, 1991). The assumption underpinning this approach is that works of art produced by people of colour fail to meet professional standards of excellence. Only when artists of colour "prove" themselves in the context of the norms and models of White elites can they overcome the great divide (West, 1990).

A review of the recent activities of art councils illustrates the above points. Between 1990 and 1992, research carried out by three of Canada's major arts councils—the Canada Council, the Ontario Arts Council, and the Toronto Arts Council—resulted in reports dealing with racism in arts-funding organizations and containing various approaches and strategies for dealing with it.[1] In addition, Metropolitan Toronto's Department of Cultural Affairs held consultations on the funding of ethno-racial and Aboriginal arts organizations. In each case it was recognized that significant barriers confronted artists of colour. However, common to each of the approaches taken by these funding organizations was some attempt to distance themselves from the issues of race and racism and to focus on cultural barriers. They seemed to have difficulty dealing with one of the most powerful components of cultural racism—the Eurocentrism of the arts in Canada. They also generally refrained from dealing with the specifics of systemic racism.

The Canada Council, for example, failed to support the committee's finding that "systemic racism is a result of the everyday functioning of all

Canadian institutions" and rejected its call for an organizational review of the Canada Council. The Ontario Arts Council report and recommendations were based on a "diversity" paradigm; "racism" appeared only once in the document. The Toronto Arts Council used the terminology of cultural equity and referred to "specific" cultural communities, to indicate differences based on culture, ethnicity, gender, language, race, and sexual orientation. However, specific systems and patterns of exclusion and discrimination are only hinted at (Bailey, 1992).

With respect to the issues of access and equity to funding, a noted Canadian recording artist and composer, commented:

> It seems that only Caucasians are allowed to sit in judgement as experts on Chinese, African, African-Canadian, South Asian, Aboriginal, Indonesian, Korean, Japanese…music, deciding who gets the grants and whose music is valuable to whose community. Until we have representation on these juries, we will only be tokens. (Nolan, 1992:28)

One of the issues raised by ethno-racial communities and artists of colour in the consultation by Metropolitan Toronto's Cultural Affairs Division is the question of professional standards. Many have suggested that the criteria and standards used by funders often screen out applicants belonging to racial communities by using Eurocentric aesthetics as a yardstick.

RESPONSES

The issues of the lack of access and barriers to writers and artists of colour have recently begun to receive more attention from funding bodies, museums, publishing houses, and other cultural agencies. The case studies of "Into the Heart of Africa" and *Show Boat* show that racial-minority communities are becoming more insistent that their cultural rights be respected and that the cultural appropriation of their experiences by the White powerbrokers in cultural organizations be challenged.

In response to these concerns, arts organizations such as the Toronto Arts Council, the Ontario Arts Council, the Canada Council, and a limited number of galleries and museums such as the Royal Ontario Museum, the Vancouver Art Gallery, and the Art Gallery of Ontario have established advisory committees consisting of people of colour. They have also attempted to increase the representation of racial minorities in their administrative structures. Among book publishers, The Women's Press has developed anti-racist guidelines.

With respect to future exhibits, the ROM appeared to learn something from the controversy over "Into the Heart of Africa." An advisory committee was established when the ROM mounted "Caribbean Celebrations" in 1991. As well, a joint staff–trustee committee on community relationships was created to examine the ROM's hiring practices.

SUMMARY

This chapter has analyzed the powerful role of cultural organizations in contributing to racism. The racism found in various forms of cultural production and transmission emanates from the dominant culture's value system. Eurocentric values, assumptions, and standards strongly influence the decisions of cultural agencies in terms of what artists, writers, musicians, and actors are supported and whose voices, words, and images are silenced.

The analyses of cultural racism and racism in cultural organizations further demonstrates the general invisibility of racism among members of the dominant culture. In almost every example cited in this chapter, efforts on the part of minority groups to identify racism in art forms and cultural productions resulted in both overt and subtle attacks on those who voiced concerns and called for change. In the cases of both "Into the Heart of Africa" and *Show Boat*, those who opposed these productions were labelled "radicals," "activists," and "troublemakers."

This chapter also illustrated the interlocking nature of various forms of racism. For example, the intrinsic relationship between racist ideology and the practices of the mass media is linked to the cultural and racial assumptions driving various cultural organizations and disciplines. This in turn is supported by police, who vigorously suppress acts of protest and resistance. Educational institutions often become another vehicle for the production and dissemination of culture. In the examples of the ROM and *Show Boat*, the participation of students became part of the debate. Racism in the arts is also inextricably linked to the marketplace and is propelled by the economic interests of the corporate elite. In the case of *Show Boat*, the profit motive was the central force driving the producers as well as the media. Racism in the arts is like racism in the other institutions of Canadian society; it is ultimately about the power of the dominant group to control cultural forms of expression.

Finally, the issue of freedom of expression was explored from the point of view of competing values. On one hand, in North American society there is great attachment to the ideal of unrestricted artistic licence for those who work in the arts and in cultural organizations. On the other hand, the act of protesting, resisting, and challenging the power of those who control cultural expression is also important. Racial-minority artists and communities believe that freedom of expression should not become the talisman under which White cultural institutions maintain and reproduce racist discourse and representation.

REFERENCES

Ames, M. (1986). *Museum: The Public and Anthropology*. Vancouver: University of British Columbia Press.

Auguste, A. (l993a). "If They Come for Me in the Morning." *Share Magazine* (Toronto) (April 1):8.

_____. (1993b). "Tired of Being Your Niggers." *Share Magazine* (Toronto) (April 29).

Bailey, C. (1992). "Fright the Power." *Fuse* 15(6):24.

Bannerji, H. (ed.).(1993). *Returning the Gaze: Essays on Racism, Feminism and Politics.* Toronto: Sister Vision Press.

Berton, P. (l993). "Let's Not Scrub Show Boat Too Clean." *The Toronto Star* (March 20): K 3.

Black Educators' Working Group. (1993). "Letter to Premier Bob Rae." (June 18).

Blatchford, C. (1990). *The Toronto Sun* (November 30).

Brant, B. (1990) "From the Outside Looking In: Racism and Writing." Panel Discussion, Gay Cultural Festival, Vancouver (August).

Browning, F. (1992). "Self-Determination and Cultural Appropriation." *Fuse* 15 (4):31–35.

Butler, S. (1993). *Contested Representations: Revisiting "Into the Heart of Africa."* Master's Thesis, Department of Anthropology, York University, North York, Ontario.

Callwood, J. (1993). "Journalism and the Blight of Censorship." *The Globe and Mail* (June 28):A13.

Canada Council. (1992). *Recommendations of the Advisory Committee for Racial Equality in the Arts and the Response of the Canada Council.* Ottawa.

Cannizzo, J. (1990). "Into the Heart of a Controversy." *The Toronto Star* (June 5):A17.

_____. (1991b). "Exhibiting Cultures: Into the Heart of Africa." *Visual Anthropology Review* 7(1):150–60.

Carby, H. (1993). "Encoding White Resentment: *Grand Canyon*, A Narrative for our Time." In C. McCarthy and W. Critchlow (eds.), *Race, Identity and Representation in Education.* New York and London: Routledge.

Clarke, G. (1991) "Whose Voice Is It, Anyway?" Symposium. Toronto: *Books in Canada* (February 20):11–17.

Clifford, J. (1990). "On Collecting Art and Culture." In R. Ferguson (ed.), *Out There: Marginalization and Contemporary Culture.* New York: Museum of Contemporary Art.

Coalition to Stop Show Boat. (1993). Reply of Coalition to Stop Show Boat to Garth Drabinsky's March 11, 1993 Press Release. (May 3).

Comaroff, J., and J. Comaroff. (1991). *Of Revelation and Revolution: Christianity, Colonialism, and Consciousness in South Africa.* Vol. 1. Chicago: University of Chicago Press.

Crean, S. (1991). "Taking the Missionary Position." In O. McKague (ed.), *Racism in Canada.* Saskatoon: Fifth House.

Da Breo, H. (1989–90a). "Da Breo Interviews Dr. Jeanne Cannizzo." *Fuse* (Winter):36–37.

_____. (1989–90b). "Royal Spoils: The Museum Confronts Its Colonial Past." *Fuse* (Winter):28–36.

Danzker, J. (1991). "Cultural Apartheid." In O. McKague (ed.), *Racism in Canada.* Saskatoon: Fifth House.

Drainie, B. (1991). "ROM Adds Insult to Injury in Debacle Over African Show." *The Globe and Mail* (April 19).

Essed, P. (1990). *Everyday Racism.* Claremont, CA: Hunter House.

Farrell, V. (1993). "Staging Show Boat is Power Play." *Share* (May 6):9.

Ferber, E. (1926). *Show Boat.* New York: Doubleday.

Ferguson, R. (ed.). (1990). *Out There: Marginalization and Contemporary Culture.* New York: Museum of Contemporary Art.

Fulford, R. (1992). "Robert Fulford Ponders the Growing Strength of the Hruska Principle." *The Globe and Mail* (September 30):C1

Hall, S. (1990). "Cultural Identity and Diaspora." In J. Rutherford (ed.), *Identity: Community Culture and Difference.* London: Lawrence and Wishart: 222–37.

_____. (1992). *Reproducing Ideologies: Essays on Culture and Politics.*

Henry, J. (1993). Presentation by the Co-Chair of the Coalition to Stop Show Boat. Toronto: Seneca College (June 15).

hooks, b. (1990). *Yearning: Race, Gender and Cultural Politics.* Toronto: Between the Lines.

Hume, C. (1989). "ROM Looks into the Heart of Darkness." *The Toronto Star* (November 17):E3, E22.

_____. (1990). "Rejection of ROM Show Not A Defeat for Racism." *The Toronto Star* (September 29):F3.

Ijaz, A. (1993). "Educators Against Show Boat." *Share* (May 27):1.

Jiwani, Y. (1992). "Local Colour Protests." *Fuse* 15(6):13–14.

Julian, E. (1992). *Cultural Equity* (June). Toronto Arts Council.

Katz, J.(1978). *White Awareness: Handbook for Anti-Racist Teaching*. Norman, OK: University of Oklahoma Press.

Lalla, H., and J. Myers. (1990). *Report on the Royal Ontario Museum's Exhibit* "Into the Heart of Africa." (May). Toronto: Toronto Board of Education.

Landsberg, M. (1993). "Blacks, Jews Must Join Forces to Sink Show Boat." *The Toronto Star* (June 12):H1.

Lee, A. (l993). "Only White Sensibilities Matter." *The Toronto Star* (May 28):A25.

Li, P. (1994). "A World Apart: The Multicultural World of Visible Minorities and the Art World of Canada." *Canadian Review of Sociology and Anthropology*.

Littman, S. (1993). "Victims Can Be Racists Too: Blacks Have Right to Proclaim their Fears over Show Boat." *The Toronto Star* (June 22):A17.

Lubiano, W. (1992). "Black Ladies, Welfare Queens, and State Minstrels: Ideological War by Narrative Means." In T. Morrison (ed.), *Race-ing, Engendering Power*. New York: Pantheon Books.

Mallet, G. (1992). *The Toronto Star* (December 15).

McMelland, J. (1990). "Uncovering A Hidden Curriculum." *Role Call* (April 10).

McCarthy, C. (1993). "After the Canon." In C. McCarthy and W. Critchlow (eds.), *Race, Identity and Representation in Education*. New York and London: Routledge.

_____, and W. Critchlow (eds.). (1993). *Race, Identity and Representation in Education*. New York and London: Routledge.

Mill, J.S. (1984). *On Liberty*. G. Himmelfarb (ed.). Harmondsworth, UK: Penguin.

Mitchell, T. (1989). "The World as Exhibition." *Society for Comparative Study of Society and History* 31(2):217–236.

Morrison, T. (1992a) *Playing in the Dark: Whiteness and the Literary Imagination*. Boston: Harvard University Press.

_____. (1992b). *Race-ing, Justice, En-gendering Power: Essays on Anita Hill, Clarence Thomas and the Construction of Social Reality*. New York: Pantheon.

Nolan, F. (l992). "Letter to Alan Gottlieb, Canada Council." *Fuse* 15(6):28.

Ontario Arts Council. (1990). *Consultations with Artists in a Culturally Diverse Society* (December).

Paris, E. (1992). "A Letter to the Thought Police." *The Globe and Mail* (March 31).

Nourbese Philip, M. (1992). *Frontiers: Essays and Writings on Racism and Culture*. Stratford: Mercury Press.

_____. (1993). *Showing Grit, Showboating North of the 44th Parallel*. Toronto: Poui Publications.

Roach, C. (1990). "Into the Heart of the Controversy." *Toronto Sun* (June 5):A17.

Slinger, J. (1993). "Show Boat Sponsorship Casts Shadow Over The Star. *The Toronto Star.* (April 20):A2.

Valpy, M. (1993). "The Storm Around Show Boat." *The Globe and Mail* (March 12):2.

Walker, M. (1993). "Multiculturalism/Oppositionality." In C. McCarthy and W. Critchlow (eds.), *Race, Identity and Representation in Education*. New York and London: Routledge

West, C. (1990). "The New Cultural Politics of Difference." In R. Ferguson (ed.), *Out There: Marginalization and Contemporary Culture*. New York: New Museum of Contemporary Art.

Williams, S. (1992). "The Appropriation of Noise." *Fuse* 15(6):15–17.

Wong, P. (1991). "Yellow Peril Reconsidered." *Fuse* (Fall):15:1–2, 48–49.

NOTES

1. The three documents include *Recommendations of the Advisory Committee for Racial Equality in the Arts and the Response of the Canada Council* (January 1992); *Consultations with Artists in a Culturally Diverse Society: A Report from the Ontario Arts Council* (December 1990); and *Cultural Equity: Report from the Toronto Arts Council* (June 1992).

Chapter 10

▼▼▼▼▼▼▼▼▼▼▼▼▼

Racism in the Media

When visible minorities do appear in our newspapers and TV public affairs programming, they emerge as villains in a variety of ways—as caricatures from a colonial past; as extensions of foreign entities; or, in the Canadian context, as troubled immigrants in a dazzling array of trouble spots; hassling police, stumping immigration authorities, cheating on welfare, or battling among themselves or with their own families. (Siddiqui, 1993)

This chapter continues the examination of cultural racism by examining how the media reinforces racist ideology and practices. It begins with a discussion of the role and function of the media and then moves to a summary analysis of some of the indicators of racism in the media. The chapter then presents an examination of the ways in which the image-makers of the Canadian media industries marginalize people of colour, reducing them to invisible status and devaluing their images and their contributions in Canadian society.

This chapter looks at the power of the media to produce and transmit the message that people of colour, especially Blacks, create social problems and jeopardize the harmony and unity of Canadian society. The example of the "racialization of crime" by the media shows how the media indulges in overt and subtle misrepresentation and stereotyping in order to influence popular opinion. The examples cited also demonstrate the close relationships and common interests of the media and elite groups such as the corporate sector and the police. The last section of the chapter analyzes each of the major sectors of the media by using data based on the practices of certain media organizations. It concludes with a summary of some of the initiatives developed as a response to racism in the media.

INTRODUCTION

The electronic and print media have become major transmitters of society's cultural standards, myths, values, roles, and images. In theory, the media provide for the free flow and exchange of ideas, opinions, and information. As such, they represent the cornerstone of democratic society and the key instruments by which its ideals are produced and perpetuated. In a liberal democracy, media institutions are expected to reflect alternative viewpoints, remain neutral and objective, and provide free and equitable access to all groups and classes.

In reality, however, while espousing democratic values of fairness, equality, and freedom of expression, the media reinforce and reproduce racism in a number of ways—negative stereotyping, ethnocentric judgements, the marginalization of people of colour, and the racialization of issues such as crime and immigration.

ROLE AND FUNCTION OF THE MEDIA

The media, as a system and process of mass communication, incorporate a number of functions, including information processing and reproduction, education, socialization, entertainment, employment, and advertising. Media institutions are expected to reflect alternative viewpoints, remain neutral and objective, and provide free and equitable access to all groups and classes. The media in general, and television in particular, hold up a mirror in which society can see itself reflected. But who is reflected in the mirror?

The media reach out and touch people of every socioeconomic level, transcending differences in age, educational background, and occupational status. The media set norms, create stereotypes, build leaders, set priorities, and educate the public in matters of national interest and concern. Because of their wide-ranging exposure, the written and electronic media have an important role in

> guiding, shaping and transforming the way we look at the world ("perceptions"), how we understand it ("conceptions"), and the manner in which we experience and relate to it ("reality"). (Fleras and Elliot, 1992:234)

Troyna (1984) suggests that for many people the mass media represent a crucial source of beliefs and values from which they develop a picture of their social worlds. Because of the marginalization of racial-minority communities from mainstream society, many White people rely almost entirely on the media for their information about minorities and the issues that concern their communities. The relationship between the White community and these groups is therefore largely filtered through the perceptions, assumptions, values, and beliefs of journalists and other media professionals.

MANIFESTATIONS OF RACISM IN THE MEDIA

Stereotypical portrayal and misrepresentation
Invisibility of people of colour in the news, advertising, and programming
Lack of representation at all levels of media operations
Racialization of people of colour as social problems
Reproduction of White values, norms, and images
Biased attitudes and practices of media professionals

THE MANIFESTATIONS OF RACISM

INVISIBILITY OF PEOPLE OF COLOUR

A brief submitted to a parliamentary subcommittee on equality rights (Canadian Ethnocultural Council, 1985) stated that people of colour are invisible in the Canadian media: "The relative absence of minority men and women in the Canadian media is remarkable" (92). The Canadian Ethnocultural Council observed that the unequal status of racial minorities in the media was reflected by their absence from on-air roles such as anchors, reporters, experts, or actors and their lack of representation at all levels of staffing operations, production, and decision-making positions in communications. Their limited participation is considered the result of both overt bias and systemic discrimination. Examples of systemic discrimination cited in the brief include the reliance on referrals in hiring from White producers, writers, and editors; the lack of comprehensive outreach programs for the employment and training of people of colour, and the lack of recognition for qualifications and experience gained outside of Canada.

A Black Canadian actor succinctly addressed the issue of invisibility by paraphrasing a famous quotation and question: "Mirror, mirror on the wall, tell me if I exist at all." The mirror is the media polished and held up by the image-makers—advertisers, radio-station owners, private and public television executives, producers, writers, artistic directors, publishers, editors, and journalists (Gomez, 1983:13).

This invisibility of people of colour is reflected in the findings of programming conducted by Deverell (1986) and commissioned by the Alliance of Canadian Cinema, TV and Radio Artists, and the Secretary of State for Multiculturalism. Several types of programs were monitored on two Canadian networks including local newscasts, network broadcasts, children's programs, drama, variety programs, and commercials. In addition, theatres were asked to list their plays for the 1984–85 season and the number of roles in the plays, and to note whether any of the roles were played by performers who were members of visible-minority groups. Radio location managers of all Canadian Broadcasting Corporation (CBC) radio locations were surveyed for the type of program produced and number of on-microphone people employed, and to tally which of those were members of audible or visible-minority groups. The findings revealed that although approximately one third of all Canadians are non-British and non-French, less than 3 percent of such Canadians appeared on the stage, less than 3 percent were in commercials, and 5.5 percent were television principals.

The invisibility of people of colour in the print media is reflected in the hiring practices of media organizations. A study of recruitment procedures and promotion channels for women and minorities was conducted in 41 English-language newspapers in Ontario in 1986. Across the entire sample, people of colour, persons with a disability, and Aboriginal peoples were negligible as newsroom employers. Of the 1731 full-time newsroom employees in the sample, 30 were from the above groups. Word-of-mouth recruitment excludes a wide range of suitable applicants. Promotion channels across all the newspapers tended to be from within. Yet, *The Toronto Star* was the only paper with a policy aimed at removing barriers to the employment and advancement of women and minorities (Mayers, 1986).

In a study of the extent of the appearances of people of colour and Aboriginal peoples in national evening news programs, particularly their participation on CBC's "The National" and CTV's "National Evening News," almost all stories in which people of colour appeared were those in which the stories were about non-Whites. There were few stories of general interest, such as sports, taxes, or political issues, in which people of colour were included. During the four weeks in which these programs were monitored, only 20 of 725 interviews solicited the opinions of racial minorities for subjects not related specifically to stories or people from their communities (Perigoe and Lazar, 1992).

In representations made to the Canadian Radio-Television and Telecommunications Commission (CRTC) by racial and ethnocultural minorities, one brief suggested: "We are here simply to point out that what we see on the television screens…makes us feel as if we are in a foreign land, not one in which we are participating citizens" (1986:26).

The invisibility and marginalization of people of colour by the media communicates the message that they are not full participants in Canadian society. Salome Bey, a prominent Black entertainer, maintained that

> Canada today is a country where men, women and children of colour want to be seen and reflected as a vibrant and valuable component of the cultural reality of Canada, in the arts, and…everywhere. But instead our people have run headlong into the harsh realities of institutionalized indifference, insensitivity and ignorance that degrades us and our children. (Bey, 1983:5)

A parliamentary task force looking at racism in Canadian society heard dozens of briefs from people of colour that racism in the media was reflected by their invisibility in terms of both their images and their representation in media organizations. Groups from across Canada spoke with a single voice about the need for people of colour to have access, participation, and equity in the print and electronic media, on media boards and commissions, and on self-regulating bodies such as press councils. Lynda Armstrong, a Black performer, commented:

> The White-only mentality of the Canadian establishment is weird when you consider that this is one of the most racially diverse societies on earth… What we get in Canadian media is a fantasy. (*Equality Now*, 1984:91)

She reflected that one of the ironic aspects of the discrimination she faced as a professional performer who happened to be Black is that she was also a fifth-generation Canadian. Yet the colour barrier continued to deny her access to the entertainment and advertising industries.

One of the primary factors in this invisibility is cultural racism and the belief in the concept of the "rightness of Whiteness." Whiteness is considered the universal (hidden) norm and allows one to think and speak as if Whiteness described and defined the world. An example of this mindset is reflected in the comments of the president of a major brewer, who, when asked why there were no non-Whites in his company's commercials, responded: "White sells." (*Equality Now*, 1984:91). This attitude characterizes the collective belief system and influences the norms and practices of the media.

STEREOTYPICAL PORTRAYAL

Studies of the media (Hall, et al., 1978; Troyna, 1984; Fleras and Elliot, 1992; Granzberg, 1982; Ginzberg, 1985; Khaki and Prasad, 1988) demonstrate that the media, in general, produce a negative view of people of colour. Contrary to myth, journalists, editors, broadcasters, and directors of media organizations are not always neutral, impartial, objective, and unbiased. The media often select events that are atypical, present them in a stereotypical fashion, and contrast them with "White behaviour" (Hall et al., 1975). The broadcaster, reporter, camera person, and editor have a context that affects the way in which they interpret images, events, and situations. This context influences what they choose to film or air, what they select, and what eventually becomes part of the story. Media professionals are often guided by a need to focus on the sensational, extraordinary, and exotic, which sell well in the marketplace. They are influenced by their own connections to the groups and institutions that have power and influence.

A pervasive theme of both news and programming is the portrayal of people of colour as "the outsiders within," reinforcing the "we–they" mindset. Research establishes the close connection between the media's conception of and construction of stories on race-related issues and their impact on public opinion (van Dijk, 1991). The writer and critic bell hooks (1990) suggests that stereotypes of people of colour are developed to "serve as substitutions for reality." They are contrived images that are developed and projected onto the "others."

One of the most common and persistent examples of racism in the media is the frequency which racial minorities and Blacks are singled out as "having problems" that require a disproportionate amount of political attention or public resources to solve or "creating problems." *They* make unacceptable demands that threaten the political, social, or moral order of society (Fleras and Elliot, 1992; van Dijk, 1991; Hall et al., 1975).

> When visible minorities do appear in our newspapers and TV public affairs programming, they emerge as villains in a variety of ways—as caricatures from a colonial past; as extensions of foreign entities; or, in the Canadian context, as troubled immigrants in a dazzling array of trouble spots; hassling police, stumping immigration authorities, cheating on welfare, or battling among themselves or with their own families. (Siddiqui, 1993:D1)

An example of how the media negatively stereotype people of colour is the coverage of the Sikh community by the mass media in Vancouver. Press coverage of issues of concern to this community are sensationalized, and

Table 10.1
IMAGES OF VARIOUS MINORITY GROUPS

Aboriginal Peoples	Blacks	Asians
✓ Savages	✓ Drug Addicts	✓ Untrustworthy
✓ Alcoholics	✓ Pimps	✓ Menacing
✓ Uncivilized	✓ Prostitutes	✓ Unscrupulous
✓ Uncultured	✓ Entertainers	✓ Subhuman
✓ Murderers	✓ Athletes	✓ Submissive
✓ Noble	✓ Drug Dealers	✓ Maiming
✓ Needing a White saviour	✓ Murderers	✓ Quaint
✓ Victim	✓ Gangsters	✓ Gangsters
	✓ Butlers and Maids	✓ Prostitutes
	✓ Simple-minded	✓ Cooks
	✓ Inconsequential	✓ Store vendors
	✓ Savages	
	✓ Primitive	
	✓ Needing a White saviour	

Sikhs are commonly depicted as militants, terrorists, and disposed to violence. For example, in *The Province* newspaper in Vancouver, headlines of articles covering Sikh issues included "Guns Alarm Cops" (March 27, 1985); "Close Watch on City Sikhs (October 20, 1985); and "Sikh Militancy Grows" (November 7, 1985). The articles conjured images of conflict, civil unrest, violent confrontation, terrorism, and destruction of property. In turn, the repetition of these images and stereotypes reinforce prejudice against not only Sikhs but all South Asians (Khaki and Prasad, 1988). The impact of stereotyping by the media is highlighted in the following case study.

CASE STUDY 10.1

THE RACIALIZATION OF CRIME

By examining the media's coverage of crime, one can see how the media shape public understanding and opinion formation and have documented the way in which racial identity is linked to deviance and crime, particularly among Black males (Daniel and Allen, 1988; Hall et al.,1978; van Dijk, 1991).

Hall identified two definitions of crime. First is the official definition, constructed by agencies responsible for crime control—the police, government agencies, and the courts. The second and equally powerful definition is the media's construction of crime. The portrayal of crime in the mass media plays a significant role in shaping public definitions of the "crime problem." The media explanations of crime are overlaid with racist ideologies that serve to "knit together…the enigma of crime and its causation" (Hall et al., 1975:15).

Following the urban disturbances of the early 1980s in the United Kingdom, the idea of Black criminality received considerable attention by the media.

> The police, aided by a hyperbolic mass media, were able to nail down their problem more precisely. Blacks, particularly young blacks, were a new force in British society and one which, unless checked, could undermine the nation's stability. A rush of lurid editorials, academic theses and television documentaries tended to confirm the police's premise: blacks were a problem. (Cashmore and McLaughlin, 1991:3).

As Black crime becomes an increasing focus of police activity, the media become willing partners in fostering the racialization of crime. As a consequence, Black life in a general sense becomes increasingly interpreted or misinterpreted by the media through the "lens which criminal signs and imagery provide" (Gilroy, 1987:76).

While the circumstances and social environment in Canada are not totally comparable to events unfolding in the United Kingdom, the United States, and the Netherlands, there is nevertheless a similar pattern of the racialization of crime, developed primarily by the police but communicated and perpetuated by the Canadian media.

EXAMPLES OF RACIALIZATION

A particularly striking example of the media's role in fostering the racialization of crime was a three-part series published by *The Globe and Mail* on Jamaican crime. The first article in this series (Appleby, 1992a), entitled "Island Crime Wave Spills Over: Criminal Subculture Exported to Canada," begins with a description of life in a Kingston slum:

> It's a sweltering Friday night—an ideal time for a plainclothes cop on the intelligence unit to look around. On one corner, Detective Corporal Mark Allen chats briefly with a man recovering from a bullet wound in the neck. It was a drive by shooting, apparently motiveless. On another a woman complains that a gang of robber rapists is terrorizing the neighbourhood. He stops in a doorway to speak with a mother whose two teen-aged sons were recently slain.... Jamaica's crime rate is among the world's highest,... "I've never seen violence to this extent—to kill for no apparent reason," said a Western diplomat. (Appleby, 1992a)

The article goes on to note that although it is now unpopular to discuss Black crime in Toronto, it is quite clear that "this criminal subculture has been exported" and is in evidence on the streets of Toronto and, to a lesser extent, in Montreal. Named and unnamed Toronto police sources are quoted as saying that Black crime is no myth; it is a reality "which manifests itself in arrest records" and is proof that "a volatile group of young Jamaican males has altered Toronto's criminal landscape...in an explosion of guns and crack cocaine." In the meantime, local Jamaican police sources maintain that this is strictly a Canadian problem and caused by "riffraff" who migrate. And local Jamaican experts are quoted as saying that crack cocaine is the result of the hopelessness of life among the poor and the breakdown of the family. It ends by offering another "expert's" opinion: that Jamaicans are aggressive and violence-prone. He explains why, as follows:

> The theory goes back to the movement of slaves from West Africa. . . . [The ones] who were offloaded in Jamaica . . . were rebellious on the trip and it was the first opportunity to offload them.

The argument is pursued in the second article, in which a number of Jamaican authorities and institutions are blamed for this violent culture. It begins by describing the "police heavy-handedness in one of the world's most violent cultures." Examples of "wholesale corruption and complicity in the drug trade" follow.

Finally, in the third article, a "divide and rule" reasoning is pursued, as disputes between Trinidadians and Jamaicans are revealed and a Trinidadian woman is quoted: "*Pressed*, she says: 'I don't know why Jamaicans are different. They just are.'" Although this article focusses on Jamaican youth in Toronto, even some born there, it nevertheless provides further explanations of the breakdowns in Jamaican society, including traditional political rivalries between its two major political parties and the "erosion of church authority."

To further add to the confusion, the writer reveals that the relationship between traditional explanations and criminal youth in Toronto is unclear, especially as more experts are cited to show that the majority of criminals are now Toronto-born. Returning to the theme of Jamaican crime, the article cites American police officials as solemnly maintaining that "Toronto's a major centre, no doubt about it."

Building on the same theme, *The Globe and Mail*, some months later, reported on prostitution in Halifax. The subheader of the article read: "Prostitution: Halifax Police Have Set their Sights on Black Pimps Who Are Sending Hundreds of Local Teen-agers to Sell Their Bodies on the Streets Across Canada." According to the reporter, most of the young *White* prostitutes work for a "loosely organized community of Nova Scotia *Black* men." (authors' italics) (Jones, 1993). A letter to the editor a few weeks later succinctly identifies the racism underlying the article and the header:

> The insinuation that a pimp's skin colour is in any way relevant is as preposterous as suggesting a prostitute's skin colour might predispose her to such a vocation. *The Globe and Mail* should be more sensitive. (Joffe, 1993)

In 1992, a tabloid in Montreal published a six-page section titled, "Whites Are Fed Up With Blacks" (because of the many crimes they commit). Details of many police–Black-community encounters were provided. Black-community leaders in the city condemned the paper for "painting all Blacks as criminals" and asked that the government press charges of hate propaganda against the tabloid. A prominent member of the community, whose picture was printed with the caption "Asshole of the week," sued the paper. Hotline radio shows were, however, deluged with callers who agreed with the article. Callers said that "Blacks are parasites of society.... They should be sent back to their islands.... Blacks are genetically prone to violence" (*The Toronto Star*, August 6, 1992).

In October 1992, the Metropolitan Toronto Police Association called for a job action to protest a new rule in which police were required to complete a report after unholstering a gun. The subtext of this job action was a protest over the issue of "race relations." While the media reported this event in great detail, a feature article in *The Toronto Star* written by "noted Canadian author" Carsten Stroud added further fuel to the issue of the racialization of crime by arguing that "cops are right to resent and resist the kinds of restrictions that the NDP and the [Black] activists are trying to place on them." He sees the police protest purely in terms of the escalating confrontation between police and Black youth:

> This is a war that's going to get a lot nastier before it gets better, because, make no mistake about it, the Metro police are the angriest police force I've seen outside of New York City. Why? For anyone who sees a Black kid being thrown into a cruiser

and automatically thinks "racist cop," the obvious answer is because the forces of goodness and racial justice have finally jerked their leashes and the cops don't like it. (*The Toronto Star*, October 17, 1992)

The implication throughout this article is that the bad behaviour of Black youth is being defended unrealistically by Black activists such as Dudley Laws and the Black Action Defence Committee, who do not represent the majority of the Black community. The police anger is further exacerbated by the NDP government, which is allegedly overinfluenced by these radical activists (or so the article claims), in its efforts to challenge the authority and restrict the powers of the police.

A columnist working at the Montreal *Gazette* provides a similar perspective on the racialization of crime. Writing about a disturbance that broke out in Montreal following a parade celebrating Caribbean culture, he observed:

A profoundly disturbing fact has emerged: If you're Black, you're subject to immense scrutiny by the public and the media. It is disturbing because only one factor directs this spotlight—the colour of your skin. Specifically Black skin. It's a scrutiny that nurtures a level of myth and misconception that defies logic because it ignores or devalues an array of hard facts about the history and the diversity of Canada's Black population. (Chandwani, 1993)

A further example of the racialization of crime by the media is the numerous instances in which newspapers identify the origin or status of criminals in reporting their crimes. One of the most blatant occurred in a story describing the conviction of a man who sexually abused women. *The Toronto Star* (December 22, 1992) identified the man twice when it noted that the "32-year-old Malaysian immigrant…" This unnecessary identification reinforces the idea in the reader's mind that immigrants of colour are responsible for the crimes committed in Canada. Stating the country of origin has become more frequent in the media because many media organizations now subscribe to the prohibition against identifying people by race.

ANALYSIS

As soon as people of colour, especially Black people, are associated with a criminal act, the event becomes newsworthy and is given significant coverage. Van Dijk (1991) suggested that the same crime committed by Whites would be ignored or given less attention. "Black crime," as it is frequently referred to, is perceived as posing a greater threat to the dominant White population. Explanations of criminal activity, although they are the acts of individuals, are frequently interpreted as a form of "group crime" for which the entire Black community is held responsible. The perspectives and "expert" opinions of White authorities (especially the police) are usually considered more reliable and unbiased than those of a person of colour.

The marginalization and stigmatization of people of colour in the media follows the same demarcation of "them" and "us" discussed elsewhere. The subtext of the discourse is that minorities and immigrants are aggressive, unlawful, disrespectful of democratic laws and values, and demanding of special treatment (van Dijk, 1991).

In many of the examples cited above, the media appear to work hand in hand with law-enforcement agencies in reporting criminal activities. In some police forces, the communication or public-affairs unit provides a continuous flow of information to local media organizations. For example, every morning CITY TV in

Toronto shows video clips of crimes committed overnight. The video is provided by the Metropolitan Toronto Police Force. Press releases are also distributed by the police to newspapers, radio, and television stations daily, providing statistics and data relating mainly to criminal activity.

The impact of this close relationship between the police and the media is that internalized racist perceptions, attitudes, and assumptions underlying police behaviour are reinforced by the biases of journalists, editors, newscasters, and their producers. Each institution's self-interests are served by this arrangement. Thus, for example, significantly more coverage was given to isolated incidents of violence during the Caribana festivities in Toronto in August 1992 than to the festival itself.

MISREPRESENTATION IN THE PRINT MEDIA

The first study to identify and document racism in the print media in Canada was made in 1977 by Rosenfeld and Spina, who examined *The Toronto Sun*'s coverage of issues relating to immigration and racial and ethnic communities. In their review of the newspaper, they found considerable evidence of racial bias and discrimination. Their analysis revealed that *The Toronto Sun* presented the reader with a single, prejudiced view of the world.

In 1982, the Canadian Arab Federation commissioned a study on the image of Arabs in political cartoons (Mouammar, 1986). Cartoons were gathered from three major Toronto dailies from 1972 to 1982. She found that Arabs were repeatedly portrayed as bloodthirsty terrorists who were blackmailing the West. They were depicted in the cartoons as ignorant, cruel, and backward. One cartoon after another over the 10-year period portrayed Arabs in a negative and stereotypical manner, using images suggesting that the Arab was tyrannical, untrustworthy, amoral, irrational, and the architect of international terrorism. The researcher pointed to the danger of this kind of racism by suggesting that the foundations of the **Holocaust** were laid by German caricaturists who commonly depicted Jews in a similar fashion (Mouammar, 1986:13).

Ginzberg's (1985) content analysis of *The Toronto Sun* was precipitated by the escalating concern and frustration felt by a number of racial-minority groups in the community who perceived that the *Sun* had consistently and repeatedly portrayed people of colour and Aboriginal peoples in a negative manner. In addition, there was a perception that the *Sun* had repeatedly distorted issues in which these communities were involved, including race relations, immigration, discrimination in employment and education, apartheid, and affirmative action. There had been a long history of minority groups expressing concerns about biased, inaccurate, and unbalanced portrayals of visible minorities to the management of this paper. In 1984, the Native Action Committee on the Media developed an information package concerning the racist coverage by *The Toronto Sun* of Aboriginal peoples. The committee's analysis of the *Sun*'s articles was that the coverage had caused hatred and misunderstanding toward Aboriginal peoples among the "majority society" by its racist commentaries. The *Sun* made no attempt to respond to these concerns.

Ginzberg (1985) studied over 200 editorials and columns covering the period 1978–85. The framework for the analysis was based on the work of Gordon Allport (1954), which emphasized that prejudice is not a single thought or behaviour, but a pattern or system of behaviours that are not independent of each other. When one is present, others are also likely to be present. Allport suggested that the component parts of prejudice include, first, negative stereotyping, which is an exaggerated, overgeneralized belief, unsubstantiated opinion, or uncritical judgement about a group of persons. Its function is to justify conduct in relation to that group of persons. Stereotypes, through repetition, become embedded in people's attitudes, reflected in their behaviour, and woven into the culture of the majority group. They can also deprive persons from racial groups of their sense of self-worth.

Stereotypes were found repeatedly in the *Sun*. People of Indo-Pakistani origin were depicted as violent, weak, passive, submissive, and barbaric. Gandhi was called a "cunning and charismatic witch doctor," and "Democracy is beyond the aptitude of the majority of Asians." Arabs were violent, uncivilized, and primitive: "A tendency to violence in the settlement of disputes characterizes the typical Muslim male." Aboriginal peoples were portrayed as immoral, drunks, useless, and primitive. Blacks were depicted as immoral, savage, uncivilized, and superstitious.

A second component of prejudice that appears regularly in the columns and editorials of *The Toronto Sun* is the writers' attempts to persistently rationalize or deny their prejudice. For example, "Gandhi did not seek peace but power"; "Apartheid represents a successful plan to save South African cities from the squalor that affects Bombay, Delhi and Calcutta through the huge, uncontrolled flux of the rural poor."

A third component of prejudice woven into the words and images used by *Sun* writers is a belief in biological racism. A view frequently shared in the newspaper was that the White race is genetically superior to non-White races.

> Those awful riots are caused by Black people who seem to be subhuman in their total lack of civility.... The Blacks of North America have diverged widely from their distant relatives in Africa. In their music and dancing and in their athletic prowess some specific genetic distinctions shine through the environmental influences. (Mackenzie Porter, July 15, 1978; cited in Ginzberg, 1985)

> Too many Afro-Asians abroad, even some of those with august rank of diplomat, possess only a veneer of civilization. (Porter, April 23, 1984; cited in Ginzberg, 1985)

Ginzberg found many examples of demagogy, a fourth component of prejudice. Repeatedly, statements appeared in the writings of editors and columnists that were likely to incite fear and hatred. The most blatant example of demagogy was found in "Our Nuremberg," in which the editorialist claimed that Toronto was gradually evolving its own set of Nuremberg race laws. Words like "gestapo," "fascist-like," "police state," "jackbooters," and "human-rights storm troopers" served to incite fear, on the part of *Sun's* readers, of human-rights policies and race-relations initiatives.

The study concluded that *The Toronto Sun* had indeed violated the fundamental freedom and responsibility that society had entrusted to the press. The potential impact of a publication that has a daily circulation of over 300 000 readers—and on Sundays more than 460 000—is enormous.

A smaller-scale study of *The Globe and Mail's* coverage of the immigration issue was conducted in 1985–86 (Ducharme, 1986). Of 70 articles written from 1980 to 1985, 12 were considered to be biased or slanted. About 86 percent of the articles focussed on the numbers of immigrants and refugees entering Canada. News stories on immigration levels and quotas appeared once a month, on average, in the 5-year period, with varying figures and contradictory estimates. Misuse of language was also noted; there was a reliance on clichés and stereotypes, such as "floods of refugees"; the need to "stem the tide of illegal aliens"; the "luring" of entrepreneurs into Canada; immigrants and refugees who "wreck" and "gatecrash" the system; the "surge" in the number of immigrants; and "job stealers."

The researcher drew attention to the way in which both the headlines and the use of language frequently distorted, confused, or hid reality. The emphasis was placed on the sensational details of immigration policy, rather than on comprehensive understanding and analysis.

In promoting and sustaining the values of the White dominant society, the media often draw a line between the "First World" and the "Third World," between the "West" and the "non-West," the "North" and the "South." This line of demarcation is created by the constant production of images that distinguish between the positive attributes, capacities, and strengths of the West and those of the countries of the East or the Third World. The First World is rational, moral, and on the side of the good and right, whereas the Third World is irrational, immoral, and uncivilized (Said in McCarthy, 1993).

CASE STUDY 10.2

THE JOURNALISTIC RIGHT TO MALIGN MINORITIES

Doug Collins, a journalist in British Columbia, has been a regular columnist with various newspapers for two decades. He has had a long history of attacking racial minorities and Aboriginal peoples, among others, in his columns for the *Vancouver Sun* and Vancouver's *North Shore News*. Some examples of the overt prejudice in his articles follow.

On immigration:

> The result is that Vancouver is becoming a suburb of Asia; Toronto, once the Queen City of English Canada, has become the tower of Babel, with every race except ours bawling for special rights and receiving them. Montreal is a target for

the enlightened folk of Haiti. And the politicians wouldn't care if voodooism became the leading religion. (Collins, 1991)

On education:

The Third World is occupying the classrooms of much of the Lower Mainland. This is clear from the statistics and the pictures on TV. Hardly a White face in sight. Which should tell you something about why we have to have free lunches. But no one wants to say it. (Collins, 1992a)

On Aboriginal peoples:

What saving the country boils down to is handing out more dough to the French and the ever-squawking Indians who know they are dealing with dummies and never had it so good until we turned up and showed them the wheel. (Collins, 1992b)

On the Holocaust:

The issue is whether the Holocaust took place. In other words, whether the Hitler regime deliberately set out to kill all the Jews it could get its hands on, and that 6,000,000 died as a result. More and more, I am coming to the conclusion that it [the Holocaust] didn't. (Darling thoughts that could land a guy in jail in this free country of ours!) (Collins, 1988)

ANALYSIS

Robin Ridington, an anthropologist, launched a complaint against the journalist with the British Columbia Press Council. His concern over Collins was based on an understanding that a journalist's language

conveys messages through the complex associations and implications of its metaphors and unstated assumptions. If a journalist's language violates the experiential reality of a minority or identifiable group within a society, it creates a conflict between public reality and the personal experience of those who come to be identified as deviant. (Ridington, 1986:6)

In his brief to the press council, he argued that

the language used by Doug Collins and supported by the *North Shore News* editorially tells the people of the *North Shore News* that it is normal to deprecate members of their community because of the ethnic group to which they belong. It implies that members of certain ethnic or other identifiable groups are inherently inferior to others as Canadians. (Ridington, 1986:7)

The press council dismissed the complaint, which led Ridington to conclude that print journalists appear to have the right to malign minority groups and be validated by their own self-regulatory institution. As a result of the complaint to the press council, the newspaper threatened the university at which Ridington was a professor with legal action, and Collins continued to attack him personally in his columns.

In 1993, the British Columbia Organization to Fight Racism (BCOFR) was appalled when it learned that the governor general of Canada had presented Doug Collins with an award that honours Canadians who have made a significant contribution to their fellow citizens, their community, or Canada. Collins was described by the member of Parliament for North Vancouver, who presented him with the medal, as a "controversial columnist for the *North Shore News* who forces people to think for themselves and re-evaluate commonly held opinions." The BCOFR circulated a petition to rescind the medal (BCOFR, 1993).

MARGINALIZATION IN PROGRAMMING

In a study by Granzberg (1982), 360 hours of prime-time television programming on two major Canadian and one American network were examined. The study concluded that the portrayal of racial minorities was characterized by misrepresentation and stereotyping. Minorities were depicted as having an image of weakness and instability. They were shown as being less maritally stable, less important, less gainfully employed, and less heroic than White people.

Studies conducted in the United States and the United Kingdom on the portrayal of racial minorities in the daily press found a scarcity of news stories that challenged racial stereotypes. According to van Dijk (1991), a comprehensive analysis of racism in the media, White newsmakers are more likely to report stories that confirm their preconceptions of Blacks as drug pushers, criminals, and troublemakers.

Daniel and Allen (1988) showed that this phenomenon also applies to leading newsmagazines. Comparing the coverage of Blacks in *Time* and *Newsweek* with issues of concern identified by Black organizations such as the National Urban League, they found that topics that are of critical concern to Blacks, such as maintaining civil rights gains or alleviating poverty, were not at all the focus of these news magazines. Van Dijk (1991) argued that given the fact that White elites control the contents and structure of the media, it may be expected that the White press shares in the overall system that sustains White group dominance.

A classic example of the kind of misrepresentation indulged in by the electronic media was a feature on a public affairs program, aired on a national Canadian network, called "Campus Giveaway." The program was filmed at the University of Toronto. By using distorted statistics and erroneous information, it communicated the notion that Chinese students were depriving Canadians of their rightful places in the university. The assumption was that anyone who was not White had to be an immigrant or "foreigner." In reality, although almost all the faces filmed belonged to individuals of Chinese descent, every individual was either a Canadian citizen or a permanent resident. Despite this, the viewer was left with the distorted impression that deserving Anglo-Canadians could not find places in medical and engineering schools because these "outsiders" were taking their place.

In recent years, although racial minorities are seen more frequently in television programming, particularly on U.S. networks, some disturbing patterns of the marginalization of racial minorities are emerging. The television critic for *The Globe and Mail* observed that where Black people were central to a television show they tended to be portrayed (even more one-dimensionally than is TV's norm) as "victim, villain, buffoon or cuddly, folksy types" (Cuff, 1990). Historically, the predominant images of Black people portrayed on both American television networks and the Hollywood film industry have been those of criminals, rioters, thieves, drug addicts, pimps, and prostitutes (Cuff, 1992). It has been suggested that the mainstream White supremacist media make it appear that a Black menace to societal safety is at large (hooks, 1990).

Actors and popular media personalities such as Arsenio Hall and Oprah Winfrey are rarely critical of or outspoken about the systemic and personal racism that is a fact of life for many minorities. Hall's clowning agreeability presents little threat to the common racial stereotype of Blacks.

The world portrayed for 9 years on "The Cosby Show" features a Black family, the Huxtables, composed of a father who is a doctor and a mother who is a lawyer. The children go to university. The show is a reassuring fantasy of both domestic life and Black upper middle-class life. The Huxtable family live in a world unknown to most Black people in the United States. They almost never encounter racial prejudice or discrimination. The lifestyle they enjoy is an unrealistic portrayal of the experiences of the majority of American Blacks.

There is little connection between the social status of Black Americans and "the fabricated images of Black people that Americans consume everyday" (Cuff, 1989). "The Cosby Show" is designed to offer an antidote to the pervasive images of Blacks, as drug addicts, criminals, and basketball players, that dominate television programming. It is intended to entertain White audiences and make them feel comfortable with Blacks (*New York Times*, 1989). On the other hand, shows such as "I'll Fly Away" and "Frank's Place" which dealt with far more realistic, complex, and relevant issues such as racism, classism, and sexism were scrapped.

Open-Line Shows

Open-line radio and television shows, which have become increasingly popular, often provide an opportunity for hosts, listeners, and viewers to publicly disseminate racist beliefs. An example of this occurred in April 1985, during Gary Bannerman's daily call-in radio program in Vancouver. The program that day provided the host and his listeners with an opportunity to express derogatory and demeaning views about Aboriginal peoples. The program was supposed to discuss self-government and land claims, but the host chose instead to start the show by delivering a diatribe against Native peoples:

> Every Native Indian alive today has got everything to do with the tragedy of the Native peoples, the fact that they have the highest rates of incest in Canada, the highest rates of crime, and misery and poverty and failure, you name it.... They have privileges that the average Canadian doesn't have, endless privileges, whether it comes to fisheries, handouts, meetings, grants. And what do they do with them? The brother has a child with his sister, is what they do with them. (Ridington, 1986:44)

In response to the mood and assumptions established by the host, callers supported and legitimized his racist comments. Under the guise of "fair comment," Bannerman abused the principle of free expression (Khaki and Prasad, 1988).

Ridington's (1986) study concluded that the very nature of call-in shows, which are growing in popularity in Canada, is a matter of concern with respect to race relations. It points out that the call-and-response format of radio and TV shows is a form of reality management, in which hosts (or columnists) "call" their audience in a language that establishes their assumptive world. The respondents (telephone callers or letter writers) are encouraged to speak in a manner and language consistent with the host/columnist's perceptions. Responses that oppose this assumptive world appear to be deviant.

LACK OF ACCESS TO MASS MEDIA

Many institutions have ready access to the media. As a result, a significant proportion of news coverage deals with information that emanates from government agencies, politicians, police forces, school boards, commissions, chambers of commerce, and labour federations (Siddiqui, 1993). This contrasts sharply with the lack of access of people of colour in making their viewpoints and voices heard. Hall et al. (1975) argue that media professionals (editors, journalists, broadcasters, producers) and their institutions control access between the elites of power and the mass audience. By controlling the qualitative aspects of the information that will become the audience's news, by determining the events that will dominate the "agenda" of new programs, newspapers, and public discussion, and by selecting which "expert" opinion will be solicited, the media assume the function of gatekeepers and agenda setters.

Black musicians and their promoters have identified significant racial barriers in their access to the Canadian broadcasting system. Despite the popularity of Black dance music, there is little opportunity for it to be heard on commercial radio-stations in Canada. This issue was highlighted in 1990, in a battle for what was then Toronto's last available FM radio license. The award of the licence to a country-music station dashed the hopes of hundreds of thousands of Metro-area fans of Black music.

The decision by the Canadian Radio-Television and Telecommunications Commission (CRTC) was opposed by three of the commissioners, including chief commissioner Keith Spicer. He wrote in his dissenting opinion that he regretted the missed opportunity to serve the public interest "by opening other minds to a vital and growing dimension of Toronto." He further stated that an opportunity was missed to "embrace these [multicultural and racial] communities by echoing new themes, new accents, new values, new music." (*The Globe and Mail*, l990). A *Toronto Star* editorial concluded:

> By rejecting dance music such as rhythm and blues, reggae, rap, calypso, salsa, and other Afro and Caribbean styles, the Commission displayed a woeful ignorance of the varied multicultural community that constitutes Metropolitan Toronto. It doesn't appear to understand that the once predominantly White days of Hogtown are no more. (*The Toronto Star*, 1990)

As even the chief commissioner noted in his dissenting opinion, the decision did not pay sufficient attention to the principles of the Multiculturalism Act (to promote policies, programs, and practices that enhance the ability of individuals and communities of all origins to contribute to the continuing evolution of Canada) or the Broadcasting Policy (Canadian Radio and Television Commission, 1986), which states the CRTC's policy to increase access by ethnic groups to conventional radio and television and to cable services.

RACISM IN THE ADVERTISING INDUSTRY

Advertising plays a crucial role in the media as a primary source of income. In a less tangible but equally significant way, advertising has enormous power, not only over mass media organizations, but also in establishing "desirable" societal standards and styles of living.

Advertising, in its multiplicity of forms, provides many of the images and experiences we take for granted, and paints a picture of our social world. Day after day, the White images circulated in newspapers and magazines, on radio and television, and on the movie screen, mould impressions and shapes perceptions. Since advertising is geared to White consumers, audiences are reminded of who counts, who is reflected in the mirror, and who is cast outside the mainstream of society.

Non-representation

The first Canadian study of the representation of people of colour in advertising was carried out by Elkin (1971) on behalf of the Ontario Human Rights Commission. The study examined the representation of visible minorities in TV commercials and revealed that only 3.7 percent of television ads contained a minority performer—usually in a group or crowd scene. A follow-up study in 1980 found only 48 visible-minority persons among the 2000 people in the commercials, and the majority of these were children or high-profile American sports and entertainment figures.

In 1982, a two-phase research project commissioned by the federal government was designed to determine the attitudes of Canadians toward the use of peoples of colour in TV advertising and provide a content analysis of commercials. This analysis revealed that only 10 percent of the over 600 commercials viewed included racial-minority performers; most again were either children or people in crowd scenes (PEAC Media Research, 1982).

In the second phase of the study, small groups of viewers in different regions across Canada (both White and non-White) were exposed to sixteen recent commercials. Half of the ads contained White characters only, and the remainder contained multiracial characters. The findings of the survey challenged many of the basic assumptions held by advertisers, many of whom assumed that using Black or Asian actors would have a negative effect on White viewers. The study found no significant differences in viewers' responses that could be attributed to the presence or absence of visible minorities. Regardless of the racial characteristics of the actors, participants in the research stressed the importance of the creative quality and realism of the commercials. There was also some concern expressed on the part of the non-White viewers about the stereotyped roles played by most non-White actors in these commercials.

Niemi and Salgado (1989) conducted an analysis of advertising on billboards in Montreal subway stations. A total of 311 billboards were analyzed. Of the 163 billboards depicting people, only 10 showed an individual from a visible-minority community. Of the 44 advertisers, only one included a person of colour, and that was the Ministry of Tourism in Ontario. The researchers argued that this "Whitewashing" of advertising reflected both ethnocentrism and discrimination. They suggested that the invisibility of racial minorities denied their existence, devalued their contribution to society, and trivialized their aspirations to participate as full members of society. The exclusion of racial minorities helped perpetuate the "White face" of Canada, "leaving others with feelings of rejection, of marginality and of non-belonging" (28).

A nationwide study conducted by the Canadian Advertising Foundation in 1992 found that 70 percent of Canadians thought that advertising is still "too geared toward White consumers" and fails to reflect the cosmopolitan reality of Canada in the 1990s. The poll found that 36 percent of respondents thought negatively about companies that excluded racial minorities from their advertising. The chairman of the firm that conducted the poll said that "Canada is a multicultural country. Our advertising should reflect that, but right now our advertisers are behind the times" (Goldfarb, 1992). The advertising industry, like other media industries, remains trapped in its self-defeating stereotypes.

Stereotyping

Another common manifestation of racism is stereotyping. Aunt Jemima, for example, has appeared on boxes of pancake mix for over 100 years. The smiling Black woman, whose head until three years ago was wrapped in a kerchief, is reminiscent of a mammy/servant ready to prepare pancakes for a White family. Rastus is still the Cream of Wheat chef, and Uncle Ben (the negative association is with Uncle Tom, a deeply offensive image to Black people) is still the smiling, grandfatherly Black man who has been pictured on boxes of rice for more than a half century. These images, created decades ago, are woven into popular culture. As Craig Neville, a Washington advertising analyst, states:

> These are symbols that are so ingrained in the society and culture that most people do not even notice them any more.... These symbols promote stereotypes. (Graham, 1993)

In the same article, sociologist Gaynelle Grant comments that "the very nature of advertising is to alter how we look at ourselves and things in our environment...and advertising that perpetrates negativity—like Blacks as smiling, simple-minded servants—affects the way our culture regards Black people."

RESPONSES TO RACISM IN THE MEDIA

The many above examples provide a significant body of evidence that racism in the media exists and that it is reflected in almost every part of the mass communication system in Canada. The following section considers some of the responses to this reality.

COMMUNITY ADVOCACY

There are many examples in Canada of the significant role of the community as a change agent. In the case cited earlier, of the racist program on a public affairs show aired by a TV network, a national protest was spearheaded by Chinese Canadian communities across Canada. It had the support and participation of many other community groups and individuals from a wide diversity of racial and cultural backgrounds. After a 7-month campaign, the president of CTV issued a public apology.

The Nisga'a Tribal Council, which had a 100-year-history of lobbying on behalf of Aboriginal issues, together with the Musqueam Band, filed a complaint with the CRTC against the Gary Bannerman program discussed earlier. The CRTC strongly condemned the radio station and its hosts. It urged the station to institute controls immediately. The council also filed a complaint with the Ministry of Justice. However, the inadequate response of the media and the legal and justice systems to this and several similar incidents of racism in the media resulted in the formation of the Ad Hoc Media Committee for Better Race Relations in Vancouver, a coalition of Jewish, Indo-Canadian, Chinese, and Black communities, in 1985.

In 1986–87, Khaki and Prasad (1988) conducted a survey of racism and the media. The study was designed to examine the portrayal of visible minorities and Aboriginal peoples in the media. The intent of the study was to create a greater awareness of the concerns of these groups regarding negative coverage in the media and to foster a more positive relationship between minorities and the media.

In Ontario over the last 15 years, community advocacy committees have been formed both to respond to particular racial incidents and to deal with the general problems of bias and discrimination in advertising, programming, and news coverage. For example, as the result of a racist incident involving a Toronto broadcaster on a weekly jazz radio program, an intensive and extensive lobbying process was set in motion. This ultimately led to a community advisory committee being established to assist the senior management of this station and to create new policies and practices that gradually led to changes in programming, hiring practices, and news coverage.

In the field of advertising, an effective strategy was developed by the Urban Alliance on Race Relations in Toronto in 1984 to deal with the almost total exclusion of racial minorities in advertising and promotions by major retail stores in Metropolitan Toronto. Seven companies were targeted, all of which were frequented by large numbers of visible-minority shoppers. A mail-back campaign was instituted after many lobbying attempts by individuals and organizations had failed to produce any changes in the glossy brochures and ads distributed daily. Letters were sent to each of the targeted companies, informing them of the campaign and of the reasons for it.

Details of the campaign were then distributed to race relations organizations and community groups across Metropolitan Toronto. Their co-operation and support were solicited. They were asked to mail back every catalogue, flyer, and promotion that did not reflect the multiracial composition of Metro, with a note to the president and advertising managers explaining why. Press releases were distributed, announcing the campaign. A content analysis of the ads 6 months later revealed positive results. Although there were no subsequent attempts to measure the representation of people of colour in advertising, evidence suggests that the numbers of racial minorities used in private-sector advertising have increased.

Public-Sector Responses

Ontario developed guidelines concerning the portrayal of visible minorities in government advertising and communications in 1983. In 1984, the federal government introduced similar guidelines, largely as a result of lobbying efforts by community groups and organizations, who urged the government agencies to ensure that their ads and promotions reflected Canada's racial and cultural diversity. However, several years after the establishment of these guidelines, there are no mechanisms in place to monitor or evaluate the governments' performance and their implementation of these guidelines. For a brief period, the government of Ontario established an advisory committee composed of community representatives and civil servants who had full-time management positions in provincial ministries, but the committee was allowed to fade away.

In 1986, a task force on broadcasting policy affirmed that Canadian broadcasting should contribute toward "safeguarding, enriching and strengthening the cultural, political, social and economic fabric of Canada." The CRTC's policy recognizes the importance of multicultural programming. Briefs presented to the task force were united in the view that cultural and racial minorities do not want multicultural programming confined to special ethnic television and radio services. They expected public broadcasters, particularly the CBC, to take the lead. The task force recommended that the CRTC create a special class of licences for minority groups that would make them responsible for program context. It recommended that the right of access to the broadcasting system by Aboriginal Canadians and other Canadians, including diverse multicultural and multiracial groups, be established in the Act.

Under federal legislation, Crown corporations such as the CBC are required to report to Parliament each year their progress toward employment equity goals for racial minorities. However, this legislation does not affect other electronic or print media.

ANALYSIS

This chapter's analysis of racism in the media reveals that the vast majority of media organizations fail to respond to the daily challenges that confront them in a multiracial, pluralistic society. Decision-makers generally have ignored or denied the existence of the racial bias and discriminatory practices in all sectors of the media. The coverage of issues affecting racial minorities are filtered through the stereotypes, misconceptions, and erroneous assumptions of largely White reporters, advertisers, journalists, editors, programmers, and producers. The media's images reinforce cultural racism, the collective belief system that divides society into "them" and "us" and sustains White group dominance.

Racism is manifested in the professional attitudes and behaviours of journalists, broadcasters, editors, publishers, program producers, directors, advertising managers, and marketing executives. It is reflected in the way in which issues are dealt with in the slant of a news story or in the use of imagery that promotes negative stereotyping (e.g., Asians are associated with gangs, Blacks and Jamaicans with crime, Tamils with immigration violations, Sikhs and Muslims with terrorism, refugees with welfare abuse). Racial bias is expressed in ethnocentric values and norms that lead advertisers to conclude that using racial minorities in an advertising campaign will have a negative impact on White consumers. It is evidenced in newspaper headlines that sensationalize issues (e.g., "Immigration Policy Called Risk to Canadian Educator's Jobs" and "Quotas, Quotas and more Quotas").

Siddiqui (1993) identifies some of the institutional barriers in media organizations that influence their coverage of racial and cultural issues:

- Although they are on the frontiers of news, journalists are rarely on the cusp of social change.
- Pretensions notwithstanding, the media are "the establishment."
- The media are not good at hearing the voices of the unorganized.
- The media's black-and-white, no greys-in-between, view of the world hurts minorities.
- Most media think of minorities only in the context of their ethnicity. Reporters and editors value their views on race relations but not on larger Canadian or world issues.
- Although race relations is clearly one of the most important issues of our time, most media do not cover it or cover it "on the run," looking for an easy hit.

Other indicators of racism in the media include the lack of recognition attributed to the qualifications and experience gained outside of Canada by media professionals; the absence of outreach and training opportunities for minorities; the way in which "facts" and "events" are selected and subsequently transformed into "news"; and the absence of programming that features the social, cultural, political, and economic contributions of people of colour.

Barriers to racial equity in the media may have the appearance of neutral practices, but in reality they reflect a preformulation of the ideas, opinions, and assumptions of the White power elite in society. Mass communication in Canada has been influenced and controlled by one dominant group and reflects its norms and values.

Racism is found in the daily operations of media organizations across the country and in every area of mass communications. As several of the studies cited in this chapter clearly demonstrate, it stems, at least in part, from the ethnocentrism that pervades the industry. The "we–they" way of thinking leads members of the dominant group to believe that the perceptions, feelings, and judgements of their group are appropriate and normative, while the beliefs and norms of "others" have less value and merit (Essed, 1991). As in other sectors, racism in the media has resulted in the denial of access, participation, and equity for racial minorities.

MEDIA REFLECT AND REPRODUCE WHITE IDEOLOGY

Canadian newspapers, magazines, and television and radio stations (with the exception of public agencies such as the CBC) are generally owned by corporate interests and are structured to sustain the economic interests of business and government elites (van Dijk, 1991; Hall et al., 1975).

Van Dijk (1991) states that the reproduction of racism by the media, particularly the press, takes the specific form of "elite racism." His thesis is that since the dominant White media's values are inextricably linked to political, social, and corporate elite groups, it is also in their interest to play a role in producing and generating consensus. He argues that the mass media have nearly exclusive control over the resources required to produce popular opinion, especially in the area of race and ethnic relations. Van Dijk suggests that the media uses distinct strategies to weaken the positions, issues, and ideas advocated by minority groups that threaten the status quo.

This analysis is consistent with that of Fleras and Elliot (1992), who observe that the media operate as powerful agents of domination, control, and propaganda. Media images of what is desirable or acceptable are absorbed, with little understanding and awareness of the indoctrination process. Thus, the media are able to establish the boundaries of social discourse from which priorities are set and public agendas are established and perpetuated.

One example of the influence of the power elite to shape the media's discourse is the debate over employment equity, a federal and Ontario government-legislated program for overcoming employment barriers affecting people of colour, Aboriginal peoples, women, and people with disabilities. Most media organizations reflect the position of the corporate elite by misrepresenting employment equity as a risk to the operation of a free marketplace, a violation of the merit principle, and a threat to White males.

FREEDOM OF SPEECH

There exists in the media a significant resistance to altering the power of the dominant culture. Attempts by racial minorities to protest and resist racist images and discourse in the media are frequently challenged by the media.

These protests are seen by the corporate elite as attempts to suppress freedom of expression and are equated with censorship. What is frequently ignored is the connection between the championing of freedom of expression and the freedom of the marketplace to operate without constraint. Van Dijk (1991) argues that freedom of expression is closely linked to freedom of enterprise.

Many see the issue of freedom of speech in the context of the lack of access that people of colour and other groups have to the communication networks. The numerous examples cited in this chapter indicate that racial minorities are largely excluded from participation in public discourse. As Nourbese Philip suggests:

> Freedom of expression in this society is underwritten not by the free flow of information, but by the fact that there are those who are powerful enough in society to make *their* voices, *their* version of history; and *their* viewpoints heard. (1993:66)

In the same way, Hill (1992) argues that the way in which "freedom of speech" is applied is really just a reference to the rights and privileges that very few groups in this society possess, in terms of their access to the media (17). The norms, values, and assumptions of White, male-dominated institutions continue to prevent the mass media from fairly and accurately reflecting and representing the multiracial reality of Canadian society.

CONCLUSIONS

Ensuring greater access, participation, and equity in the mass communications industries continues to challenge Canadian society. The responsibility for change belongs both to the individuals working in the advertising, print, and electronic media and to the media organizations. Advertisers, editors, journalists, and broadcasters have personal biases; their attitudes, perceptions, and values are influenced by numerous social and cultural factors. However, professional standards should prevent these attitudes from being expressed in their work.

Policies to promote fairness and equity must address the underrepresentation of minorities in all areas of mass communication. Without greater access to employment opportunities, racial minorities will continue to have virtually no influence in determining how they are represented by others.

Research findings and the work of anti-racism advocates and practitioners suggest that there are a number of barriers to change:

- Freedom of the press is considered so sacred a trust that the media believe they have the right to communicate racist content in both print and broadcasts.
- The diverse and diffuse nature of the media makes them difficult to target, access, and penetrate.
- Self-regulating media agencies are either non-existent or extremely weak. Unions, press councils, and advertising boards exercise limited power and authority over media corporations.

- Significant resources are needed to effectively lobby such agencies as the CRTC. Regulations are complex and demand a high level of expertise.
- There is an absence of consistent monitoring processes and mechanisms in the media.
- Advocacy across Canada is erratic and generally limited to reactions to specific incidents.
- Few substantive, practical media anti-racism models and strategies exist. Where new approaches have been initiated, there is little dissemination of information.
- The law and the justice system provide only limited redress for libel and defamation.

SUMMARY

This chapter examined how the mass media in Canada have perpetuated and reproduced racism while maintaining an image of neutral, objective, and unbiased purveyors of the truth. Racism in the media is reflected in the racist ideologies and practices of media organizations. Media professionals are often guided by their need to support special and powerful interests, such as government and business, to promote their positions and agendas.

Numerous examples were provided of how the media create and reinforce negative stereotypes of people of colour to influence public opinion. Minorities are commonly depicted as outsiders who make unacceptable demands and pose a threat to the stability, harmony, and unity of Canadian society.

Racism is manifested in the underrepresentation of racial minorities in the advertising, print, and electronic media. People of colour are not in decision-making positions, they are largely invisible in newsrooms, and they have less access to television and radio programming. Actions by racial minorities to challenge racism in the media are dismissed as attempts to deny freedom of expression.

REFERENCES

Allport, G. (1954). *The Nature of Prejudice*. New York: Doubleday.
Appleby, T. (1992a). "Island Crime Wave Spills Over." *The Globe and Mail* (July 10):A7.
_____. (1992b). "The Twisted Arm of the Law." *The Globe and Mail*. (July 11):A1, A7.
_____. (1992c). "Identifying the Problem." *The Globe and Mail* (July 13):A1, A6.
Bey, S. (1983). "Visible Minorities in the Media." *Currents: Readings in Race Relations* (Toronto) 1(2):5–8.
British Columbia Organization to Fight Racism. (1993). "Petition." Surrey, BC.
Canadian Ethnocultural Council. (1985). "Brief to the Parliamentary Subcommittee on Equality Rights." Ottawa.
Canadian Radio and Television Commission. (1986). *Report of the Task Force on Broadcasting Policy*. Ottawa.
Cashmore, E., and E. McLaughlin, (eds.). (1991). *Out of Order: Policing Black People*. London and New York: Routledge.
Chandwani, A. (1994). "Do Blacks Attract Unfair Scrutiny?" *The Toronto Star* (July 13):A14.
Collins, D. (1988). *Vancouver Sun* (August 8).

_____. (1991). *Vancouver Sun* (September 11).

_____. (1992a). *Vancouver Sun* (January 22).

_____. (1992b). *Vancouver Sun* (August 26).

Contenta, C. (1992). "Furor Rages Over French Tabloid's Attack on Blacks." *The Toronto Star* (August 6).

Cuff, J.H. (1989). "Crossing TV's Colour Line." *The Globe and Mail* (June 15):C3.

_____. (1990). *The Globe and Mail* (August 21):C1.

_____. (1992). "Putting a Lid on the Mean Streets" *The Globe and Mail* (May 9).

Daniel, J., and A. Allen. (1988). "Newsmagazines, Public Policy and the Black Agenda." In G. Smitherman-Donaldson and T.A. van Dijk (eds.), *Discourse and Discrimination*. Detroit: Wayne State University Press.

Deverell, R. (1986). *Equal Opportunities to Perform: The Alliance of Canadian Cinema, Television and Radio Artists*. Ottawa: Secretary of State.

Ducharme, M. (1986). "The Coverage of Canadian Immigration Policy in *The Globe and Mail*." *Currents: Readings in Race Relations* (Toronto) 3(3):6–11.

Elkin, F. (1971). *The Employment of Visible Minority Groups in Mass Media Advertising*. Toronto: Ontario Human Rights Commission.

Equality Now. (1984). Report of the Special Committee on Visible Minorities in Canadian Society. Ottawa.

Essed, E. (1991). *Understanding Everyday Racism*. Newbury Park, CA: Sage.

Ewart, D., et al. (1983). *Ontario Government Task Force Report on Racial Diversity in Government Advertising and Communications*. Toronto.

Fleras, A., and J. Elliot. (1992). *Multiculturalism in Canada*. Scarborough, ON: Nelson Canada.

Gilroy, P. (1987). *There Ain't No Black in the Union Jack*. Chicago: University of Chicago Press.

Ginzberg, E. (1985). *Power Without Responsibility: The Press We Don't Deserve*. Toronto: Urban Alliance on Race Relations.

The Globe and Mail. (1990). "A License Denied to Dance Music." Editorial. (August 11).

Goldfarb, M. (1992). "Ads Still Too Geared to Whites, Poll Finds." *The Toronto Star* (December 15):D1.

Gomez, H. (1983). "The Invisible Visible Minorities." *Currents: Readings in Race Relations* (Toronto) 1(2):12–13.

Graham, R. (1993). "We Are What We Eat and the Box It Comes In." *The Toronto Star* (January 30):D5.

Granzberg, G. (1982). *The Portrayal of Visible Minorities by Canadian Television During the 1982 Prime-Time Season*. Ottawa: Secretary of State.

Hall, S. (1973). *The Structured Communications of Events*. Birmingham, U.K.: Centre for Contemporary Cultural Studies.

_____, C. Critcher, T. Jefferson, J. Clarke, and B. Roberts. (1975). *Newsmaking and Crime*. Paper presented at NACR0 Conference on Crime and the Media, Birmingham: University of Birmingham, Centre for Contemporary Cultural Studies.

_____, C. Critcher, T. Jefferson, J. Clarke, and B. Roberts. (1978). *Policing the Crisis: Mugging, the State and Law and Order*. London: Methuen.

Henry, J. (1983). "Typecasting." *Currents: Readings in Race Relations* (Toronto) 1(2):10–11.

Herman, E.S., and N. Chomsky. (1988). *Manufacturing Consent: The Political Economy of the Mass Media*. New York: Pantheon.

Hill, R. (1992). "One Part Per Million: Native Voices and White Appropriation." *Fuse* 15(3):17.

hooks, bell. (1990). *Yearning: Race, Gender, and Cultural Politics*. Boston: South End Press.

Indra, D. (1979). *The Production and Legitimization of South Asian Stereotypes by the Vancouver Press*. Lethbridge, AB: University of Lethbridge.

Joffe, H. (1993). "Offensive Premise." Letter to the Editor. *The Globe and Mail* (May 1).

Jones, D. (1993). "Skirmishes in the Skin Trade." *The Globe and Mail* (April 24):D3.

Khaki, A., and K. Prasad. (1988). *Depiction and Perception: Native Indians and Visible Minorities in the Media.*Vancouver: Ad Hoc Media Committee for Better Race Relations.

Mayers, A. (1986). *Minorities in Ontario Newsrooms.* MBA thesis. McMaster University, Hamilton, ON.

Mouammar, M. (1986). "When Cartoons Are Not Funny." *Currents: Readings in Race Relations* (Toronto) 3(3):20–21.

Niemi, F., and M. Salgado. (1989). *Un visage Français, oui, mais . . . multiculturel et multiracial, aussi!* Montreal: Centre for Research Action on Race Relations.

Nourbese Philip, M. (1993). *Showing Grit: Showboating North of the 44th Parallel.* Toronto: Poui Publications.

PEAC Media Research. (1982). *The Presence and Portrayal of Non-Whites in English-Language Television Advertising in Canada.* Ottawa: Secretary of State.

_____. (1982). *The Presence and Portrayal of Non-Whites in English-Language Television Advertising in Canada.* Ottawa: Multiculturalism Canada.

Perigoe, R., and B. Lazar. (1992). "Visible Minorities and Native Canadians in National Television News Programs." In M. Grenier (ed.), *Critical Studies of Canadian Mass Media.* Toronto and Vancouver: Butterworths.

Ridington, R. (1986). "Texts that Harm: Journalism in British Columbia." *Currents: Readings in Race Relations* (Toronto) 3(4) (Summer).

Rosenfeld, M., and M. Spina. (1977). *All the News That's Fit to Print: A Study of the Toronto Press's Coverage of Immigration, Ethnic Communities and Racism.* Toronto: Cross-Cultural Communication Centre.

Said, E. (1993). "The Politics of Knowledge." In C. McCarthy and W. Crichlow (eds.), *Race, Identity and Representation in Education.* London and New York: Routledge.

Secretary of State. (1984). *A Matter of Balance: Visible Minorities in Government Communication.* Ottawa.

Siddiqui, H. (1993). "Media and Race: Failing to Mix the Message." *The Toronto Star* (April 24):D1, D5.

Stroud, C. (1992). "Handcuffing the Police." *The Toronto Star* (October 17):C1.

Tator, C. (1984). "Mail Back Campaign." *Currents: Readings in Race Relations* (Toronto) 3(4) (Summer).

Teachman, G. (1988). *The Portrayal of Canadian Cultural Diversity on English-Language Television.* Ottawa: Secretary of State.

The Toronto Star. (1990). "Music for Everyone." Editorial. (August 10).

Troyna, B. (1984). Media and Race Relations. In E. Cashmore (ed.), *Dictionary of Race and Ethnic Relations.* London: Routledge.

Van Dijk, T. (1991). *Racism and the Press.* London: Routledge.

PART FOUR

▼▼▼▼▼▼▼▼▼▼▼▼▼▼▼▼▼▼▼▼▼▼▼▼▼▼▼▼▼▼▼▼▼▼▼▼▼

The Impact of Democratic Racism on Canadian Institutions

▼▼▼▼▼▼▼▼▼▼▼▼▼▼▼▼▼▼▼▼▼▼▼▼▼▼

This part analyzes the impact of democratic racism on Canadian organizations and institutions. Chapter 11 describes and analyzes government responses to racism, and stresses the inadequacies of laws, public policies, and state agencies in dismantling structural inequality. Chapter 12 examines the powerful methods used to resist anti-racist change in organizational culture, policies, and practices. Chapter 13 discusses the ways in which democratic racism has maintained racial inequality. The concluding pages of this book identify some strategies for change.

▼▼▼▼▼▼▼▼▼▼▼▼▼▼▼▼▼▼▼▼▼▼▼▼▼▼▼▼▼▼▼▼▼▼▼▼▼▼▼

Chapter 11

▼▼▼▼▼▼▼▼▼▼▼▼▼▼

State Responses to Racism in Canada

The law has been used through direct action, interpretation, silence and complicity. The law has been wielded as an instrument to create a common-sense justification of racial differences, to reinforce common-sense notions already deeply embedded within a cultural system of values...and to form new social constructions. (Kobayashi, 1990:49)

This chapter explores the role of the Canadian state in promulgating and controlling racism. It begins by analyzing Canada's legislation, public policy, and international commitments to eliminate racial discrimination.

First, this chapter examines the role and effectiveness of the Canadian Charter of Rights and Freedoms, human-rights codes and commissions, and the Multiculturalism Act. Second, it reviews public-sector employment equity initiatives. Third, it reviews contract compliance as the principal means by which the state uses its power, as Canada's foremost buyer of goods and services, to influence private-sector employment practices. Fourth, it examines the role of the state as a provider of essential services.

INTRODUCTION

The state has many functions and responsibilities. One of its main roles is to proscribe behaviour. It also influences public opinion through its public-policy and legislative functions and helps thereby to define national ideology. Among its many responsibilities is the responsibility to support the social, cultural, and economic development of communities that suffer racial discrimination by helping them to achieve full participation, access, and equity.

THE STATE'S ROLE AS PUBLIC-POLICY-MAKER AND DECISION-MAKER

The influence of state policies and practices at various levels (federal, provincial, and municipal) is critical to the eradication of racism and the promotion of racial equity. As such, the state has a special responsibility to assert leadership.

The fundamental rights and freedoms to which Canada adheres include the right of all residents to full and equal participation in the cultural, social, economic, and political life of the country. This right is based on the principle of the fundamental equality of individuals. The rights to equality of access, equality of opportunity, and equality of outcomes[1] for all communities are therefore implicit. They are entrenched in a number of state policies and statutes, as well as the international covenants to which Canada is a signatory.

The ideal of racial equity is a relatively new and still fragile tradition in Canada because racism has only recently been acknowledged as a serious social concern. Both federal and provincial governments have, however, enacted legislation that reflects their abhorrence of racism as a form of behaviour antithetical to a democratic state. The legislation includes the Canadian Charter of Rights and Freedoms, the Canadian Multiculturalism Act, and provincial human-rights and labour codes.

Racism is a humiliating and debilitating experience for its victims. Its destructive forces affect individuals, groups, and communities, rendering them powerless and disadvantaged. Racism also is a threat to the viability and stability of the broader society. This has been recognized by many countries; Canada has, therefore, participated in international movements to stem racism and guarantee human-rights.

INTERNATIONAL DECLARATIONS OF HUMAN RIGHTS

The Canadian government has participated in several international declarations concerning human rights. The Universal Declaration on Human Rights, was the first international covenant protecting human rights that was ratified by Canada. Since then, the United Nations has adopted a number of international covenants on human rights, including the International Convention on the Elimination of All forms of Racial Discrimination, which was ratified in 1970. The convention is based on the conviction that any doctrine of superiority based on racial differentiation is scientifically false, morally condemnable, socially unjust, and dangerous.

Signing these international conventions creates the impression that Canada is committed to the development of an equitable society based on fairness and non-discrimination. International human-rights covenants provide Canada with global standards to which all federal legislation is expected to conform, but they do not bind the provinces. Moreover, most international instruments respecting human-rights do not constitute a legally binding set of rules, and many contain no enforcement mechanisms.

THE CANADIAN CHARTER OF RIGHTS AND FREEDOMS

Before the patriation of the Constitution Act of 1982, Canada's Constitution contained no explicit prohibition of racial discrimination. Although the Canadian Bill of Rights did prohibit racial discrimination, it neither had constitutional status nor applied to provincial activities. Thus, before 1982, constitutional issues of race and civil liberties were resolved under the division-of-powers provisions of the British North America Act through what became known as the "implied bill of rights."

In 1982, the Canadian Charter of Rights and Freedoms was enshrined in Canada's Constitution. It stipulates constitutional rules to which all government action must conform with respect to anti-discrimination. Enshrining the Charter in the Constitution was hailed as a triumph. It was expected to end racial discrimination in society.

Section 15 of the Charter (the "equality rights" clause) is perhaps the most significant equality provision in the Charter. It provides that people cannot be discriminated against on the basis of "race, national or ethnic origin, colour (or) religion," among other factors. While s.15(1) prohibits discrimination and provides for equality before and under the law, equal protection of the law, and equal benefit of the law, s.15(2) also protects affirmative action programs from constitutional litigation. Arguably, s.15(2) recognizes societal inequalities and permits affirmative action measures to assure equity for all Canadians.

While the Charter outlaws discrimination on the basis of race, it defines neither discrimination nor race. The job of interpreting the Constitution has been left to the courts. The interpretation of the Charter has been an important vehicle through which ideas of racial discrimination have been explored, expanded, and restricted.

Despite its proponents, the Charter remains a seriously flawed instrument. Its equality-rights guarantee is subject to the legislative override in s.33. As a vehicle for protecting citizens against discrimination, the Charter has also been seriously criticized. Matas (1990) notes that it is an inadequate instrument for addressing racism. He suggests that, while the Charter prohibits racial discrimination in law (s.15(1)), it does not require governments to promote racial equality. Thus, a government that did absolutely nothing about racial equality would be in full compliance with the Charter. According to Matas, positive efforts to combat racial discrimination are completely absent from the Charter. He further asserts that every law is subject to Charter scrutiny, regardless of its intent. Thus, a law designed to ameliorate the effects of discrimination must pass the negative prohibitions of the Charter by clearly demonstrating that it does not contravene rights already secured in the Charter.

Duclos (1990) makes a similar point regarding the weakness in the constitutional equality-rights process. She maintains that the constitutional equality-rights system, through its procedures, makes the same flawed assertion as the human-rights system, that is, equality exists; only lapses from it need to be addressed. Kallen (1982) notes, to the contrary, that there is a covert status hierarchy among the enumerated minorities who are eligible to receive specified protection for their human rights in s.15. Ethnic and multicultural minorities, Aboriginal peoples, and women have specified human-rights protection under other Charter provisions (ss.25, 27, and 28, respectively), whereas other enumerated minorities (e.g., racial minorities) do not.

Lack of a support structure for victims of inequality and the absence of a public agency capable of challenging inequalities on behalf of disadvantaged groups is another major deficiency in the Charter. Perhaps one of its most important limitations is its failure to guarantee funding to pursue a challenge. To raise a Charter issue, a litigant must be willing and able to fight its case to the Supreme Court of Canada. A challenge of federal legislation on Charter grounds can cost $100 000 or more. Few citizens have the necessary funds, and the disparity in resources available to minority groups exacerbates social inequalities. (The Charter Challenges Program, which was supported by the federal government to help disadvantaged groups pursue Charter cases was discontinued in Febuary 1992) (*The Globe and Mail*, 1992). At the time of the writing of this book (August 1993), the prime minister had indicated a willingness to re-establish the program.

In terms of Charter equality-rights litigation, thus far, only one case has been initiated by a racial minority and four members of national or ethnic minorities. Part of the problem is the previously mentioned lack of resources, which limits access to the Charter for most of citizens, especially racial minorities, who generally occupy lower socioeconomic positions in society. This trivializes the s.15 provision and affirms that court actions are largely brought by wealthy litigants. It can be argued that a significant reason for the lack of Charter challenges by visible minorities is that justice is economically inaccessible.

A further limitation of the Charter in relation to the protection of minority rights is the passivity of the courts. Gibson (1985) argues that the Charter "stands against a backdrop of the courts' passive tradition of self-restraint" (39). Historically, the courts have deferred to elected representatives.

HUMAN-RIGHTS CODES AND COMMISSIONS

Ontario's Racial Discrimination Act of 1944 was the first provincial legislation to prohibit racial discrimination. In 1962, the Ontario Human Rights Code was the first such provincial legislation to be enacted. The code prohibited discrimination on the grounds of race, creed, colour, nationality, ancestry, or place of origin. Today, each province, the two territories, and the federal government maintain a human-rights code and most have a human-rights commission to administer their codes.

Provincial human-rights codes have quasi-constitutional status. The Canadian Human Rights Code is, of course, subject to the Canadian Charter of Rights and Freedoms, which in s.52 states that the Constitution is the supreme law of Canada.

Human-rights laws are codes of conduct to which society is expected to abide. While the prohibited grounds of discrimination vary from province to province, several jurisdictions prohibit discrimination in accommodation, facilities, services, contracts, and employment. All the codes prohibit discrimination on the basis of race, creed, colour, ethnicity, religion, gender, and, in Ontario, sexual orientation.

Canada's system of human rights is activated by the complaint mechanism. Under various human-rights codes, claims must be handled by a human-rights commission which investigates claims and attempts to settle them by conciliation and mediation. If this is not possible, the commission either dismisses the claim or sends it to hearings conducted by a human-rights board of inquiry. The board of inquiry is a quasi-judicial tribunal and an independent body.

If a claim goes to a board of inquiry, lawyers acting for the commission present the case and argue for the "appropriate" remedy. Boards of inquiry make decisions to uphold or reject claims and can order redress, such as back pay and damages (Ontario Human Rights Code Review Task Force, 1992:17)

The present model of human rights has been criticized (Day, 1990; Duclos, 1990; Equality Now, 1984) for being a reactive model that comes into play only when a complaint is launched. Critics argue that commissions do not have a sufficiently broad mandate to combat discrimination effectively. A principal criticism is that a complaint-motivated system cannot effectively address a problem which is so widespread in society.

The Canadian human-rights commissioner reinforced the criticism of the complaint model: "I am convinced that one of the reasons our scheme of human-rights laws has become prey to bureaucratic delays and judicial haggling is that it is so predominantly a complaint-driven model," which requires several conditions to be met: a victim must come forward; that person must be able to relate particular actions to one or more of the forbidden types of discrimination; and the treatment must be demonstrably discriminatory, not just unfair or different. He proposes that the commissions complement the complaint systems by creating a non-discriminatory environment that includes employment equity (Yalden, 1990:2).

A review of the Ontario Human Rights Commission in 1992 found that the system of enforcing the human-rights code in Ontario was so flawed that it had lost the confidence of the public it was supposed to serve. The report concluded that the province was "not providing effective human-rights protection" and that the commission itself was not free from allegations of racist attitudes and behaviour (*The Globe and Mail* July 10, 1992:A3).

In resolving human-rights complaints the present model allows for persuasion and conciliation where necessary and, alternatively, for punitive measures when such persuasion fails. Human-rights commissions are therefore under tremendous pressure to settle complaints. In attempting to reach conciliation, staff are often unaware of the impact of their behaviour on victims. In the hearings of a task force established to examine the procedures of the Ontario Human Rights Commission, delegations representing various community groups stated that the "process can be coercive and unfair. Claimants argued that sometimes they are specifically told that if they do not accept a settlement, which in their view is unjust, their case will be dismissed by the commission. Since they have no other choice, they feel forced to accept the settlement" (Ontario Human Rights Code Review Task Force, 1992:116). Often, settlements involve the payment of a certain sum of money. Several people believe that such settlements are offensive and unprincipled, as it appears that human rights are being bought and that the underlying questions of discrimination are not being addressed.

This complaint-driven approach is viewed as inadequate in addressing the complex, pervasive, and intractable forms of racism in Canadian society. Further limitations of the model relate to the weakness and excessively bureaucratic nature of commissions. Complainants rarely are able to tell a respondent what it felt like to be discriminated against in a non-adversarial, confidential process (Day, 1990).

Race and Gender Issues

Duclos (1992) noted that where race and sex were alleged as grounds for discrimination, "racial-minority women disappear from" the body of law. Despite the fact that they clearly experience discrimination, they are generally absent from human-rights cases. She cited a number of reasons for the underrepresentation of racial-minority women, including their lack of awareness of their rights in the legal system and their lack of trust in it. Immigrant women have the additional fear of jeopardizing their immigration status. The complaints-adjudication process may not respond to the reality of women's lives. Employment, accommodation, and other services covered by discrimination prohibitions may be so essential to racial-minority women, and the discrimination so pervasive, that an individual complaint may seem hopelessly idealistic.

Systemic forms of discrimination and racism, which are deeply rooted in institutional policies and practices, cannot be addressed by a procedure that is designed for individuals, essentially passive in nature, and activated only when victims complain. While some commissions have the mandate to deal with complaints of systemic discrimination, they appear to be so overwhelmed with backlogs of individual complaints (some lasting over a period of years) that very limited resources are available to challenge systemic racism.

The most recent and arguably strongest indictment of the human-rights system in Canada appears in a report commissioned by the Ontario Human Rights Commission in 1992. Young (1992) analyzed the disposition of racial-discrimination cases in the period 1980–92 and concluded that "the treatment of race discrimination cases at the commission confirmed that individual and systemic racism exists at the commission." She noted further that "although my analysis uses as examples the discriminatory assumptions and practices of individuals, my conclusion implicates the commission as a whole, thereby leading to a collective responsibility for change" (3). The irony of this situation is that the public agency established to be a watchdog over race-based complaints has been implicated in perpetuating racial discrimination.

MULTICULTURALISM POLICY AND LEGISLATION

Multiculturalism as a state policy had its official beginnings in 1971, when the then prime minister, Pierre Trudeau, announced in Parliament that his government had accepted the recommendations of the Royal Commission on Bilingualism and Biculturalism (Fleras and Elliot, 1992). Recognizing that Canada was both a culturally and ethnically "plural" society, in that it contained Canadians of British and French origin, Aboriginal peoples, and "others," the commission recommended that Canada's diversity be recognized and maintained. "Multiculturalism within a bilingual framework commends itself to the government as the most suitable means of assuring the cultural freedom of Canadians."

Since then, the policy has become enshrined in the federal Multiculturalism Act, and a Ministry of Multiculturalism was established. The act committed the government to a policy of preserving and enhancing the multicultural identity and heritage of Canadians, while working to achieve equality of all Canadians in economic, social, cultural, and political life.

Subsection 3(2)(a) of the act recognizes discrimination in Canadian society and articulates the federal government's commitment to ensure that no unfair barriers exist to employment and career advancement. The act commits federal institutions to enhance the ability of individuals and communities to contribute to Canadian society by ensuring that government policies and programs respond to the needs of all Canadians. Subsection 3(2)(c) provides assurances that government services will be delivered in an accessible manner to everyone (Multiculturalism and Citizenship, Canada, 1989–90).

The act requires federal government agencies to develop and implement multicultural and racial-equality policies and programs as they apply to their respective mandates. Examples of initiatives cited in the 1991 annual report tabled in Parliament include:

- The solicitor general established a police race-relations centre to serve as a resource both to federal and provincial police forces.
- The Canada Council audited its advisory committees and juries to ensure that they reflected Canadian diversity, and it increased support to minority artists.
- Employment and Immigration increased its funding of programs for immigrant integration.
- The Federal Business Development Bank established ethnocultural advisory committees to assist small businesses owned by minorities and immigrants.

As a result of changes in the leadership of the Government of Canada in July 1993, multiculturalism was subsumed into an overarching heritage ministry.

Federal multicultural initiatives have been described as providing symbolic support, setting the tone for what is acceptable ("behaviour clues"), establishing a legal basis for action, and sending out signals regarding the notion of justice and equality. By legitimizing the presence of racial minorities, multiculturalism has furthered Canada's experience with nation-building from a mosaic of cultures and races (Tepper, 1988).

Critics have argued, however, that the government has failed to "appreciate the nature, scope, and impact of racial discrimination on the victims"

(Fleras and Elliott, 1992:320). Federal decision-makers regard the prevailing norms and institutions of Canadian society as fundamentally sound, and racial discrimination is considered either as a minor aberration in the system or as the random behaviour of a few anti-social individuals. In commenting on the Multiculturalism Act as an inadequate instrument for addressing racism, Li and Bolaria (1983) suggested that

> the failure of multiculturalism...is not so much a sound policy misman-aged. Rather, it is a failure to solve non-cultural problems with cultural solutions. Issues of ethnic inequality and racial discrimination have polit-ical and economic roots in the history and social institutions of Canada, and the solutions lie beyond what multiculturalism can offer.

A related criticism is that multiculturalism is focussed on lifestyles rather than life chances. Research on the problems facing immigrants and refugees, as Fernando (1991) pointed out, demonstrates that the promise of multiculturalism is much greater than the reality. He provided examples of inadequate provision of language training, insufficient access to counselling, failure to recognize foreign educational credentials, and insecure funding of settlement organizations as evidence of the failure of multiculturalism in British Columbia.

Despite the policy of multiculturalism, the legacy of "White settler" colonialism continues to provide some citizens with greater power, privilege, and entitlements; to define who is a "real citizen" in Canada; and to shape the organization of major institutions (Creese, 1993).

Buchignani (1983) maintained that the driving force behind multicultural policy was the "mainline" (White) ethnic groups. Having largely vanquished personal problems of discrimination, representatives of these groups have become increasingly concerned with symbolic cultural preservation, group cultural rights, and the promotion of a group identity in the larger Canadian society. Racial-minority communities' concerns are subordinated to their individual quests for jobs, advancement, housing, and education. This split is seen as having a potentially significant impact on the support of White ethnic groups for programs and initiatives directed at ending racism.

Members of minority communities are particularly critical of multicul-tural policies: "Multiculturalism, as we know it, has no answers for the prob-lems of racism, or White supremacy—unless it is combined with a clearly articulated policy of anti-racism" (Nourbese Phillip, 1992). It has also been suggested that multiculturalism is premature as a policy and should be put on hold until racism in Canadian society is addressed.

EMPLOYMENT EQUITY

THE EMPLOYMENT EQUITY ACT

In 1986, the federal government adopted the Employment Equity Act, s.2 of which states that its purpose is to achieve equality in the workplace so that no person shall be denied employment opportunities or benefits for reasons unrelated to ability, and in the fulfilment of that goal, to correct the conditions of disadvantage in employment experienced by women, Aboriginal peoples, persons with disabilities, and persons who are, because of their race or colour, in a visible minority in Canada by giving effect to the principle that employment equity means more than treating persons in the same way but also requires special measures and the accommodation of differences.

The Employment Equity Act applies to about 1250 federally regulated companies that employ about 1.5 million people. It requires employers to gather statistics on the number of employees who are members of "**designated groups**," which include women, visible minorities, Aboriginal peoples, and people with disabilities. Employers are required to submit an employment equity plan annually, setting out goals and timetables for hiring persons from designated groups, with the goal that their workforces should eventually reflect the Canadian population.

THE STATE AS EMPLOYER

The parliamentary committee established to review the legislation recommended broadening it to include all federal departments, the RCMP, the Canadian armed forces, Parliament, all political parties, and all federal agencies and commissions. It also recommended that private companies be required to comply with the principles of employment equity if they wanted to bid on government contracts of $200 000 or more. The parliamentary committee report identified a need for higher fines for those who failed to comply with employment equity goals and recommended that the power of enforcement of employment equity plans should be included in new legislation and given to the Canadian human-rights commission.

At the time of the act's enactment, the federal government exempted itself from the provisions of the act. As a result, the entire federal workforce, as defined under the Financial Administration Act, has no statutory mandate to pursue employment equity. The Treasury Board operates a voluntary employment equity program, but federal civil servants have no formal directive to achieve employment equity goals and timetables.

A survey released by the Canadian Ethnocultural Council (1992) found that the federal public service had fewer racial minorities in its senior management jobs in 1991 than it had in 1990. The council stated that the government's equity record was worse than that of the industries it regulated—racial minorities held more than 7 percent of the jobs with private employers that were regulated by Ottawa. The study concluded that progress under the federal government's voluntary program had been less than minimal.

The act contained no penalties for failure to implement programs, nor criteria for measuring success in terms of meeting goals; it included no performance standards and set no benchmarks. Although the Canadian Human Rights Commission assumed a monitoring role, it had no enforcement role under the legislation. The act contained no provisions for enforcement except for failure to comply with the reporting requirements.

In passing the act, the government cited the need to avoid more bureau-cratic regulation and argued that all that was required was procedures involving publicly accessible data collection on individual employers; criti-cal public opinion was to be the driving force for change (Reitz, 1988).

Enforcement by public opinion was not effective. The lack of progress of the designated groups in employment was documented in the fifth annual report of the parliamentary committee to the House of Commons (Par-liamentary Committee on the Review of the Employment Equity Act, 1992). The report indicated that the legislation failed to identify clearly the type and extent of changes expected of employers. It noted that an element of enforcement within the process was required to ensure that employment equity was taken seriously in Canada.

CONTRACT COMPLIANCE

Contract compliance is a method of influencing private companies to imple-men an employment equity program. Under contract compliance, a condition of a vendor's contract is contingent on the existence of an equity program. The penalty for non-compliance is loss of the contract with the federal government.

The federal government has specific criteria governing contract compli-ance. A company must design and implement a program that will identify and take steps to remove barriers in the selection, hiring, promotion, and training of select minority groups. As in employment equity, compliance is largely voluntary; each company is expected to establish special programs in areas where imbalances exist (Jain, 1988).

This program can be criticized on many grounds; for example, the equi-ty programs are not legislated and operate at the discretion of government, and government conducts only random audits of companies that have promised to implement employment equity programs, which allows compa-nies to avoid developing a program until an audit occurs. What develops, therefore, is a cycle of delay in which federal bureaucrats and their corporate counterparts negotiate to delay the implementation of employment equity.

Some companies that supply highly specialized services are not audited. Corporate clients are permitted to set their own goals and timetables to match what is considered reasonable for their peculiar settings, but anti-racism is not a high priority for some companies. Since the government has not applied a criterion of success to this process, companies proceed at their own, often slow, pace.

THE STATE AS PROVIDER AND FUNDER OF SERVICES

EQUALITY OF ACCESS

Communities affected by racial discrimination continue to feel excluded from public services. They also perceive little support in their efforts to develop the community infrastructures and support systems required to meet the needs of their communities (*Equality Now*, 1984). Studies on access to government services carried out in the past decade (Mock and Maseman, 1987) suggest that racial minorities and Aboriginal peoples do not have equal access or participate adequately in government programs and services.

Notwithstanding this concern, all levels of government for many years have provided some support to racial-minority community-based service organizations. Generally, however, the funding is in the form of short-term project support. Despite varying levels of support and varying criteria, this support is a recognition by the state that racial-minority organizations play a critical role in ensuring that the community derives equal benefit from public services.

From one perspective, such support is an appropriate bridging strategy, until all communities are adequately served by public structures and programs. On the other hand, it encourages the development of parallel services that existing public institutions should be offering. The question of whether satisfactory service can only be effected by separate provision continues to be debated. Would separate service agencies along racial lines meet minority needs, or would they further fragment the state's delivery system? Would matching rather than mixing racial clients provide more emphatic help to people in need? Is "separate services" a euphemism for segregation?

Another concern is that in providing support to racial-minority organizations, the level of public support is grossly deficient. Separate services have become synonymous with inferior services. Expecting far too much for far too little, minority organizations have been exploited by the state as an expedient way to deliver public services to people of colour (Doyle and Visano, 1987).

Arrangements made within public organizations determine to whom services are provided, facilities are made available, and resources are allocated. The attitudes and actions of those who direct these institutions determine who gets what, where, and when. Since people of colour are generally absent from the key decision-making processes in these organizations and in the delivery of services, to what extent do public institutions treat people of colour less favourably?

Although considerable resources have been expended on the training of public servants in "multiculturalism," "race relations," or "managing diversity," to what extent have the special needs of minorities been identified? And to what extent have they been adequately considered and provided for? To what extent have the resources of the state been reallocated in favour of minorities as part of a commitment to equity? Within a framework of genuine, equal sharing of public resources, it appears that the scale on which this has been done by any state agency or institution in Canada is insignificant in redressing the imbalances caused by racially discriminatory policies, programs, and practices.

Initiatives taken to measure and address racial minorities' inequalities of access to public programs and services in Canada have been tentative and piecemeal.

A study of access to government services (1989) carried out by the Ontario Anti-Racism Secretariat found that racial minorities experienced significant barriers in obtaining government services. The barriers to equitable treatment in service delivery included

- the insensitivity of government employees;
- a lack of understanding of racial minorities;
- poor telephone reception skills;
- a lack of referrals to other departments;
- a lack of information provided in appropriate language; and
- overt racial discrimination.

The study also found a lack of representation of racial minorities in government politically (on boards and commissions), at the management level, and in civil-service staff positions.

THE ROLE OF MUNICIPALITIES

In many ways, municipal government is the most important level of government for ordinary citizens. Municipal governments, as service providers, are responsible for many of the key services that determine the quality of life in a community. The scale of municipal activity is reflected in the fact that in 1982, total municipal expenditures amounted to almost $33 billion, representing over 9 percent of Canada's gross national expenditure (Rees, 1985).

Municipalities are often the largest employers in their area. Without counting seasonal employees or those employed in municipal enterprises, utilities, or educational institutions, the municipal workforce makes up 25 percent of all public-sector employees in Canada. As influencers of public opinion, municipalities are well positioned to positively affect community attitudes and practices. Local governments have the capacity to identify specific local issues and needs, to develop consensus and mobilize action.

As purchasers of goods and services, municipalities have the capacity to influence the employment practices of local employers. As grant-aiding authorities, they can ensure that their financing and grants are equitably allocated to meet minority needs.

As the most direct, open, accessible, and accountable level of government, municipalities have increasingly become the most important vehicle for resolving the community's most pressing concerns. In recent years, several municipalities have begun analyzing the barriers experienced by racial-minority communities and Aboriginal peoples in their efforts to access municipal services. The barriers include a lack of effective communication vehicles, including linguistic interpretation; a lack of culturally and racially sensitive programs; disproportionate funding to mainstream, established, and traditional organizations; insufficient channelling of resources to groups and agencies representing minorities; a lack of core funding support; a lack of effective consultation and participation by people of colour and Aboriginal peoples in the decision-making process; and a lack of clear anti-racist policies and implementation plans aimed at ensuring access to grants and other services (Municipality of Metropolitan Toronto, 1993). In the case of Metropolitan Toronto, efforts have been made to ameliorate these barriers by implementing comprehensive policies and programs in all departments to increase the access of racial minorities and Aboriginal peoples.

A growing number of municipalities have established advisory committees of lay people to improve "race relations," "ethnic relations," and/or "community relations." Some of these are referred to as "mayor's" committees. Some committees report to the municipal council through one of its standing committees, and some are chaired by the mayor. Committee members are usually appointed by the mayor on advice from a nominating committee.

These committees appear to have been ineffective in producing broad and substantive changes in the status of racial minorities. Reitz (1988) suggested that they often co-opt minority leaders and marginalize racial politics:

> When politicians appoint minority group members to race advisory bodies, both have a vested interest in a perception of close links to the respective minority community.... In the long run, co-optation reduces conflict, not inequality. (436)

None of these committees have significantly addressed racism in the municipal corporation itself. Most of them become sterile because they are consumed by the larger politics of the municipality. Moreover, many serve as a training ground for those with political aspirations. Committee members are expected to be loyal; they are not expected to publicly criticize the ineffectiveness of the body of which they are members. A number of these committees become paralyzed by the politics of race within the committee itself. In camera meetings ensure that politically sensitive agenda items are explored and defused; motions are contrived and prepared. Thus, many community consultative committees have been subject to criticism (Keith and Murji, 1989).

None of these committees uses the term "anti-racism," which symbolizes their orientation to the subject. Committees whose names cover both community relations and race relations frequently experience tensions with respect to their priorities. Since "community relations" is a broad, all-encompassing subject, issues unrelated to racism can easily assume priority.

Programs sanctioned by these committees can easily be eliminated when they disturb, or threaten to disturb, the centres of power in the municipal corporation. In one such situation, the Mayor's Committee of the City of Toronto was instrumental in establishing the Multicultural Access Program. Ironically, the committee was also instrumental in dismantling the initiative when its activities began penetrating deeply into the organization's core.

Some municipalities have introduced employment equity programs to improve their recruitment practices, conducting (in some instances) workforce audits and providing training (e.g., Toronto, Vancouver). Montreal has an employment equity program targeted at "cultural minorities." Regina has attempted to increase the representation of Aboriginal employees. Ottawa's efforts have been concentrated on information dissemination. It has provided forums for representatives from community groups to meet with potential employers and service providers to facilitate employment opportunities for racial minorities.

Generally, municipal committees are powerless to address employment equity in the municipal corporations. Their advisory status means that they make no decisions, can hold none accountable, and have a discretionary mandate revokable at the whim of the mayor. Thus, despite their significant level of activity, municipal committees are by and large incapable of forging policies and programs, and they have been very tentative in pursuing them.

CASE STUDY 11.1

THE ONTARIO HUMAN RIGHTS COMMISSION

The Ontario Human Rights Commission has a mandate to investigate and resolve complaints of racial discrimination. Since its inception, it has been subject to a number of reorganizations, but it continues to be plagued by allegations of ineffectiveness, mismanagement, and perpetuating racial injustices. These criticisms come from various segments of the community—lawyers, advocacy groups, consultants, the media, and a variety of other sources—and have led to a significant loss of confidence in the commission.

EVENTS

In 1982, the prohibited grounds of discrimination in Ontario were broadened. Between 1982 and 1985, the volume of complaints rose dramatically. This led to an operational review in 1985 by Coopers and Lybrand, who made a number of recommendations. The commission responded to the report's recommendations by setting up a policy committee on operational review. When Coopers and Lybrand were called in again in 1987 to conduct a second review, they found that little progress had been made on implementing the 1985 recommendations. The improvements that had been made were overwhelmed by the increased caseload.

Despite the Coopers and Lybrand recommendations, the commission continued to operate without sufficient staff. New staff did not receive adequate training, and incoming complaints continued to exceed the number of cases closed. This led to delays in the processing of complaints, which in turn led to complaints to the ombudsman of Ontario that the commission's inefficiency prejudiced complainants' cases.

In addition, the commission itself was charged with allegations of racially discriminatory hiring practices. In 1989, Chief Commissioner Raj Anand was forced to resign. The charges came after the commission engaged in a recruitment campaign. It hired seven new staff members, none of whom was from a minority group, although there were several qualified minority applicants.[2]

On April 8, 1991, *The Toronto Star* published a report in which human-rights critics in the Ontario legislature attacked the commission for the manner in which it handled complaints against T.E.S. Contracting Services and Ian Martin Group, both of which were employment agencies operating in Toronto. The controversy over the commission's handling of this case came about because it had conclusive evidence that both these companies engaged in discriminatory hiring practices. A recruiter who worked at both agencies provided the commission with no less than

200 documents of damaging evidence of racism in both firms. The commission's own investigations concluded that staff and workers at T.E.S. agreed to refer candidates to jobs on the basis of race, among other things. Rather than making this a model case, the commission settled with both companies. Critics in the legislature referred to the commission's approach as a "slap on the wrist" (Armstrong, 1991a).

By 1991, the commission's statistics painted a grim picture of its effectiveness in processing complaints. Although the commission closed 1763 cases in 1990, at the same time it received 1971 new complaints—almost 170 each month. According to human-rights lawyers, many people who sought help from the commission were discouraged and dissatisfied with its process. Complainants often felt pressured to accept settlements they found unsatisfactory.

Increasingly, the commission came under attack from community activists, some of whom claimed that it was in a conflict of interest by advocating for human rights on the one hand and investigating and negotiating on the other hand. The broader concerns raised by community activists was that the commission assumed too many, and sometimes conflicting, roles (Brent, 1992).

The suspicions and allegations of community activists were partially substantiated by a confidential report leaked to the press. Equal Opportunity Consultants (EOC) was contracted to review racial tensions among staff at the commission's Mississauga office. In its report (1990), EOC noted that the commission's huge backlog had put an unbearable strain on investigators working on the front lines. The report concluded that damaged relations, distrust, and lack of communication and interaction were all the result of an organizational culture that had not promoted co-operation, collaboration, participation, and equity. Allegations of racism in the workplace had been ignored by management and created a hostile environment.

The report cited a legacy of what appeared to have been preferential treatment toward White staff members and identified racism in the ranks of the commission, citing as examples racial slurs and demeaning behaviour toward racial minorities (Armstrong, 1991b). Moreover, nothing positive was added to the commission's sagging public image when a judge accused it of trying to coerce a 62-year-old woman into accepting a settlement she found unacceptable. The commission told the woman that it would dismiss her racism case if she didn't accept a $1500 settlement (Armstrong , 1991b).

In August 1991, an ad hoc collection of human-rights workers and lawyers formed a coalition to reform the commission. Over 50 groups joined the coalition, which called itself the Human Rights Reform Group. This group called for a task force to hear public submissions and report to the government. Along with other individuals and groups, it called for an overhaul of the human-rights system in Ontario. The group called for more teeth in the Ontario Human Rights Code, tougher and faster penalties, and wider access to a board of inquiry (Armstrong, 1991c).

The government responded by appointing the Ontario Human Rights Code Review Task Force. The mandate of the task force was to examine the system of enforcing human-rights complaints in Ontario. At several of the 900 hearings held across the province, the task force was told that racism, discrimination, and bureaucratic insensitivity plagued the operations of the commission. In one of the presentations to the task force, it was suggested that dogs, cats, and pigeons had better protection in Ontario than did human beings, particularly if the humans belonged to an oppressed and exploited race.

By the end of 1992, the task force had produced a scathing report of the system of investigating human-rights complaints. The study suggested that the system of enforcing the Ontario Human Rights Code was so flawed that it had lost the confidence of the public it was supposed to serve. It concluded that discrimination was entrenched in Canadian society and that the government was not providing effective protection from violations of human rights, and it implied that the commission was rife with prejudice, reflecting the pervasiveness of prejudice in Canadian society. The task force recommended that penalties for obstructing the tribunal or violating its orders should be raised from the current $25 000 maximum to a $200 000 maximum.

Finally, a report sponsored by the commission to act as an internal discussion paper was made public. Young (1992) examined the manner in which race-related complaints were handled and disposed of by the commission. She examined, among other things, all reported decisions involving racial discrimination from 1980 to early 1992. She evaluated the decisions in terms of their strengths and weaknesses in analysis, evidence, citations, arguments presented, policy statements, and assumptions made.

Although the report was dated October 23, 1992, it remained confidential until July 1993. It made several important findings about the assumptions made with respect to the disposal of race-based complaints. The report stated that the commission's practice of considering the respondent innocent at the investigatory stage skewed the results. Young argued that a legal standard was inappropriate at the investigatory stage, at which one is attempting to collect evidence. Moreover, she pointed to the presumption that a complainant lacks objectivity and that corroboration is necessary. She also noted that boards of inquiries trade the interests of business' reputation with those of the complainant. The commission, she argued, was reluctant to make a finding of racism because it might be damaging to the reputation of a business. This trend was adhered to even when there was evidence of racial name-calling, slurs, and epithets.

Young concluded that "the commission should consider offering a public apology for its mishandling of race complaints, accompanied by a statement guaranteeing a better record in the future" (1992:28).

CONCLUSION

A number of critical issues are highlighted by this case study. First, it provides an example of how a government agency established to protect the rights of individuals appears to be severely hampered in its work. The numerous studies and reviews of the commission identified several factors that undermined the functioning of this important agency, including:

- lack of effective leadership;
- structural and organizational constraints;
- the underfunding of the agency, in terms of both human and material resources;
- the inadequately trained and unqualified staff;
- the existence of racist attitudes on the part of staff and management, contributing to a hostile working environment for racial minorities;
- poor service delivery to clients;
- ineffective, cumbersome, and time-consuming procedures and mechanisms for processing complaints; and
- a vague and unclear mandate.

This case study demonstrates that establishing a human-rights code and commission to combat racism may be inadequate ways to achieve that goal.

SUMMARY

This chapter analyzed the roles and functions of the state as law-giver, policy-maker, employer, purchaser, and provider of goods and services. It noted, however, that much of the legislation and public policies developed by the federal and provincial governments are weak, flawed, and ineffective in addressing racism. The Canadian Charter of Rights and Freedoms, human-rights codes, the Multiculturalism Act, employment equity, and the development of public agencies to combat racial discrimination have not fundamentally altered the barriers that limit the full participation of racial minorities in Canadian society.

Many of the measures reflect a certain amount of tokenism; for example, the Employment Equity Act fails to apply to the public service. Others have been built on the wrong premise. Human-rights commissions, in attempting to deal with individual cases, fail to address systemic, institutional, and ideological racism. Thus, the state, which is founded on the principles of equality and justice, plays an important role in maintaining democratic racism in Canada.

It appears that the Canadian state response to racism has been considerable. In principle, legislation and the establishment of human-rights complaints procedures should have gone a long way to ensure racial equality in Canadian society. Canada has entrenched anti-discrimination in its laws and public policies. Yet the pursuit of racial equity in Canada appears to be fragmented and hampered by an inability to translate policy into practice and legal requirements into effective procedures that have a measurable impact on eradicating racism. This chapter's case study illuminated some of the difficulties of translating the state's commitment to equality into practices that ensure the protection of the rights and freedoms of racial minorities.

REFERENCES

Abella, R. (1984). *Report of the Commission on Equality in Employment*. Ottawa.

Access: Task Force on Access to Trades and Professions (1989). Toronto: Government of Ontario.

Armstrong, J. (1991a). "Job Firms 'Slap on Wrist' Anger Critics of Bias Probe." *The Toronto Star* (April 8).

———. (1991b). "Rights Commission Hit By Racial Strife." *The Toronto Star* (May 24).

———. (1991c). "50 Groups Join Fight To Reform Rights Agency." *The Toronto Star* (August 19).

Berry, V., and A. McChesney. (1988). "Human Rights and Foreign Policy Making." In R.O. Matthews and C. Pratt (eds.), *Human Rights in Canadian Foreign Policy*. Kingston and Montreal: McGill-Queen's University Press.

Brent, B. (1992). "Task Force Tries to Solve Rights Balance." *The Toronto Star* (March 10).

Buchignani, N. (1983). "Some Comments on the Elimination of Racism In Canada." *Canadian Ethnic Studies* 15(2):119.

———, and D. Inda. (1985). *Continuous Journey: A Social History of South Asians in Canada*. Toronto: McClelland and Stewart.

Bolaria, S., and P. Li. (1991). *Racial Oppression in Canada* (2nd ed.). Toronto: Garamond Press.

Canada Employment and Immigration Commission. (1991). *Annual Report, Employment Equity Act*. Ottawa: Supply and Services Canada.

Canadian Ethnocultural Council. (1992). *Employment Inequity: The Representation of Visible Minorities in the Federal Public Service 1989–1991*. Ottawa.

Cohen, T. (1987). *Race Relations and the Law*. Montreal: Canadian Jewish Congress.

Creese, G. "The Sociology of British Columbia." Forthcoming 1994 in *BC Studies*.

Day, S. (1990). *Human Rights in Canada: Into the 1990s and Beyond*." Ottawa: Human Rights Research and Education Centre.

Doyle, R., and L. Visano. (1987). *Access to Health and Social Services for Members of Diverse Cultural and Racial Groups*. Toronto: Social Planning Council.

Duclos, N. (1990). "Lessons of Difference: Feminist Theory on Cultural Diversity." *Buffalo Law Review* 38:325.

———. (1992). "Disappearing Women: Racial Minority Women in Human Rights Cases." In *Western Judicial Education Centre Material for Seminar on Racial and Cultural Equity*. Saskatoon: Western Judicial Education Centre.

Equal Opportunity Consultants. (1990). *An Organizational Review of the Mississauga Office*. Toronto: Ontario Human Rights Commission.

Equality Now. (1984). Report of the Special Committee on Visible Minorities in Canadian Society. Ottawa: Government of Canada.

Fernando, T. (1991). "'Mosaic Madness' or Sensible Public Policy? Some Reflections on Canadian Multiculturalism." In N. Guppy and K. Stoddart (eds.), *Sociological Insights*. Vancouver: Department of Anthropology and Sociology, University of British Columbia.

Fleras, A., and L.E. Elliott. (1992). *Unequal Relations: An Introduction to Race and Ethnicity in Canada*. Scarborough, ON: Prentice-Hall.

———, and J. Elliot. (1992). "Statement by the Prime Minister in the House of Commons on October 8, 1992." In *Multiculturalism in Canada*. Appendix A. Scarborough, ON: Nelson.

Gibson, D. (1985). "Protection of Minority Rights Under the Canadian Charter of Rights and Freedoms." In N. Neville and A. Kornberg, *Minorities and the Canadian State*. Oakville, ON: Mosaic Press.

The Globe and Mail. (1992). "Discontinuance of Court Challenges Program." (March 11).

The Globe and Mail. (1992). (July 10):A3.

Jain, H. (1985). *Anti-Discrimination Staffing Policies: Implications of Human Rights Legislation for Employers and Trade Unions*. Ottawa: Secretary of State.

———. Affirmative Action Employment Equity Programmes and Visible Minorities in Canada." *Currents: Readings in Race Relations* 5(1)(4):3.

Kallen, E. (1982). "Ethnicity and Human Rights in Canada." In P. Li (ed.), *Race and Ethnic Relations in Canada*. Toronto: Oxford.

———. (1989). *Label Me Be Human: Minority Rights of Stigmatized Canadians*. Toronto: University of Toronto Press.

Keith, M., and K. Murji. (1989). "Race, Racism and the Local Politics of Policing." In W. Ball and J. Solomos (eds.), *Race and Local Politics*. London: Macmillan.

Kobayashi, A. (1990). "Racism and the Law." *Urban Geography* 11(5):447–473.

Li, P., and S. Bolaria. (1983). *Racial Minorities in Multicultural Canada*. Toronto: Garamond Press.

Matas, D. (1990). "The Charter and Racism." *Constitutional Forum* 2:82.

Mattis, W. (1990). "Canada's Immigration Policy, 1867–1990: More of the Same." Unpublished manuscript. Toronto.

Mock, K., and V. Maseman. (1987). *Access to Government Services*. Toronto: Ontario Ministry of Citizenship.

Multiculturalism and Citizenship Canada (1989-90). *Annual Report of the Operation of the Canadian Multiculturalism Act*. Ottawa.

Municipality of Metropolitan Toronto. (1993). A Framework for Action: Principles and Implementation Guidelines for Ethnoracial and Aboriginal Access to Metropolitan Grants. Draft report. Toronto: Municipality of Metropolitan Toronto.

Mittelstaedt, M. (1992). "Ontario Indicted on Human Rights." *The Globe and Mail* (July 10):A3.

Nourbese Philip, M. (l992). *Frontiers: Essays and Writings on Racism and Culture.* Stratford, ON: Mercury Press.

Ontario Human Rights Code Review Task Force. (l992). *Achieving Equality: A Report on Human Rights Reform.* Toronto: Ministry of Citizenship.

Parliamentary Committee on the Review of the Employment Equity Act. (1992). "A Matter of Fairness." Ottawa.

Rees, T. (1985). "Municipal Government and Race Relations." *Currents: Readings in Race Relations* 3(1) (Spring):1–2.

Reitz, J. (1988). "Less Racial Discrimination In Canada, Or Simply Less Racial Conflict? Implications of Comparisons with Britain. *Canadian Public Policy* 14(4):424–441.

Samuel, J. (1988). "Immigration and Visible Minorities in the Year 2001: A Projection." *Canadian Ethnic Studies* 20(2):90–100.

Tarnopolsky, W. (1982). *Discrimination and the Law in Canada.* Toronto: Richard DeBoo.

_____. (1991). "Discrimination and the Law in Canada." Seminar on Race, Ethnic and Cultural Equity. Vancouver: Western Judicial Centre.

Tepper, E. (1988). "Changing Canada: The Institutional Response to Polyethnicity." In *Review of Demography and Its Implications for Economic and Social Policy.* Ottawa: Carleton University.

Yalden, M. (1990). "Canadian Human Rights and Multiculturalism." *Currents: Readings in Race Relations* (Toronto):6(1):2.

Young, D. (1992). *The Handling of Race Discrimination Cases at the Human Rights Commission.* Toronto: Ontario Human Rights Commission.

NOTES

1. The Abella (1984) report on equality in employment distinguished equality of opportunity and equality of outcomes by noting that treating all people the same (equality) does not necessarily achieve equity.

2. Among the rejected candidates was one who was later appointed chief commissioner.

Chapter 12

▼▼▼▼▼▼▼▼▼▼▼▼▼

Organizational Resistance to Anti-Racism

> White people still invite people of colour to participate in social actions as subordinate to the organization as a whole. The bureaucratic machinery to ensure continuity is withheld from people of colour. We remain a peripheral validation of the lack of racism in White organizations. (Maracle, 1993:128)

This chapter examines change within institutions and institutions' effectiveness in dismantling racism within their organizations. Various forms of organizational resistance are analyzed as examples of institutionally specific forms of democratic racism. These are the commonly used mechanisms that have been employed in organizations to maintain racist behaviour and practices and to resist, evade, or sabotage anti-racism initiatives. The chapter concludes by noting that a race-conscious model of organizations is required, and by describing three models of organizational change: assimilationist, multicultural, and anti-racist.

INTRODUCTION

An organization can be defined in various ways: in terms of its structure, its function, or a multitude of other characteristics. For our purposes, "organization" is defined as a sociopolitical system in which people act together under an imposed structure and ideology and use a specific set of technologies to achieve a specific objective.

The dominant theme of this definition is that an organization is a social system in which human beings do specific jobs. An important aspect of the definition is the fact that an organization is a social construct; it does not have a physical existence. Furthermore, an organization is a series of subsystems that are inextricably linked. A change in any one of the subsystems affects the entire organization.

Organizations are social systems within which individuals act through a network of social relations. Behaviours in this social system are influenced by the organization's values, the values of the individuals within the organization, their functional responsibilities, and the society's prevailing ideology, which determines what is considered "right" and "proper." One of the important characteristics of organizations is that they resist change. This aspect of organizational behaviour is discussed in this chapter.

RESISTANCE TO CHANGE[1]

Resistance is human behaviour that either actively or passively attempts to undermine any aspect of the change initiative. The ideology of democratic racism, which sustains two conflicting values—one that espouses fairness, equity, tolerance, and justice; another that maintains and reproduces racism—has been instrumental in sabotaging efforts to eradicate racism. The opposition shows itself not through an overt display of intolerance but through subtle, sustained, and refined resistance to anti-racism.

The arguments of democratic racism may be applied at a number of points and take many forms. Figure 12.1 shows the points at which resistance may occur.

Figure 12.1

THE CYCLE OF RESISTANCE

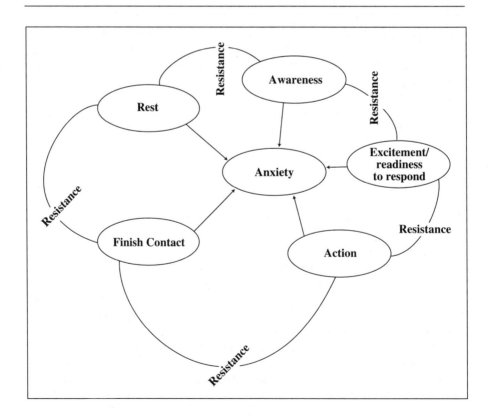

While resistance is generic to all large-scale change initiatives, a major factor of resistance to anti-racism change is rooted in the extent to which organizational leaders believe that "anti-racism" is a legitimate force to motivate change. Resistance to anti-racism initiatives in organizations takes many forms:

1. Reluctance to create an anti-racist vision
2. Lack of commitment
3. Inadequate policies
4. Inadequate training
5. Lack of representation
6. Limited access to goods and services
7. Absence of sanctions
8. Lack of individual accountability
10. Structural rigidity
11. Ineffective monitoring and evaluation mechanisms
12. Insufficient resources
13. Tokensim
14. Minority change agents
15. Lack of organizational accountability
16. Limited public accountability

One of the recurrent themes of organizational resistance to anti-racism is the reliance on cultural explanations of difference. Decision-makers in organizations often refuse to recognize that physiological racial differences (which are socially constructed into racism) account for much of the structured inequality both in organizations and in society. Identifying cultural differences leads to the provision of cultural programs and policies of change. Refusing to recognize the role of racism leads to cultural responses that cannot adequately deal with racial inequality. Cultural solutions—for example, providing translation services in court—do not necessarily lead to equity, and the provision of cross-cultural communications training does little to address the institutional and structural nature of racial disadvantage.

RELUCTANCE TO CREATE AN ANTI-RACIST VISION

The need for a clear and concise vision statement is critical to the success of an organization. A vision statement sets out the organization's goal and binds it and its members to work toward achieving that goal.

Very few of the organizations examined in the previous part of this book explicitly incorporated anti-racism in their visions. Such an omission occurs partly because anti-racism is not considered important to the overall mandate of the organization. When an organization consciously omits anti-racism from its vision statement, it clearly wishes to retain a reactive stance to anti-racism. Even if the organization has progressive programs, the absence of a vision statement shaped by anti-racism principles and goals results in an inadequate framework for the changes required. When an organization responds purely on the basis of political or social pressures, it is often unwilling to link the change process to its mandate. On the other hand, anti-racism as a guiding organizational framework suggests a commitment to examining not only programs and practices, but also the ideology motivating the programs and practices.

LACK OF COMMITMENT

A commitment to anti-racism is a desire on the part of decision-makers and power-brokers to act consistently and systematically to challenge and redress racism. Lack of commitment is illustrated in many ways; for example, many organizations embark on anti-racism initiatives through coercion rather than by design. Thus, forces either within the organization or outside it demand a response in order for the organization to maintain its credibility.

A common form of coercion is a race-related complaint to a human-rights commission. Many of these complaints originate in organizations whose managers maintain that "there are no problems here"—an approach that results either from wilful blindness or from ignorance of the manifestations of racism in organizations. The coercion resulting from the settlement of a human-rights case does not require an organization to change its ideology, but only to create programs or develop practices that give the appearance of change.

Lack of commitment is demonstrated when formal studies expose racism in an organization and management adopts a defensive position. This defensiveness takes various forms: discrediting the findings, suggesting that the researcher misinterpreted the mandate or overstepped the boundaries of the project, "sanitizing" the results so that they do not appear so "negative." The latter strategy allows management to practise damage control by deflecting attention from the issue. A striking example of this strategy occurred when a government-ministry unit asked that the word "racism" be removed from a final report investigating employee complaints of racial discrimination.[2]

Often, vision statements are vague, "motherhood" statements of high-sounding principles that are difficult to put into practice. The intent of the organization (to maintain the status quo) is often masked in the vision statement because the organization has mastered the language, the vocabulary of the trade. The words become empty promises, nothing more than symbolic gestures. Thus, the commitment to anti-racism rarely goes further than a *verbal* commitment to equality, which in most cases means equality of opportunity rather than a commitment to action and equity.

None of the organizations examined in the previous section was committed to both the process and the content of anti-racism change. Although all sectors of society have responded to the pressures motivating change, organizational structures have remained untouched; the ideological underpinnings of their actions have remained intact.

Of those organizations that do recognize the need to respond to racism, most choose not to use the term anti-racism. They prefer instead labels such as "multiculturalism," "managing diversity," and "race relations." Their strategy may be identified as one of resistance. Avoiding the term "anti-racism" circumvents the need to identify "racism."

Adopting euphemisms provides the organization with a rationale for limiting its responses to cosmetic changes. Multicultural approaches suggest that gaining an understanding of other cultures is sufficient to combat racism. Diversity labels cushion the organization by allowing it to hide behind the rationalization that managing diversity is all that is required. Such a view implies that racism results from diversity, and that it can be managed. Thus, racism is considered something to be "managed," not necessarily opposed. A more constructive approach would be one in which racism is acknowledged and anti-racist strategies are adopted.

Resistance to anti-racism is often very subtle. It may entail the setting of unrealistic goals. It may show itself in the context of last-minute, crisis-oriented planning, such as appending anti-racism plans to other plans, after all the other plans have been made. It may exist in the simplistic "fix it now" mentality; and it may show its preference for delay in requests for how-to guides and requests for more data.

INADEQUATE POLICIES

In all areas of organizational and institutional life there is an intrinsic relationship between policy and practice. Every institution is governed by a policy, "whether stated or unstated" (Brandt, 1986:103). Although Brandt found no organization with an explicit racist policy, strong evidence of the existence indicated covert racist policies that reflected deeply entrenched values, ideals, and assumptions. In each institution Brandt studied, racist ideologies influenced policies as well as individual behaviours and organizational practices.

In reviewing the formation of policies aimed at eliminating racism in the past two decades in Canada, it is possible to conclude that policies do not always lead to substantive and sustained change. Many of the policy documents are framed in the context of racial and cultural diversity and pluralism. Issues are conceptualized in terms of improving "relations" between different racial and ethnocultural groups, and there is often a reliance on rhetoric and euphemisms such as "race and ethnic relations" and "multicultural and race relations." Policy statements often lack specificity and clarity in relation to their goals, objectives, and implementation strategies.

For example, the focus of both the policy and the implementation of many educational agencies is, on one hand, the "needs" of racial- and cultural-minority students, and on the other hand, the "problems" of racial-minority students. Thus, it is not the educational system that is the "problem"; the problem is the difficulties that racial-minority students create for the system. The language of many of the policies suggests a preoccupation with creating, promoting, and encouraging greater tolerance, understanding, and harmony among racial-minority students and staff, rather than ensuring fairness and equity as the outcomes.

A survey of policy development and implementation sponsored by the Ontario Ministry of Education (Mock and Masemann, 1989) found that 39 boards had a policy and that 25 boards were currently developing policies.

A study of these policies revealed that most school boards preferred positive language in the policy document and that there was a strong reluctance to refer to "anti-racist education."

Many educators have viewed the concept of anti-racism as too polemical and political and leading to unnecessary conflict and resistance (Tator and Henry, 1991). Instead, policy statements and documents choose to ignore, deny, and deflect the reality and persistence of racism in educational structures, processes, and ideologies.

A study of policy implementation in schools and boards noted that the desired outcome of many race relations policies in boards of education is the maintenance of the status quo—racial harmony—rather than systematic and systemic change (Anderson and Fullan, 1984). But policy-driven goals such as racial harmony, tolerance, and understanding, while appearing positive, avoid the need to deconstruct racist ideology, practices, and procedures.

Even an institution's use of the term "anti-racism" in policy documents does not necessarily ensure that it is supportive of or committed to actions and initiatives that will produce substantive change. In some cases, the issue of the racism is framed in such a way that it fails to take into account how racism is specifically linked to the role and function of the organization (e.g., the school) or institution (e.g., a board of education).

Another common weakness of policy documents is that they neglect to delineate the ways in which an anti-racism agenda will be pursued throughout all levels of the organization. The most common flaw, however, is the failure to link the anti-racism policy to the mission and mandate of the organization. For example, policing organizations have developed policies that fail to be explicit about the nature of the problem they are seeking to address. They have also not been specific about the kind of changes expected to occur at the various levels in the policing organization. As a result, many police officers appear to believe that their force's race relations policy is inconsistent with the work of policing and that it does not further the goals of law enforcement "to serve and protect."

An audit of the Metropolitan Toronto Police Force (Andrews, 1992) found that most of the force's race relations policies, programs, and undertakings were framed in a way that encouraged the view that the force itself did not really require fundamental ideological or structural changes. The report suggested that efforts were mainly directed toward changes that affected only the fringe of the daily operations of policing. It identified attempts to engage in some form of accommodation of differences in the community. However, what was really required was a commitment to changing the values and culture of the institution.

Similarly, policies in human-service agencies do not appear to have transformed human-service agencies in Canada. For example, although the United Way of Metropolitan Toronto had been involved in promoting multicultural and anti-racist organizational development in its social agencies for more than 6 years,[3] most of Metro's ethno-cultural and racial communities continued to experience an "appalling lack of services"(Medeiros, 1991).

What is the potential for a policy to serve as an agent of individual or institutional change? Policies are perhaps a useful starting point, but policy statements in and of themselves are of limited value in actually combatting racism. They cannot function as mechanisms to promote change.

INADEQUATE TRAINING

Training is the development of specific skills to meet policy and program objectives. Most programs for combatting racism fail to meet these specifications. By and large, these programs have been ineffective because they treat anti-racism like any other subject—to be learned by employees in a three-hour, one-day, or, at most, three-day workshop. Learning about racism is placed into the same category as developing skills to manage a new computer program. Training is commonly delivered by trainers who are inexperienced and unskilled in anti-racism theory and practice. Often the training is unrelated to the daily roles and functions of the participants.

Training has drawn upon many different models, from developing cultural sensitivity and racial awareness to creating management skills for managing diversity and implementing employment equity. Some of these approaches are briefly described below.

Human-Awareness Training

Human-awareness training models perceive the goal of training to be the promotion of positive relations between the organization and groups from different cultural backgrounds. These programs focus on acquiring sensitivity to the values, customs, and practices of different groups. Most race relations training programs use some combination of human-awareness training with cultural awareness training, and both are based on three false premises. The first assumption is that when people understand the customs of another group, they will be able to deal with them more effectively. Second, is the assumption that an understanding of the complexities of culture can be learned in a few hours of training. Third is the assumption that only those who come into daily contact with racial-minorities need to be trained.

Cultural-Awareness Training

The goal of cultural-awareness training is similar to that of human awareness training. It has a strong emphasis on transmitting information about ethnic groups and their cultural patterns. This emphasis on transmitting "snapshots" of cultural information ignores the more important study of the complexities of culture. The crucial problems experienced by people of colour in organizations and institutions are not simply the result of a White lack of understanding of non-European cultures. Cultural awareness or cross-cultural training commonly ignores the systemic and individual barriers created by racism.

Race-Awareness Training

The premise of race-awareness training is that racism is a White problem. The purpose of the training is to help participants understand examine their attitudes and behaviours and the implications of their own racism. Energy is directed toward self-examination rather than toward fundamental changes in the structure and ideology of the organization. Self-examination is only the initial phase of problem identification. Effective training should move on to ways in which the entire organizational ideology can be challenged.

Legislative Compliance

The goal of legislative compliance training is merely to understand human-rights and employment-equity legislation so that the organization and its employees can comply with it. These programs rarely address the issue of racism nor seek to change racist attitudes and behaviours.

Managing Diversity

While legislative compliance stresses the avoidance of unlawful discrimination, managing diversity focusses on organizational management. These training programs see racism as simply a management problem, something that can be managed and contained. Thus, the emphasis is on changing institutions by providing people-management skills, interviewing skills, and so on. These programs are not designed to bring about a greater understanding of race issues per se, but attempt to relate general understandings about diversity to the professional and practical world of the organization.

Many organizations in Canada have been fearful of even using the term "anti-racism" in their definition of training. For the most part, the objectives of their training are to enhance sensitivity and understanding, to provide ethno-racial information on diverse groups, or to provide knowledge and tools to manage employment equity programs. Basic to these approaches is the view that racism stems simply from a failure of Whites to understand Blacks and other groups. Many organizations feel that once they have offered such training, they have met the goals of an anti-racist organization. A further flaw in many of the training programs is that the initiative is introduced into an organizational environment that is not particularly supportive. As a result, it is usually front-line staff who receive the training. Thus, training is generally provided to new police recruits, teachers, and human-service providers, but rarely to supervisors and senior managers.

Little research on training has occurred in Canada. The evidence from the United Kingdom and the United States, however, as well as the experience of anti-racist trainers in Canada, suggests that training as currently constituted has little chance of success in creating an anti-racist environment. In Canada, police–race relations training has been studied by Ungerleider and McGregor (1992), who examined studies of interventions designed to "change the attitudes and behaviours of police and military personnel towards minority groups." The study found a small measure of attitudinal or behaviourial change exhibited by little more than half of the training participants. In many instances, however, the impact of the training was minimal, compared with the effects of learning by experience, by absorbing the values of the occupational culture, and other factors.

Training is perhaps the most common institutional response to racism. It is often used by organizations because it is an easy way to show that some action is being taken to improve the organizational climate for racial-minority members. However, it does little to change the ideology that creates the framework within which the organization operates. That ideology is, for the most part, drawn from and influenced by the value system of the larger, mainstream society.

The value conflict that characterizes democratic racism is as evident in organizations as it is in the wider society of which they are a part. Training does not challenge that ideology; at best, it tinkers with it. Training is merely an organizational mechanism to adjust to the changing environment without changing or transforming any aspect of it. Thus, it is an essential element of an assimilationist organizational model, but it does little to move an organization toward anti-racism.

LACK OF REPRESENTATION

The evidence of widespread and systemic racial discrimination in employment in the public and private sectors is inimical to the fundamental tenets of a liberal democratic society. However, it is in this area of organizational change that resistance is most evident. Even *proposed* race-conscious measures generate enormous tension, hostility, and dissension within organizations.

In the limited number of institutions in which either anti-racism or employment equity programs are in place—such as some boards of education, universities, and police forces—there have been negative reactions, especially from White males. With the implementation of the Employment Equity Act and the contract compliance program at the federal level of government and the proposed employment equity legislation in the Province of Ontario, it is clear that huge obstacles will be faced. The inadequacy of the legislative and regulatory requirements, the lack of monitoring of implementation of employment equity programs, and the weak enforcement mechanisms are some of the significant flaws in the current approach to equity. Even more problematic is the powerful backlash to these initiatives, manifested in the attitudes and behaviours of White male employers, managers, and staff.

In many institutions, such as universities, the media, police forces, and other public-sector agencies, initiatives designed to fundamentally alter discriminatory barriers are rigorously opposed. Resistance is framed within the ideological construct of a set of beliefs that rationalize and justify the maintenance of the status quo. Efforts to increase the representation of people of colour in the workforce as well as in appointments to boards, commissions, and other public bodies are thus deflected.

A recent example of resistance occurred in the Toronto Fire Department. The department is 99 percent male, 96 percent of whom are White. In an effort to redress this situation, the personnel committee of the Toronto city council recommended that the department give preference in the hiring of thirteen *qualified* women and racial-minority candidates, ahead of the White men who had scored only slightly higher in the qualification process. Despite the fact that the thirteen candidates were drawn from a pool of 140 fully qualified individuals selected from 4000 applicants and that all the candidates had passed the physical, health, and aptitude tests, the chief of the department protested vigorously. The motion was defeated by city council. Many of the arguments used by the firefighters and the media were based on the following myths.

Employment Equity Is Reverse Discrimination.

According to this view, employment equity requires employers to discriminate against better-qualified Whites and gives an unfair advantage to people of colour. However, what is required is not reverse discrimination but the end of a long history of employment practices that result in preferential treatment for White males.

Employment Equity Ignores the Merit Principle.

This myth is perhaps the most widely believed and promoted. It is based on the assumption that employment equity and other anti-racist measures will result in the hiring and appointment of unqualified individuals and bring an end to the merit principle. In reality, however, equity programs do not require the abandonment of standards and qualifications. Rather, they eliminate irrelevant criteria such as the colour of one's skin, cultural background, and gender.

Employment Equity Stigmatizes Minorities.

According to this misconception, minorities will never know if they have been selected on the basis of their qualifications or because of their group membership. One could argue that White males for 200 years should have been asking themselves the same question. Implicit in the above assumption is the perception that there are no meritorious persons in this group. As one observer notes,

> Do all those corporate directors, bankers etc., who got their job for extraneous reasons—first because they were somebody's son, second, because they were male, third because they were Protestant, and fourth because they were White—feel demeaned thereby? It would be interesting to ask them—or to ask the same question of those doctors who managed to get into good medical schools because there were quotas keeping out Jews, the skilled tradesmen who were admitted to the union because two members of their families recommended them and so on. (Green, 1981:79)

Clearly implicit in the standard critique of these pro-active programs is the notion that being rewarded is the natural result of being in the majority or the elite. Rewards are only demeaning when one is a member of a minority or a marginalized group (e.g., women).

Equality is Best Achieved Through the Free Market.

Although abundant evidence demonstrates that the free market does not lead to equality (Abella, 1984), this view is still widely held. However, at the current pace of change it would take women and minorities hundreds of years to achieve equality with White able-bodied males. The reliance on slow measures such as education, information sharing, and dialogue with employers will not reverse centuries of bias and disadvantage that are built into employment systems and are generally invisible to all but those who suffer from their adverse impacts.

Fairness Is Best Achieved by Treating Everyone in the Same Way.

Opponents of equity measures argue that in a democratic society, treating everyone equally is sufficient to ensure fairness in the workplace. However, as Abella (1984) points out, "We now know that to treat everyone in the same way may offend the notion of equality" (3). She suggests that ignoring differences and refusing to accommodate them is a denial of equal access and opportunity; it is discrimination.

Employment Equity Means Hiring by Quotas.

Although mandatory quotas are not required in employment equity programs, a widespread perception exists that governments require specific numbers of racial minorities to be hired, promoted, or appointed in specific organizations. Instead, employment equity in Canada requires employers to set goals for their organization, taking into account the number of qualified individuals from target groups that are available in the potential workforce as well as the composition of the internal workforce. Flexible goals and timetables are used to establish benchmarks toward representative hiring and promotion.

Finally, concerning employment equity as a strategy to eliminate racism, there is some doubt about its efficacy in achieving this goal. The experience of the authors suggests that employment equity measures generate such a racist backlash that many people of colour suffer even greater discrimination after their introduction. Moreover, employment equity programs include other designated groups (women, Aboriginal peoples, people with disabilities), thus the potential for competition among these groups for the limited number of available positions is very high.

LIMITED ACCESS TO GOODS, PROGRAMS, AND SERVICES

The lack of access to goods and services has been illustrated in the chapters dealing with institutional racism. The lack of support for ethno-racial agencies in the human-service delivery system is an example of the failure of government and other funding bodies to address racism in the mainstream delivery system. Another manifestation of the lack of access to goods, programs, and services is seen in the power of mainstream cultural and arts organizations to marginalize and exclude racial minorities in the production and transmission of literature, music, visual art, dance, theatre, and film. The Eurocentric funding criteria and priorities of art councils relegate artists of colour to the margins of the dominant culture. The streaming of Black students in schools and bias in curricula and teaching methods further demonstrate the lack of access and equity for racial minorities in the educational system. The absence of people of colour in print and electronic media organizations, and the racialization of their communities in the images and stories transmitted by the mainstream media, reinforce racism in Canadian institutions.

ABSENCE OF SANCTIONS

Rewards and sanctions are important ways of changing behaviour in organizations. No organizations in Canada, however, are known to impose wage sanctions on staff or management for racist behaviour. Typically, the sanctions that do exist are those mandated by race relations or anti-racism policies, but few of them include staff accountability mechanisms. Even where anti-racism policies exist, adequate sanctions have been lacking; and, where sanctions are in place, they tend to be weak and ineffective.

The Ontario Human Rights Commission has recently instituted a system authorizing organizations to conduct internal investigations of complaints based on prohibited grounds of discrimination. Organizations are free to develop strategies to respond to such complaints as they see fit. Unfortunately, most organizations do not have the expertise to conduct such investigations; moreover, complaints, unless they are serious, are likely to be dismissed. Sanctions are likely to be inadequate, and continuous monitoring may be non-existent. In some situations, the victim of discrimination may be punished and labelled a troublemaker.

LACK OF INDIVIDUAL ACCOUNTABILITY

Many organizations assume that their members are fair-minded, that they subscribe to the principles of equity and equality of treatment. This assumption leads to a lack of accountability for individuals. Few organizations require their employees to be held accountable for racist behaviour. Even organizations that have an anti-racism policy believe that their employees are tolerant and without prejudice. For example, in the case of teachers who are alleged to have demonstrated racist attitudes or behaviours, there are few mechanisms to deal with the problem. In many schools and boards, students, parents, and the community have little recourse.

A common problem with many organizational responses to racism is that individual members are not held accountable for their actions. Sanctions and accountability differ. Sanctions refer to the penalties imposed as a result of an infraction of organizational policies and norms. Accountability, on the other hand, refers to the assignment of responsibility for a specific set of actions for which non-compliance may result in specific sanctions. Thus, there can be accountability without sanctions.

It is difficult to find job descriptions that specifically prescribe anti-racist behaviour. Most often, the expectation is that those employed as equity practitioners[4] are the only ones accountable. The task of creating equity in the organization is frequently understood to be the job of the equity practitioner and no else. As Thomas (1984) notes in a review of the implementation of Toronto Board of Education's policy and program, race relations is often perceived by the rest of the organization as the work of the adviser on race relations: "It is where all the complaints, disputes, questions, and fears about racism go, even if they are connected to personnel or curriculum... Whose business is race relations anyway?" (18)

There are therefore two competing philosophies of equity in the organization. Since most members are considered tolerant, there is a need to prove that intolerance or racism was, in fact, intended. Since racism is defined by senior decision-makers very narrowly in most organizations, it becomes necessary to prove that employees, policies, and practices *intended* to discriminate or otherwise act in a racist manner. Often this results in a situation in which the innocence of the offender, already reinforced by the ideology of fairness, must be protected. Thus, an individual's reputation must not be tarnished by allegations of racism, nor must his or her fairness and objectivity be questioned. Anti-racism policies therefore provide an investigatory framework for which there is a strong presumption of innocence.

The presumption of innocence at the investigatory stage is peculiar to anti-racism allegations. A police investigation, on the other hand, is directed by a strong presumption of non-innocence. When a police officer arrests a suspect, it is usually assumed that the suspect is the correct person, and evidence is gathered to prove the police case. At the investigative stage in a charge of racism, however, the result of the presumption of innocence is a search for alternative explanations for the act of racism. Any other "reasonable" explanation negates a claim of racism, not simply for that case, but for all cases like it, regardless of the parties involved. The elusive nature of racism means that an alternative explanation can almost always be found. Thus, the notion of impact is eradicated and the result is a reduction in the level of individual accountability for actions that have a racist impact.

In addition, in racially hostile work environments, those most affected by racism are unlikely to complain about it. Overt racism may be so entrenched in the organization's operation that victims are expected to comply. In correctional institutions, for example, both inmates and staff often engage in overt racist acts. Minority staff find it difficult to complain for fear of reprisal, despite the existence of a policy forbidding racist acts.

STRUCTURAL RIGIDITY

Anti-racism requires fundamental changes to the structure of organizations. Yet, a characteristic response is the maintenance and preservation of traditional structural arrangements. In some instances, organizations have responded to the challenge by creating advisory bodies but not altering the basic structure of the organization. By definition, these bodies have limited power and exist at the discretion of those who appointed them.

Anti-racism is rarely considered important in the restructuring of ministries and government departments. The recent restructuring of the federal government proceeded without much attention to anti-racism. Thus, anti-racism initiatives and policies operate at the periphery. They are not considered as "really" important by senior decision-makers. When they are initiated, they are "add-ons." For example, pay equity legislation proceeded with little discussion of the relationship between race, gender, and pay.

INEFFECTIVE MONITORING AND EVALUATION MECHANISMS

The pursuit of racial equality demands that the mechanisms for measuring change be put in place. It means moving from discussing the principles of equality of opportunity to measuring achievement.

Equal-opportunity policies, mass "sensitization" training programs, and glossy public-relations campaigns are not especially effective unless they are combined with concrete programs that are regularly monitored, evaluated, and publicly reported. The use of effective monitoring systems—which can be mere progress reports—can begin to provide information on whether the goals of a program are being reached.

The most important measure of any initiative is its results. Extensive efforts to implement training and develop procedures, data-collection systems, report forms, and finely written policy statements are meaningless unless measurable improvement takes place. Just as the success of a private business is evaluated in terms of increases in sales, the only realistic basis for evaluating a program to increase equity for racial-minorities is its actual impact on these groups.

In Canada, the little evaluation that has been done on race relations training programs has focussed on evaluations by participants. The key indicator of effective training seems to be whether the participants found the trainers credible, balanced, and fair. The effectiveness of training for better interracial attitudes has, however, provided ambivalent results.

Efforts are needed to develop appropriate methods of "impact evaluation"—that is, measures of the extent to which an anti-racism initiative produces various results. The emphasis must be on an initiative's "return on investment" in relation to predetermined goals. From that basis, one can begin to establish legitimate and meaningful performance standards. The emphasis must be on determining whether the activity had the impact that it set out to have.

Measuring results with some degree of comfort and certitude requires the goals to be defined in specific, concrete, and realizable terms. Measuring results is impossible when the goals and objectives are nebulous generalizations.

INSUFFICIENT RESOURCES

The anti-racism initiatives discussed above suffer from inadequate resources, both material and human. To achieve a racially just and equitable society requires large-scale change and concerted commitment. In periods of economic restraint, many programs are cut due to lack of funds. Anti-racist initiatives are often the most vulnerable, and often the first programs to be reduced or eliminated.

The Ontario government's Anti-racism Secretariat has been given the responsibility of administering anti-racism programs in Ontario. It provides small grants to organizations and institutions to undertake initiatives aimed at addressing racism. The secretariat has limited power in influencing ministries to take more active steps to combat racism. It also lacks the funding to provide ministries with substantial help. Although it has the power to develop guidelines for ministries to follow, it has little power to ensure compliance. Nor does it have the authority to intervene in the affairs of a ministry.

The test of the effectiveness of anti-racist measures is their success in reducing racism. Using this criterion, the secretariat has had a very limited impact on reducing racism in Ontario. At the very least, it requires more authority and more power to influence decision-making in government ministries.

Similarly, at the federal level, the Multiculturalism Act makes no provision for the multiculturalism department to dictate the scope of activities performed by individual ministries with respect to anti-racism. Both the federal multiculturalism department and the provincial anti-racism secretariat function as internal consulting bodies to government and as minor funding bodies to organizations. Since these agencies do not have the statutory power or substantial financial resources to intervene in government affairs, the net effect is that government institutions are free to take whatever initiatives they deem sufficient.

TOKENISM

Tokenism often involves the practice of appointing or hiring one or two members of designated minority groups for relatively powerless positions in order to demonstrate the organization's tolerance of diversity. Tokenism circumvents substantive change. It is the most commonly used organizational mechanism to resist pressures for change and "an essential element in the ideological hegemony of the institutional process of racism" (Phillips and Blumberg, 1983:34).

With respect to the employment of racial minorities, tokenism takes several forms. For example, minorities may be ghettoized in certain positions. The segregation of ethnic employees is well documented (Reitz et al., l981; l982). Women of all ethnic and racial backgrounds are employed in factories as wage workers. Increasingly, Black men are hired as security guards and Black women are found in segregated occupations such as nursing aide, factory worker, and food service provider. In addition to these well-known methods of segregation is the racialization of occupation.

Stereotypes about the skills of certain groups of people have structured the occupational categories in which minorities tend to be found. Many organizations today hire minorities for certain specific type of jobs. It is common to find a disproportionate number of persons from Southeast Asia employed in jobs that involve computation, such as computer science and accounting. A disproportionate number of Black people employed in the public service are in jobs related to racism, anti-racism, equity, diversity, and so on.

This kind of job ghettoization of racial-minority professionals is partly related to a reluctance to value the universal skills that people of colour possess. It is also related to the desire of many firms to relegate minorities to occupational categories in which they are deemed to be efficient workers. Thus, Asians are thought to be especially good at math-related jobs, and Blacks, because of their size and alleged strength, are thought to do well at security. (When both physical strength *and* quick thinking are required, as in policing and fire marshalling, Blacks, oddly enough, are not considered.)

MINORITY CHANGE AGENTS

The people in an organization who are responsible for initiating and developing strategies of change have been called "change agents." Their position is fraught with difficulties, since change agents rarely occupy a position of power in the hierarchical structure of the organization. Although they are responsible for advocating and implementing new policies and practices, their role is often marginal.

Their role may evoke resistance. For example, change agents of colour engaged in anti-racism work, purely because of their identity, elicit resistance from White members of the organization. To organizational leaders, change agents of colour represent a paradox. On the one hand, White people see them as "successful," unlike others of their community. Implicit in this assumption is that the individual does not possess the negative qualities of members of his group. On the other hand, change agents of colour represent the targets of racism. Consequently, resistance is engendered in ways that White people engaged in this same work do not experience.

Change agents of colour are particularly subject to scrutiny and to challenges of their position. They are seen as "looking for problems." They are subject to accusations such as "having a chip on their shoulder" or seen as "being too sensitive." Their knowledge, skills, resilience, and ability to mediate between various groups is constantly tested. Their "objectivity" is questioned, and their "favouritism" toward their own group, or toward racial minorities in general, is suspected. Their boundaries of responsibility are narrowed or expanded, depending on the situation.

Their methodologies or strategies are often held suspect. Their reports are often censored and altered until they are unrecognizable, as issues are restated so as not to sound so "negative," or their recommendations are set aside because they are viewed as being unrealistic, inaccurate, or unreasonable. All of these behaviours are manifestations of resistance to the anti-racism effort, exacerbated by the presence of minority change agents.

Even when persons of colour hold positions of power, their words and actions are closely scrutinized and their actions are frequently criticized. The intense criticism and the overwhelming scrutiny by the media, members of the police establishment, and others of Susan Eng, chair of the Metropolitan Toronto Police Service Commission, is a powerful example of the vulnerability of people of colour who achieve positions of power. Recently, another minority member of that board, in reacting to criticism of comments he made to a Bermuda newspaper about the well-documented problems between the police and Toronto's Black community, noted:

> This is what happens, in part, when people of colour make comments about a situation that exists. I expect it is still not nice for us to say these things, as if I should be grateful for having the opportunity to say anything at all. The vituperative, hostile reaction is so out of proportion. (Minors, 1993)

The lack of support and the powerlessness experienced by change agents results in a significant incidence of "burn out." Individuals suffer both physical and emotional exhaustion in their work as change agents; their "suffering or stress is a natural consequence of the dilemmas and paradoxes inherent in playing or resisting the token role" (Phillips and Blumberg, 1983:36).

ORGANIZATIONAL ACCOUNTABILITY

Many of Canada's public institutions appear to have become increasingly bureaucratized, institutionalized, specialized, and isolated not only from the public, but from each other. They often operate as if they were separate and distinct from the larger society and far removed from the concerns and issues of importance to people of colour. Functioning in this framework results in a lack of accountability not only to the public but also to the political process.

The criminal justice system, for example, has been criticized for assuming that it can pursue the goal of upholding community standards only by being above the community. Its legitimacy is gained from a general acceptance of the laws and regulations it enforces, the values it embraces, the morality it is supposed to support, and the order it maintains. Many other professional groups, such as those in education, human services, and the media, feel a stronger sense of accountability to their self-defined codes of conduct than they do to those they serve.

Public-sector organizations are administered by bureaucrats whose roles, functions, and responsibilities appear to be largely unaffected by the issue of racism in their systems. Bureaucrats perform with relative autonomy and most of their jobs involve making informed decisions in the interest of preserving democratic institutions. They are technocrats whose judgements are valued and trusted and they are probably among the most mobile of public servants. Their judgements help determine the priorities of governments and other public-sector institutions. The judgements and ideology of senior bureaucrats dictate what is fair, reasonable, and achievable in the organization. As a group, therefore, they are perhaps the least accountable of all public servants but the most trusted. They are most capable of designing strategies to undermine any attempt to achieve a different conception of equity. In a government ministry, for example, some well-designed anti-racism training models developed with the help of international "experts" in the field were quietly "killed" by a handful of senior bureaucrats who thought them too radical.[5]

LIMITED PUBLIC ACCOUNTABILITY

One of the underlying tenets of Canadian democracy is the obligation of its public institutions to explain and justify their activities. This accountability might be said to provide legitimacy to the democratic state. It entails an acceptance of the notion of community participation in and control of the decision-making processes of public institutions.

But how does a public-sector organization develop these relationships? How does it include a diverse clientele, a diverse group of constituents, into the system? What are the mechanisms for bringing the community into the decision-making process? Do the institutions and organizations examined in this book demonstrate public accountability?

A number of public-sector agencies have responded to this issue by initiating a range of public-consultation mechanisms. These mechanisms have included:

- needs-assessment surveys
- consultation with key informants
- opinion polls
- community focus groups
- advisory councils and committees
- commissions and task forces
- public hearings
- conferences and workshops
- public information programs
- advertising
- neighbourhood meetings
- support to community groups
- telephone information hotlines
- community relations offices

Although many of these activities have been useful, others have not. Their objectives have frequently lacked clarity, their implementation has often been ineffective, and their impact has rarely been evaluated with any rigour.

There exists in racial-minority communities an increasing sense of mistrust, apathy, and anger toward these exercises, especially community consultations. Reactions such as "We have been consulted to death" and "What happened to our recommendations?" are the result of too many minor, cosmetic improvements. Community consultations require the expenditure of enormous time and resources by community groups and organizations that are already hard pressed. The growing scepticism and distrust of consultation initiatives are the result of the widespread view that public institutions are simply "going through the motions," that they continue to devote most of their resources to support "mainstream" organizations.

The spirit and commitment with which public consultations are carried out are therefore questioned. When goals are not clearly identified, when expectations are not articulated, and when no substantive action is initiated as a result of the exercise, these consultations are considered pseudo-democratic exercises to distract minorities from the real organizational goal of maintaining the status quo. When attempts made to improve community relations involve the community in an unplanned, undisciplined, and unprofessional manner, the notion of community participation in the decision-making processes of public institutions moves that much further from reaching fruition.

Figure 12.2
ADDRESSING RESISTANCE AND ENLISTING SUPPORT

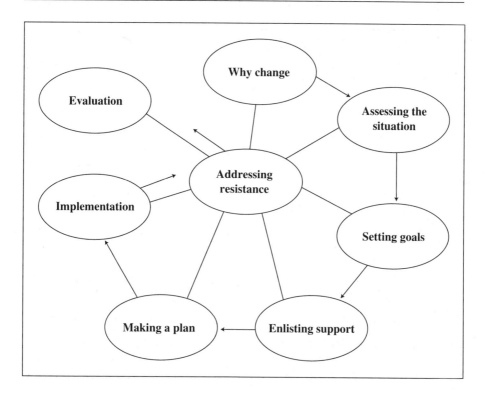

RACE-CONSCIOUS THEORY OF ORGANIZATIONS

Overcoming resistance to anti-racist change can best be accomplished in an organization that has become conscious of race. In a race-conscious theory of organizations, the nature of social relations is influenced by race. Interests deemed legitimate have a racial component. Compliance, and the risks of non-compliance, are assessed in terms of the importance and legitimacy of the interests, power, and/or lack thereof, as well as social status both within the organization and outside of it. To what extent are Canadian organizations race conscious? Most organizations fall within a continuum that starts at monoculturalism, gradually changes to assimilationism or multiculturalism, and finally assumes an anti-racist organizational stance. The majority of Canadian organizations appear to fall within the first two categories. Few, if any, have developed a genuine anti-racist model of organizational behaviour.

Figure 12.3

A RACE-CONSCIOUS THEORY OF ORGANIZATIONS

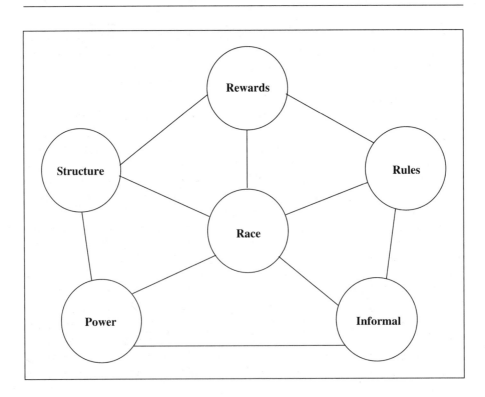

THREE ORGANIZATIONAL PARADIGMS OF CHANGE

In a heterogeneous society, race affects every aspect of organizational life. For this reason, some analysts view organizations along a race-cultural continuum as a method to categorize organizational responses to racism. These approaches have a variety of labels, but are identified here as the assimilationist (exclusionary, monocultural, ethnocentric, homogeneous); multicultural (add-on); and anti-racist (racial equity) approach. Each of these approaches has very different implications in relation to the organization's development of strategies and initiatives for dealing with racial bias and discrimination.

The various responses by institutions to racism are based on different assumptions about the nature of racism and reflect broader perspectives underlying people's thoughts and behaviour. They also reflect the ideology of the organization, that is, the collective belief and value system that weaves its way through the institution and shapes and affects all its aspects. Particularly in large and complex organizations, more than one model may operate concurrently. For example, a board of education might have a very innovative approach in one unit, such as curriculum development, and an extremely resistant group in the department responsible for placement and assessment issues.

ASSIMILATIONISM

Organizations that do not recognize racial and cultural diversity generally operate on the assumption of homogeneity among people. They assume, for example, that even in a predominantly multiracial society such as Canada, individuals belonging to racial minorities have been assimilated into the mainstream of Canadian society.

Consequently, these organizations have a monocultural perspective (Jackson and Holvino, 1989). Their policies and practices are expressed in universal terms that emphasize the underlying values and norms of the dominant culture. Such organizations focus on preserving and maintaining the control of those in power, and their efforts are directed to protecting the status quo (usually reflecting the interests of White males, but not always). The existing mission, policies, and practices of the assimilationist institution are perceived as the only "right" ones, and no consideration is given to other groups' perspectives or interests. Thus, the concerns of racial and cultural minorities are constantly ignored or deflected (Jones, 1986). There is no sense of accountability to external constituencies.

Mighty (1992) suggests that this form of cultural imperialism often unconsciously but sometimes consciously seeks to homogenize non-dominant cultures and transform them into a single one. It fails to consider both the sociocultural context in which the organizations operate and the diversity of perspectives that co-exist within them. They undertake no efforts to respond to diversity issues in general. Moreover, there is a total absence of interest in addressing the issues or concerns of racial minorities or the other constituencies that the organization is supposed to serve. Assimilationist organizations do not see the need to participate in any fundamental alteration in their organizational culture (Jackson and Holvino, 1989).

This paradigm continues to be widespread (Adler, 1983; McDonald, 1991). Assimilationist institutions may recognize that racial diversity exists in society, but they perceive its impact as negative. They assume that their way of viewing the world is the best way and that all other perspectives are essentially inferior (Adler, 1983; Kanter, 1977).

Assimilationist organizations try to minimize diversity by selecting a workforce that is as homogeneous as possible. When external pressures such as anti-racism policies or employment equity are imposed, organizational decision-makers may find themselves coerced into allowing a few members of racial minorities to gain access to their organizations. They then seek to assimilate the newcomers into their world (Holvino and Jackson, 1989).

The biases in such organizations' perspectives are reflected in inequitable policies, inaccessible services, and discriminatory practices, all of which are considered immutable. "Outsiders" must conform without disturbing the existing organizational culture. As a result, newcomers are usually confined to the lower ranks of the organization, where they remain powerless to change the status quo. Occasionally, the recruitment of a "token" woman or racial minority into a higher-level position may occur after ensuring that the person is an exceptional member of the out-group, a team player who will conform to the organizational culture and not challenge the status quo (Mighty, 1992; Jackson and Holvino, 1989; Kanter, 1977).

MULTICULTURALISM

The principle underlying multicultural change strategies is a willingness to make limited modifications in the organization or institution but not to alter its fundamental structure, mission, and culture. A variety of initiatives may be undertaken from time to time, such as recruiting a "minority" for a staff position or as a member of the board, and translating materials into various languages.

Multicultural organizations and their members learn to master the equity rhetoric while engaging in cosmetic changes. Homeostasis characterizes these organizations, and it is very often reactive rather than proactive. Diversity is useful in such organizations. For example, they may draw on ethno-racial staff to assist in the translation of materials or to work with members of their own culture.

These organizations see diversity as a product and are therefore image conscious. They often proclaim their programs and initiatives. They therefore make a point of hiring minorities, most of whom will have responsibility without power, limited control, and impressive titles without access to the centres of power. In many cases, these minorities will be physically and structurally isolated from the rest of the organization.

In this type of organization there is a recognition that certain changes must be made in order to comply with new policies, regulations, or legislation.

However, issues related to racism are considered distinct from the day-to-day life of the organization. The needs, interests, and perspectives of racial minorities are dealt with on an ad-hoc basis rather than being integrated into the programs and services of the organization.

Responsibility for change is often delegated to the front-line worker, who may then function in an unsupportive environment. The multicultural organization may seek to remove some discriminatory barriers by providing greater access to racial-minorities, but its members are expected to conform to the dominant group's values and worldview (Jackson and Holvino, 1989).

Despite recognizing diversity, multicultural organizations rarely make conscious efforts to create organizational climates that support diversity or establish systems that enable different types of employees to succeed (Copeland, 1988). For example, they may introduce training initiatives (human rights, cross-cultural, intercultural, race relations, anti-racism, organizational management, employment equity). But, while the training creates an awareness of diversity, it rarely creates new behavioural norms and organizational procedures that would promote access, participation, and equity; eliminate discrimination; and effectively manage diversity (EOC, 1990).

ANTI-RACISM

An anti-racist organization is not one in which racism is absent. Rather, it takes a proactive stand against racism in all its forms. It is oppositional in nature and addresses racism at both the organizational and individual levels. Commitment in these organizations is based on an acknowledgement that racism exists, that it manifests itself in various forms, at the individual, institutional, and systemic levels, and that it is embedded in the mass culture of the dominant group. An anti-racist perspective begins by accepting that the perceptions of people of colour are real and that there may be a multiplicity of realities in any one event.

The anti-racism approach to change is based on a commitment to eradicate all forms of social oppression and racial disadvantage in the organization. The anti-racist organization includes members of racial minorities as full and equal participants. It follows through on decisions that affect its broader social responsibilities and external relationships.

Anti-racism emphasizes a holistic approach to the development of anti-racist ideologies, goals, policies, and practices. As an organizational response requires the formation of new organizational structures; the introduction of new cultural norms and value systems; changes in the power dynamics and the implementation of new employment systems; substantive changes in the services delivered; support for new roles and relationships at all levels of the organization; new patterns and more inclusive styles of leadership and decision-making; and the reallocation of resources. Strategic planning, organizational audits and reviews, and monitoring and accountability systems are all considered an integral part of the management of anti-racist change.

Of prime importance in the anti-racist institutional process is a commitment to the empowerment of racial minorities both within the organization and outside of it. Policy development and new mission statements are not considered an end in themselves; adequate attention, priority, and resources are given to implementation strategies and programs. Effective monitoring mechanisms are put in place to ensure accountability throughout the organization. Evaluation of the change effort is an ongoing process. Resistance to change is anticipated, and strategies to overcome it are planned.

Finally, anti-racism recognizes that no institution operates in isolation from other institutions and that racism in one arena of social life, such as education, will affect others, such as employment; that racism in police forces can be fostered by the media and in turn that the media can be influenced by market forces and government "propaganda." Thus, the anti-racist approach to change seeks to encourage and facilitate linkages and partnerships among institutions in order to identify and dismantle racial barriers and racial inequalities.

(For more on diagnosing and removing institutional racism, please see Table 12.1 on pages 304–305.)

SUMMARY

This chapter presented reasons why organizations have been slow in enacting anti-racist initiatives. It was suggested that although organizations generally resist change, they are especially reluctant to initiate and implement anti-racist change. The reasons for this include a lack of vision or mandate, a lack of upper-level managerial commitment, inadequate policies, a lack of individual accountability, and insufficient resources.

Some organizations are not accountable to the public, nor do they listen to the requests made of them, especially by members of minority groups. Even agencies of government whose mandate is anti-racism lack the resources and especially the power to influence the decisions of other ministries. Anti-racist initiatives must have a strong organizational commitment in order to reach their goal.

The chapter concluded with a discussion of various models of organizational change and noted that most Canadian organizations can be described as either assimilationist or multicultural. Few have moved to a genuine race-conscious or anti-racist model of organizational behaviour.

REFERENCES

Abella, R. (1984). *Report of the Commission on Equality in Employment*. Ottawa.

Adler, N.J. (1983). *Cross Cultural Management Research: The Ostrich and the Trend* 8(2):226–232.

Andrews A. (1992). *Review of Race Relations Practices of the Metropolitan Toronto Police Force*. Toronto: Municipality of Metropolitan Toronto.

Anderson, S., and M. Fullan. (1984). *Policy Implementation Issues for Multicultural Education at the School Board Level*. Toronto: Ontario Institute of Studies in Education.

Brandt, G. (1986). *The Realization of Anti-Racist Teaching*. London: Falmer Press.

Copeland, L. (1988). "Learning to Manage A Multicultural Work Force." *Training* (May):31–35.

Equal Opportunity Consultants (EOC). (1990). *Race Relations Training Review*. Ontario Ministry of the Solicitor General, Race Relations and Policing Unit. Unpublished.

Green, P. (1981). "The New Individualism." *Christianity and Crisis* 41 (March 30):79.

Jackson, B.W., and E. Holvino. (1989). *Working with Multicultural Organizations: Matching Theory and Practice*. Proceedings of Workshop on Diversity: Implications for Education and Training. Toronto: 109–21.

Jones, E.W. (1986). "Black Managers: The Dream Deferred." *Harvard Business Review* (May–June):84–93.

Kanter, R.M. (1977). *Men and Women of the Corporations*. New York: Basic Books.

Maracle, L. (1993). "Racism, Sexism and Patriarchy." In H. Bannerji (ed.), *Returning the Gaze: Essays on Racism, Feminism and Politics*. Toronto: Sister Vision Press.

McDonald, B. (1991). *Managing Diversity: A Guide to Effective Staff Management*. Winnipeg: Cross Cultural Communications International.

Medeiros, J. (1991). *Family Services for All*. Toronto: Multicultural Coalition for Access to Family Services.

Mighty, E.J. (1992). "Managing Workforce Diversity: Institutionalization and Strategic Choice in the Adoption of Employment Equity." Ph.D. dissertation, York University.

Minors, A. (1993). *The Toronto Star* (September 6):A7.

Mock, K., and V. Masemann. (1989). *Survey of Race and Ethnocultural Equity Policy Development and Implementation in Ontario School Boards*. Toronto: Ontario Ministry of Education.

Phillips W., Jr., and R. Blumberg. (1983). "Tokenism and Organizational Change." *Integrateducation* 20(1 & 2) (March):34–39.

Reitz, J., et al. (1981). *Inequality and Segregation in Jobs*. Toronto: Centre for Urban and Community Studies, University of Toronto.

————.(1982). *Ethnic Group Control of Jobs*. Toronto: Centre for Urban and Community Studies, University of Toronto.

Tator, C., and F. Henry. (1991). *Multicultural Education: Translating Policy into Practice*. Ottawa: Multiculturalism Canada.

Thomas, B. (1984). *Race Relations Program Review*. Toronto: Toronto Board of Education.

Ungerleider, C., and E. McGregor. (1992). *Issues in Police Intercultural and Intercultural Race Relations Training in Canada*. Ottawa: Canadian Centre for Police Race Relations.

NOTES

1. Many of the examples of organizational resistance are drawn from the authors' experiences in working with public- and private-sector institutions.

2. This incident occurred when the authors were working with an agency of government.

3. In 1986, the United Way of Greater Toronto first piloted its Multicultural/Anti-Racist Organizational Development Program, which is designed to assist health and social service agencies in identifying and dismantling barriers to the full participation of ethno-racial groups as volunteers, staff, and clients. Its goal is to enhance the capacity of agencies to respond effectively to the needs of a diverse community.

4. The term "equity practitioner" is used here to mean any individual involved in the pursuit of equity. Such a person could exist in an organization under a variety of labels, including, but not restricted to, race relations, employment equity, human rights, cross-cultural, diversity, and intercultural communications.

5. Personal communication from the "expert" contracted by a ministry of government.

Table 12.1

A MODEL FOR DIAGNOSING AND REMOVING INSTITUTIONAL RACISM AND OTHER BARRIERS TO ETHNO-RACIAL ACCESS

Indicators For Measuring Institutional Racism

Employment	Service Provision	Purchasing
1. Is there an over- or underrepresentation of ethno-racial minority employees in some job categories?	1. Do services present barriers to ethno-racial access? Are these barriers located in occupational practices and procedures or in staff attitudes or behaviour, or are they simply the outcome of decisions on different ethno-racial groups?	1. Is there evidence of denial of contracts to minority business?
2. Is there consistent over- or underemployment of ethno-racial minority employees in terms of matching job qualifications (e.g., education experience) with job category?	2. Do the organization's communications materials and methods present barriers to ethno-racial communities (e.g., lack of translation, inappropriate portrayal, racial insensitivity, cultural inappropriateness)?	2. Is there evidence of past discrimination in the contracting customs, systems, etc.?
3. Do employee evaluations show consistent biases in favour of or against a particular race?	3. To what extent, and how, does the organization target information to and receive information from ethno-racial communities?	3. Do contracting requirements have a disproportionately negative impact on minority businesses?
4. Does race affect the degree of agreement between employees and their supervisors on the employee evaluations?	4. To what extent do the organization's communications strategies recognize the specific information needs of and barriers to information experienced by ethno-racial communities?	4. Is there a failure to distribute bidding information to potential minority businesses?
5. Does race affect the type of employment actions taken?	5. Do the information materials portray ethno-racial diversity?	5. What is the percentage of contractors that are minority-owned?
6. Is there differential access to in-service training?	6. Are ethno-racial communities involved in planning, designing, developing, and delivering information activities?	6. Is there a lack of notification of bid opportunities?
7. Is there differential enrolment in in-service training?		7. Is there a repeated use of a restricted number of vendors?
8. Are there adequate mechanisms to handle discrimination complaints?		8. How large is the minority-business supplier base?
9. What are the findings of grievance settlements?		
10. Are there policies and procedures to facilitate employee relations?		
11. Is there a failure to recruit ethno-racial minorities?		
12. What are the hiring criteria?		

Indicators For Measuring Institutional Racism		
Employment	**Service Provision**	**Purchasing**

Employment	Service Provision	Purchasing
13. Is there consistent hiring of non-minorities? 14. Is there an employment equity plan? 15. Is race an important functional variable within the organization from both the employees' and employers' perspective?	7. Are the service-delivery processes equitably reflective of the ethno-racial communities? 8. In what way are services sensitive to the life experiences and reflective of the needs of various ethno-racial communities? 9. Do ethno-racial communities participatee in the planning, design, and delivery of services? 10. Do ethno-racial communities receive equal benefit from the services?	

Categories of Information Required for this Paradigm		
Employment	**Service Provision**	**Purchasing**

Employment	Service Provision	Purchasing
1. Demographic statistics and ethno-racial workforce profile. 2. Policies and practices: job and performance factors. 3. Employer–employee relations. 4. Administrative procedures. 5. Perceptions of personnel and organization climate.	1. Demographic statistics. 2. Percentage of minority clients served by program i.e., their under-utilization or overutilization of the program. 3. Percentage of resources allocated to minority communities. 4. Communication efforts to reach minority communities. 5. Level of participation by minorities in the decision-making process.	1. Demographic statistics. 2. Percentage of minority firms in the private sector by industry sector. 3. Percentage of the organization's contractors (and prime subcontractors) that are minority-owned. 4. Percentage of total contracting purchasing dollars that goes to minority contractors.

Chapter 13

▼▼▼▼▼▼▼▼▼▼▼▼▼

The Paradox of
Democratic Racism

> In general the talk around race...has only moved as far as it its own nega-
> tion; "I am not a racist"...becomes a common and accepted disclaimer on
> the tip of everyone's tongue.... This allows for the avoidance of deep ques-
> tioning and critical thinking. (Farman, 1992:7)

This concluding chapter of the book briefly summarizes the ways in which democratic racism is expressed in individual ideologies, in organizational and institutional values and practices, and in the collective beliefs, assumptions, and norms shared by the dominant culture of Canadian society. The second part of this chapter discusses anti-racist strategies. These approaches have been developed in the context of a pervasive denial of racism and a strong resistance to a fundamental alteration in the positions of power and privilege that White Canadians occupy in relation to persons of colour.

INTRODUCTION

The various forms of resistance to anti-racism—lack of commitment; inadequate policies, programs, and practices; insufficient resources, monitoring, and eval-uation; lack of individual, organizational, and public accountability—are all strongly influenced by democratic racism and the values associated with it. These values fuel the action or inaction of the individuals working in organi-zations that make up the institutions in Canadian society.

One of the main reasons why organizations, and the individuals who work for them, fail to move toward an anti-racist model of organizational change is the overarching ideology of democratic racism. Its values provide a justification for avoiding any action that might lead an organization to make progressive changes that not only challenged racism but deconstructed it.

The hegemonic ideology of democratic racism is articulated, transmit-ted, and reproduced in every sector of Canadian society. "It is in...ideology that we live, move, and have our being" (McCarthy, 1993). In each of the central institutions of Canadian society analyzed in this book, racist myths and misconceptions continue to be generated, recycled, and replayed. These myths reinforce the racist attitudes and behaviours of individuals; fortify biased and discriminatory organizational policies, practices, and processes; and weave their way into societal belief and value systems. These processes result in collective denial, defensiveness, and a determination to maintain the status quo.

The myths that form the basis of democratic racism include the following:

- Racism cannot exist in a democratic society.
- Discrimination is a problem faced by everyone from time to time.
- White European immigrants also experienced discrimination.
- Racism is a result of immigration; racial conflict occurs because races mix.
- Minority groups refuse to fit in and adapt to Canadian society.
- Minority groups cannot fit into Canadian society; they change the national identity.
- People of colour have cultural problems. Race is not the issue.
- Non-Whites lack the skills and motivation to succeed.
- Multicultural policies are sufficient.
- Racism comes from ignorance; therefore, education about other people will eradicate it.
- Racism is a problem for non-Whites to solve.
- All we need to do is to treat everyone equally.
- Although racism exists, individuals have the right to freedom of speech.
- Anti-racism is racism in reverse.

In each of the institutional sectors examined earlier in this book, the various forms of racism influence the manner in which organizations are structured. This book has attempted to make clear that the ideology of democratic racism reinforces and maintains racism in these institutions. It has demonstrated that democratic ideals and fundamental precepts such as fairness, tolerance, and equality often conflict with the realities of injustice, inequity, and racial discrimination. The remainder of this book discusses how democratic racism is manifested in Canada's major social institutions.

THE MANIFESTATIONS OF DEMOCRATIC RACISM

EDUCATION

In the area of education, racism is woven into the formal and informal curriculum, influencing the ways in which knowledge is structured, valued, and transmitted. Racial bias is reflected in the attitudes, assumptions, and behaviour of educators. Racism in education mirrors the racism of the dominant culture. It is reflected in the learning environment and forms an intrinsic part of the learning process. The evidence of racist ideology and differential treatment that negatively affects students of colour is documented by studies and reports and recorded in the testimonies of students and parents.

Educational practices that maintain Eurocentric biases and ignore the histories and contributions of racial-minority groups are maintained by a value system that allegedly emphasizes fairness and equality for all students. Canada's educational system is based on the premise that a well-constructed learning environment benefits students of all racial and cultural backgrounds. Despite the persistent belief and claim that the educational system is based on the principles of liberal democracy, substantial numbers of racial-minority students are disadvantaged and treated as though they were inferior. This is democratic racism.

Inequity and differential treatment continues at the university level. Lack of minority representation in faculties and administrations, the teaching of a Eurocentric curriculum, and incidents of harassment and overt racism continue to plague minority students. These practices are maintained in an institution that prides itself on its academic freedom and emphasis on freedom of expression. The latter freedom has enabled faculty to conduct research that allegedly demonstrates the inequality of races, students to publicly insult members of racial minorities, and administrators to ignore issues that relate to inequity. The usual response of the university has been to deny and resist change in the name of academic freedom, freedom of expression, and the merit principle. These basic tenets of democracy allow racism to continue to flourish in the academic environment.

THE MEDIA

The media are regarded as a pillar of democratic society and the key instrument by which its ideals are produced and perpetuated. Democracy depends on a free flow and exchange of ideas, opinions, and information. In a liberal democracy, media institutions are expected to reflect alternative viewpoints and to provide equitable access to all groups.

In reality, the media are directed by the marketplace and are therefore subject to its constraints and demands. As a result, the Canadian media industries marginalize people of colour by making them invisible, devaluing their contributions, and perpetuating the White face of Canada. Media organizations play a key role in producing and disseminating the myth that people of colour, especially Blacks, threaten a well-ordered society, create social problems, and generally jeopardize the harmony of Canada.

Television cameras often show close-ups of Blacks in both the foreground and background of scenes in which the topic is crime. The media create and reinforce negative and stereotypical images to influence public opinion. Thus, issues such as crime, immigration, and housing become racialized and result in the further marginalization and exclusion of people of colour. Freedom of the press provides a licence for journalists, editors, and broadcasters to communicate racist views.

Yet, as the president of the Canadian Broadcasting Corporation stated in the introduction to the CBC's *Journalism Policy*:

> Freedom of the press...is a cornerstone of our society, since freedom itself cannot flourish without the full flow and exchange of ideas, opinion

and information. This is a tradition central to the democratic ideal and it has been accepted in that context as vital to the defence of individual liberty. (Canadian Broadcasting Corporation, 1982)

Freedom of the press has, however, continued to allow the media to include ideas, images, and words that demean and malign people of colour and that encourage fear and hatred against them.

THE ARTS

In the arts—literature, sculpture, painting, music, theatre, dance, and other creative achievements—work generated by people of colour is often judged inferior and relegated to the margins of mainstream public culture. Cultural appropriation—the use of another culture's images or experiences by artists from the dominant culture—is a particularly important example of the ways in which the culture, traditions, and history of minority artists are valued only after they have been appropriated. The prevailing ideology of cultural racism leads to the view that true art can only be produced by those with Eurocentric aesthetic values; all others produce folklore and exotica.

As is the case in the media, freedom of expression provides a rationale for silencing certain voices and ignoring particular images. Attempts to protest and resist the dominant culture's marginalization, stereotyping, and objectification of people of colour in theatre, film, television programming, and writing are met with allegations of censorship and political correctness.

POLICING

In the area of law enforcement, many racist attitudes and behaviours lead to a polarization between police and racial-minority communities. The culture of policing is based on a "we–they" mindset and emphasizes law and order, a concept that conflicts with the idea of a service-oriented police force.

In addition, the police play an important role in the racialization of crime and the criminalization of minorities. The overpolicing of racial-minority communities leads to a substantial number of charges being laid against their members, which in turn leads to the view that members of these groups commit more crimes than others do. This unsubstantiated notion creates a negative, destructive, and unfair image that is disseminated among the public by the media. The racial minority (especially the Black) as criminal is a construct particularly well suited to the production and reproduction of racist ideology.

One of the major barriers to an improvement in police–race relations is the fact that people of colour do not have access to, and are not able to participate in, the decision-making processes of policing institutions. If the police are not directly accountable to the diverse communities they serve, they are less likely to reflect and respond to the concerns of these communities.

The fall 1992 protest against the Ontario government by the Metropolitan Toronto Police Association was symptomatic of police outrage at "political intervention." The government's attempts to introduce mechanisms for greater community accountability were actions that, in the association's view, should be discouraged. They were considered either a socialist conspiracy or the result of unreasonable demands by special-interest groups. The demands for greater accountability tended to be seen as opposing the police and therefore as subverting the democratic process. Citizens' demands for change are frequently seen by the police as challenging the maintenance of law and order and therefore a threat to the security of the state.

THE JUSTICE SYSTEM

The justice system, which is based on the value of dispensing "justice" fairly and without bias, has been severely criticized for its inability to do so. Specific issues of concern include alleged differential treatment in the courts—as in the granting of bail, in sentencing disparities, in jury selection procedures, and in the attitudes of justice officials. Members of the legal profession, including the judiciary, have been cited for their prejudiced and biased attitudes toward various groups, despite their responsibility to be impartial. In minority communities, especially among Blacks, there is a fundamental absence of faith in the fairness of the system.

The justice system espouses an ideology based on long-established laws and historical and legal precedents. For example, mandatory anti-sexism training for judges was rejected by the justice minister "because of constitutional guarantees of judicial independence" (*The Globe and Mail*, 1993). Evidence continues to show that adherence to these honourable traditions and guarantees work to the disadvantage of, and dispenses injustice to, persons of colour.

HUMAN SERVICES

Social and health-care service organizations are characterized by a lack of representation of people of colour. Those who are employed by these organizations experience marginalization and differential treatment. The prevailing ideology of the human services is exclusionary and racist. It is based on the provision of appropriate service to all, regardless of colour or creed, yet its delivery is inconsistent with these principles. The assumption of a common set of needs among very different groups, which is usually accepted as a basic requirement for the equal and accessible provision of services, can have a negative impact on minority clients. People of colour often find the traditional mainstream human-service delivery system inaccessible and inequitable.

Current modes of service continue to reflect the values, norms, and practices of the dominant culture and therefore are of limited effectiveness for people coming from diverse racial and cultural backgrounds. By limiting the role and resources of ethno-racial agencies, funders and other institutional authorities have perpetuated inequality within the system. Mainstream organizations remain unable or unwilling to provide the special social and health-care services that many ethno-racial communities require.

Moreover, these helping professions are staffed by people who have been socialized to believe that since all human beings are equal and valuable, their needs can be met by the same methods and procedures. Therefore, minority workers working in mainstream services frequently find themselves isolated and marginalized, their skills and credentials undervalued.

THE STATE

At the level of the state there is also evidence to demonstrate fundamental value conflicts. As Kobayashi (1990:447) pointedly argues, "The law itself has been an instrument used in the construction of racism as a hegemonic social relationship." Despite the development of human-rights legislation and codes, the glaring inadequacies of the Canadian Charter of Rights and Freedoms, the Multiculturalism Act, the Employment Equity Act, human-rights codes and commissions, government ministries, and public agencies at all levels demonstrate a lack of commitment to truly eliminate racism.

CONCLUSIONS

The conflict of values that characterizes the hegemonic ideology called "democratic racism" is at the root of racial inequality in Canadian society. The very values that define a democracy—freedom of expression, reliance on merit, the rights of individuals, the primacy of human dignity, and the rights of all citizens to equality—are used to combat, resist, and denigrate efforts to deconstruct racial barriers and inequalities. There is a constant and profound moral tension between the reality of the everyday experiences of people of colour and the responses of those who have the power to redefine that reality. White politicians, bureaucrats, educators, judges, journalists, social workers, the corporate elite, and others pay lip service to the ideal of racial equality but are far more committed to maintaining the status quo.

The transformation of Canadian institutions and the organizations that serve them into anti-racist bodies is hindered by a reliance on the traditional values that such changes allegedly threaten. The paradox of "democratic racism" is that in the midst of a society that professes racial equality, there is racial inequality; instead of fairness, there is unfairness; instead of freedom of speech, there is the silencing of voices advocating change; instead of impartiality, bias; instead of multiculturalism, ethnocentrism. Diversity becomes assimilation, the rule of law results in injustice, service means lack of access, and protection increases the vulnerability of racial-minority communities.

STRATEGIES FOR CHANGE

Given the evidence of the collective denial of racism in Canadian society, what alternatives can be offered? What strategies can be implemented?

Given the complex, interactive nature of the Canadian social structure, no single institutional response, policy, program, or other type of intervention can ensure that racism will be eliminated or even reduced. This book has identified numerous measures that have been undertaken, such as state policies on multiculturalism, human rights, immigration, and employment equity, as well as institutional initiatives in education, policing, human services, and the media. Some measures have had the appearance of success in the short term, but none has succeeded in controlling racism in a way that ensures full access, participation, and equity for people of colour.

Most of the approaches to combat racism in Canada have, in practice, been "too little, too late." They have frequently been underfunded, short-term, ad hoc, and isolated interventions that lack co-ordination and do not address "root causes." Having been framed in an ideology of democratic racism, they have too often addressed symptoms without changing the conditions that produced the symptoms in the first place.

Although there are no sure formulas, the following four strategic approaches to anti-racism hold hope for change:

- responding to allegations of racism;
- empowering communities;
- monitoring anti-racism initiatives; and
- emphasizing the role of institutions.

The following pages offer some tentative suggestions in each of these areas to address inequalities and racist attitudes and behaviours.

RESPONDING TO ALLEGATIONS OF RACISM

Democratic racism allows individuals to hold and espouse liberal democratic values while believing and practising racist ideology. It is often subtle, elusive, and insidious. It is usually invisible to White people and readily apparent to people of colour. Thus, allegations of racism in organizations elicit anger, shock, disbelief, and pain. Every allegation of racism has both individual and organizational consequences. In developing strategies to deal with racism, the individual is an essential part of the equation.

Allegations of racism are accompanied by a series of emotional responses from both the complainant and the subject of the complaint. Allegations of racism often remain unresolved because people become involved in trying to prove that an incident was or was not discrimination. The individual accused of racism commonly believes that racism cannot occur without an intent to discriminate. The immediate organizational response is often denial, which is expressed in a number of counter-productive behaviours. The person who alleges racism generally feels isolated, unsupported, and vulnerable. He or she may have expended enormous energy in trying to decide whether to launch a complaint or bring the issue to the attention of the organization.

Thus, in the first stage, the response to allegations of racism must begin by identifying and acknowledging the deeply felt emotions of both parties. Exposing these feelings and rigorously addressing them allows the incident to be used to create opportunities both to build individual relationships and to facilitate organizational growth.

The second stage is to uncover the underlying facts upon which these emotions are built. The social facts underpinning racism cannot be readily understood by White Canadians, who do not experience discrimination based on the colour of their skin. Thus it is very difficult for many White Canadians to understand the impact of constant, everyday racism on persons of colour and to identify the ways in which bias, exclusion, marginalization, and differential treatment function in their organizations. On the other hand, racism shapes the intellectual, professional, and personal lives of many people of colour. These distinctly different social realities must be taken into account in trying to determine the social facts underlying an allegation of racism.

The third stage requires a commitment to negotiating, implementing, and institutionalizing change. Finding common ground and identifying the mutual interests of the parties is an essential part of rebuilding relationships. Both the individuals and the organization must be able to identify the benefits of seeking a resolution to race-related conflicts. Often the experience and expertise of the community provide organizations with an important resource for developing effective strategies.

EMPOWERING COMMUNITIES

Organized opposition by the offended group and/or community is a major catalyst to change. If societal institutions are to be free of racism, they need to be pushed to this level of change by organized, direct community action.

In a democratic society, where conflict is valued and rewarded as long as it occurs within socially approved limits, public-sector support for anti-racism community advocacy and lobbying activities is necessary. Competition in Canadian society is encouraged and institutionalized. Only when resources are scarce and inequitably distributed can such competition lead to disintegrative forms of conflict. Canadian democratic values encourage political dissent and opposition, again as long as they are expressed through proper channels and the conflict is "peaceful." Constructive conflict includes the recognition of different needs and interests (individual and collective) and provides for participation, negotiation, arbitration, and settlement. The establishment of such mechanisms may avoid violent confrontation.

A racial incident or series of incidents can act as triggers to direct reaction by the community, which often becomes the most salient agent of institutional and societal change. Thus, opposition and conflict may play a beneficial role in initiating the process of change toward racial equity.

A society in which integration is more advanced will have greater group interaction. As a result it may also have more frequent incidents of behavioural discrimination. However, the increasing numbers of such cases might indicate an improvement, rather than a worsening, in racial equality. Thus, ensuing conflicts should be recognized as signs of progress, not deterioration, because efforts to reduce racial inequalities may increase the short-term potential for conflict (Benyon and Solomos, 1987:156). In Canada, a society that promotes the democratic racist myths of progress through dialogue, mediation, and conciliation, the reduction of racial inequalities through increased racial conflict and tension will clearly be an uncomfortable but perhaps inevitable new direction.

The achievement of racial equity will not come about as a result of a rational, intellectual process of understanding. Nor will it occur through an "invisible hand" of organizational dynamics. Anti-racism efforts need to acknowledge the full complexity of the system they are attempting to change and to locate those efforts in the context of the obstacles to racial equity. Anti-racism strategies need to address the institutional constraints and the personal and occupational ideologies and values reflected in the arguments of democratic racism.

While national and international conditions can precipitate social change, a major impetus has been and will continue to be community pressure. It is therefore misleading to denude the pursuit of racial equity of any political dimension. Social change is often precipitated by political imperatives. Does it matter whether the motivation is prevention, fear, moral panic, or altruism? Does it matter whether the response is based on attempts to appease, to defuse discontent, to manage a crisis, to repair the meritocratic credibility of institutions, or to avoid the development of separate institutions along lines of race?

What does matter is that the response will have an appreciable impact on reducing racial injustice.

The case studies cited in this book show that the initial response of Canadian institutions and organizations to demands for change is to make cosmetic changes, and even then to make them only to defuse protest. Real improvements come about only through sustained external pressure.

Parekh (1987), in writing about anti-racism efforts in the United States, concluded that no reform had been secured without powerful and constant Black pressure.

> It was the Black agitation, initially the non-violent civil rights campaigns and the later riots, that activated the moral impulse, energized and mobilized the liberals, provided a political counterweight to the highly influential racial lobby, threatened disorder, changed the equations of White self-interest and resulted in reforms. (x)

Parekh argued that no American reform was secure unless Black organizations and their leaders were able to consolidate, defend, and build on it. His analysis of the American experience suggests that reforms secured in the teeth of opposition by vested interests are fragile, vulnerable to subversion, and generally lack the resources to implement them. Moreover, they are unlikely to be fruitful and achieve the desired goal unless they are carefully formulated and part of a well-conceived strategy.

The frenzy of activity on March 21 each year—the day set aside to commemorate the International Day for the Elimination of Racial Discrimination—is symbolic of the kinds of institutional initiatives that are often little more than public-relations exercises. "Eliminate racism," "Remove racial discrimination," "Create equality of opportunity," "Manage diversity," and "Implement anti-racist training" are empty slogans, incapable either of guiding those who genuinely wish to help or of restraining those determined to resist them.

One of the most important conclusions that can be drawn from the anti-racism activities described in this book is that immediate, consistent, and well-developed community mobilization and action strategies can be highly successful in influencing political, institutional, and social action. Progress toward race equity is therefore unlikely to be attained unless concerned citizens and communities are able to co-operate to combat racism.

Community infrastructures and support systems need to be in place to combat racism, to monitor organizational and institutional initiatives, to ensure their implementation, and to overcome resistance, both systemic and individual.

Parekh (1987) argued that any progress toward race equity is achieved only by sustained and direct community involvement. Sustained community advocacy and lobbying activities require:

- *organizational resources*: financial and human;
- *legitimacy*: support from the media and other communities;
- *expertise*: legal, media, and organizational; and
- *leadership*: training and development.

Political representation and the participation of people of colour in the decisions that affect them must also be regarded as necessary preconditions for the non-violent resolution of racism in Canadian society. For example, the issue of police behaviour raises questions that go to the heart of democratic accountability and government by consent. People of colour must be represented in the police force at all ranks and on the boards that manage them.

The use of police or the armed forces to deal with protest reflects a "legitimation crisis" in which inequalities of power and status undermine loyalty and create contradictions that threaten social integration. When such conflicts result in violent protest and a coercive response by authorities, they undermine the moral basis of society and the integrity of the state. Only through a comprehensive approach that addresses the underlying conditions that foster democratic racism and that facilitates constructive responses will a repetition of such crises in the future be avoided. The first precondition is that people of colour must participate in the decision-making process.

MONITORING ANTI-RACISM INITIATIVES

Public policies on multiculturalism and race relations, legislation on employment equity and human rights, and systems and agencies to promote racial equality have all had the impact on altering the appearance, if not the reality, of racial inequality in Canada. Canadians, including people of colour, are encouraged to believe in the myths of goodwill, tolerance, and racial harmony. The maintenance of these democratic racist myths continues to hamper citizens' readiness to measure and dismantle racism. Although the extent of racial discrimination and inequality in Canada is similar to that of the United

States and the United Kingdom, Canada has not yet experienced the level of violence and unrest that these other countries have.

An increasing number of institutions and agencies in all sectors of Canadian life are articulating finely worded commitments and policies with regard to equity issues. Unfortunately, these commitments have seldom been translated into good practices. The pursuit of racial equality in Canada appears to be hampered by an inability to translate policy into time- and cost-efficient procedures that have a measurable impact on controlling racial disadvantage and discrimination. There is a danger that the impetus and commitment to equity will unravel in a collection of uncertain, cumbersome, and misdirected activities that do not achieve any real results in removing racial inequalities. These responses may indeed reinforce and even exacerbate the existing racial inequality.

The activity that has taken place in Canada in the last while in pursuit of racial equity has largely consisted of determining whether racism is occurring, how it is occurring and to what extent, and on proposing ways of prevention. While data on these issues is far from adequate and considerable research is still required, more emphasis should be placed on analyzing the issues from the perspective of outcomes.

The most important measure of any initiative is its *results*. Extensive efforts to implement training and develop procedures, data-collection systems, report forms, and finely written policy statements are worse than meaningless unless the end product is measurable improvement. Just as the success of a private business is evaluated in terms of increases in sales, the only realistic basis for evaluating a program to combat racism and increase racial equity is its actual impact on these issues. To accelerate the process of change, more careful consideration needs to be given to particular issues in sectors where there is a real prospect of effecting change quickly.

In addition to focussing on strategic targeting, any strategy for improving policy and practices must incorporate mechanisms for monitoring and measuring their impact. In other words, initiatives must show definable results that reduce racial injustices in a measurable way. New techniques and mechanisms are required to assess whether anti-racist policies and practices are in fact achieving racial equity. There is a lack of rigorous monitoring in the field of anti-racism in Canada, and few criteria of evaluation have been developed. The consequence of this is that limited public dollars and community energies are wasted on irrelevant exercises that do little to control or eliminate racism.

Too many community activities are concerned with "promoting," "encouraging," "co-ordinating," "heightening," "improving," and other similarly imprecise and vaguely worded objectives. Sometimes, project evaluation consists merely of a loose "process evaluation" activity in which, for example, conference participants are asked to rate the speakers. The little evaluation that has been done on training programs indicates that efforts are needed to develop appropriate methods of "impact evaluation"—that is, evaluations of the extent to which anti-racism initiatives produce desirable outcomes. In terms of measuring results, the emphasis should be on an initiative's "return on investment" in relation to predetermined goals. Only then can legitimate and meaningful performance standards be established.

To be able to measure the results with some degree of comfort and certitude requires stated goals to be defined in specific, concrete, and realisable terms. Measuring outcomes is impossible if the goals and objectives consist of nebulous generalizations.

There is a need in Canada to collect and disseminate the knowledge—strategies, technology, and technical skills—that is required to achieve racial equity. Unfortunately, the degree of information sharing in Canada across institutional, racial, and geographical boundaries is relatively insignificant. This isolation, in not drawing on the experience of other effective initiatives, methods, programs, and approaches, also separates Canadians from the international community.

Canada cannot afford to persist in pursuing racial equity on an insecure foundation of inadequate knowledge. Nor can it, through its public and private sectors and its various social agencies and institutions, afford to continue to devote resources to "improving opportunity" for people of colour if the impact on these persons continues to be negligible.

The failure to address the problem of racism in Canadian society might therefore be said to be largely due to a lack of information about the problem. A coherent response is more likely, and more likely to be effective, if Canadians have complete information on the extent and nature of racism. If effective preventive measures are to be formulated, then this kind of basic data is critical.

EMPHASIZING THE ROLE OF MAJOR INSTITUTIONS

The first task of an institution committed to racial equity is to make a clear statement that racism in any form will not be tolerated. Unfortunately, most major Canadian institutions operate as if the realities of a racially diverse population have nothing to do with the way they carry out their activities. They rely on "traditional management initiatives" or respond to incidents in an ad hoc manner.

In focussing on institutional strategies and in light of the previous observation regarding community involvement, an important factor is the degree to which an institution is open to *community pressure*. Some institutional sectors are more closed off from the public than are others. For example, the police are more accountable to the public because they are supported by tax dollars. Other public-sector agencies are accountable to elected representatives who are concerned with staying in office. The education system is accountable as a public service and has additional obligations to parents.

Other public-sector institutions, however, such as the justice system, are less easily affected by public pressure. The tradition of judicial independence is difficult to overcome when combatting racial inequalities in the justice system.

Similarly the tradition of freedom of speech is frequently used by the media to protect and defend themselves from community pressures. In addition, since the media are not highly organized, the mechanisms for seeking public redress are either ineffectual or non-existent.

Universities and colleges have decentralized authority structures, and old academic traditions guide their culture. Greater priority is given to the tradition than to the students or the broader population.

Museums and cultural institutions are also susceptible to being isolated from the populations they serve. The structure of and representation on the boards of these institutions suggests that they are not accountable to the larger community.

The case studies cited in this book indicate institutional ill-preparedness in dealing with issues of racism. Strategies need to be developed that respond to incidents of racism that are largely the result of discriminatory institutional structures and customs. Institutional change strategies are fundamentally "local" in their orientation, in that they focus on one organization at a time. This is not to suggest, however, that there is not a generic organizational response model.

Progress toward racial equity can be measured by the degree to which an organization:

- reflects the contributions and interests of all racial groups in Canada in its mission, operations, and service delivery;
- acts on a commitment to eradicate all forms of racial discrimination and disadvantage within itself;
- involves members of all its racial groups as full participants in all its levels; and
- fulfils its broader external responsibilities to promote racial equity.

In moving toward this ideal, appropriate organizational responses include:

- an immediate and strong condemnation of racism, and of those responsible for it, by the head of the organization;
- the development of a coherent implementation strategy to combat racism within the organization. This strategy should not merely deal with managing individual incidents, but strive to overcome the causes of racial incidents and eradicate systemic and structural discrimination in the organization;
- the establishment of an internal monitoring mechanism to record and monitor racism in all its forms; and
- taking action against those responsible for racism, serving notice on perpetrators, and informing the victims of all actions being taken.

Internal monitoring systems are generally located in organizations human-resource policies and programs. They generally involve the filing of complaints, a multistep procedure to attempt to resolve them, and a final decision by a senior official. In some organizations, an independent arbitrator is appointed to adjudicate complaints. In union settings, the collective agreement often includes a non-discrimination clause that subjects any discrimination complaint to grievance and arbitration procedures. In the Ontario Public

Service Employees Union, for example, this procedure culminates in a hearing before the Crown Employees Grievance Settlement Board.

A "coherent strategy" for addressing systemic issues may include structural diagnosis (e.g., data collection and problem identification, customer/client audits, and employment equity audits), public and policy commitments, the appointment of an adviser and/or committee, the establishment of goals and timetables, training, monitoring, and evaluation.

Developing a coherent anti-racist strategy for an organization therefore entails:

- a total system effort that must be comprehensive, systematic, and long-term; and
- clearly enunciated goals, not so much concerned with maintaining order and harmony as with dealing with grievances and correcting inequities.

Within the organization and its activities, the responsibility for race equity initiatives should reside not with one person or office, but with all the organization's members. The development of anti-racism values that could be integrated in the organization's culture and procedures should be considered. In summary, achieving race equity and a racism-free organization entails:

- an acknowledgement that racism exists in the organization and that certain groups have been, and continue to be, hurt by it;
- an acknowledgement of the need to move beyond racially inexplicit analyses that deflect the issue of racism by interpreting it in human-relations or cultural terms; and
- an acknowledgement of the need to move beyond policy statements and articulations of principles. Organizational and administrative measures will be required to provide appropriate conditions for progress toward race equity. Guidelines and procedures that include clearly identified responsibilities and accountability measures are required.

It may seem superfluous to state that the first step for all organizations, particularly those in the public sector, is to establish the need for a service for people of colour. It is clearly of major importance that the needs of the community be accurately assessed by systematic studies.

Secondly, in order to establish the relevance of services for people of colour, their provision must be monitored. A regular check must be made to ensure that a correspondence between need and service does in fact exist. The assessment must include the collection of data on the racial origins of clients, staff, and decision-makers.

The organizational arrangements of both public and private institutions determine the people or groups to whom services are provided, facilities are made available, and resources are allocated. The attitudes, actions, and practices of those who control these institutions determine who gets what, where, and when. Given the fact that people of colour are generally absent from these organizations' key decision-making processes and in the delivery of services, to what extent do the institutions treat them less favourably?

To what extent have the different and special needs of people of colour been identified and quantified? And to what extent have they been adequately considered and provided for? To what extent have existing resources been redirected in favour of people of colour as part of a commitment to equality?

The pursuit of racial equality also demands that institutional mechanisms for measuring change be in place. Adopting formal employment equity policies, implementing mass "sensitization" training programs, and undertaking glossy public-relations campaigns are generally ineffective methods unless they are combined with concrete programs of action that are regularly monitored, evaluated, and reported on publicly. Effective monitoring systems can begin to provide the information needed to answer the question of whether progress is occurring.

Increasing the amount of resources for anti-racism in and of itself is not a measurement of progress. Increasing the amount of "feel good" rhetoric contributes only to further obscuring the measurement of progress. Collecting evidence, although dry and tedious, is certainly cheaper and more honest than performing glamorous public-relations exercises. More resources should be devoted to research and evaluation and less to "communications strategies."

Ensuring that the multiracial dimension of Canadian society is incorporated into organizatonal decision-making in a comprehensive and systematic manner is not that difficult. But if it is not addressed directly, the notions of democratic racism and assumed equality will continue to be a major obstacle to race equity and will continue to contribute to the disadvantaged position of people of colour in Canada.

SUMMARY

Although all the strategies identified in this chapter are positive mechanisms for dismantling racism in organizations and institutions, it must be acknowledged that they must be linked to a comprehensive transformation of the cultural values and norms that shape Canadian society.

Clearly, Canada's racial heterogeneity is a demographic and social reality historically and currently, and, in all likelihood, will be so in the future. However, racial inequality and injustice continue to limit the participation of people of colour. Despite various policies, programs, and other initiatives, the evidence in this book suggests that racial barriers to equity in organizations and social structures have not been significantly reduced; that membership in the dominant White culture confers cultural, political, and economic power; and that racist ideology and discourse operate freely, without constraint.

The existence of democratic racism suggests that we can expect increasing resistance from those who now enjoy the power and privilege of membership in the dominant group to efforts by people of colour and other anti-racism advocates to alter the status quo. Simultaneously, those who are deprived of their rights as Canadians can be expected to become increasingly impatient with the slow rate of change.

Dealing with racism in an effective way requires us to deal with the dissonance in values that underlies our current understanding of democracy. At this point in the history of Canada, we have an opportunity to redefine and redistribute power and to eradicate the structured inequality propelled by the hegemonic ideology that we have called democratic racism.

REFERENCES

Benyon, J., and J. Solomos. (1987). *The Roots of Urban Unrest*. Oxford: Pergamon Press.

Canadian Broadcasting Corporation. (1982). Journalism Policy. Toronto.

Farman, A. (1992). "An Archaeology of Interracial Relations." *Fuse* 15(3) (Winter):7–11.

"Judges' Training Program Rejected." (1993). *The Toronto Star* (September 8):A6(CP).

Kobayashi, A. (1990). "Racism and the Law." *Urban Geography* 2(5):447–473.

McCarthy, C. (1993). "After the Canon." In W. Critchlow and C. McCarthy (eds.), *Race, Education, Identity and Representation*. New York and London: Routledge.

Parekh, B. (1987). In J. Shaw et al., (eds.), *Strategies for Improving Race Relations*. Manchester: Manchester University Press.

Appendix A

▼▼▼▼▼▼▼▼▼▼▼▼▼

Racial Groups in Canada

Various racial groups make up the Canadian population. They can be categorized as follows:

Aboriginal—Métis, Inuit, status and non-status Canadian Indian, North and South American Native peoples

Black—African Black, American Black, Canadian Black, West Indian and Caribbean Black, other Black

East Asian—Chinese, Fijian, Japanese, Korean, Polynesian

South Asian—Bangladeshi, Indian (India), Pakistani, Sri Lankan

Southeast Asian—Burmese, Cambodian, Filipino, Laotian, Malaysian, Thai, Vietnamese

West Asian—Arab, Armenian, Egyptian, Iranian, Israeli, Lebanese, North African Arab, Palestinian, Syrian, Turkish

White—British, European, Latin and North American of Caucasian background, Russian, Ukrainian, others of Caucasian background

Other—Mixed racial heritage; racial groups not referred to above

Glossary

▼▼▼▼▼▼▼▼▼▼▼

One of the difficulties of discussing racism is arriving at a common understanding of terminology. Unfortunately, the definitions and interpretations of terms vary considerably. Racism is an elusive and volatile issue, and our understanding of it continues to evolve. As such it is inevitable that our understanding of common, agreed-upon terms will also evolve.

Labelling groups of people is a difficult task because of the emotional significance of the names by which groups of people choose to identify themselves in Canadian society. And racism, by its very definition, addresses the evolving nature of that identity.

Another issue that needs to be considered in framing a discussion of racism is the scientific argument that there is only one "race" to which all members of human society belong, whatever their origin, colour, or other physical features. Anti-racism in this context is therefore concerned with eradicating the notions of race and racism and the myths of multiple "races" that have been used as the justification for one group to exert power over another.

The following glossary of terms is offered, not as the final word on the topic, but to explain the more commonly used terms and phrases now being used in the constantly changing discussion on racism.

Aboriginal Peoples   In Canada, status Indians, non-status Indians, Inuit, and Métis.

Acculturation   A process of adaptation and change whereby a person or an ethnic, social, religious, language, or national group integrates with or adapts to the cultural values and patterns of the majority group.

Adverse Impact   The extent to which policies, procedures, and practices disproportionately exclude certain groups.

Affirmative Action   A set of explicit actions or programs designed to eliminate systemic forms of discrimination by increasing the opportunities of individuals and groups who have historically been excluded from full participation in and access to such areas as employment and education.

Anti-Racism   A process of identifying and eradicating racism in all its various forms.

Anti-Racist Education   A perspective that addresses all aspects of the educational system and school practices, including all areas of the curriculum, and is aimed at understanding and eradicating racism in all its various forms.

Anti-Racism Organizational Change   A process of identifying and eradicating organizational values, policies, procedures, and behaviours that exclude people of colour from full participation as employees, customers, or clients.

Assimilation   A process by which an individual or group completely adopts—or is absorbed by—the culture, values, and patterns of another social, religious, linguistic, or national group.

Attitude   A consistent pattern of thought, belief, or emotion toward a fact, concept, situation, or group of people.

Bias   An opinion, preference, prejudice, or inclination formed without reasonable justification that then influences an individual's or group's ability to evaluate a particular situation objectively or accurately; an unfounded preference for or against.

Censorship   The suppression of information and ideas—such as literature, the performing arts, criminal court cases, and ideologies—that are considered unacceptable or dangerous for political, moral, or religious reasons.

Contract Compliance   Compliance with a binding, written agreement between two or more parties. Within the context of anti-racism, it normally entails compliance with an anti-discrimination clause that may ask companies to take definite steps such as employment equity to redress imbalances in the workforce. Failure to comply or act in good faith could result in penalties or exclusion from future contracts.

Culture   The totality of the ideas, beliefs, values, knowledge, and way of life of a group of people who share a certain historical, religious, racial, linguistic, ethnic, or social background. Manifestations of culture include art, laws, institutions, and customs. Culture is transmitted and reinforced and it changes over time.

Culture may refer to a lifestyle of a group of people who tacitly acknowledge their differences from others in terms of beliefs, values, worldviews, and attitudes about what is right, good, and important.

Culture is a complex and dynamic organization of meaning, knowledge, artifacts, and symbols that guide human behaviour, account for shared patterns of thought and action, and contribute to human, social, and physical survival.

Colonialism   A process by which a foreign power dominates and exploits an indigenous group by appropriating their land and resources, extracting their wealth, and using them as cheap labour. Also refers to a specific era of European expansion into overseas territories between the sixteenth and twentieth centuries. Racial doctrines that reinforce patterns of superiority and inferiority have often been invoked to justify, explain, and promote the exploitation of indigenous minorities.

Democratic Racism   The term refers to an ideology that permits and sustains the ability to justify the maintaining of two apparently conflicting values. One set of values consists of a commitment to a democratic society motivated by egalitarian values of fairness, justice, and equality. Conflicting with these liberal values are attitudes and behaviours including negative feelings about people of colour, and which carry the potential for differential treatment or discrimination against them.

Designated Groups   Social groups whose members have historically been denied equal access to such areas as employment, accommodation, health care, and education because of their membership in the group. Under employment equity legislation, the designated groups have been identified as women, visible minorities, Aboriginal peoples, and persons with disabilities.

Disadvantage   Unfavourable and unequal access to resources such as employment, education, and social services.

Discrimination   The denial of equal treatment and opportunities to individuals or groups with respect to education, accommodation, health care, employment, and services, goods, and facilities. Discrimination may occur on the basis of race, nationality, gender, age, religion, political affiliation, marital or family status, physical or psychiatric disability, or sexual orientation.

Dominant/Majority Group   The group of people in a given society that is largest in number or that successfully shapes or controls other groups through social, economic, cultural, political, or religious power. In Canada, the term has generally referred to White, Anglo-Saxon, Protestant males.

Employment Equity   A set of practices designed to identify and eliminate discriminatory policies and practices that create unfair or unequal employment opportunities and to provide equitable opportunities in employment for designated groups. Employment equity means more than treating persons in the same way; it also requires special measures and the accommodation of differences. Thus, the quality of the results, not the equality of treatment, is important.

Equality of Opportunity   The rights of individuals to be free from discrimination when competing for opportunities or services.

Equity   The rights of individuals to an equitable share of the goods and services in society. In order to ensure equality of outcome, equity programs treat groups differently when the situation in society precludes equal treatment. Equity programs are more inclined to accept the priority of collective rights over individual rights.

Ethnic Group   A community maintained by a shared heritage, culture, language, or religion; a group bound together by ties of cultural homogeneity, with a prevailing loyalty and adherence to certain beliefs, attitudes, and customs.

Ethnocentrism   A tendency to view events from the perspective of one's own culture, with a corresponding tendency to misunderstand or diminish other groups and regard them as inferior.

Exclusion   A process of disempowering, degrading, or disenfranchising a group by discriminatory practices and behaviour.

Genocide   Deliberate actions of a nation or group of people to exterminate another nation or group.

Ghettoization   The conscious or unconscious act of isolating members of an ethnic or racial minority group from the larger community.

Harassment   A persistent and continuing communication (in any form) of negative attitudes, beliefs, or actions toward an individual or group, with the intention of disparaging that person or group. Forms of harassment include name-calling, jokes and slurs, graffiti, insults, threats, discourteous treatment, and written and physical abuse.

Hegemony   Social, cultural, religious, or moral traditions and ideas that reinforce the power of the dominant group at the expense of other groups.

Holocaust   A widespread destruction and loss of life; particularly refers to the genocidal extermination of six million European Jews in concentration camps during World War II.

Identity   A subjective sense of coherence, consistency, and continuity of self, rooted in both personal and group history.

Ideology   A complex set of ideas that attempts to explain, justify, legitimate, and perpetuate the circumstances in which a collectivity finds itself. It provides a basis for guiding behaviour, making sense of the world, imparting meaning to life, instilling a common bond among group members, and explaining situations.

Institutions   Organizational arrangements and practices through which collective actions are taken (e.g., government, business, media, education, health and social services).

Integration   The process that allows groups and individuals to become full participants in the social, economic, cultural, and political life of a society while at the same time enabling them to retain their own cultural identity.

Intolerance   An unwillingness to consider and/or respect the beliefs and practices of others. Racial intolerance prevents members of other racial groups from sharing equally and benefitting fully from the opportunities available in a community, while religious intolerance refuses to accept or respect the religious beliefs of others.

Mainstream   In the context of anti-racism, the dominant culture and the political, social, educational, cultural, and economic institutions through which its power is maintained.

Marginal   The status of groups who do not have full and equal access to the social, economic, cultural, and political institutions of society.

Minority Group   A group of people that is either relatively small in number or has little or no access to social, political, or economic power.

Multiculturalism   Multiculturalism has different levels of meaning. It is a description of the composition of Canada both historically and currently, referring to the cultural and racial diversity of Canadian society. It is an ideology that holds that racial, cultural, religious, and linguistic diversity is an integral, beneficial, and necessary part of Canadian society and identity. It is a policy operating in various social institutions and levels of government, including the federal government.

Oppression   The domination of certain individuals or groups by others through the use of physical, psychological, social, cultural, or economic force.

People of Colour   (See Racial Minority)

Pluralism   An approach in which some degree of cultural, linguistic, ethnic, religious, or other group distinction is maintained and valued by individuals.

Prejudice   A mental state or attitude of prejudging, generally unfavourably, by attributing to every member of a group characteristics falsely attributed to the group as a whole.

Race   A category used to classify humankind according to common ancestry and reliant on differentiation by such physical characteristics as colour of skin, hair texture, stature, and facial characteristics.

Race Relations   The quality and pattern of interactions between people who are racially different.

Racial Discrimination   Any distinction, exclusion, restriction, or preference based on race that has the purpose of nullifying or impairing the recognition, enjoyment, or exercise, on an equal footing, of human rights and fundamental freedoms in the political, economic, social, cultural, or any other field of public life.

Racial Incident   Any incident in which it appears that there is an element of racial motivation, or any incidents that include an allegation of racial motivation made by any person. Racial incidents may involve verbal abuse (such as banter, jokes, name-calling, harassment, teasing, discourteous treatment), or defacement of property, or physical abuse and assault.

Racial Minority   A group of persons, other than Aboriginal peoples, who are non-Caucasian in race or non-White in colour, and who so identify themselves or agree to be so identified. Their minority status is the result of a lack of access to power, privilege, and prestige in relation to the White majority group.

Racism   A system in which one group of people exercises power over another group on the basis of skin colour; an implicit or explicit set of beliefs, erroneous assumptions, and actions based on an ideology of the inherent superiority of one racial group over another, and evident in organizational or institutional structures and programs as well as in individual thought or behaviour patterns.

Individual racism is a form of racial discrimination that stems from conscious, personal prejudice.

Systemic racism consists of policies and practices, entrenched in established institutions, that result in the exclusion or advancement of specific groups of people. It manifests itself in two ways: (1) institutional racism: racial discrimination that derives from individuals carrying out the dictates of others who are prejudiced or of a prejudiced society; and (2) structural racism: inequalities rooted in the system-wide operation of a society that exclude substantial numbers of members of particular groups from significant participation in major social institutions.

Cultural racism is deeply embedded in the value system of a society. It represents the tacit network of beliefs and values that encourages and justifies discriminatory actions, behaviours, and practices.

Racist   An individual, institution, or organization whose beliefs, actions, or programs imply or state that certain races have distinctive negative or inferior characteristics.

Racist Ideology   Includes the whole range of concepts, ideas, images, and institutions that provide the framework of interpretation and meaning for racial thought in society. It creates and preserves a system of dominance based on race and is communicated and reproduced through agencies of socialization and cultural transmission such as the mass media, schools, and universities, religious doctrines, symbols and images, art, music, and literature.

Skin Colour   Skin colour carries with it more than the signification of colour: it also includes a set of meanings attached to the cultural traits of those who are a certain colour.

Stereotype   A false or generalized conception of a group of people that results in an unconscious or conscious categorization of each member of that group, without regard for individual differences.

REFERENCES

Mock, K.R. (1988). Race Relations Directorate, Government of Ontario. Toronto.
Ontario Ministry of Citizenship. (1988). *Intercultural Communications Workshop*. Toronto.
_____. (1993). *A Guide to Key Anti-Racism Terms and Concepts*. Toronto.
Thomas, B., and C. Novogrodsky. (1992). *Combatting Racism in the Workplace: A Course for Workers*. Toronto: Cross-Cultural Communication Centre.
Toronto Mayor's Committee on Community and Race Relations. (1993). *Race Relations Myths and Facts*. Toronto.

Index

▼▼▼▼▼▼▼

Reader Reply Card

We are interested in your reaction to *The Colour of Democracy: Racism in Canadian Society*, by Frances Henry, Carol Tator, Winston Mattis, and Tim Rees. You can help us to improve this book in future editions by completing this questionnaire.

1. What was your reason for using this book?

    ☐ university course   ☐ college course   ☐ continuing education course
    ☐ professional   ☐ personal   ☐ other _____
        development   interest   _____

2. If you are a student, please identify your school and the course in which you used this book.

3. Which chapters or parts of this book did you use? Which did you omit?

4. What did you like best about this book?

5. What did you like least about this book?

6. Please identify any topics you think should be added to future editions.

7. Please add any comments or suggestions.

8. May we contact you for further information?

    Name: _____

    Address: _____

    _____

    Phone: _____

(fold here and tape shut)

MAIL ✈ POSTE

Canada Post Corporation / Société canadienne des postes

Postage paid
If mailed in Canada

Port payé
si posté au Canada

**Business
Reply**

**Réponse
d'affaires**

0116870**99**   01

0116870399-M8Z4X6-BR01

Heather McWhinney
Publisher, College Division
HARCOURT BRACE & COMPANY, CANADA
55 HORNER AVENUE
TORONTO, ONTARIO
M8Z 9Z9